The Diplomatic Presidency

The Diplomatic Presidency

AMERICAN FOREIGN POLICY FROM
FDR TO GEORGE H. W. BUSH

Tizoc Chavez

University Press of Kansas

© 2022 by the University Press of Kansas
All rights reserved

Published by the University Press of Kansas (Lawrence, Kansas 66045), which
was organized by the Kansas Board of Regents and is operated and funded by
Emporia State University, Fort Hays State University, Kansas State University,
Pittsburg State University, the University of Kansas, and Wichita State
University.

Library of Congress Cataloging-in-Publication Data

Names: Chavez, Tizoc Victor Hutchinson, author.
Title: The diplomatic presidency : American foreign policy from FDR to George
H. W. Bush / Tizoc Chavez.
Description: Lawrence, Kansas : University Press of Kansas, 2021 | Includes
bibliographical references
Identifiers: LCCN 2021012550
  ISBN 9780700632862 (cloth)
  ISBN 9780700632879 (ebook)
Subjects: LCSH: United States—Foreign relations—1945–1989. | Presidents—
United States—History—20th century. | World politics—1945–1989.
Classification: LCC E744 .C466 2021 | DDC 327.73009/04—dc23
LC record available at https://lccn.loc.gov/2021012550.
British Library Cataloguing-in-Publication Data is available.

Printed in the United States of America

10 9 8 7 6 5 4 3 2 1

The paper used in this publication is recycled and contains 30 percent
postconsumer waste. It is acid free and meets the minimum requirements of
the American National Standard for Permanence of Paper for Printed Library
Materials Z39.48-1992.

To my mother and father

Contents

Acknowledgments

It might be a cliché to say that this book is the product of many years and that many debts were accrued along the way. But it is true. First and foremost, I must thank Tom Schwartz. He read (always cheerfully) more drafts of this project than anyone, providing thoughtful comments and suggestions to improve it. I could not ask for a more patient, kind, and encouraging mentor. His intellectual guidance and friendship have been invaluable. I am also profoundly grateful to Dave Lewis. I took Dave's presidency seminar in my first semester of graduate school, and it was extremely influential on my development as a scholar. It was my favorite course in grad school and led me to focus my research on the presidency. Since that first class, I have relied on Dave's insights and knowledge of the executive branch, but more importantly, he has always been a source of encouragement and support. I am indebted to other scholars as well who took the time to read drafts of this project at different stages and offer their advice and feedback, especially Sarah Igo, Paul Kramer, Andy Johns, Mitch Lerner, and Nicholas Evan Sarantakes.

My graduate school cohort was present for the origins of this project, and their great questions and comments helped shape it. Thanks to Jason Bates, Michell Chresfield, Alex Jacobs, Sonja Ostrow, Lance Ingwerson, and Ashish Koul.

As a DAAD (German Academic Exchange Service) postdoctoral fellow, I was fortunate to spend a year at the Johns Hopkins School of Advanced International Studies as part of the United States, Europe, and World Order program led by Dan Hamilton and Kristina Spohr. Both of them read parts of the book and offered invaluable feedback. For providing a wonderful intellectual community as I finished the book at SAIS, I thank Cornelia-Adriana Baciu, Frank Stengel, David Kleimann, Jason Moyer, Wilhelmina Hindström, Māris Andžāns, Faruk Ajeti, Iulia-Sabina Joja, Maria Snegovaya, and Sofia Jern.

I made final revisions of the book while teaching in the Department of Social Sciences at the United States Military Academy at West Point. It was a fantastic place to spend a year, and I feel lucky to have had the opportunity to do so. One would be hard-pressed to find a more supportive department or group of colleagues.

I was fortunate to have multiple professors during my undergraduate years at California State University–Stanislaus who provided me with the intellectual foundation and support to continue my studies and make this book possible. Richard Weikart was the first person to suggest I pursue postgraduate studies, and his courses were great preparation. Marjorie Sanchez-Walker was a source of support both inside and outside the classroom. Bret Carroll's classes taught me what it means to be a historian. Samuel Regalado delivered some of the most captivating lectures and guided my senior thesis. Stephen Routh sparked my interest in political science, and I took every class I could with him.

I received valuable assistance from archivists at the Roosevelt Library in Hyde Park, New York; the Truman Library in Independence, Missouri; the Eisenhower Library in Abilene, Kansas; the Kennedy Library in Boston, Massachusetts; the Johnson Library in Austin, Texas; the Nixon Library in Yorba Linda, California; the Carter Library in Atlanta, Georgia; and the Reagan Library in Simi Valley, California. I would particularly like to thank Ray Wilson at the Reagan Library, who was exceedingly generous with his time and made helpful suggestions.

The research and writing of this book were made possible by financial assistance from the Department of History and Graduate School at Vanderbilt University and the Lyndon B. Johnson Foundation. A postdoctoral fellowship funded by the DAAD allowed me to finish the book.

Thank you to the entire team at the University Press of Kansas for all their work to make this book possible, and in particular, thanks to David Congdon for taking on this project and guiding it.

I am very grateful to friends who provided a much-needed respite from the challenges of researching and writing. I will never forget trivia at Corner Pub, parties at the Anthro House, Vandy sporting events, intramural softball, and nights on Broadway with Scotti Norman, Brian McCray, Sarah Eckhardt, Will Bishop, Steve Harrison, Emily Beugelmans Cook, Erin Stone, and Matt Owens. Graduate school would not have been the same without you all. Derrick Burnett deserves a special mention. I have known him since high school, and I could not ask for a funnier, more dedicated and caring best friend. I can never repay all he has done for me. I am lucky to have him in my corner.

This book would not have been possible without my family. Franchesca is the best big sister anyone could ask for. She is the most generous person I know. Her love, support, and friendship are a constant source of strength. My brother-in-law Frank and I joke a lot, but like my sister, he is extremely giving, and I am thankful for him. I owe the greatest debt to my parents, Vickie and Felipe. Their work ethic has always been an inspiration to me, and I would not be where I am today without their encouragement and sacrifices. Their love and support are endless. I am also thankful to my in-laws, who are the best anyone could ask for. From day one, they have been incredibly welcoming, generous, and supportive. Thank you Susan, Paul, Joey, Chrissy, and Daniel for making me part of your family.

I met my wife, Kelly, in grad school as I began this project. She was also pursuing a Ph.D. in history, and the demands of academia required us to be in a long-distance relationship for much longer than either of us wanted. Though the miles between us were many, they never lessened her support or encouragement of me and this project. Despite her own work, she always made time to read drafts and listen as I bounced ideas off her. She constantly amazes me with what she accomplishes, both personally and professionally. I aspire to be as good a scholar as she is. Her faith in me gives me strength, and without her love, this project would not have been possible. I could not ask for a better life partner.

Introduction:
The Pull of Personal Diplomacy

On December 14, 1918, Woodrow Wilson rode down the Champs-Élysées as an estimated two million ecstatic Parisians welcomed him to the city. A hundred-gun salute cracked the air. Violets and roses littered the street. He was the first American president to visit Europe while in office—it was his "paramount duty," he said.

It had been a month since the signing of the armistice ending World War I, and Wilson believed *his* attendance at the postwar peace conference would ensure a new world order based on liberal principles. With banners reading "Honour to Wilson the Just," it was clear Parisians supported the president's mission. French leaders, though complimentary in public, were less enthusiastic. Wilson's presence at the peace conference caused them concern; together with British and Italian leaders, the French worried about the American president's ability to compromise on his idealistic vision.[1]

In the United States, Wilson's European sojourn also caused unease. As the first sitting president to visit Europe and personally negotiate at a conference with world leaders, Wilson was shattering precedent. But his diplomatic mission was a sign of America's growing international power and prestige. As a former US attaché noted at the time, America's enhanced global standing "carries with it a number of obligations of an international character," which included "the maintenance of personal relations with the rulers of the other great powers."[2]

In the second half of the twentieth century, such interactions between the American president and other heads of state and government would become commonplace. But Wilson was a man ahead of his time. For most of American history, personal diplomacy by presidents had been rare. Although US presidents directed foreign policy, direct engagement with foreign counterparts was not considered a central duty. Today, by contrast, face-to-face meetings, telephone calls, videoconferences, and letters to foreign chief executives are part of the president's routine. If a president did not do those things, it would be seen as a dereliction of duty. Modern presidents consider diplomacy more than a responsibility; they see value in the practice.

The "modern presidency," characterized by rising expectations, sensitivity to public opinion, activism in the legislative arena, a propensity to act unilaterally, and a vast executive branch bureaucracy, emerged during Franklin D. Roosevelt's administration.[3] Overlooked is how the modern presidency also witnessed the rise of personal diplomacy, as men with vastly different political ideologies, policy objectives, leadership styles, partisan affiliations, and personalities engaged in this practice to advance American foreign policy.

Historians have long written about presidential diplomacy. They have focused on presidents' relationships with particular leaders, presidential personalities and preferences, and famous conferences and summits.[4] This scholarship is valuable and has deepened our understanding of how individual presidents used personal diplomacy. But it has largely failed to explore the practice as a larger phenomenon of the American presidency, and it has not examined why presidents made personal foreign policy central to the nation's conduct of international relations. This is not to deny that some historical works have placed leader-to-leader engagement in a broader context—as a significant element in explaining global change, with a focus on exploring the significance and influence of change agents at pivotal moments.[5] But they have not concentrated on America alone, nor has the existing historical literature answered the question why, since Franklin Roosevelt, all American presidents have resorted to diplomacy at the highest level when previously that was not the case. What changed, and what did twentieth- and twenty-first-century presidents seek to achieve? How did US public expectations change?

Political scientists have been more apt than historians to explore personal diplomacy as a practice of international politics that transcends individual leaders.[6] They have also examined it as an institutional practice of the presidency. Foremost among them is Elmer Plischke, who has covered the modes of personal diplomacy, details about specific interactions between presidents and world leaders, and the outcomes, advantages, and risks of the practice. But like most historians, Plischke provides little analysis of why presidents resorted to the practice in the first place. For example, in *Diplomat in Chief*, he merely notes that personal diplomacy increased after World War II but offers no explanation.[7]

My aim is to explore why the presidency, as an institution, resorted to diplomacy at the highest level. I argue that regardless of who occupied the postwar White House, presidents were driven to use personal diplomacy for the same reasons: international crises, domestic politics, foreign leaders' requests, and a desire for control. I study particular episodes in various administrations, while offering a novel explanation of the institution of the presidency and its functionality. Overall, the goal is to provide a better understanding of presidential behavior and US foreign relations today.

The term *personal diplomacy* is commonly used, but there is no clear definition. The term conjures up images of leaders engaging in intimate and perhaps even friendly conversations, but that is often not what happens when heads of state and government interact. Meetings between world leaders often include a phalanx of advisers and interpreters. The same is true for telephone calls, which are far less private than we might think. Letters may be written in a leader's own hand, but they are often composed by bureaucrats. Some leaders are more transactional in their approach and less interested in "friendship," while others cherish the "personal" part of diplomatic relations. Thus, personal diplomacy is not always particularly personal. But regardless of the level of intimacy, and even if others are involved, each leader's power and authority are invoked when two of them interact. And because the American president is at the top of the US bureaucracy and is both the head of government and head of state, the president's personal involvement matters. If it were not important, presidents would rarely interact with other world leaders in any capacity. In this book, *personal diplomacy* denotes direct communication between presidents and their foreign counterparts, whether face-to-face, through correspondence, or on the telephone, and regardless of how intimate the exchange is.

Leaders can interact in various ways, but there is a hierarchy. Face-to-face meetings are the ultimate form of personal diplomacy. For those who see the practice as a valuable means to build rapport, trust, and understanding, face-to-face interactions are most effective. As international relations scholars Todd Hall and Keren Yarhi-Milo argue, an in-person meeting "provides a setting in which leaders not only exchange information by the content of what they say, but also through myriad other channels. These include facial expression, body language, tone of voice, even unconscious movements or reactions."[8] Other modes of personal diplomacy, such as letters, telephone calls, and even contact through personal representatives, also play an essential role. They reinforce the discussions held and the relationships built during face-to-face encounters.[9] If leaders met only occasionally and had no contact in between, those in-person meetings would be less meaningful.

THE HISTORY OF PERSONAL DIPLOMACY AND
THE US PRESIDENCY

Leader-to-leader diplomacy is an ancient practice and has been used in Europe for centuries.[10] But the United States is a different story. At its founding in 1776, America saw itself as a nation set apart. The diplomatic ways of Europe—"the pest of the peace of the world," according to Thomas Jefferson—held no allure for the fledgling nation.[11] This is not to say that the early United States wanted nothing to do with the rest of the world. From its founding, it sought robust trade relations with other countries, but political connections across the oceans were anathema to early Americans. Even as the United States established itself as a rising global power at the start of the twentieth century, it remained wary of Europe and its politics. Combined with this ideological aversion to connectedness was geographic separation. Vast oceans to the east and west and weak neighbors to the north and south meant that US security and prosperity were less dependent on diplomatic engagement, and the nation could afford to distance itself from traditional customs and procedures during the nineteenth century.[12]

America's isolation also meant that its presidents had fewer opportunities to communicate with foreign leaders. On occasion, they corresponded with other heads of state and government; however, these interactions were more the exception than the rule, and even if greater contact had been possible, the public would have been skeptical. There was an unspoken rule that travel abroad and close contact with foreign leaders did not constitute proper presidential behavior. It was considered unbecoming for a democratic leader to be feted by monarchs and engage in private discussions with them. Some worried that such behavior threatened the president's, and perhaps even the nation's, republican simplicity.[13] Some even believed that presidential travel abroad was unconstitutional. "I am under the impression that there is a Statute, or some provision, against the president leaving the territory of the U.S.," Ulysses S. Grant wrote to the Speaker of the House in 1871. Even without a legal prohibition, President Grant did not want to "be the one to establish the precedent of an Executive going beyond the limits of his country."[14] Thus, as the United States entered the twentieth century, an "ironclad" custom had developed: presidents did not travel abroad. There was no such prohibition against foreign leaders coming to the United States, although the Department of State discouraged such visits over concerns about costs and the safety of foreign guests. Not until 1874, when Grant welcomed the king of Hawaii, did a head of state visit the United States. But this did not become a regular occurrence. In the almost sixty years between the king's visit and Franklin Roosevelt's presidency, foreign leaders visited America only twenty-four times—a few European leaders, but mostly Latin American chief executives.[15]

The United States welcomed few foreign visitors in the first decades of the twentieth century, but two presidents, Theodore Roosevelt and Woodrow Wilson, experimented with the practice. Roosevelt engaged in direct correspondence with European leaders such as Kaiser Wilhelm II, King Edward VI, and Tsar Nicholas II.[16] He also organized international gatherings to reduce world tensions, such as the Portsmouth Conference in 1905 to end the conflict between Japan and Russia and the Algeciras Conference in 1906 to mediate European imperial rivalries. Although Roosevelt did not attend these conferences, he worked behind the scenes to ensure their success, including writing to his foreign counterparts.[17] Roosevelt became the first sitting president to leave the country when he visited the Panama Canal in 1906. While there, he met with Panama's president, an encounter that included public speeches, a fireworks display, and an elaborate reception—exactly the type of activities modern presidents would engage in.[18]

Even more than Roosevelt, President Wilson practiced personal diplomacy when he traveled to Europe to negotiate peace agreements after World War I. He represented a shift from "traditional" or "old" diplomacy to what scholars have labeled "new" diplomacy. Whereas traditional diplomacy was characterized by the interaction of professional diplomats, usually bilaterally and in private, new diplomacy featured multilateral engagement, international organizations, greater openness, and the personal participation of world leaders.[19] Wilson engaged his European counterparts even before the peace conference. Shortly after war broke out, he sent messages to the emperors of Germany and Austria-Hungary, the Russian tsar, the president of France, and the British king, offering to serve as a mediator. Over the next few years, as the United States stayed out of the conflict, Wilson sent many notes to the belligerents. "Whatever else the present war may be accomplishing, it is revealing a great writer of despatches [*sic*] in the President of the United States," wrote one newspaper.[20]

But in the early twentieth century, Americans were not ready for an active president on the global stage, and both Roosevelt and Wilson faced political attacks for their actions. Roosevelt grumbled that Americans were too insular and lamented, "I sometimes wish that we did not have the ironclad custom which forbids a President ever to go abroad." Otherwise, he would have set sail to visit his European counterparts.[21]

Wilson encountered even more trouble. When he announced in November 1918 that he would travel to Europe to attend the peace conference, opposition was widespread. Days before the announcement, a survey of thirty-five major newspapers found that only ten supported a potential presidential trip to Europe. The concerns ranged from breaking with tradition to the president's need to deal with important domestic issues to fears that Wilson would become disconnected from his fellow citizens.[22] Secretary of State Robert Lansing opposed the trip, stating, "the President's place is here in America"; in his opinion, Wilson was "making one of the greatest mistakes of his career." Lansing predicted that Wilson would lose his commanding international stature and that Congress would be unsupportive.[23] Indeed, when Wilson delivered the State of the Union address two weeks after announcing his trip, he argued that he had to go because the leaders of other nations "very reasonably desire my personal counsel." The applause was scant.[24] The next day, Republican senator Lawrence Sherman proposed a joint resolution seeking to strip Wilson of his presidential powers. He argued that because the president could not fulfill his constitutional duties while abroad, his powers should be transferred to the vice president—and not just temporarily but until the next election. Sherman's resolution failed, but it showed the political headwinds buffeting the president. As Democratic senator Henry Ashurt told Wilson, the House of Representatives "would impeach you and the Senate convict you if they had the courage. Their lack of nerve is all that saves your removal from office."[25]

Roosevelt's and Wilson's behavior raised several potentially troubling questions. How safe would the chief executive be far from American shores? Could the president properly fulfill his constitutional duties thousands of miles away? What business did America have getting involved in European politics? Would it lead to the "entangling alliances" George Washington had warned against? Was it even proper for a republican leader to engage in private talks with other leaders, many of whom were autocrats?

The pushback against Roosevelt and especially Wilson demonstrates the fundamental change that personal diplomacy would bring to the American presidency and the conduct of US foreign affairs. The uproar over Wilson's actions made his Republican successors refrain from similar behavior, but they could not avoid world leaders entirely and welcomed thirteen of them to the United States. They even went abroad themselves, although they stayed in the Western Hemisphere.[26] Times were changing. But the personal diplomacy of the early twentieth century was quantitatively and qualitatively different from the diplomacy that occurred in the second half of the twentieth century.

MOTIVATIONS FOR THE USE OF PERSONAL DIPLOMACY

In his classic work *Presidential Power and the Modern Presidents*, Richard Neustadt argues that the presidency's formal powers are not enough to meet the demands placed on the office.[27] Presidents have to rely on their personal skills, and their ability to bargain, enhance their reputation, and gain political capital can determine their success. Other scholars have explored the traits and characteristics necessary for the successful exercise of presidential power in the United States, and the study of personal diplomacy seemingly fits into this personalized approach to the presidency.[28] Analyzing how a US president performs when interacting with foreign leaders is very much about the president's skill, personality, and style.

When it comes to examining why presidents, as a group, engage in personal diplomacy, a different approach is necessary. Neustadt has been extremely influential, but others have challenged his focus on personal qualities and argued that although the president is a single individual, he is also an institutional actor with "a role well specified by law and expectations. . . . Some portion of presidential behavior, then, and perhaps a very large portion, is quite impersonal. All presidents, whatever their personalities or styles or backgrounds, should tend to behave similarly in basic respects."[29] This is how I conceptualize personal diplomacy in this book. In the period under consideration—the second half of the twentieth century—all presidents, regardless of their personality, leadership style, or partisan affiliation, engaged in personal diplomacy, and they all did so for similar reasons.

The basis for personal diplomacy derives from the president's constitutional role as diplomat in chief. According to Clinton Rossiter, during the Cold War it became "the most important and exacting [role] . . . we call upon the President to play." Between the intelligence briefings, national security meetings, consultations with Congress, and meetings and correspondence with foreign leaders, "it is a wonder that he [the president] had a moment's time for any of his other duties."[30] Even if they had more time, it is not clear that presidents would choose to spend it on domestic matters. As Aaron Wildavsky has argued, "two presidencies" exist. One is focused on the domestic arena and is constrained by Congress and other actors on the home front. The second, which concentrates on foreign policy, is freer to act and more successful in imposing its will. In the international arena, the executive has first-mover and informational advantages.[31] I contend there is also a personal diplomacy advantage. By its very nature, presidential personal diplomacy is something that only the president can do. It is a unilateral tool the White House can employ, much like its ability to conclude executive agreements or deploy military forces. Congress's ability and will to challenge the president on these fronts are often limited.[32]

Yet the Constitution does not explicitly spell out presidential diplomatic practice. This is one of the ambiguities in the nation's founding document that presidents have exploited and, in the process, have used to increase their power and dominance in foreign affairs.[33] The desire for power is something all presidents share. "No matter their ideological commitments or partisan affiliations, regardless of their personal backgrounds or philosophies of governing," William G. Howell writes, "all presidents nearly all of the time seek to guard and expand their base of power." And the search for "power—both its attainment and maintenance—infuses all presidential actions."[34]

I argue that the rise of presidential personal diplomacy accompanied the rise of the modern presidency—all in the Cold War context of the United States as a world power. When Franklin Roosevelt took office, leader-to-leader diplomacy was not the norm, and the presidency was a small enterprise. But the New Deal's advent to tackle the Great Depression caused the operations of government to expand and exposed "the presidency's institutional shortcomings." In 1936 Roosevelt appointed a committee, led by Louis Brownlow, to study the executive branch and its organization. The following year the Brownlow Committee released its conclusion: "The President needs help." It made proposals to bolster the presidency's managerial capabilities and help the president deal with government's increased responsibilities. Initially, Congress balked at plans to empower the president, but it eventually passed a compromise measure. The Reorganization Act of 1939, along with Roosevelt's Executive Order 8248, resulted in the Executive Office of the President, which over time came to house a multitude of offices designed to help presidents govern, including the National Security Council (NSC).[35]

The National Security Act of 1947 created the NSC to improve the coordination and management of the nation's foreign policy. It was a reaction against the management style of Franklin Roosevelt, who often worked in secret with a small group of advisers to maintain control. For critics, the president's penchant for personal politics—both domestically and internationally—was part of the problem, since it often left the rest of the government in the dark about what Roosevelt had discussed and agreed to. By the end of World War II, there was a consensus that the demands of America's new global dominance made this personalized system dangerous and outdated.[36] However, far from containing the president's ability to dominate the foreign policy process, the NSC provided the White House with increased resources and power. It became "the hub of all U.S. international engagement." Moreover, it became "both the policy creation mechanism and the policy implementation mechanism that helped harness and coordinate the actions of an increasingly complex government in an increasingly complex word."[37]

As the presidency's power grew institutionally, it also grew in practice through the president's interactions with foreign leaders. On a basic level, the growth of institutional resources facilitated personal diplomacy; the means to handle voluminous correspondence with world leaders, provide analysis, prepare briefing materials for face-to-face meetings, and handle logistics for presidential trips abroad were made possible by the office's growth.[38] Simultaneously, more personal diplomacy meant the need for more resources. The expansion of the institution and the intensifying pace of personal encounters and engagement were self-reinforcing.

Still, presidents could have continued to leave the bulk of diplomacy to the Department of State while only occasionally resorting to interactions at the leader level. In the State Department, presidents possess a vast and deep bureaucratic machine. Today it consists of tens of thousands of foreign service officers and civil service employees and operates hundreds of embassies and consulates around the globe in hundreds of countries. The department carries out many functions, but representing the nation abroad, analyzing foreign developments, and negotiating with foreign governments have long been central to its work.[39] After World War II, the State Department continued to perform these roles. Indeed, presidential personal diplomacy did not eradicate other actors or other means of conducting foreign policy. Instead, it was layered on existing practices, creating both new opportunities and new tensions.[40]

So why did American presidents feel the need to increase their interactions with foreign leaders? As noted, an underlying desire for power played a role in the growth of personal diplomacy, and the growth of institutional resources helped facilitate it. But I argue that other forces also influenced presidential behavior.

One cannot make sense of the development of presidential personal diplomacy without acknowledging the advancement in communications and travel technology, which shrank the vast distances between presidents and their foreign counterparts. The telephone allowed real-time communication with capitals all over the globe, but not until the 1960s did telephone conversations between American presidents and world leaders become increasingly common.[41] But from its earliest uses, presidents realized the telephone's diplomatic potential. When Calvin Coolidge placed the first presidential transatlantic call to King Alfonso XIII of Spain in October 1928, he extolled the benefits of the technology and introduced the arguments that future presidents would make in defense of personal diplomacy: "I believe it to be true that when two men can talk together the danger of any serious disagreement is immeasurably lessened and that what is true of individuals is true of nations. The international telephone, therefore, which carries the warmth and the friendliness of the human voice, will always correct what might be misinterpreted in the written word."[42] And that sentiment came from someone who believed the telephone to be beneath the "dignity of the [president's] job."[43]

Advancements in transportation technology also made leader-to-leader engagement easier. With the arrival of the airplane, travel that would have taken weeks was cut to hours. Franklin Roosevelt made the first presidential flight in 1943 when he attended the Casablanca Conference to meet with British prime minister Winston Churchill. This feat captured Americans' imagination. Some expressed admiration, while others worried about the president's safety. Roosevelt was not a fan of air travel, which was still relatively slow compared with today's flights, and the planes were small and uncomfortable. In 1959 the Boeing 707 "transformed" presidential air travel. In addition to being more comfortable, it allowed the diplomat in chief to fly in inclement weather and to bring along more advisers and staff. More work could now be accomplished in the air, making the plane "a second Oval Office . . . that kept the president in touch with the world."[44]

These communications and travel advancements made it easier for presidents to engage in personal diplomacy in the second half of the twentieth century. But they do not explain the frequency, scope, or depth of leader-to-leader interactions in this period. If these technological advancements were the main drivers of personal diplomacy, the practice's novelty would have worn off over time and its use declined. Other forces were at play. I argue that four factors, both international and domestic, influenced modern US presidents to make personal diplomacy a central feature of how America engages with the world.

The first factor was the challenge of the Cold War and the crises it produced. The United States emerged from World War II a superpower. But as one war ended, another began, and the nation quickly became entangled in a decades-long struggle with the Soviet Union. The Cold War created a bipolar international system. Even though the period was seemingly stable, this "long peace" did not mean that crises could not get hot in the periphery.[45] Furthermore, in the view of officials in the Truman administration, "the distinctions between peace and war had disappeared, leaving America in a world of perpetual crisis."[46] As leader of the Western bloc, the United States was at the helm when dealing with global flare-ups. It was the dominant power, and other countries looked to the White House for leadership because the United States was often the only entity with the political, military, and economic clout to intervene effectively. When trouble arose in places like Berlin, the Middle East, or Southeast Asia, presidents frequently found themselves writing letters, making telephone calls, or meeting with their foreign counterparts to mediate disputes between rival nations, consult with allies, or negotiate with adversaries.

Even when the United States seemingly had little at stake, such as the dispute between Turkey and Greece over the small island of Cyprus, the president often felt compelled to get involved. In an era when the watchword was *stability* and any crisis had the possibility of leading to Cold War entanglements, American presidents felt pressure to do something, and this often took the form of personal diplomacy. Sometimes their efforts were successful; other times, not. But the key is that presidents felt obliged to try.

The specter of nuclear Armageddon provided added impetus for leaders to engage. If a local conflict became ensnared in the superpower confrontation, or if there was a direct confrontation between the United States and the Soviet Union, nuclear weapons lurked menacingly in the background. Leaders on both sides knew that nuclear war would be devastating, yet this understanding did not prevent American and Soviet leaders from threatening the use of nuclear weapons for political gain. But when they were on the brink, personal diplomacy provided an avenue of communication and understanding that could lessen tensions, such as during the Cuban missile crisis, when Nikita Khrushchev and John F. Kennedy exchanged numerous messages.[47] The showdown in Cuba revealed the need for greater communication during a crisis and led to a formal method of leader-to-leader diplomacy with the installation of the "hotline" between the United States and the Soviet Union.

The second factor influencing the use of personal diplomacy was domestic political incentives. Presidents seek to dominate foreign policy in part because, more so than any other political actor in the US system, they are likely to be blamed or praised for whatever occurs globally; as a result, foreign affairs play a significant role in presidential elections but not in congressional contests.[48] Presidents rarely admit that domestic political considerations influence their foreign policy decisions, because that would make them seem crass, self-serving, and opportunistic. But those calculations exist. Anthony Lake, Bill Clinton's national security adviser, compared the influence of domestic politics on foreign policy to the relationship between the Victorians and sex: "Nobody talks about it but it's on everybody's mind."[49] As politicians, presidents seek every opportunity to enhance their political clout, their standing with the public, their reelection prospects, and their legacy.[50] In the second half of the twentieth century, personal diplomacy assisted in these endeavors.

In this period, as the power and prestige of the presidency increased, so did expectations. "Since the president has become the embodiment of government," presidential scholar Theodore Lowi observed, "it seems perfectly normal for millions upon millions of Americans to concentrate their hopes and fears directly and personally upon him."[51] The problem was that, even with greater resources and power, there was no way presidents could meet all the demands placed on them. And the American people's high expectations were often contradictory.[52] This meant that presidents had to find ways to maintain public support, even as they failed to meet expectations.[53] Personal diplomacy was one way to do that. It allowed presidents to create spectacles that, though perhaps not relevant to governing, at least made them look active and in charge.[54] During the Cold War, presidential personal diplomacy received widespread news coverage, and the pomp and ceremony that often accompanied the practice allowed presidents to appear statesmanlike and enhance their leadership appeal. And the strategy often paid off, albeit on a small scale. Foreign travel and high-level meetings with world leaders frequently boosted presidential popularity, though fleetingly.[55]

For modern presidents, concentrating on foreign policy becomes more attractive when their domestic agendas are stymied. So whether the occupant of the White House is a lame duck or the opposing party controls Congress, focusing on foreign policy and personal diplomacy allows the president to better shape the narrative.[56] For instance, presidents have used their leader-to-leader interactions to portray themselves as apostles of peace and to buttress their image as commander in chief. During the Cold War, when the world lived in the shadow of nuclear conflict and presidents had their fingers on the proverbial nuclear button, engaging other world leaders in the cause of peace showed them to be wise stewards of that responsibility, thus reinforcing their role as wartime leaders.

Personal diplomacy sent other signals as well. It is a type of "theater" in which leaders play a significant role. As Raymond Cohen has written, "As a national symbol . . . the leader is placed in an unrivalled position to perform the role of dramatic communicator." Diplomacy at the highest level is a visual manifestation of a president's foreign policy. While the public might struggle to grasp the intricacies of foreign affairs, interactions between leaders send easily digestible messages about the state of relations between the United States and other countries. Although this simplifies the nuances of foreign policy, this personalization by presidents "is a succinct and most expressive means of dramatizing—and hence better communicating—policy."[57]

The third factor influencing presidential diplomacy was foreign leaders themselves. During the Cold War, the US president was the leader of the Western superpower, a position of political might, status, and prestige that was backed up by unique military and economic prowess.[58] Thus, other heads of state and government increasingly sought to engage the White House on political, military, and economic issues. Though lobbying Congress might also pay dividends, its decentralized nature made this difficult, and few nations had the resources to do so effectively. By comparison, engaging the president was easier, and because he was the dominant figure in the US political system, it was often the most effective means to gain assistance. Indeed, one scholar found that, during the Cold War, a country whose leader met with the president was more likely to receive aid than a nation whose leader did not. A summit with the president increased not only the odds of getting aid but also the amount.[59]

Interacting with the US president was also a way for foreign leaders to boost their own stature. It was a political boon for leaders, both at home and abroad, to meet with the head of a superpower. Even for adversaries of the United States, engaging with the American president could have benefits. For example, during the Cold War, the Soviet Union—which was always concerned with its international standing—believed that summits conveyed equality and respect. The Soviets took particular pride in the 1972 summit in Moscow, where Richard Nixon and Leonid Brezhnev signed the "Basic Principles," which the Kremlin viewed as US recognition of Soviet superpower status.[60]

Although foreign leaders' desire to interact with the White House bestowed a certain amount of power and leverage, it also increased the demands on the presidency. Presidents' time is finite, but the issues they face are infinite. Ann Lewis, director of communications and counselor to Bill Clinton, summed up the dilemma: "the most valuable resource we have is the president's time, and we'll never have enough of it."[61] The more time presidents spent engaging with foreign leaders, the less time they had for other issues. But the role of diplomat in chief, just like the role of commander in chief, cannot be delegated. Presidents must do it themselves.[62]

During the Cold War, the White House often welcomed overtures by heads of state and government, but sometimes it did not. Perhaps the issue a foreign leader wanted to discuss did not interest the president or was politically toxic. Maybe the president did not like the other leader. Or maybe he simply did not have enough time. Rejection of a foreign counterpart's outreach, however, could be perilous. If the president refused to engage in personal diplomacy or did so halfheartedly, it could harm relations. Amid a global struggle in which accumulating allies was key, presidents had to keep their old friends happy and try to win new ones. Personal diplomacy helped in this endeavor, and its absence could be damaging.

The last factor influencing presidential personal diplomacy was the desire to control US foreign affairs. As a group, modern presidents believe they are preeminent in crafting American foreign policy. And although presidents are dominant in the international arena, they do not always have an easy time. In theory, the Department of State is the executive branch's official instrument of diplomacy and foreign policy. Yet in every modern presidency there has been at least one moment when the president was frustrated by the State Department. Much of this has to do with the general nature of large bureaucracies, and presidents' troubles with the State Department are similar to their complaints about other executive branch departments. McGeorge Bundy, national security adviser to John F. Kennedy and Lyndon Johnson, once remarked that the executive branch "more nearly resembles a collection of badly separated principalities than a single instrument of executive action."[63]

Control is not the only issue. Presidents often distrust the bureaucracy. Richard Nixon "distrusted the bureaucracy, particularly the State Department, figuring they were a bunch of either thoughtless bureaucrats or left-wing Democrats or both. But . . . even if they weren't, he wanted to control it [foreign policy]," recalled former NSC staffer and ambassador Winston Lord.[64] One might expect such sentiments from the paranoid and secretive Nixon. However, even Jimmy Carter, a president with a vastly different personality, often lacked faith in Foggy Bottom. When he moved to normalize relations with China, he was "leery" of going through the State Department and did not believe he "had full support there." Instead, he worked mainly through the NSC so his "efforts would not be subverted."[65]

Nineteenth-century presidents did not confront this problem, as the nation's bureaucratic machinery remained minimal. But as America transformed from an agricultural society to an industrial one in the twentieth century, this changed. As society transitioned, the presidency grew, as did the president's need and desire to control the bureaucracy. "Presidents are driven to take charge," writes Terry Moe. What bureaucracies do, or do not do, can affect a president's agenda and cause political headaches.[66] But maintaining control requires a constant effort, because once "presidential attention shifts, bureaucratic policy once again prevails . . . even though it may in serious respects contradict presidential policy of only days before."[67]

The desire for control led to greater centralization in the White House.[68] This meant increasing reliance on the NSC rather than the State Department. Whereas the NSC is seen as looking out for the president's interests, the State Department has a different constituency. "The State Department has 180 clients [i.e., other countries]," Henry Kissinger observed. Its job is "basically answering cables," he said, and with its numerous daily tasks, the State Department is unable to think long term and focus on the president's priorities.[69]

Though not traditionally conceptualized as a way to gain control, personal diplomacy allowed presidents to centralize their foreign policy. They not only crafted policy in the White House but also executed it from there. By directly engaging with foreign leaders, presidents could avoid distortion of their views, information leaks, and bureaucratic stagnation. The result was an increase in presidential power.

Throughout this book, these four factors are explored, and their influence on presidential behavior is explained. No factor was necessarily more important than another in elevating personal diplomacy. In some instances, one factor might have been dominant, but in most cases, presidents were influenced by a mix of motives. For example, a global crisis might lead a president to reach out to another world leader, who in turn might desire an ongoing dialogue, forcing the president into more direct interactions. Despite the greater demands on the president's time, this type of engagement allowed more control over the US response. That personal diplomacy could then be used for political gain to depict the president as a statesman. Thus, the four factors combine to provide a portrait of an institution resorting to personal diplomacy for myriad reasons to accomplish multiple objectives. They demonstrate that, regardless of personality, leadership style, or partisan affiliation, postwar presidents behaved similarly when it came to personal diplomacy. Clark Clifford, an adviser to several presidents, observed that the presidency is "like a chameleon. To a startling degree it reflects the character and personality of the President."[70] But in deciding to engage with world leaders, modern presidents were remarkably of one color.

Personal diplomacy thus became the norm. The more presidents interacted with foreign leaders, the more natural it seemed. Though critics persisted, future presidents did not question whether to engage in personal diplomacy. There was no need to mobilize support for the practice. Debates over its constitutionality ceased. It was understood as proper and, for many, essential presidential behavior. And over time, the cost of abandoning the practice became too high.[71] The more presidents engaged in it, the harder it was to stop. The public and the media saw it as evidence of presidential leadership. Thus, not engaging in personal diplomacy could hurt a president's standing at home and harm his reputation abroad. Foreign leaders expected presidents to engage and frequently sought them out. And because personal diplomacy was so useful in various situations, ranging from crisis management to rapprochement, its abandonment would take away a tool in the president's national security arsenal and adversely affect US foreign relations.

It can be debated whether personal diplomacy was a positive element in the nation's handling of foreign affairs and in the presidency as an institution. Although some presidents, such as Dwight Eisenhower, considered how their personal diplomacy might affect the presidency and their successors' behavior, modern presidents as a group generally used the practice to handle the challenges of the day and gave less thought to the long-term consequences of directly engaging with their foreign counterparts. Short-term considerations, such as dealing with crises, meeting foreign leaders' demands, and capturing political gain, trumped long-term thinking about what personal diplomacy meant for the presidency.[72] But regardless of whether adherents considered the long-term consequences of the practice, the result was the same: the institutionalization of presidential personal diplomacy.

THE PRESIDENT AS COUNSELOR

This book also explores Cold War presidents' most common role when engaging with foreign leaders—that of counselor. After World War II, the United States became a status quo power seeking global stability. But the crises and pressures of the Cold War—not to mention the ever-present specter of nuclear war—caused fear and insecurity throughout the world. As leaders of the world's most powerful nation, presidents and their advisers saw it as their responsibility—and in the national interest—to address these concerns. Military and economic aid helped, but there was also an emotional and psychological element involved. Diplomats are supposed to be rational individuals, immune from the vagaries of human emotions, but personal feelings cannot be completely shut out.[73] So presidents sought to ease their foreign counterparts' minds and, by doing so, forestall actions or inactions that might lead to volatility in the international sphere.

This was not something presidents did casually. Almost every interaction between an American president and a foreign leader involved the former trying to ease the latter's concerns by conveying US support, strength, determination, and reliability. When presidents did this, they acted as "counselors." The American Psychological Association defines a counselor as someone who helps people with "physical, emotional and mental health issues improve their sense of well-being, alleviate feelings of distress and resolve crises."[74] No American president was trained in this field, but they sought the same ends as a counselor. Nor did foreign leaders necessarily ask the president to perform this role; in fact, if some of them knew how officials in the White House described their mental states, they would have taken offense. Instead, this was a function US presidents performed because they believed it was in America's national interest to soothe other leaders' minds.

The role of counselor was connected to the larger issue of credibility, which was and is central to US world leadership. Both allies and adversaries had to believe that the United States would act when necessary to protect its interests. As historian Robert McMahon argues, in "an inherently dangerous and unstable world," American presidents believed that "peace and order depend[ed] to a great extent on Washington's ability to convince adversaries and allies alike of its firmness, determination, and dependability."[75] Interaction with world leaders played a central role in sending these signals. And projecting credibility extended not just to other world leaders but to the American people as well. A president's credibility abroad influenced his credibility at home, and vice versa.

Presidents employed all the various modes of personal diplomacy to play the counselor role, including the use of letters, telephone calls, and surrogates. But it was in face-to-face encounters where the emotional and psychological elements of diplomacy were most evident. Using insights from social psychology and social neuroscience, international relations scholars have shown the value of face-to-face interactions in promoting understanding and empathy and clarifying intentions.[76] There is a reason why leaders want to meet in person and size up their counterparts. The words spoken during a meeting matter, but leaders are also sensitive to other cues. "Face-to-face encounters are seen as potentially more honest and open than those conducted by other means," writes Jenny Edkins, because "we pay attention to reading each other's faces—reading people's moods, personalities and origins into their facial appearance. We search for clues as to who the person opposite us may be and what they may be thinking." People regularly make these assessments in everyday life. So do world leaders. The reliability of such nonverbal cues is debatable, but studies suggest that humans are quite perceptive when reading others.[77] And regardless of how reliable such signals may be, foreign leaders use them to assess the American president's reliability. Thus, when the president's goal is to reduce the anxiety of another leader, meeting face-to-face provides an opportunity to offer comforting words, and it allows the foreign leader to assess the sincerity of those words.

When presidents performed the role of counselor, it was not because of altruistic impulses. Some presidents formed genuine friendships with other world leaders and wanted to help them as much as possible. But the breadth and depth of the counselor role meant that presidents had to deal with leaders they were not close to. Regardless of the intimacy of the relationship, presidents sought the same objective: to further American interests. Acting as a counselor was strategic. A president's natural affinity for personal relations could make him more effective, but this function was about the position he held, not his personality. Undoubtedly, foreign leaders welcomed a personable president, but even more, they valued the resources a president could assemble to confront global challenges. It was the president's job, no matter his personality, to convince foreign leaders that he could and would stand tall.

How effective presidents were in this role is questionable. The White House thought presidential reassurances were valuable, but presidents had to do it a lot. A president might meet with a leader and feel confident that he had played the role of counselor well, only to be asked to address those same fears and worries soon thereafter.

ORGANIZATION OF THE BOOK

The following chapters cover the presidency from Franklin Roosevelt to George H. W. Bush. The first chapter examines how Roosevelt established a pattern of personal diplomacy for modern presidents. Part of FDR's use of leader-to-leader diplomacy was based on his personal predilection for the practice. However, during his presidency, the four factors outlined earlier and the counselor role began to emerge. Rather than focusing on FDR's well-known wartime interactions with Winston Churchill and Joseph Stalin, chapter 1 examines the broad scope of his interactions with a range of leaders both before and during World War II.

Chapter 2 explores the administrations of Harry Truman and Dwight Eisenhower. Despite the backlash against personal diplomacy during the late 1940s and early 1950s due to Roosevelt's dealings, particularly his interactions at the Yalta Conference, the practice did not disappear. By the end of Eisenhower's presidency, thanks to his informal style and global goodwill tours, personal diplomacy had been revived.

Each of the next five chapters focuses on a single administration and examines how one particular motivation influenced the presidency. Chapter 3 looks at the president as counselor, using John F. Kennedy's attempts to ease the concerns of West German chancellor Konrad Adenauer and the shah of Iran. This required constant effort, and Kennedy was frequently frustrated and only temporarily successful. However, the counselor role was deemed to be in the US national interest and essential to maintaining stability in two vital regions of the world.

Chapter 4 focuses on how world crises can push presidents to engage with their foreign counterparts. It examines Lyndon Johnson's struggles to manage crises in Cyprus and Yemen and his attempts to reduce tensions with the Soviet Union. In confronting these challenges, the administration believed the president's personal diplomacy was its most potent tool. It was not always successful, but from the US perspective, Johnson at least had to try.

Chapter 5 explores Richard Nixon's use of high-profile visits to Beijing and Moscow to boost his electoral prospects in 1972. The summits improved his image as a statesman and peacemaker and helped him win reelection. But there were limits to what personal diplomacy could do. It could not save Nixon from the Watergate scandal and only minimally helped his successor, Gerald Ford.

Chapter 6 illustrates how foreign leaders can make demands on presidential time by examining Jimmy Carter's relations with Japanese prime ministers Takeo Fukuda and Masayoshi Ōhira and Egypt's Anwar Sadat. Fukuda and Ōhira often irritated Carter by their frequent and occasionally public requests for his attention. And although Carter welcomed Sadat's engagement, he was pulled into a level of personal diplomacy he could not have imagined at the start of his presidency.

Chapter 7 centers on Ronald Reagan's engagement with Soviet leaders. He faced hard-liners in his administration who were opposed to improved US-Soviet relations, and he possessed little faith in foreign policy bureaucrats' ability to pull off bold diplomatic moves. Thus, Reagan resorted to personal diplomacy to assert greater control and push his policy forward.

Chapter 8 examines personal diplomacy at the end of one global era and the beginning of another. George H. W. Bush, motivated by the same factors as his predecessors, engaged with leaders at the end of the Cold War to achieve administration objectives such as German unification and the assembly of an international coalition against Iraq's Saddam Hussein.

Chapter 9 discusses how to assess the importance of presidential personal diplomacy. It looks at the benefits and risks of the practice, its relationship to policy, the lessons to be learned from its history, and how to evaluate an individual president's impact.

Overall, the book demonstrates that, regardless of personal preferences, American presidents in the second half of the twentieth century engaged in personal diplomacy for the same reasons. In doing so, they made it a central part of the office of the presidency and US foreign relations. The practice continues today, as presidents rely on personal diplomacy to deal with traditional Cold War concerns and twenty-first-century transnational challenges.

Like his father, George W. Bush made interactions with world leaders a hallmark of his foreign policy. After 9/11, terrorism catapulted to the top of US global concerns. Although this was a new foreign policy focus for the nation, Bush's diplomatic tools were familiar. In pursuing the war on terror, he relied heavily on personal diplomacy (with varying degrees of success) to garner support from other leaders for his actions, such as the war in Iraq.[78] Barack Obama did not evince the same enthusiasm for leader-to-leader engagement as his predecessor, but he relied on it for one of his top priorities: the Paris Climate Accord. He built relationships with Chinese leader Xi Jinping and Indian prime minister Narendra Modi and spoke with them frequently.[79] As Donald Trump, the most unconventional of presidents, said, "It is very important that if you are the president, you should be with the foreign leaders."[80] Indeed, faced with a global pandemic in 2020, Trump and other chief executives found value in consulting, even if they could not do it face-to-face. In dealing with COVID-19, world leaders relied on advancements in communications technology to hold emergency meetings virtually.[81]

With Joe Biden in the White House as of 2021, personal diplomacy will continue to be central to the American presidency. Biden's decades-long career, including his eight years as vice president, make it clear that he will emphasize personal relations with foreign leaders.[82] But even without his affinity for personal diplomacy, Biden would still find value in the practice, for the same reasons his predecessors did.

1. FDR's Wide-Ranging Personal Diplomacy

The man of steel seemed nervous. As Soviet leader Joseph Stalin prepared to meet American president Franklin D. Roosevelt for the first time in 1943, he wanted everything to be perfect. His clothes were neatly pressed, his boots were polished, and inserts had been placed in his shoes to make him appear taller. To hide his pockmarked face, Stalin had prearranged the seating so he would not be too close to the light. His interpreter had never seen Stalin act this way. When the two men finally met, both turned on the charm and got along well. They furthered their bond over dinner by riling up British prime minister Winston Churchill about the end of colonial empires and joked (perhaps Stalin was somewhat serious) that the Allies should deal with a defeated Germany by killing its military officers en masse.[1]

When Stalin and Roosevelt met a year and a half later, they greeted each other like old friends. The president hoped this relationship would prove beneficial not only during the war but also after. In light of future developments, however, his embrace of Stalin may seem naïve and nearsighted.[2] But FDR's wartime diplomacy was crucial in maintaining the alliance and demonstrates his penchant for personal diplomacy. In the words of one diplomatic historian, he "took special pleasure in his direct contact with world leaders such as the sinister and Sphinx-like Joseph Stalin and the bulldog Churchill."[3]

Other forces also pushed Roosevelt toward engagement with his counterparts, including a volatile international environment, domestic political incentives, the wishes of other leaders, and a desire for greater control. These factors did not develop all at once or in equal proportion during the Roosevelt years. However, all took on greater significance and continued to do so in the postwar period. FDR did not interact with world leaders simply because he enjoyed it. He did so because it was a tool that furthered American interests.

Roosevelt's interactions with Churchill and Stalin have, understandably, received much attention.[4] This wartime focus, however, neglects FDR's contact with other world leaders, obscuring the totality of his leader-to-leader diplomacy. His wartime encounters were more consequential and had a more desperate quality than prewar contacts, but when we look at the pre- and postwar periods together, the wide scope of FDR's personal diplomacy becomes clear.

The importance of exploring Roosevelt's leader-to-leader contacts goes beyond simply deepening our understanding of how he conducted foreign affairs. His extensive engagement with heads of state and government had implications for the institution of the presidency and its conduct of foreign affairs. He established a pattern of behavior that postwar presidents followed. Historian William Leuchtenburg has argued that FDR's successors were in his "shadow." Whether it was the policies they pursued, how they presented themselves, or the coalitions they formed, comparisons to Roosevelt have been unavoidable.[5] Though it is not generally thought of as part of FDR's legacy, his personal diplomacy set an example for future presidents, as the practice became a feature of the modern presidency.

This chapter explores Roosevelt's wide-ranging use of personal diplomacy both before and after the outbreak of war. Rather than covering the same terrain as so many other works, I look at FDR's connections to world leaders other than Churchill and Stalin. The influence of international crises, domestic politics, other world leaders, and FDR's desire for control are evident. In various regions of the world, and with different world leaders, certain factors took on more prominence and importance than others. Most often, however, there was a confluence of motivations. By the end of his presidency, Roosevelt had ushered in not only the modern presidency but also the practice of personal diplomacy.

ROOSEVELT IN THE WORLD

When Roosevelt became president in 1933, economic recovery from the Great Depression, not foreign policy, was the priority. His inaugural address made this clear. The "greatest primary task is to put people to work," he declared. This did not mean he had no thoughts on foreign affairs. In the 1920s he had been a strong internationalist. He supported the League of Nations and wrote an article for *Foreign Affairs* demonstrating his knowledge and awareness of international developments.[6]

Roosevelt understood that the United States could not withdraw from the world; it needed to be involved in some manner. He also believed that a president needed to have public support. Those two views were at odds throughout the 1930s. While FDR wanted the United States to take a more active role in world affairs, he knew the public had little desire for such an agenda. He was also concerned that battles over foreign policy would alienate members of Congress whose votes he needed to pass his economic program.[7]

As FDR struggled to improve the economy and battled Americans' desire to turn inward, he was left with little room to maneuver in the international arena. At the 1933 World Economic Conference in London, Roosevelt chose economic nationalism over global cooperation, dooming the last real international attempt to deal collectively with the worldwide financial crisis. Before the gathering, he had given signs that the United States would work with other countries and would be amenable to the conference's proposals. In the days leading up to the London talks, the *New York Times* noted optimistically that the United States was coming out of its isolationist shell. Thus, FDR's rejection of the conference's plan for currency stabilization was a "bombshell." Conference attendees fumed and came close to formally denouncing the United States.[8] The sabotaging of the World Economic Conference was followed two years later by the first Neutrality Act, and throughout the 1930s the United States seemed ambivalent to the aggression of fascist dictators in Europe and a militant Japan. This led to the perception of a weak America that was on the decline. As one reporter described, "Never within memory . . . has American prestige and American influence been at a lower ebb. . . . In international affairs there can be noted an increasing tendency to forget at times that the United States exists at all."[9]

To characterize Roosevelt's foreign policy in the 1930s as pure isolationism and weakness, however, would be a mistake. He could have been bolder in the international arena, but there would have been political costs. As long as the American economy remained dismal, an intrepid foreign policy would have alienated large segments of the population. Isolationist elements in Congress would have been incensed, threatening the economic recovery Roosevelt needed to make the public more receptive to international engagement. If FDR had pursued an internationalist foreign policy in his first term, he might have been a one-term president. Pursuing the New Deal at home and internationalism abroad were not compatible.

Despite the lack of a bold foreign agenda early on, Roosevelt did not completely shun international affairs. Too often the narrative of his twelve years in office goes something like this: for most of the 1930s he was aimless, changing course only at the end of the decade as he saw the world heading toward war;

only after Pearl Harbor did he provide imaginative and courageous global leadership. Though partly accurate, this account obscures FDR's contacts with world leaders before World War II and ignores his use of personal diplomacy as a defining feature of his foreign policy from the beginning of his presidency.

EUROPE AND CANADA

In February 1933, a little less than a month before Roosevelt was sworn into office, British prime minister Ramsay MacDonald wrote to the president-elect: "I am making bold to write you this letter explaining some of our difficulties here, so that you may understand them at first hand. It is in no sense official. I repeat that this is purely a personal communication which I have been emboldened to make." The prime minister then asked that the letter not be used in official diplomatic channels.[10] Thus began FDR's extensive communication with foreign leaders.

MacDonald's caution makes it clear that personal communication of this sort between world leaders was uncommon in the 1930s. Roosevelt, however, was "delighted" with the letter and quite comfortable with the diplomatic back channel. He did not fully trust his ambassadors and had disdain for professional diplomats. Thus he sought direct channels of communication with his foreign counterparts. FDR told the prime minister he hoped their informal contact would continue and expressed a desire to meet soon. A meeting, he believed, would be invaluable for Anglo-American relations, and he was sure they "would not find it difficult to establish a personal relationship of absolute confidence."[11]

The two men met a few months later. In April the prime minister spent a week in the United States discussing economic issues related to the upcoming World Economic Conference. Considering that gathering's failure, the long-term value of these talks is questionable. Yet they did have value for FDR, who benefited politically. Interest in the prime minister's visit was high, and press coverage of the president was laudatory. It portrayed him as a wise sage whom MacDonald hoped to learn from. As one newspaper wrote, the prime minister sought Roosevelt's "aid and counsel" to solve the problems confronting Europe and the world. This early venture in personal diplomacy also allowed the president to contrast himself favorably with his predecessor. "Repeatedly, since he was elected," the *New York Times* noted, "the President has remarked that the Prime Minister is an 'old friend,' who would vastly prefer to deal personally with him and was entirely willing to wait for effective negotiations until the Hoover administration expired."[12]

After Roosevelt and MacDonald conferred, they released a joint statement praising their "unity of purpose and method." As the economic conference in London almost two months later made clear, however, that harmony was fleeting. In fact, the limits of personal diplomacy were illustrated about a month before the conference when Roosevelt sent a message to more than fifty heads of state appealing for peace and resolution of the world's economic ills. The message garnered wide acclaim in the press, which portrayed the president as a great statesman. He received twenty-one replies, but no tangible actions were taken.[13]

Despite the lack of results, Roosevelt's early endeavors showed that he was more than willing to engage his foreign counterparts. Throughout his time in office, he established ties with numerous European leaders. During World War II the heads of Poland, Greece, Yugoslavia, Czechoslovakia, and Iceland all visited the White House. Queen Wilhelmina of the Netherlands, King Peter of Yugoslavia, King Leopold of Belgium, and King George of Britain frequently corresponded with the president, and in 1939 he hosted King George at his home in Hyde Park, New York. This was the first time a British monarch had visited the United States, and it symbolized the two nations' unity as the situation in Europe deteriorated. FDR became quite close with Wilhelmina's family, particularly her eldest daughter, who referred to him as "Uncle Franklin" and named him the godfather of her third daughter.[14]

Roosevelt also engaged with Churchill's predecessor, Neville Chamberlain, a fact that is often overlooked. From the beginning of the prime minister's tenure in 1937, the two men wanted to meet. As Europe descended into war, the president offered words of support and encouraged Chamberlain to write to him outside official diplomatic channels. The prime minister welcomed FDR's encouragement and friendship but had little confidence that the president would help in any tangible way.[15] Indeed, though he offered support during critical moments, Roosevelt never provided material assistance to Britain until Churchill took power.

As Roosevelt engaged the Allies, he also communicated with leaders of the Axis powers. Before war erupted, and even after the United States entered the conflict, he communicated directly with Adolf Hitler and Benito Mussolini in an attempt to ease tensions and avoid conflict. As Roosevelt biographer

James MacGregor Burns notes, this engagement was partly for the record, but it also sprang from FDR's immense confidence in his ability to persuade and convince abhorrent dictators to change their ways.[16]

As early as 1933, the president communicated with Mussolini. "I only wish that I might have the opportunity to see you myself," he wrote, "to give you my greetings and to talk over many things in which you and I have a common interest." By the time of Roosevelt's reelection, their correspondence had trailed off, a development the Italian leader "regretted." He was hopeful that, going forward, their relationship would "not undergo any further interruption."[17]

Roosevelt's contacts with Mussolini were not based on affection but were aimed at benefiting American interests. If the president could establish a modicum of goodwill, future cooperation might be possible. Even as Italy became increasingly aggressive throughout the 1930s, Roosevelt never sharply condemned Mussolini or cut ties with him. Rather, according to one Italian historian, "Until the eve of Italy's entry into the war, Roosevelt tried to build a personal relationship with Mussolini as a way to distance the Italian dictator from Germany."[18] Indeed, months before World War II broke out, Roosevelt met with the Italian ambassador and said, "He regretted that he himself had not had the opportunity of personally meeting and of talking with Mussolini because he believed that such an opportunity for discussion between the two might be useful and because he believed that they would find that they 'spoke the same language.'" Even after hostilities began, Roosevelt sent a letter through his personal envoy, Sumner Welles. Mussolini was very pleased with the president's message, particularly his expressed desire to meet. The dictator noted that he too had long desired the same thing.[19]

Similarly, though to a different degree, Roosevelt communicated with Hitler and tried to prevent war. In September 1938, as conflict between Germany and Czechoslovakia seemed imminent, Roosevelt appealed to the German leader to continue negotiations. Though Hitler "appreciate[d] the lofty intent" of FDR's message, he put the onus for war or peace on the Czechs.[20] Even so, a month later Hitler met with Mussolini, Chamberlain, and French prime minister Édouard Daladier, delaying bloodshed. The result of that gathering was the infamous Munich Pact, which averted war by sacrificing part of Czechoslovakia. American diplomat Joseph Davies, the ambassador to Belgium, told FDR that many in Europe saw his "energetic timely action" before Munich as "the deciding factor in the Fuhrer's decision for peace."[21] Davies, however, was an incessant flatterer, and other factors weighed more heavily on Hitler's mind than any personal appeals by Roosevelt. Although it is now seen as a dark chapter in world diplomacy, the Munich agreement was initially praised, and Roosevelt told Chamberlain he was a "good man."[22]

In March 1939 the German dictator violated the promises made at Munich and annexed the rest of Czechoslovakia. Roosevelt appealed to Hitler to cease further aggression, volunteered to serve as a mediator, and asked him to pledge not to attack a list of more than thirty countries. Noting his message's "spirit of frankness," Roosevelt ended with an emotional plea: "Heads of great Governments in this hour are literally responsible for the fate of humanity in the coming years. They cannot fail to hear the prayers of their peoples to be protected from the foreseeable chaos of war. History will hold them accountable for the lives and the happiness of all—even unto the least."[23]

Unlike the message sent in September 1938, this one received no direct reply. One newspaper reported that the Nazis considered Roosevelt's communication a "long winded document" that the German leader was too busy to be bothered with.[24] But Hitler did respond two weeks later in a virulent public speech before the Reichstag, mockingly rejecting Roosevelt's proposal point by point. The rebuff came as no surprise, and other nations were also critical of FDR. Unsurprisingly, Germany's fascist ally Italy viewed the president's message as a diplomatic "faux pas." The Italian consensus seemed to be, if it "were not attributable to Mr. Roosevelt's inexperience in foreign affairs his message would be positively insulting." Even elements in friendly nations were critical. One British newspaper reported that some nations were "puzzled" by Roosevelt's message because it made no sense to attack Hitler verbally and then offer to mediate.[25] Some in Europe, however, praised FDR's message, according to one US ambassador, as did nations in the Western Hemisphere.[26]

Domestically, Roosevelt's plea for peace also received a mixed reaction. Critics in Congress derided it as simply the president "seeking publicity" and believed it would lead the United States into war. Especially disparaging was the conservative *Chicago Daily Tribune*, which compared Roosevelt to Woodrow Wilson: "Mr. Wilson played the same kind of game and wrote better notes. They cost us 50,000 American lives and 20 billion dollars of debt."[27] However, many in Congress were supportive, and a Gallup poll found that Roosevelt's message aligned with the opinion of the majority of Americans. Seventy-three percent supported a peace conference of world leaders. Indeed, Roosevelt's message was as much for domestic consumption as it was for Hitler. It allowed the president to appear to be a peacemaker and show the belligerency of the two fascist leaders, slowly preparing the American public for war and framing the confrontation in moral terms.[28]

In August 1939 Roosevelt tried to engage Hitler again and sent the Führer two messages seeking peace.[29] A week later, Hitler invaded Poland. The president, however, did not give up. Through an informal emissary, James D. Mooney, FDR made overtures to the German leader. "I started out the discussion by presenting to the Chancellor your personal respects and greetings to which he responded warmly," Mooney reported. He then told Hitler that FDR believed informal communication between leaders allowed better understanding. Roosevelt, he explained, "wanted to be informed as to what the leaders in various countries in Europe really and actually had in their minds. In this way preliminaries could be developed for the formalities that must be arranged."[30] Roosevelt's attempts to persuade and reason with Hitler failed; if anything, the personal touch antagonized the Führer. In his 1941 speech declaring war against the United States, the German leader personally attacked FDR. "I cannot be insulted by Roosevelt," he averred, "for I consider him mad, just as [Woodrow] Wilson was."[31]

While poor personal relations with adversarial leaders were to be expected, that was also the case with some allies, such as Charles de Gaulle.[32] As leader of the Free French Forces during World War II, de Gaulle's international stature rose as the war progressed. By the time the fighting was over, everyone recognized that he would be a force in French politics. Roosevelt and others in the US government, however, were not keen on the Frenchman. They saw him as arrogant and anti-American, a demagogue with an authoritarian streak and an overall pain. As Roosevelt told Churchill, he was "fed up" with the French leader and considered him a "very dangerous threat." De Gaulle also had several grievances. The United States maintained ties with the German puppet regime of Vichy France until late in the war. De Gaulle was angry that he was not included more extensively in political and military planning, and he believed the United States wanted to keep France weak in the postwar era. Finally, initial US support for his main rival was something he never forgot or forgave.[33]

Whatever issues Roosevelt had with de Gaulle, he could not ignore the Frenchman. In June 1944 the head of the Office of War Information wrote to Roosevelt and warned that the "De Gaulle situation" was the most "dangerous point in American foreign policy—dangerous because of reactions at home as well as abroad." The problem was that de Gaulle successfully portrayed any US issues with his leadership as a personal matter, one of "'De Gaulle and

France versus Roosevelt.'" This view was disseminated not only in France but also in the United States, "with the President pictured as a stubborn man waging a feud against De Gaulle because of personal dislike." The Office of War Information recommended that Roosevelt go on the offensive and urged a public relations campaign. The president needed to change public perceptions and show that he was "a man exercising the greatest possible patience with General De Gaulle because of his service as a rallying point of resistance."[34]

Even though de Gaulle was a headache, the Roosevelt administration worked with him for two reasons. First, from a public relations standpoint, Roosevelt had no choice. The French leader was genuinely popular, and France was an ally. Thus, the projection of unity—especially in wartime—was imperative. Second, an acrimonious relationship with de Gaulle could have real-world consequences. It was in the United States' interest to have stability in France, and as Ambassador Jefferson Caffery told Roosevelt, "While perfectly willing to call deGaulle [*sic*] all the names in the devil's calendar, I would like to say that it is essential for us, with so many troops at the front, to have order maintained in France."[35] By 1945, de Gaulle was seen as the person best able to deliver stability.

In contrast to Roosevelt's rocky relationship with de Gaulle, he was perhaps closest to Canadian prime minister William Lyon Mackenzie King. Throughout his presidency, FDR met with King at least thirteen times, and they carried on a vast correspondence full of warmth and expressions of friendship. Initially, however, King's opinion of Roosevelt was quite negative. In the years before they met, he wrote in his diary that the American president was a "dictator" whom he "greatly disliked" and whose policies were "absolutely wrong, amateurish, half-baked and downright mistaken."[36]

Like most presidential relationships, their first contact was for political purposes. In November 1935, mere weeks after assuming office, King visited the White House to finalize a trade agreement that had recently stalled. Completing the deal had been one of King's campaign promises, and its importance was evident in his first meeting with the US minister in Canada. The prime minister suggested that he travel to Washington to meet with the president. US officials warned they could give "no assurances" that a trade agreement would be reached during his visit, and King would be taking "something of a chance" if he expected to finalize the deal.[37] King made the trip anyway, and although they did not finalize an agreement during that visit, one was concluded soon thereafter. Most important, this initial meeting proved to both men that they could work together. One Canadian historian describes this period as the "turning point" in US-Canada relations, and the rapport they established proved to be an asset once World War II broke out.[38]

The following year, Roosevelt and King met in Canada. Substantive issues were on the agenda, but symbolism was also important, and some saw the visit as a gesture of American friendship. It was only the second time a US president had made the trek north, and FDR was the first to do so for an official visit. The two men met again the next year, after Roosevelt sent King a handwritten letter inviting him to the White House. The president indicated they would discuss "everything," although both leaders remained vague about the exact content of their talks. By the end of the visit, though, it was clear that whatever they discussed, they did so in the "friendliest spirit."[39] Indeed, after their meeting, King wrote to Roosevelt, "I cannot begin to say how much I enjoyed my visit to the White House. The talks we had together . . . will live in my memory always. I am sure they will prove to be of great value."[40]

For the rest of Roosevelt's presidency, King visited the United States every year but one, and they met four times in Canada. The two men became partners. They consulted on significant world problems and developed a close relationship. After a trip to the White House a month before Roosevelt's death, King told the president how "large a part of the memories I shall ever most cherish have had their associations with my visits to the White House, or Hyde Park, or to Warm Springs, and how large a part of my interest and thought is wrapped up in all that pertains to your life and work and the friendship so intimately shared with you over so many years."[41] The prime minister was the more emotional and sentimental partner, but Roosevelt's feelings toward King were also evident. "One of our mutual friends who saw you recently," the president wrote, "told me that he thought you looked a wee bit tired and that it would do you good to run down to the United States for a little while 'to get your gas tank refilled.' . . . I hope that when you are able to you will come down to see me."[42]

According to one Canadian historian, King had an "obsequious relationship" with Roosevelt.[43] That may have been somewhat true, but King's flattery and submissiveness served a purpose. During the late 1930s, although Canada still had strong ties with Britain and Europe, it began to draw closer to the United States, particularly in the realm of hemispheric security. As Britain declined economically and militarily, the United States was Canada's best bet. Indeed, even in the prewar period, the British realized that Canada was in the American sphere. For Roosevelt, friendship with King was part of a larger effort to cultivate ties with hemispheric neighbors to counter the growing threats from Japan and Germany. In the years leading up to World War II, the United States and Canada increasingly cooperated on security issues, culminating in the Hyde Park Declaration of 1941, which gave Canada access to Lend-Lease aid. Throughout the war, the US interest in Canada waned, and Canadians grumbled about their exclusion from wartime planning.[44] Roosevelt and King's personal relationship, however, remained strong and illustrated how the political and the personal are intertwined.

A GOOD NEIGHBOR IN LATIN AMERICA

In Roosevelt's 1933 inauguration speech, he proclaimed that the United States would be a "good neighbor" who "respects the rights of others—the neighbor who respects his obligations and respects the sanctity of his agreements in and with a world of neighbors."[45] This approach applied to the entire world but came to be associated with Latin America, where the United States rejected an interventionist approach and pursued a policy of cooperation and reciprocity. From the US perspective, the Good Neighbor policy was a success. It was "the one bright spot in the troubled world," declared Josephus Daniels, the retiring US ambassador to Mexico, less than a month before the United States entered World War II.[46]

Roosevelt's wartime diplomacy often overshadows his foreign policy in the 1930s, but the Western Hemisphere was central to America's global agenda in the prewar period. "Among the foreign relations of the United States as they fall into categories," the State Department wrote in 1933, "the Pan American policy takes first place in our diplomacy."[47] Latin America's proximity and the US desire to avoid the travails of Europe made engagement with the region acceptable in a period when the United States often sought to keep contact with the rest of the world to a minimum.

In the early 1930s relations with Latin America were improving, thanks to Herbert Hoover's withdrawal of troops from the region and his avoidance of the use of force. But Roosevelt developed new policies and officially renounced military intervention as a tool of US policy. He also relied heavily on personal diplomacy to change perceptions in the region. During FDR's first term, of the eight foreign leaders who came to the United States, half were from Latin America. In that same period, he visited six Latin American countries.[48]

Panamanian president Harmodio Arias was the first Latin American leader to visit. He came in October 1933 to discuss America's presence in the Canal Zone, an issue that he characterized as a "matter of life or death" for his nation. He wanted to meet Roosevelt face-to-face to "appeal to his noble sentiments of justice and humanity."[49] As Arias left for Washington, the Panamanian press described his trip as "the most important since the birth of the republic," and the archbishop of Panama issued a decree urging the nation's Catholics to pray daily for success.[50] Whether attributable to the faithful's devotions or something else, Panamanians deemed the visit a triumph. On the ceremonial side, Arias was an official guest, staying at the White House and attending a state dinner held in his honor. Substantively, the two presidents agreed to general principles for the US-Panama relationship. Arias's fellow citizens received this news with joy, and he returned home to a hero's welcome. Tens of thousands of Panamanians filled the streets, cheering and waving flags to greet him. In addressing the crowd of supporters, he praised the American president as a "good neighbor."[51]

Six months later, Haitian president Sténio Vincent visited to discuss his nation's finances and the American marines stationed on the island. Like Arias, he left content. Vincent received assurances that Haiti could control its own finances without US interference, and Roosevelt agreed to withdraw the marines by the end of the year and improve trade relations.[52] In July 1934 Roosevelt solidified the goodwill established a few months earlier by making a brief visit to Haiti, where he bolstered the agreement on the marines' withdrawal. Vincent received him warmly as thousands of Haitians lined the street to greet the American president. Both men's speeches—Roosevelt delivered part of his in French—emphasized friendship between the two nations. FDR was "greatly pleased" by the visit, and the US minister in Haiti deemed it "an unqualified success from every point of view."[53] The US president impressed Vincent, who declared Roosevelt's approach toward America's southern neighbors enlightened: "What a splendid policy this new policy of good will is!"[54]

Four days later, Roosevelt stopped in Colombia—a nation still smarting over the US role in Panama's independence in 1903—where he met with President Enrique Olaya Herrera. A month earlier, when asked if there was any particular reason for the visit, Roosevelt had said, "Just to say, 'How do you do?'"[55] That simple response, however, downplayed the visit's significance. It was the first time a sitting US president had traveled to South America, and Colombia was "honored," according to its acting foreign secretary.[56]

Many saw the informal visit as significant for the region. Explaining the diplomatic importance, the *New York Times* noted that FDR's visit was "a cordial gesture, the importance of which cannot but be considered as the greatest ever made by the Executive of the United States in the interest of closer relations and deeper amity between" the United States and Latin America.[57] Indeed, it was a public relations success. Cheering crowds greeted Roosevelt as he rode through the streets of Cartagena with the Colombian president, and his brief remarks garnered praise. FDR said he had dreamed of visiting the city since he was a child, noting that it "signifies so much to all Americans in every part of our continent."[58] Overall, his message was one of solidarity, equality, and cooperation. This delighted the Colombian president, who praised American policies.[59]

Roosevelt's next stop was Panama, where he rededicated the Panama Canal to "all Nations in the needs of peaceful commerce."[60] He acknowledged that although tensions had arisen in the past and new challenges might develop, the United States and Panama would solve them together. As in Colombia, the locals hailed Roosevelt as he drove to the presidential palace for a state dinner. With worldwide press coverage, the stops in Haiti, Colombia, and Panama reflected a clear improvement in America's image south of the border. Many Latin Americans began to regard FDR as "the world's best neighbor."[61]

After his reelection in November 1936, Roosevelt again headed south in another highly visible act of personal diplomacy. Less than a week after winning a second term, he announced that he would attend the Pan-American Peace Conference in Argentina and make stops in Brazil and Uruguay. Widespread approval greeted Roosevelt's plans, and the trip was the culmination of the Good Neighbor policy in his first term. Even those critical of American policy were supportive, such as one Argentine newspaper that wrote, "President Roosevelt's visit to our country will be the most eminent distinction the United States ever has extended to Argentina." FDR's role at the Pan-American Peace Conference, however, was limited to delivering the opening address, where he referred to all nations of the Americas as "family."[62] The real personal diplomacy occurred outside the conference.

In Buenos Aires, the government declared a national holiday, and millions came out to greet Roosevelt and shower him with flowers. The Argentine government planned a massive military and naval exhibition, "a triumphal entry worthy of a victorious Roman monarch," according to one American newspaper.[63] But Roosevelt requested a simpler reception. When he and the president of Argentina, Agustín Justo, met for the first time, FDR greeted Justo as "*mi amigo*," and Justo responded by hugging Roosevelt before formal introductions had been completed.[64] Similar scenes marked other moments. At the executive palace, both men stood on the balcony as hundreds of thousands cheered while FDR "dramatically wrung Justo's hand." When he departed three days later, Roosevelt again embraced the Argentine leader. Thousands had come out in the heavy rain to bid him farewell, and FDR, "almost as if he were on stage," thrilled the crowd by pulling out a handkerchief in Argentine colors and waving it.[65] After years of America's southern neighbors fearing the "colossus of the North," goodwill visits like this made the United States seem less menacing, and they were a boon to US–Latin America relations.

Of all the Latin leaders Roosevelt engaged with, Mexican president Manuel Ávila Camacho became perhaps his closest ally. This was not foreordained. In 1940, the year Ávila Camacho was elected, US-Mexico relations were cool. His predecessor had expropriated foreign oil and mining properties in 1938, some of which were owned by US companies. Even though Mexico had agreed to provide compensation, two years later, the United States was still unsatisfied. In the 1940 election, Ávila Camacho was the candidate of the outgoing president's party and supported his policies. After a disputed election that some feared might lead to upheaval, Ávila Camacho emerged victorious and proved to be a moderate.[66]

Shortly after the election, Ávila Camacho announced his intention to visit the United States, expressing hope that US-Mexico relations would become closer than ever. Even though the proposed visit was canceled, his words set a positive tone. The Roosevelt administration reciprocated by announcing that it would send Vice President–elect Henry Wallace to attend Ávila Camacho's inauguration.[67]

Once in office, Ávila Camacho and Roosevelt sought closer ties. For FDR, a warmer relationship with Mexico would bolster hemispheric solidarity, which was becoming a priority as the situation in Europe worsened. Thus, after Ávila Camacho took office, the two nations quickly resolved the outstanding dispute over compensation for American oil companies. Soon thereafter, Japan attacked Pearl Harbor, and the United States entered World War II. Immediately, Ávila Camacho announced that he stood united with his northern neighbor and sought to coordinate the hemisphere's defenses. Five months later, Mexico declared war on the Axis powers, which Roosevelt praised in a letter to the Mexican president.[68]

Shortly after Ávila Camacho assumed office, in March 1941, FDR tentatively planned a fishing trip in the Gulf of Mexico and hoped the Mexican president could join him. According to Ambassador Josephus Daniels, upon receiving the invitation, Ávila Camacho said "nothing would please him better, and . . . he sincerely hoped . . . he could have the pleasure of welcoming [FDR] . . . to the waters and shores of his country."[69] Although the proposed fishing trip never materialized, they met two years later to great fanfare.

Early in 1943 Ávila Camacho sent a message to Roosevelt through the new US ambassador, George Messersmith. The Mexican president noted that "a great psychological change had taken place among the Mexican people," who now viewed the United States much more positively. This made it an opportune time for Roosevelt to visit. It would not only give Ávila Camacho "personal satisfaction," he said, but "would consolidate in a most marked way the changed relationship between Mexico and the United States."[70]

A few months later, secret planning for a Roosevelt visit began. As both countries made preparations, Messersmith frequently brought up three points: how much Roosevelt's planned visit to Mexico thrilled Ávila Camacho; that the Mexican president wanted the visit to have the greatest public impact, which included a radio broadcast, addresses by both leaders, and having FDR wave to crowds from a balcony; and how important the trip was for US-Mexico relations. One word that showed up multiple times in Messersmith's communications was "transcendental."[71] For officials in both countries, the meeting was expected to be a defining moment.

The April 1943 meeting was the first time an American and Mexican president had met in thirty-four years. Unlike the previous meeting in 1909 between William Howard Taft and Porfirio Díaz, which had taken place at the border, Roosevelt traveled more than a hundred miles into Mexico. Ávila Camacho also traveled to Corpus Christi, Texas. Although the two presidents discussed substantial issues such as economics and war, the visit's imagery and what it represented took center stage. As one Mexican official noted, the meeting had "done more to improve relations . . . than any single gesture on the part of Washington in this century." Ambassador Messersmith concurred. "It is safe to say," he wrote, "that there has been no event in Mexican history in many years which has made so profound an impression on so great a mass of Mexican people." He added that the Mexican press's positive coverage was more than he could have hoped for, and the fact that Roosevelt had traveled into Mexico rather than meeting at the border was particularly gratifying to the journalists.[72]

The trip also symbolized Pan-American solidarity. By that point in 1943, Roosevelt had met with British prime minister Winston Churchill multiple times to discuss war-related matters, and though he had yet to meet Soviet premier Joseph Stalin or Chinese leader Chiang Kai-shek, his desire to do so was well known. But except for a brief stop in Brazil on his return home from a conference with Churchill, the US president had not visited any Latin American country since the start of the war. Meeting with Ávila Camacho helped demonstrate US appreciation of its southern neighbors and their contribution to the war effort.[73]

The visit was full of fanfare, including a twenty-one-gun salute, an open car ride through the city as confetti and roses rained down, a military parade, and a banquet. At the dinner, both presidents gave speeches that were broadcast over the radio to an international audience. Roosevelt praised Mexico's war contributions and proclaimed a "brotherhood in arms," and he championed hemispheric solidarity. Ávila Camacho praised the visit as evidence of how far US-Mexico relations had come; he praised FDR's leadership and expressed hope for the future.[74]

In the months and years that followed, Ávila Camacho and Roosevelt often reflected on their 1943 meeting.[75] And within months of their get-together, the two presidents were discussing plans for a fishing trip. At the time of Roosevelt's death in April 1945, concrete arrangements had been made. After attending the United Nations Conference in San Francisco, Roosevelt intended to drive across the border and meet Ávila Camacho.[76]

"There is no Chief of State in the other American Republics," Messersmith wrote, "who is a sounder and firmer and more convinced friend of our country than President Avila Camacho . . . what an understanding friend our country has in the President of Mexico."[77] With World War II raging, Roosevelt undoubtedly appreciated a friendly leader on the southern border. Ávila Camacho was predisposed to this position, but Roosevelt met him halfway, allowing cooperative relations between Mexico and the United States to flourish. The two men's relationship was also symbolically significant, as it demonstrated the changing nature of US-Mexico relations and encouraged a positive impression of the United States.

A NEW ROLE IN AFRICA AND ASIA

Unlike in Latin America, the United States' ties to Africa and Asia were minimal in the 1930s. Though trade and commerce occurred, close political connections were absent. During Roosevelt's first three terms, there was not much
need for US political involvement in those regions, nor would the American
public have allowed it. Except for a 1938 visit to the United States by the sultan of Muscat and Oman, who was on a leisurely global sojourn, face-to-face
interactions with leaders of Asia and Africa did not occur. World War II
changed this. With the United States involved in a global conflict, the extent
of the nation's interests grew immensely. Both politically and militarily, the
United States was no longer confined to the Western Hemisphere. As its international role began to change, the American public began to accept that
the United States would have a global presence, not only during the war but
also after it. "The knowledge of the world which this war has provoked among
Americans is not the least of its side products," the *Washington Post* wrote.
"One of the countries we have become aware of is little Liberia. . . . It went its
way in obscurity till war broke out, and then we realized Liberia's importance
to our Atlantic security."[78]

As America increased its global activity, Roosevelt arranged meetings with
Asian and African leaders, such as Liberian president Edwin Barclay. Traveling back from the Casablanca Conference in January 1943, FDR stopped at
the small nation on Africa's west coast. He lunched with Barclay and toured a
large Firestone rubber plantation that produced large quantities of war materials. Four months later, the Liberian president reciprocated the visit, becoming the first black leader to sleep in the White House. A Liberian official stated
that Barclay's visit "will do much toward creating international and interra-
cial goodwill."[79] That official was overly optimistic, but in a nation plagued
by rampant racial discrimination, the US president hosting a black man and
treating him as an equal was no small matter. With US interests now spanning
the globe, the issue of racial equality became increasingly important. And for
many, Roosevelt's meetings with Asian and African nationalists were symbolic
expressions of support for decolonization, a message that was not missed by
non-Western nations and Europeans.[80]

When Roosevelt journeyed to and from the Tehran Conference in November 1943, he made time to meet with the leaders of China, Turkey, and Iran.
In Turkey, Roosevelt met President Ismet Inönü for the first time, although

the two had previously exchanged letters. Turkey was still neutral, and there was much talk about whether it would finally declare support for the Allies. Indeed, Roosevelt used the meeting with Inönü to try to persuade him to provide greater assistance to the war effort. Though sympathetic to the Allied cause, the Turkish president remained noncommittal and would not declare war against the Axis powers until 1945. Still, the conference allowed Roosevelt and Inönü to get to know each other and set the stage for future cooperation. A few months later, FDR told the Turkish leader how "very happy" he was that they had met and could now "talk to each other as old friends." He also lamented that they were thousands of miles apart. "There are many matters," Roosevelt wrote, "I would like to talk with you about almost every day."[81]

Though the meeting with Inönü was more substantive and garnered more attention, Roosevelt's encounter with the shah of Iran, Mohammad Reza Pahlavi, was in many ways more interesting and illustrative of how personal gestures—and their absence—can have serious consequences. As head of the host nation for the Tehran Conference, the shah called on the Allied leaders. It was a simple courtesy call, but Roosevelt's failure to make a reciprocal visit to see the Iranian leader created tension. According to the Office of Strategic Services (the forerunner to the Central Intelligence Agency), that oversight might make the Iranians less cooperative. "Moreover, since the Shah's visit with the President was not a[s] long as that with Stalin . . . the prestige of America has been lowered. . . . The prestige of Russia has increased."[82] In a memo to Roosevelt, Secretary of State Cordell Hull added that the Iranian leader was "bitterly disappointed and even felt humiliated that you were unable to make a return call . . . and receive the hospitality and the honor which he was eager to accord you."[83] Even so, the US-Iran relationship endured. Soon after the president left, he sent a letter to the shah that was well received. In response, the Iranian leader expressed his friendship and desire to accept FDR's invitation to visit the United States.[84]

When Roosevelt traveled to the Yalta Conference in 1945, he again met with a number of non-Western leaders. Over two days, Roosevelt conferred with three monarchs on a naval ship in Great Bitter Lake near Cairo: Egypt's King Farouk, Emperor Haile Selassie of Ethiopia, and King Ibn Saud of Saudi Arabia. These meetings were substantive as well as symbolic of America's growing global interests. They also represented a meeting of different cultures that fascinated the American public.[85]

Of the three monarchs, Ibn Saud most interested the public. With his flowing robe and team of servants—including bodyguards armed with swords—he most closely conformed to Americans' expectations of how a ruler from the "Orient" looked and behaved.[86] For the Saudi king, it was the first time he had ever left his own country. To facilitate the meeting, the United States sent a naval vessel to pick him up and bring him to Great Bitter Lake. Once on board, rather than sleep in a cabin, Ibn Saud and his party set up tents on the ship's deck. They even brought their own food, which included seven live sheep, and special water for the king that came from two holy wells.[87]

These stories captivated the public, but Roosevelt had serious matters to discuss. The administration had prepared for the meetings by producing biographical sketches of the monarchs, background reports of the countries, and proposed discussion topics. In the second half of the twentieth century such documents would become institutionalized, but in the Roosevelt administration, they were ad hoc.[88]

Roosevelt had previously corresponded with Ibn Saud (as he had with Farouk and Selassie), discussing issues such as the British presence in the region and the situation in Palestine.[89] FDR had even sent a special representative to Saudi Arabia in 1943 to sound out the king and investigate the US position in the Middle East more broadly. "The United States does not have a similar [comparable to the British and French] coordinated political set-up in the Middle East," the envoy reported, "and, as a result, American political interests tend at times to suffer." With the United States developing long-term economic interests in the region, particularly in the oil industry, this situation could not continue in the postwar period.[90] To secure its interests, the United States needed to increase its organization and influence in the region. Ibn Saud also sought something from America: he wanted to counterbalance the British, get American support for the Arabs in Palestine, and receive American assistance for numerous domestic projects.[91]

When the two leaders met, they discussed important regional issues such as Palestine and the king's fear that France was threatening Syria's and Lebanon's independence.[92] On a personal level, FDR and Ibn Saud quickly developed a rapport. As the American minister in Saudi Arabia noted, "The King spoke of being the 'twin' brother of the President, in years, in responsibility as Chief of State, and in physical disability." On that last point, Roosevelt offered the king one of his wheelchairs so they could truly be "twins." After the meeting, the US minister reported that Ibn Saud repeatedly commented, "I have never met the equal of the President in character, wisdom and gentility." The king also favorably compared Roosevelt to Churchill: The prime minister, he said, "speaks deviously, evades understanding, changes the subject to avoid commitment. . . . The President seeks understanding in conversations; his effort is to make two minds meet; to dispel darkness and shed light upon the issue."[93]

Of all the non-Western leaders Roosevelt engaged with, he had the most contact with China's Chiang Kai-shek. Churchill and Stalin receive the bulk of attention in analyses of Roosevelt's wartime relationships, but Chiang and FDR carried out an extensive correspondence before and during the war.[94] American familiarity with Chiang dated back to the 1920s, when China was fractured and brimming with warlords. American newspapers carried frequent accounts of developments in China and often wrote profiles of Chiang, describing him in various ways: young, modern, temperamental, modest, scholarly, and pleasant. But above all, he was a nationalist, and he was seen in the West as the best person to unify his country.[95]

The relationship between Roosevelt and Chiang began in 1937 with the start of the Sino-Japanese War.[96] After Pearl Harbor, and as the conflict between China and Japan morphed into the larger Pacific theater of World War II, the volume of communication between the two men increased. In addition to various tactical and strategic issues, their correspondence had three main features: Chiang's frequent emotional pleas, Roosevelt's constant reassurances, and Chiang's desire that China be recognized as a world power on a par with the other Allies.

In many ways, Chiang was the catalyst for the relationship. Personal diplomacy was at the heart of his war strategy and US-China relations. He believed that forming a bond with the American president was vital. In many of Chiang's letters he praised Roosevelt and tried to ingratiate himself. "I feel impelled to seek your counsel and assistance," he wrote to FDR in 1940. A year earlier, he had claimed the American president held "the key" to solving global problems.[97] After Roosevelt's reelection in 1940, Chiang was especially effusive, writing that news of the president's victory gave him "the greatest gratification. . . . This is good tidings for the cause of human justice and world peace . . . rejoicings are shared by all those nations who love freedom and are striving to defend themselves."[98]

Months before Pearl Harbor, White House adviser Lauchlin Currie reported on the situation in China and offered insight into dealing with its leader. Chiang was driven by "sentiment" and "self-interest," Currie noted, and with "a little care and attention from America," he would follow America's lead.

The generalissimo greatly admired the United States and Roosevelt. Thus, "to be treated as an equal or ally would mean a great deal to him," Currie advised. In addition to providing material support, FDR needed to make a concerted effort "to say nice things about China and to speak of her in the same terms now used toward England."[99]

Whether because of Currie's advice or his own instincts, FDR followed that strategy. He continuously reassured and encouraged Chiang and heaped praise on him. For example, in January 1943 Roosevelt wrote that he hoped Chiang would visit the White House after the war "to accept tribute of the citizens of the United States to your heroic leadership of the Chinese people." In another letter, he wrote of the Chinese leader's "far sighted vision, which has guided and inspired."[100]

Whether Roosevelt truly believed what he wrote is secondary to the aims he hoped to accomplish. He wanted to bolster Chiang's and, by extension, the Chinese people's morale to keep them fighting against the Japanese, which the president believed was imperative. With American attention focused on Europe, it was crucial for Chinese forces to keep at least some Japanese troops occupied. But Roosevelt struggled to get Chiang to fight. The Chinese leader was more concerned with battling his communist rivals than the Japanese, and he was never satisfied with the aid he received from the Allies. He always wanted more.

Roosevelt, however, remained patient with Chiang, unlike some of his subordinates. Joseph Stilwell, the American general assigned to the China-Burma-India theater, regularly interacted with Chiang but had a poor relationship with him. Lacking the president's patience, Stilwell wrote to his superior, General George Marshall, that Chiang was worried about low morale and had concerns that the prestige of the rival communists was on the rise. The Chinese leader also said that if Japan attacked, he would need more assistance. "He would not listen to reason, logic or argument," Stilwell grumbled. "He complains about the little help the United States is giving him. My impression is that it is partly acting, that he is also getting wind up."[101]

In another letter, Stilwell stated that the United States needed to take a harder line with Chiang. Roosevelt, however, disagreed. In a memo to Marshall he wrote:

Stilwell has exactly the wrong approach in dealing with Generalissimo Chiang. . . . When Stilwell speaks about the fact that the Generalissimo is very irritable and hard to handle, upping his demands, etc., he is, of course correct; but when he speaks of talking to him in sterner tones, he goes about it just the wrong way. . . . All of us must remember that the Generalissimo came up the hard way to become the undisputed leader of four hundred million people. . . . He is the Chief Executive as well as the Commander-in-Chief, and one cannot speak sternly to a man like that or exact commitments from him the way we might do from the Sultan of Morocco.[102]

Roosevelt recognized that Chiang needed to be approached in a particular way. Though he was sometimes frustrated, FDR knew that it was in the United States' long-term interest to have a friendly leader in China. Roosevelt also believed that there was no alternative. As he told his son Elliott, "Who is there in China who could take Chiang's place? There's just no other leader." So despite his "shortcomings," FDR believed he had to "depend" on Chiang.[103] If that meant continually providing a psychological boost, Roosevelt was more than willing to do so.

But even as he sought to assuage Chiang's worries and reassure him of Allied support, the president could never completely alleviate the generalissimo's concerns. In letter after letter, Chiang consistently described dire situations and the need for more assistance. In one particularly evocative telegram, he appealed for 300 planes. He had never seen such "deplorable unpreparedness, confusion and degradation. . . . There was an intolerable stench from the corpses of those killed in the raid and from the carcasses of animals which had not been removed. The same was the case with the corpses in the houses. . . . The whole scene was therefore one of desolation and disorder."[104] Despite Roosevelt's continual encouragement and his attempts to convey how valuable China was to the war effort, these reassurances had limits. In October 1942 Roosevelt sent a letter pledging more aid to China, but it fell short of what Chiang wanted. "For your renewed assurance of aid to the Chinese I am deeply grateful," the generalissimo wrote. "However, in order to reach the greatest efficiency in our combined operations, I am firmly convinced that further action is necessary."[105]

Roosevelt also had trouble convincing Chiang that the Allied powers recognized China as an equal. As late as 1943, the two men had not yet met, and from the Chinese perspective, this was evidence that China was not viewed as an equal, given that the American and British leaders had met many times. When Roosevelt and Churchill gathered at Casablanca in January 1943,

Chiang, while publicly supportive, was privately angry that he had not been invited.[106] According to an American intelligence report, a Chinese official was puzzled by Roosevelt's failure to meet with Chiang, which demonstrated that the Allies viewed "China as an inferior power." The Chinese official argued that even if a Chiang-Roosevelt conference were convened simply to exchange pleasantries, it "would enhance Chinese morale to such an extent that it would be even better than all the Lend-Lease materials the United States could get into China."[107]

Whether because of that report or Roosevelt's own inclinations, in the months that followed, he assured Chiang of his "anxiety" to meet. "I am sure there are many things that can only be satisfactorily settled if we can meet face to face," the president wrote.[108] The two men finally did get together in November 1943 in Cairo, a few days before Roosevelt flew to the Tehran Conference. A somewhat disgruntled Churchill joined them. The prime minister had hoped to meet with Roosevelt alone before Stalin joined them, and he did not appreciate having to entertain Chiang and discuss matters of secondary importance.

For FDR, the meeting was mainly about making Chiang feel important. Secretary of War Henry Stimson wrote in his diary that, to Roosevelt, the conference's most crucial aspect was "the psychological benefits which would come from such a meeting rather than the solution of any concrete special problems."[109] If Roosevelt's goal was to give Chiang and China their place in the sun, it worked—at least temporarily. The conference's press coverage was extremely positive, with headlines such as "China's Triumph" and "China Gets Her Place in 'Big Four' Councils."[110] Back home, Chiang's position was greatly enhanced. It had an "electric" effect in China, according to Chiang's wife, and "was hailed everywhere as a great diplomatic and political triumph . . . that would establish the country's position as a major power."[111]

In addition to the publicity and China's symbolic elevation to a world power, Chiang received promises that Japan would be removed from all territory it had taken by force and that China would reclaim its lost land. Additionally, Roosevelt verbally committed to a billion-dollar loan to China, and a new military operation was planned (Operation Buccaneer). But the loan never materialized, and after the Tehran Conference, Churchill and Roosevelt met again in Cairo and decided to cancel Buccaneer and focus solely on upcoming operations in Europe.

A frustrated Chiang considered it "a breach of faith."[112] After receiving

Roosevelt's letter breaking the bad news, Chiang responded by stating that "the repercussions would be so disheartening that I fear of the consequences of China's ability to hold out much longer . . . my task in rallying the nation to continue resistance is being made infinitely more difficult."[113] Though privately angry, Chiang remained publicly positive and continued to praise Roosevelt. To make up for Operation Buccaneer's cancellation, Chiang tried to extract some concessions, mainly increased loans and credits. Though unsuccessful in that effort, he was able to achieve one of his goals. For years he had been trying to have Stilwell replaced as the top American general in the region, and finally, in October 1944, Roosevelt removed him. This pleased Chiang and boosted his domestic standing.[114]

Though angry and disappointed with the American president, Chiang never publicly broke from FDR. He had put too much effort into the relationship, and it was the central aspect of his wartime strategy. As one Chinese scholar described, "Chiang gave personal diplomacy such a preeminent role because, in his view, the president had practically become the only one in the US government who was both sympathetic to China's cause and capable of satisfying China's needs."[115] This calculation never changed. He did not get everything he wanted, but just as FDR saw no alternative to Chiang, Chiang had no alternative to Roosevelt.

The Chinese leader saw the American president as key to getting the aid and support he needed. For Roosevelt, confronted by a large, complicated, divided country thousands of miles away, dealing with one individual was the simplest solution. The connection between FDR and Chiang was the defining feature of US-China relations during the war, as confirmed by a 1944 report on US aid to China: the bulk of its sixty pages documented the ebb and flow of the two leaders' relationship. Their vast correspondence, the report stated, "brought about understanding and mutual confidence, and faith in their ability to solve their problems easily."[116] Both Roosevelt and Chiang engaged in personal diplomacy because their personalities and management styles predisposed them to do so, but in the particular case of US-China relations, cultivating a personal relationship with the other was also seen as the best policy.

Roosevelt's personal diplomacy touched every continent and numerous leaders. As of January 31, 1943, Roosevelt had logged 252,335 miles of travel (both foreign and domestic) in his ten years in office. Many marveled at the distance he had trekked, and laudatory newspaper articles cheered his use of conferences.[117] Others, however, were critical, especially the conservative *Chicago Daily Tribune*. His "junkets are becoming tiresome," it wrote. "Mr. Roosevelt's touring had no counterpart in history. Nero fiddled as Rome burned, but at least he stayed in Rome."[118] Many saw Roosevelt's personal diplomacy as both new and exciting, but others viewed it as suspect.

Whether people loved it or hated it, presidential personal diplomacy was here to stay. Roosevelt's successors would engage in the practice, and they would do so for similar reasons. During the 1930s and 1940s the features that would define and encourage leader-to-leader interactions in the second half of the twentieth century became clearer: a changing international environment in which the United States became the leader of a growing global community, foreign leaders' eagerness to establish relationships with the US president, the aggrandizement of presidential power and the desire for control, and domestic political incentives. And as presidents engaged with foreign leaders, they often had to deal not only with military, economic, and political issues but also with the emotions and anxieties of their counterparts.

2. Truman, Eisenhower, and the Retreat and Resurgence of Personal Diplomacy

When Franklin Roosevelt died in April 1945, the Allies were well on their way to victory. The Grand Alliance, however, began to crack. In the aftermath of the Yalta Conference in February, Soviet intentions came under increased scrutiny. In the weeks leading up to Roosevelt's death, it became clear that Stalin was not meeting his responsibilities under the Yalta agreements, and he accused the United States and Britain of attempting to negotiate a separate peace with Germany. Such accusations filled Roosevelt with "bitter resentment." However, he was still committed to working with the Soviet leader.[1]

If Roosevelt had lived, perhaps these difficulties would have been resolved, but under his successor, Harry Truman, it was not to be. Insecure and unsure how to handle the Soviets, Truman increasingly relied on the State Department, which had been relegated to the sidelines by FDR. As the previous chapter demonstrated, personal interactions with foreign leaders were central to Roosevelt's management of foreign affairs. This was not the case with Truman. During his time in office, the practice of personal diplomacy declined. Truman still interacted with foreign leaders, but the grand summits of World War II and the place of personal diplomacy in the public's imagination faded. And as tensions with the Soviets increased, Roosevelt's style of personal diplomacy was subjected to increased scrutiny. Some saw his dealings with Stalin at Yalta as treasonous, turning leader-to-leader engagement of the FDR variety into a political liability.

Truman's successor exhibited a similar revulsion to the type of grand summitry and personal diplomacy Roosevelt delighted in. By the end of Dwight D. Eisenhower's second term, however, there had been a revival of great-power conferences. But because they failed to produce concrete results or live up to public expectations, personal diplomacy once again fell out of favor. Less controversially, the Eisenhower years saw a rise in informal personal diplomacy, where the president would meet with world leaders, often outside the capital, with no formal agenda. This practice was not cheered by all, but many ordinary Americans and political elites accepted it as a useful diplomatic tool.

This chapter explores the evolution of personal diplomacy during the Truman and Eisenhower years. The period began with leader-to-leader diplomacy in retreat, followed by a resurgence and then a return to disrepute. However, the practice proved to be resilient and was more firmly entrenched by the end of the period than it was at the beginning. Truman and Eisenhower were not necessarily opposed to interacting with their foreign counterparts, especially with allies. It was personal diplomacy with adversaries, particularly Soviet leaders, that gave them pause.

As the two presidents increasingly engaged in personal diplomacy—both in person and through correspondence—it became the norm. With every face-to-face interaction between the president and an ally, the public became more accustomed to the practice. There was criticism at times, especially during bouts of great-power summitry, but the practice proved adaptable. Critics could do nothing to stop it, especially when the occupants of the White House saw the practice's value and usefulness in achieving various objectives. And the more presidents engaged in personal diplomacy, the less they questioned whether they should be doing so.

TRUMAN PULLS BACK

From the moment he took office, Harry Truman was in a difficult spot. Replacing Roosevelt would have been hard under any circumstances, but the suddenness of FDR's death made the problem acute. Truman had no time to prepare, and neither did foreign leaders. As Truman attempted to find his footing, his foreign counterparts sought to reaffirm the commitments Roosevelt had made. Chiang Kai-shek reminded the new president that, at the 1943 Cairo Conference, "after long and careful deliberations," FDR had agreed that, even if the war ended earlier than anticipated, the United States would provide military aid to China for ninety divisions of troops. The king of Saudi Arabia pressed Truman on "the promise made by your late predecessor" regarding French control of Morocco. Churchill reminded the new president that Roosevelt had agreed to visit Britain before he visited France.[2]

With the United States still waging a global war, Truman's direct communications with his foreign counterparts remained crucial. A day after Roosevelt's death, Truman told Churchill that he wanted to meet soon and hoped to "continue the loyal and close collaboration" the British prime minister had enjoyed with FDR. Truman also said he was familiar with the vast correspondence among the Allied leaders.[3] But in fact, Truman had been left in the dark with regard to FDR's exchanges with Churchill and Stalin. So in May 1945 Harry Hopkins—Roosevelt's close adviser—came to the White House and briefed Truman on aspects of the former president's personal diplomacy.[4]

Despite his inexperience, Truman seemed eager to engage his allies. A day after FDR's death, he proposed to Churchill that they have "another go" at Stalin and send him a joint message about the makeup of the provisional Polish government.[5] After Germany's defeat in May, he agreed with Churchill's view that another Big Three summit was needed to settle any outstanding issues among the Allies. Stalin, however, did not seem particularly interested, and the United States and Britain had to persuade him. Churchill sent Stalin a message, while Truman sent Hopkins to confer with Stalin about US-Soviet relations and raise the prospect of a Big Three meeting.[6]

Truman also sent diplomat Joseph Davies to confer with Churchill. Both Hopkins and Davies acted as surrogates for the president, who wanted to know whether Roosevelt's death had caused Churchill's and Stalin's thinking to change. Truman wanted "personal, on-the-spot reports" that would provide more information "than I was able to get from messages and cables or even from telephone conversations," he wrote in his memoirs.[7]

Truman soon got the opportunity to make his own assessments. When Hopkins broached the topic of a Big Three conference, Stalin "indicated that he was anxious to meet."[8] Less than two months later, the president was face-to-face with the Soviet leader at Potsdam. Despite pushing for a summit, Truman was not looking forward to it. Still insecure in his new role as president, he was worried about how his interactions with Stalin and Churchill would go. Others were also worried; the new president was inexperienced in high-level diplomacy, while the other two were "tough old hands."[9]

Whatever Truman's concerns, his first impression of Stalin was positive. He found the Soviet dictator "honest" and "smart as hell," someone he could "deal with."[10] Truman, however, did not make a good first impression. At the president's direction, Davies had set up a preconference meeting with Stalin, which Truman abruptly canceled. Instead, he met with advisers about the successful testing of the atomic bomb—news that boosted Truman's spirits. But when he was finally ready to meet with Stalin, the Soviet leader declined.[11]

Once the conference got under way, the participants discussed issues such as Poland's border and German reparations and disarmament, and they

reaffirmed their commitment to defeating Japan. Most observers and participants were optimistic about the outcome. Truman felt he had established a
relationship with Stalin and was confident about the future.[12] Reporting to the
nation, he touted the "mutual understanding and friendship" he had achieved
with the Allies and their "fundamental accord." He ended on a hopeful note,
telling Americans that the great powers were closer than ever and "shall continue to march together to a lasting peace and a happy world!"[13]

Despite the upbeat assessment of the conference, according to those close
to Truman, "he came away from it with a feeling of dislike for a big shot personal diplomacy."[14] Truman had been homesick and missed his wife. Lacking Roosevelt's temperament, he abhorred the prolonged discussions that
diplomacy often required. Although Truman invited Stalin to visit the United
States twice, once at Potsdam in 1945 and again in 1946, four months after
Potsdam he declared, "I am not in favor of special conferences, and never have
been." Rather, he wanted the fledgling United Nations to take the diplomatic
lead and avoid the fate of the League of Nations, which he believed had been
"ruined by a lot of special conferences."[15] Others agreed.

During the last half of the 1940s, personal diplomacy became a much-
criticized practice. New York governor Thomas Dewey, the Republican presidential nominee in 1948, declared, "I would not have gone [to summits]
myself, if President, because that is the way we always lose our shirts."[16] The
Democratic National Committee, sensing Truman's vulnerability, produced a
fact sheet to defend the president. It argued that he and Roosevelt "stood up
strongly" for American war aims, and those critical of their handling of Stalin
"do not know the truth—or they are lying for political purposes."[17]

As the Cold War intensified, Roosevelt's wartime diplomacy came under increased scrutiny, particularly the agreements reached at Yalta in 1945.
Within a year, the secret deals with Stalin, such as the Soviets' agreement to
enter the war in the Pacific in exchange for Japanese islands, became public
knowledge and turned many against diplomacy at the highest level. Yalta was
"not only incompatible with democratic principles but also recklessly ineffi-
cient," syndicated columnist Roscoe Drummond wrote.[18]

Truman never met Stalin again, but Churchill's return to power in 1951 re-
kindled the idea of a Big Three gathering. A well-known advocate of personal
diplomacy, Churchill suggested that a summit might lower tensions and solve
outstanding problems between the Soviet Union and the West.[19] Vincent Au-
riol of France was of a similar mind. In the United States, however, there were

skeptics. As one newspaper editorialized, "In today's world illusions are risky; and none is more dangerous than the one which assumes that high policy for great states can be manipulated successfully as a personal affair by three or four leading personages."[20]

If Truman's attitude toward leader-to-leader diplomacy and the public backlash against it were not enough, Secretary of State Dean Acheson also expressed a "deep dislike and distrust" of it. Though diplomacy at the highest level might be "glamorous," he believed that leaders often arrived at such summits unprepared. And by meeting face-to-face, presidents lost the advantage of distance and weakened their bargaining position. If a diplomat makes a bad agreement, the president can veto it. When a president negotiates, there is no safety valve. As Acheson mused, "When a chief of state or head of government makes a fumble, the goal line is open behind him."[21]

For these reasons, personal diplomacy is absent from most accounts of Truman's foreign policy, with the exception of the Potsdam Conference.[22] This makes some sense, as Truman did not evince the same enthusiasm for the practice as his predecessor, and he traveled abroad less often and met with world leaders more sparingly than his successors.[23] But it neglects the interactions Truman did have with other heads of state and government and how his administration's use of the practice was similar to that of other modern presidents. Truman and Acheson distinguished between meeting with leaders of friendly nations and high-profile summits with the Soviet Union. During Truman's presidency, relations with the Soviets would be conducted mainly through the State Department, but the administration recognized personal diplomacy's potential value in other settings.

In the Middle East, for example, the administration sought to bolster Iran against communist aggression and keep its oil fields in friendly hands. The State Department's Middle East experts suggested that the shah visit the United States because he needed to be "constantly encouraged" to remain firm, and a meeting with the president would provide the necessary boost.[24] Less than a month before the visit, the US ambassador to Iran, John Wiley, provided Truman with an analysis of the shah. Because the young Iranian leader was impressionable, "personal contact with you . . . will be of great value," Wiley wrote. The ambassador believed the visit "may exercise a decisive influence upon" the shah and enhance America's position in the region.[25]

When newly independent Pakistan and India seemed to be on the verge of war over Kashmir, the administration tried to ease tensions. After the

United Nations' attempts to mediate the dispute stalled, Acheson suggested in the summer of 1949 that Truman send letters to the leaders of both nations, urging them to cooperate with the UN. He believed a presidential message "would lend vigorous support" to UN efforts.[26] Truman approved, and the letters were dispatched. But as all presidents learn, personal diplomacy does not always work. Indian prime minister Jawaharlal Nehru was "surprised at the intervention" of Truman—but not in a good way. Both Pakistan and India were "cool" to the president's proposal of UN mediation. Pakistan eventually consented, but India did not.[27]

Closer to home, Truman went on well-received goodwill trips to Mexico, Canada, and Brazil in 1947. The trip to Mexico was the first official state visit undertaken by an American president. A survey of US editorials showed widespread approval of the trip, which was Truman's idea.[28] Reaction in the Mexican press was even better. The State Department deemed the visit an unqualified success, and Truman's honoring of the Niños Héroes—teenage soldiers who had died in 1847 during the Mexican-American War—"had tremendous emotional appeal, [and] was deeply appreciated."[29] The trip to Canada was just as successful. The president's three-day visit was front-page news in Canadian newspapers, with "unanimously highly favorable" editorials. The approximately thirty-five US correspondents who traveled with the president also reported positively.[30] And during the state visit to Brazil, Truman was given a raucous reception, as a million Brazilians lined the streets to welcome him.[31]

Although generating goodwill in the Western Hemisphere was important to the administration, European issues remained central. In Truman's last year in office, his most high-profile visitor was Winston Churchill, newly returned to power. Some observers predicted a strengthening of Anglo-American ties, but the president and the prime minister had different outlooks. Churchill favored summit diplomacy with Stalin. Truman did not.[32] Churchill's visit recalled the days of World War II and his conferences with Roosevelt, but times had changed. The Soviet Union had gone from ally to enemy, and British power was waning. Churchill now came as less of an equal and more of a supplicant. The mood in the United States had also changed. The prime minister, the *Washington Post* wrote, "will come in contact with a reaction against the personal policymaking on the part of the wartime Roosevelt. In none is the reaction more pronounced than in the present occupant of the White House."[33] Nevertheless, Truman greeted Churchill graciously and later toasted him as "the great man of the age." And despite reports of discord, the visit appeared to go well, as both sides agreed on various political and military matters.[34]

Even with this successful meeting, high-profile personal diplomacy during the Truman years lacked the glamour, drama, and political effect of the Roosevelt era. Many Americans viewed the practice suspiciously, as did the president himself. The administration, however, believed personal diplomacy could serve larger policy objectives and employed it where possible. But Truman never became associated with personal diplomacy in the same way his predecessor was or his successors would be.

After the Truman-Churchill parley, the *Washington Post* chided a group of Republican senators who criticized the talks, noting that they would have done better to pick a different issue for their partisan attacks. Though "the personal diplomacy of the Roosevelt era has left a bad taste," the newspaper wrote, "if there is anything that differentiates the Truman regime from its predecessor, it is the absence of this sort of personal diplomacy."[35] Truman's successor would display a similar ambivalence to the practice at first, but by the end of his term, he would be fully immersed in it.

EISENHOWER'S INFORMAL STYLE

Dwight Eisenhower's contacts with foreign leaders are part of any account of his presidency, although works specifically dealing with his personal diplomacy are lacking.[36] This absence obscures Eisenhower's role in making the practice a central part of the conduct of foreign affairs.

In Eisenhower's first State of the Union message in 1953, he sketched his administration's approach to the Cold War. In proclaiming a new direction in US foreign policy, he averred that the United States "shall never acquiesce in the enslavement of any people . . . [and] recognizes no kind of commitment contained in secret understandings of the past with foreign governments which permit this kind of enslavement."[37] To the conservative *Chicago Daily Tribune*, it was clear that the president "intended a resounding repudiation of Tehran, Yalta, and Potsdam, and the personal and unconstitutional diplomacy of Mr. Roosevelt and Mr. Truman." However, the newspaper was not pleased with Eisenhower's resolution on enslaved peoples that he submitted to both houses of Congress. Rather than forcefully criticizing his predecessors' dealings, the president simply said that the problem with past agreements was not the agreements themselves but the Soviets' failure to live up to their end of the bargain. By not directly attacking Roosevelt's and Truman's personal diplomacy, the newspaper claimed, Eisenhower "has adopted the apologia of the New Dealers and has made it his own and seeks to make it that of the Republican party."[38]

The *Chicago Daily Tribune* saw Eisenhower's lack of condemnation as tacit approval of his Democratic predecessors' behavior, but in fact, the opposite was true. "This idea of the President of the United States going personally abroad to negotiate—it's just damn stupid," Eisenhower said. "Every time a President has gone abroad to get into the details of these things he's lost his shirt." He was not in favor of a Yalta- or Potsdam-type meeting with Soviet leaders. In his first two years in office, Eisenhower left the country only three times to visit neighboring Canada, Mexico, and Bermuda.[39]

Despite the president's caution, the prospect of a great-power summit lingered. Weeks before Eisenhower took office, Churchill visited the United States. Although he called on Truman, the prime minister's main purpose was to confer with the president-elect about a summit. Eisenhower had to reassure Republican senators that his meeting with Churchill was simply a social visit, not a policy meeting. The prime minister received the same message. While Eisenhower was happy to rekindle their close wartime partnership, all agreements had to go through official diplomatic channels.[40]

Calls for a meeting with the Soviets—especially by Churchill—grew after Stalin's death in March 1953. The Eisenhower administration was hesitant and did not want a hastily arranged meeting. Rather, it wanted to lay the diplomatic groundwork at lower levels, which would increase the likelihood of a successful meeting at the highest level. "I am not afraid to meet anybody face to face to talk," Eisenhower told the prime minister, "but the world gets in a habit of expecting a lot."[41]

Eisenhower was "ready to do anything" for peace, including meet with his foreign counterparts, as long as the possibility of progress existed. But he believed that in foreign affairs, the State Department was paramount: "I suppose there are times when the highest authorities, taking great questions of policy, might do better by meeting, establishing personal contacts. . . . But, by and large, I think that these things must be done through the Foreign Offices and State Department, because they are so complicated. . . . It would be unwise to depend entirely on just meeting of the heads of state."[42]

Eisenhower also made a constitutional argument for the limitation of personal diplomacy. He maintained that his duties in the United States prevented him from leaving the country for extended periods. It was "an awkward thing" to leave for more than a day, he told the British prime minister.[43] In addition, the American people were simply not used to it. As Secretary of State John Foster Dulles explained to his British counterpart, while the British public may be accustomed to their prime minister negotiating at a summit, "it is unusual" for the president, and "there is considerable sentiment against his doing so at all."[44]

In July 1955, however, Eisenhower found himself at a four-power summit. In May the new British prime minister, Anthony Eden, had written to the president and informed him that it was time for a summit, which, he noted, "could play a useful part in the reduction of world tension."[45] Eisenhower and Dulles did not completely dismiss the idea, but they continued to insist on preparation at lower diplomatic levels. Their resistance slowly eroded as British and French insistence intensified. Then the Soviet Union helped move things along when it finally signed the Austrian State Treaty after years of intransigence. According to Eisenhower, many saw this as "a deed auguring well for melting the Soviet ice that had frozen fruitful negotiation."[46] The president also warmed to the summit because of the type of gathering envisioned. Rather than hard negotiations, the meeting would merely set the agenda for future talks at lower levels.[47]

In a meeting with members of Congress, Eisenhower noted that the United States was going to the summit "with hope, and not with false expectations," and he assured them "there is no sentiment for appeasement."[48] He had a similar message when he spoke to the American people on radio and television, telling them his goal was "to change the spirit" that had existed since the end of World War II. He spoke eloquently of peace and hope, but he also felt compelled to defend his mission. Eisenhower tried to distinguish between the upcoming Geneva meeting and top-level summits of the past. This was the first time a president would be attending such a conference in peacetime, and rather than dealing with issues of war, he was going to "prevent wars."[49]

The Geneva talks were amicable, and both the Soviets and the Western powers were pleased with the outcome. The conference allowed the Soviets to demonstrate equality with the West, and the United States was pleased that its allies remained united. There were no major agreements, but this was by design. Neither the Kremlin nor the White House wanted to discuss substantive matters such as German reunification. Both were more interested in the propaganda aspects of the summit and how it played domestically. As presidential adviser Nelson Rockefeller told Eisenhower, the central aim was "to capture the political and psychological imagination of the world." Thus, "the propaganda stakes" were more important "than the actual conference results."[50] Eisenhower tried to win the public relations battle with his Open Skies proposal, which would have allowed each side to conduct aerial surveillance over the other's territory. The administration knew there was little chance the Soviets would agree, but it hoped to score a public relations victory. Although the idea was popular in Europe and among members of Congress, one poll showed Americans split on the proposal.[51]

In the end, nothing came of the "spirit of Geneva." It was Eisenhower's only high-profile summit in his first term, but he welcomed a steady stream of foreign leaders to the United States.[52] Sometimes these meetings proved problematic. "It seems to me this business of entertaining Heads of State can be run into the ground a little bit," Eisenhower told Dulles. "In fact the more we do of it, the more there seems to be done." He particularly lamented "the agony of the state dinner," followed by the reciprocal dinner at the visiting leader's embassy. Dulles acknowledged that Eisenhower's "calendar has been crowded with foreign visitors," but he assured the president that the State Department had been instructed to limit official state visits. Fortunately for Eisenhower, reciprocal dinners were required only for formal visits; for informal talks, they were not necessary.[53] And it was in the realm of informal visits that Eisenhower truly made his mark on the development of presidential personal diplomacy.

Before becoming president, Eisenhower had acquired years of practice cultivating relationships. During his illustrious military career, he demonstrated a deft touch with superiors and subordinates alike. He frequently communicated with world leaders during World War II and then later as supreme allied commander of the North Atlantic Treaty Organization (NATO) in the early 1950s. Throughout his military service, he demonstrated a knack for collaboration and consultation. As he told Lord Louis Mountbatten during the war, effectively leading a multinational force "involves the human equation. . . . Patience, tolerance, frankness, absolute honesty in all dealings, particularly with all persons of the opposite nationality." Eisenhower's wartime contemporaries recognized his skill in this area, and it became obvious to all during his presidency.[54]

In Eisenhower's first three years in office, thirty-seven world leaders visited the United States. His successor, John F. Kennedy, would welcome nearly that many in his first year in office. But at the time, Eisenhower set a new record, exceeding Truman's eighteen world leaders and FDR's seven during their first three years. As the *New York Times* reported, the president and his advisers were "convinced that these personal meetings and intimate tête-a-têtes are a most valuable lubricant to the wheels of world diplomacy."[55] Rather than formal conferences, Eisenhower favored casual talks that often took place outside of Washington and involved few advisers, no formal agenda, and little protocol. He believed this type of personal diplomacy promoted trust and goodwill and counteracted Soviet propaganda.[56] According to one administration official, these private, informal talks also gave the president "a freshness of viewpoint and a sense of familiarity" with international issues. Despite their informal nature, these high-level talks made professional diplomats nervous, as they worried what the president might say or do without their guidance.[57]

A March 1956 meeting with the leaders of Mexico and Canada at White Sulphur Springs, West Virginia, is illustrative of Eisenhower's informal diplomacy. As White House press secretary James Hagerty noted, there was no formal agenda, and the gathering had been "called for the purpose of getting to know each other better." After two days of talks, there were no agreements or communiqués, yet Eisenhower called the meeting "a great success" because it achieved its purpose of enhanced understanding and friendship.[58] Although the outcomes of such talks were often intangible, the American public was supportive. It, like the president, saw value in promoting goodwill through personal contact. But, as the *Washington Post* reminded readers, Eisenhower's "homely chats" would not solve world problems.[59]

In addition to face-to-face meetings, the administration sought to leverage other forms of personal diplomacy. Vice President Richard Nixon was often sent abroad as Eisenhower's surrogate.[60] Correspondence was another tool. "You might wish to consider sending personal communications from time to time to those heads of state or government who have visited the United States and have had the opportunity to become acquainted with you," Secretary of State Dulles told the president. Doing so would "prove very effective in promoting closer relations with our friends."[61] Eisenhower found that writing to allies was a useful way to stay in touch and helped him formulate ideas. He also maintained a steady correspondence with Soviet leaders beginning in September 1955, although it eventually devolved into more of a public relations campaign than serious diplomacy. Important topics were covered in the president's correspondence, and many issues were raised that were typically discussed at lower diplomatic levels. These letters were often released publicly, sometimes even before the recipient received them. Instead of being a means to gain understanding, the correspondence became propaganda.[62]

EISENHOWER'S SECOND TERM

In Eisenhower's second term, the scope and scale of his personal diplomacy increased dramatically. Gone was the reluctance to go abroad for extended periods. In his last year in office, he went on multiple world tours, visiting Europe, Latin America, Africa, the Middle East, and Asia. These journeys were about generating goodwill rather than hard negotiating, and they signaled a shift in the development of presidential personal diplomacy. Explaining his missions to another world leader, Eisenhower said his aim was "to strengthen the ties which bind the nations of the Free World together. I have found from experience that there is no substitute for personal contact in furthering understanding and good will."[63] After Eisenhower's first world tour at the end of 1959—which kept him out of the country for three weeks—he told the nation the trip was not part of "normal diplomatic procedures." He went not to negotiate but "to improve the climate in which diplomacy might work more successfully."[64]

Eisenhower said the origins of his goodwill missions lay in conversations with Dulles. The secretary of state recognized the "world prestige" of the presidency and believed the United States could benefit from Eisenhower's engagement with foreign leaders. "Dulles was very clear," Eisenhower recalled, "that he did not think such visits would solve any particular problems—and was not in favor of going somewhere just to solve a problem." He also thought summits "were not only futile but had many dangers," a sentiment the president shared. The rise of new nations in Africa and Asia changed the secretary's thinking. Dulles believed the international clout of these nations would grow, so it was important for the United States "to establish a foothold of friendship." Presidential visits provided the opportunity to generate favorable attitudes toward the United States and aid the West in its battle with the Soviets.[65]

As Eisenhower resorted to personal diplomacy more frequently in his second term, he also faced a succession of crises. During his reelection campaign in 1956, there was trouble in the Suez, and the Soviets brutally crushed an uprising in Hungary. The following year brought the Soviet launch of the satellite *Sputnik* and domestic turmoil as Eisenhower sent federal troops into Little Rock, Arkansas, to enforce desegregation. Crises in Lebanon and Iraq followed in 1958, as did renewed tension with China in the Taiwan Strait. And the specter of communism loomed in Cuba, Congo, and Laos.

The most crucial issue of the late 1950s, however, was Berlin. If the Cold War turned hot, most believed the divided German city would be ground zero. "Trouble was always afoot," Eisenhower recalled.[66] For both the United States and the Soviet Union, Berlin was a strategic liability. Soviet leader Nikita Khrushchev referred to it as "a cancer" and a "bone in my throat," yet he also saw Berlin as the "testicles of the West." When he wanted a reaction, he just had to "give them a yank."[67] In late 1958, as East Germany's economy eroded and it hemorrhaged skilled workers fleeing to West Berlin, Khrushchev hastily issued a six-month ultimatum to settle the city's status. The deadline passed without a word from the Kremlin, but the provocation was designed in part to lure Eisenhower into a summit. Since the Geneva Conference three years earlier, little had changed in US-Soviet relations. This was a problem for Khrushchev, who wanted progress on numerous fronts. West Germany's continued integration into the West and fear that it would acquire nuclear weapons was his top priority. An escalating arms race that increasingly drained the Soviet economy also concerned him.[68]

As discussed, Eisenhower was leery of high-stakes summitry. By the summer of 1959, however, progress on any aspect of US-Soviet relations had stalled. The only idea Eisenhower could come up with was to invite Khrushchev to the United States. What the outcome might be was unknown. Khrushchev's visit, the first to the United States by a Soviet leader, was "an experiment," according to a top State Department official, and the administration confessed that it might be a mistake.[69] Explaining to French president Charles de Gaulle what he hoped to accomplish, Eisenhower said a visit to the United States might give the Soviet leader "a better picture of our strength and way of life. It would also serve to reduce the atmosphere of crisis" if diplomacy at lower levels failed to make progress. Eisenhower was under no illusion that their talks would solve every problem, and he "regretted that normal diplomatic channels . . . were being so markedly ignored." But he also believed the "effect [of the meeting] might be considerable" and could lead to a four-power summit.[70]

Before facing off with Khrushchev, Eisenhower consulted with European allies. In the weeks leading up to the Soviet leader's visit, the president traveled to West Germany, the United Kingdom, and France. As the State Department noted, the trip "serve[d] a necessary psychological function." The Continent was a mix of hope and fear, and part of Eisenhower's goal was to reassure Europeans that "the West will not succumb" to Khrushchev's pressure.[71] Complicating the president's journey was the fact that each leader he met had a different view. Leaders in West Germany and France reacted to the news of Khrushchev's visit with "consternation," while the British "applauded" it.[72] West German chancellor Konrad Adenauer feared a weakening of US support and worried that Eisenhower—with British prodding—might make concessions to the Soviet Union that adversely affected his nation. Thus, the US ambassador in West Germany saw the president's trip as a chance to "soothe [the] Chancellor's apprehensions."[73] In Britain, Prime Minister Harold Macmillan greatly favored a formal four-power summit, and Khrushchev's visit to the United States quieted the demand for one. However, the State Department believed Macmillan would want "some public assurance" that a four-power meeting would eventually occur, especially with parliamentary elections quickly approaching.[74] And in France, Eisenhower dealt with the irascible de Gaulle. The French leader was "rather rigidly opposed" to a summit and wanted to know the administration's thinking on and purpose for Khrushchev's visit, which he considered "a futile gesture." De Gaulle also wanted assurances that Eisenhower would be speaking only for the United States and not the West as a whole.[75]

Overall, Eisenhower's European sojourn was successful. In Bonn, he and Adenauer had private talks that were so "absorbing" they never bothered to bring in their advisers.[76] Eisenhower found his time with de Gaulle "more than rewarding," and the US ambassador reported the president's trip to France "was [an] unqualified success" that resulted in a "vastly improved atmosphere."[77] From Britain, the US ambassador noted that the president's "personal impact . . . was enormous," and the visit "left Anglo-American relations in [a] rosy glow" and "unquestionably enhanced British confidence in United States leadership."[78] Though differences remained, Eisenhower's European junket reassured his allies, and it was called a "personal triumph." To observers, Eisenhower's European trip and his pending talks with Khrushchev demonstrated that he was now his own secretary of state.[79]

With his European allies satisfied, Eisenhower welcomed Khrushchev in September 1959. In their first private meeting, the president expressed his desire for harmonious relations. Flattering the Soviet leader, he said Khrushchev "had an opportunity to become the greatest political figure in history" if he used his power for peace. Eisenhower spoke on "such a personal basis," he explained, because the matter was "very close to his heart."[80]

After their initial talks, the Soviet leader toured the United States, visiting New York, Iowa, and California before returning to Washington for more talks with the president at Camp David. "My purpose in these man-to-man talks," Eisenhower recalled, "was to learn more about his intentions, objectives, and personal characteristics." Despite Khrushchev's reputation for colorful language and actions, he was on his best behavior.[81] The focus of their discussions was Berlin, as Eisenhower refused to address other issues until he thought Khrushchev would be willing to ease pressure on the city. They also discussed a presidential visit to the Soviet Union and a four-power summit the following year. In Eisenhower's opinion, the talks went well. Their only "real argument," according to Eisenhower, was over a summit: Khrushchev wanted to convene one quickly, and the president did not. "Like mountain summits, political summits are normally barren, but . . . under proper circumstances, I would have no particular objections to such a meeting," Eisenhower said. Still, he warned the Soviet leader that he would never agree to a summit based on any threat or ultimatum related to Berlin.[82]

The talks were widely popular, with 66 percent of Americans approving of Khrushchev's visit and 71 percent approving of Eisenhower going to the Soviet Union.[83] But the "spirit of Camp David" was short-lived. Two weeks before a planned four-power summit in May 1960, the Soviets shot down a U-2 spy plane. At first, the administration tried to deny that it was involved in aerial espionage, but Khrushchev forced the Americans' hand when he unveiled captured pilot Francis Gary Powers. The Soviet leader demanded an apology, and Eisenhower refused. Khrushchev's rhetoric became increasingly inflammatory and undiplomatic, yet he still wanted to have a summit.[84]

When Eisenhower, Macmillan, de Gaulle, and Khrushchev gathered in Paris for a "pre-summit" meeting, the Soviet leader opened with a lengthy statement attacking the United States. He said the summit needed to be postponed for six to eight months, as did Eisenhower's visit to the Soviet Union. Macmillan and de Gaulle tried to convince Khrushchev to participate in the conference, but to no avail. The Soviet Union had suffered a public insult, he declared, and there could be no summit "until the United States has publically removed the threat it has imposed."[85] After Khrushchev's outburst, the Western leaders met among themselves to decide whether to invite him to another round of talks. They believed that if they did, and he failed to attend, this "would help the West to dramatize" Soviet intransigence.[86] Khrushchev was a no-show at subsequent meetings, dashing the hopes of millions. The Soviet leader bore the brunt of responsibility for the failed summit, but American prestige had been damaged as well.[87]

Though politically wounded, Eisenhower went on a previously planned goodwill tour of Asia, visiting the Philippines, Taiwan, and South Korea.[88] At home, his personal diplomacy continued unabated as well. In September he went to New York for the opening of the UN General Assembly and held ten bilateral meetings, ushering in a practice his successors would follow.[89] But despite all the high-level talks held in his final year, presidential personal diplomacy was under attack.

The events in Paris had left a bitter taste in Americans' mouths. The *Washington Post* noted that although the president had handled himself well, he "ought not to be greeted as a conquering hero. He did not conquer; he, and the country with him, suffered a humiliating rebuff." The *New York Times* sounded the death knell for summitry: "The Paris fiasco is not merely the fiasco of a single conference. It casts new doubt on the wisdom of the whole concept of 'summitry' as practiced in the past.... Certainly no American President should again be exposed to the verbal assaults, abuses and humiliations heaped upon" Eisenhower.[90]

Even the president's postsummit goodwill trip was not without controversy. Initially, Japan had been part of the itinerary, but intense, weeks-long demonstrations over a US-Japan security treaty caused the Japanese prime minister to request a postponement of the president's visit to Tokyo. Eisenhower did visit Okinawa, however, which was home to a US military base; though technically Japanese territory, it was essentially a US military colony. An estimated 200,000 people greeted Eisenhower warmly, but thousands of protesters also came out, scuffling with US marines and causing the president to change his route.[91]

What had been a boon to Eisenhower's popularity six months ago was now a millstone. Initially, he had bipartisan support for his goodwill tours, and at the start of 1960, a Gallup poll reported his approval rating at 71 percent. He was seen as a "master diplomat" whose "program of simple and direct personal diplomacy has made a deep impression on many."[92] In the aftermath of the canceled Tokyo visit, the president's approval rating dropped seven points. Although 61 percent of Americans still approved of Eisenhower's performance, that drop represented the largest one-month decline since the 1958 midterm elections. George Gallup declared that the decrease was a direct result of the president's dealings with world leaders. Americans had "misgiving about the merits of personal diplomacy efforts."[93]

By mid-1960, it was clear that personal diplomacy had "fallen to low repute," and the administration was reevaluating the practice's usefulness.[94] While defending Eisenhower's recent goodwill trip to Asia, Secretary of State Christian Herter announced that the president would not be going on any more grand tours. Instead, US diplomacy "should return to traditional channels and procedures of international contact." According to one journalist, Herter was admitting that "presidential touring and personal diplomacy is ill-conceived, and unproductive and . . . [should] be discontinued."[95] Privately, the administration did a postmortem on superpower summitry. The State Department examined the pros and cons of the practice and concluded, "It is generally in our interest to avoid summit meetings and pursue our objectives by other means, including negotiations at other levels." If the president needed to interact with the Soviet leader, "it should generally be sought in the guise of informal exchanges—e.g., during visits or attendance at the UN— rather than of summit conferences."[96]

As the administration sought to put superpower summitry on the back burner, other world leaders had different thoughts. Toward the latter part of 1960, the biggest names in the nonaligned movement put forth a resolution at the United Nations, urging Eisenhower and Khrushchev to meet. The proposal irritated the president.[97] He did not understand how these leaders could place Soviet and American actions on equal footing, and when he had met with four of them the previous week, they had made no mention of any such proposal.[98] Eisenhower responded by stating that he was more than willing "to meet with anyone at anytime if there is any serious promise of productive results." But, he argued, Soviet words and actions made this highly unlikely.[99]

Eisenhower's high-profile personal diplomacy was over, but his engagement with foreign counterparts continued behind the scenes. For example, as the end of Eisenhower's second term neared, the administration sent farewell messages to leaders all over the globe. Initially, only leaders the president knew personally received such messages, but the State Department worried about offending others, especially those who had been "friendly and cooperative." The State Department therefore recommended that less intimate messages be sent to other heads of state and government. In total, farewell messages went out to the leaders of more than eighty nations.[100]

When Eisenhower returned from his final goodwill tour in June 1960, he addressed the nation, delivering a speech that was fundamentally a defense of personal diplomacy. He explained the origins of his goodwill journeys, spoke of his trips' objectives, and contrasted them with official summitry. The goodwill tours demonstrated the United States' desire for peace and helped create understanding, he declared. Diplomacy at the highest level was not always the best means of producing international accords, and informal visits "frequently bring about favorable results far transcending those of normal diplomatic conferences." They create a "more friendly atmosphere and mutual confidence between peoples" and bring "closer together nations that respect human dignity and are dedicated to freedom." Though critics might scoff, Eisenhower believed these intangibles were a powerful product of personal diplomacy and reason enough for future presidents to continue in his footsteps. "So long as the threat of Communist domination may hang over the free World," he proclaimed, "I believe that any future President will conclude that reciprocal visits by Heads of friendly Governments have great value in promoting free World solidarity."[101] The president's philosophy impressed the *Los Angeles Times,* which wrote that his "words on this vital aspect of his office might well serve as a guide for future chiefs of state. . . . His experiences are a major contribution to a fuller understanding of the power and responsibilities of his office and future Presidents would do well to pay them heed."[102]

Toward the end of 1959, as the nation prepared to enter a presidential election year, some speculated on the role that personal diplomacy might play. If Eisenhower visited the Soviet Union and reduced tensions, Republicans would have "tremendous political talking points . . . [and] inspiration for the sloganeers could be fabulous," wrote the *Washington Post.* Presidential contenders from both parties appeared eager to experiment with leader-to-leader diplomacy, as almost all of them had met with Khrushchev either at home or abroad. "Altogether it looks as if a personal mission to Moscow, or at least some acquaintance with Mr. K, may become as familiar a political badge as the log cabin, red galluses or respect for motherhood," the newspaper mused. This was not a development it championed.[103]

After the failed summit in Paris, the aura of diplomacy at the highest level wore off. As John F. Kennedy assumed office in January 1961, his administration appeared to be moving away from personal diplomacy. The message from the White House was that the new president preferred "quiet diplomacy" through traditional diplomatic channels, rather than a summit with Khrushchev.[104] This approach earned praise from the press, although there were questions about how long Kennedy could resist the pull of summitry.[105] As it turned out, the restraint was short-lived. Four months after his inauguration, Kennedy was face-to-face with Khrushchev in Vienna.

Despite the backlash against personal diplomacy at the end of the Eisenhower era, the practice was here to stay. Eisenhower relegitimated the practice through meetings in the United States, extensive travel, and meditations on personal diplomacy. Thus, unlike the hostility toward personal diplomacy that developed in the wake of the Yalta and Potsdam Conferences and caused a retrenchment of leader-to-leader contacts, Eisenhower's successors would increasingly interact with heads of state and government. Some, like Kennedy and Richard Nixon, welcomed it. Others, like Lyndon Johnson, were less enthusiastic. But every future administration engaged in personal diplomacy to some extent and was driven by similar motives. Whether they hoped to bolster a foreign leader's spirits and confidence, deal with the exigencies of world crises, reap the potential political benefits, satisfy a push by a foreign leader, or maximize control of US foreign relations, occupants of the White House frequently turned to personal diplomacy.

3. John F. Kennedy and the President as Counselor

When John F. Kennedy traveled to Canada for his first trip abroad as president, his briefing book warned, "The essential element in problems involving Canada is psychological." America's economic and military power gave its northern neighbor an "inferiority complex," and Canadians viewed America as having "a trigger-happy military . . . not [being] regardful of cultural values . . . [and] absent-minded and neglectful of the interests of Canada." Kennedy needed to establish a "frank working relationship" with the Canadian prime minister and project a reassuring, positive image of the United States. It was impossible to completely change the Canadians' minds with one visit, but the administration believed the president's presence would go a long way toward dispelling negative perceptions. And it seemed that Kennedy was successful, as he "charmed Canadian officialdom and populace alike."[1]

When Italian prime minister Amintore Fanfani visited Kennedy in January 1963, the administration saw it as an opportunity "to build up the prestige and self-confidence of Italy" and help it "overcome her chronic worries about the role of a second rate power in Europe."[2] The Italians felt like they were "left out of everything," presidential adviser Arthur Schlesinger Jr. noted, and they wanted "a greater sense of participation." Kennedy needed to confide in Fanfani and ask for his views.[3] The focus on the Italian leader's psyche seemed to pay off. The US ambassador in Italy reported that Fanfani "was profoundly pleased with [the] reception he got especially from [the] president personally. Long-range benefits may flow to us from this."[4]

The importance of psychology was not unique to Canada, Italy, or Kennedy. The relationship between psychology and international relations is deep, and concepts such as deterrence and credibility are rooted in psychology.[5] Throughout the second half of the twentieth century, American presidents and their advisers were very concerned about the mental conditions of heads of state and government and recognized the importance of tending to their fears and anxieties. Whether dealing with a European ally, a nonaligned leader, or a non-Western partner, presidents sought to soothe their worries and concerns and convince them of America's credibility and reliability.

Foreign leaders might not have noticed the president performing this function, but presidents and their advisers were well aware of it.

This chapter examines how President Kennedy acted as a "counselor" for world leaders. In the thick of the Cold War, this period offers an especially useful case study of how American presidents use personal diplomacy to ease their counterparts' concerns. The United States was locked in a decades-long struggle with the Soviet Union, and the fear of nuclear war permeated international politics in the early 1960s. After eight years of dealing with Dwight Eisenhower, a war hero and elder statesman, world leaders were now faced with a young, inexperienced former senator. Questions about Kennedy's leadership were acute. He had to convince foreign leaders of his mettle while expressing sympathy and understanding for their economic and security problems and addressing concerns about their political standing back home.

Approaching foreign leaders, particularly the heads of non-Western nations, through the lens of psychology seemed more valid to the Kennedy administration than older approaches. "Psychoanalysis was not necessarily more accurate, but it was more convincing," Andrew Warne notes, "in part because it allowed policy-makers to use a scientific language considered legitimate at a time when the racial language that characterized traditional Orientalism was becoming less acceptable."[6] Furthermore, a psychological rather than a racial lens offered US policy makers greater hope. If a nation's problems were "mental," they could be fixed, and presidential counseling might improve the situation.[7]

In particular, this chapter examines Kennedy's relationships with German chancellor Konrad Adenauer and the shah of Iran. In both instances, Kennedy's outreach was required to counteract Bonn's and Tehran's perceptions that the United States was no longer a reliable partner. At times, the Kennedy administration advanced policies that were at odds with Adenauer's and the shah's preferred positions. Thus, Kennedy's personal diplomacy was needed to persuade both leaders to accept US action or at least temper their criticism.

A NEW FRONTIER IN PERSONAL DIPLOMACY

In his short time in office, Kennedy took personal diplomacy to new heights. Whereas Truman and Eisenhower were initially less inclined to follow in Franklin Roosevelt's footsteps, Kennedy made personal diplomacy a fixture from the beginning, despite promising the opposite on the campaign trail. As a candidate, JFK emphasized his plans for the home front rather than summitry, and he declared that official State Department channels would handle the bulk of diplomatic activity. Politically, this made sense. Compared with his opponent's, Kennedy's domestic policy proposals were viewed favorably by twice as many voters.[8] In a campaign speech, Kennedy proclaimed:

> I want to be the President known . . . as one who not only held back the Communist tide but advanced the cause of freedom and rebuilt American prestige . . . not by tours and conferences abroad, but by vitality and direction at home. My opponent promises, if he is successful, to go to Eastern Europe, to go perhaps to another summit, to go to a series of meetings around the world. If I am successful, I am going to Washington, D.C., and get this country to work.[9]

Like Eisenhower, Kennedy had no problem welcoming foreign leaders to the White House to enhance cooperation and understanding. But trips abroad for negotiations were problematic and conjured images of secret backroom deals by Woodrow Wilson and Franklin Roosevelt, which critics believed hurt the nation and were improper for a democracy. Echoing Eisenhower's stance, Kennedy required diplomatic progress at lower levels before any summit with the Soviets. Secretary of State Dean Rusk was also cautious. Summitry, he argued, should be "approached with the wariness with which a prudent physician prescribes a habit-forming drug—a technique to be employed rarely and under the most exceptional circumstances, with rigorous safeguards against its becoming a debilitating or dangerous habit."[10]

The administration's stance quickly changed. Less than five months into his presidency, Kennedy traveled to Europe for a state visit to France, an encounter with Soviet leader Nikita Khrushchev in Vienna, and talks with British prime minister Harold Macmillan in London. This was in addition to his earlier state visit to Canada. By the end of the year, he had also been to Venezuela, Colombia, and Bermuda.[11]

Unsurprisingly, among Kennedy's first-year travels, his meeting with Khrushchev garnered the most interest and scrutiny.[12] Little diplomatic groundwork had occurred at lower levels, and although a meeting might allow the two leaders to get acquainted, the risks seemed quite high. The *Los Angeles Times* worried about high expectations: "The danger . . . is that while the President might regard his trip as only a limited excursion in personal diplomacy, the rest of the world would attach far greater significance to the meeting. Desperate optimism would make of it something it is not, and the advantage would go to our adversary."[13] The conservative *Chicago Daily Tribune* had a different concern. Playing on the perception of Kennedy as young, brash, and full of bluster, it argued that he would get in trouble if he tried to tough-talk Khrushchev. The newspaper doubted that the Soviet leader would take the president seriously. "We do not have any confidence," it opined, "that Mr. Kennedy, alone and by any presumed force of will and personality, is the man to make Khrushchev think twice . . . [Kennedy] is insufficient to arouse either dread or caution in the Kremlin."[14]

Critics were right to be concerned. Kennedy's first venture into the "big leagues of personal diplomacy," coming shortly after the Bay of Pigs fiasco in Cuba, did not go well.[15] Khrushchev saw Kennedy as weak and hoped to bully his younger and less experienced counterpart. The American president was mentally unprepared for the Kremlin leader's bellicosity and hard-line approach. Rather than reduce Cold War tensions, the meeting raised them. Kennedy admitted that Khrushchev "beat the hell out of me," and a month later, partly in response to the summit, JFK increased defense spending, expanded draft callups, and extended military enlistments. He also advocated a program for the building of fallout shelters. From the Kremlin, these actions looked like a prelude to war.[16]

Kennedy also ran into trouble when corresponding with Khrushchev. In the spring of 1962 the president's military aide, Chester Clifton, warned that the Soviets were upset by the speed with which JFK responded to Khrushchev's messages. Whereas the administration thought quick responses demonstrated the United States' eagerness for dialogue and the importance of the exchange, Khrushchev thought the opposite. He believed the rapid responses meant that his letters were not being taken seriously or given careful consideration. This posed not only a political quandary but also a potential public relations problem. "Because the President is young—and the press has capitalized on this—he is very vulnerable to the unwarranted accusation that he shoots from the hip," Clifton wrote. To avoid adding to this perception, he advised the administration to issue a "message received" note before responding more fully to Khrushchev at a later date.[17]

Kennedy's experience with Khrushchev did not turn him off personal diplomacy. He frequently met with leaders at the White House. He welcomed foreign leaders to the United States seventy-six times throughout his presidency, including thirty-four in his first year.[18] Kennedy also carried out a vast correspondence that was "frank," "warm," and "often even intimate." According to one journalist, he "was establishing a precedent to be followed by every successive President."[19] Indeed, while Franklin Roosevelt created the mold of presidential personal diplomacy and Eisenhower relegitimized it, the Kennedy years solidified the practice. Even though skeptics remained, his successors did not retreat from the use of personal diplomacy.

KENNEDY AND ADENAUER

For all nations, the Cold War caused great anxiety. This was particularly true of America's European allies because, in a very literal sense, they were on the front lines. If the Cold War heated up, the Soviet Union would invade their countries, not the United States. Thus, the president had to reassure them constantly that the United States would defend the Continent from the Soviet Union with both conventional military forces and nuclear forces. For Europeans, the fear was multifold. They worried about the robustness of the US response if the Soviets crossed the Iron Curtain. European leaders doubted that the United States would actually use its nuclear arsenal to attack the Soviet heartland, because a nuclear strike on Moscow would inevitably lead to a counterstrike on American territory. Their fear was that the United States would use its nuclear forces in Europe, minimizing the risk of a direct assault on America but raising the likelihood that the Continent would become a nuclear wasteland. Another worry was that the United States might cut a deal with the Soviets that was detrimental to European interests. Europeans feared the United States would make peace with the Soviets, leaving them to deal with Moscow on their own. And at various times, different countries thought the United States was not doing enough to support them militarily or economically.

European leaders also appealed to the American president for more personal reasons. In addition to assurances about US security commitments to their countries, they sought support for their political positions back home. Often it was not enough for the president to signal his support for a nation; he had to provide personal encouragement and backing to an individual leader as well. Although political and personal support was offered to all of Europe, in the early 1960s a troika of leaders stood at the forefront of European politics: Britain's Harold Macmillan, France's Charles de Gaulle, and West Germany's

Konrad Adenauer. Through letters and face-to-face meetings, Kennedy sought to comfort, reassure, cajole, and convince his European counterparts of America's support and good intentions. This was not easy, and Kennedy had to do it often. The most intractable of the three was de Gaulle, the president's most frequent visitor was Macmillan, and the one needing the most reassurance was Adenauer. The Kennedy administration put significant time and effort into dealing with these three leaders, but Adenauer and West Germany were especially important.

As Europe became an increasingly tense Cold War battleground in the late 1950s and early 1960s, Germany was on the front lines. Security concerns were paramount, and Adenauer needed constant affirmation that the United States would not abandon his nation. There had been concerns about American reliability during the Eisenhower years, but he was a known quantity and a peer of the chancellor. Kennedy was young enough to be Adenauer's grandson.[20] Revealing the generational divide, Kennedy felt he "was talking to a man who had lived in another world, another era, and that it was difficult, therefore, for the two of them to understand each other in a very real sense."[21] At the same time, Schlesinger recalled that Kennedy initially had "great respect" for Adenauer, but as the chancellor became more difficult to deal with, the president looked forward to the day when the senior statesman stepped aside.[22] Although the Kennedy administration was committed to West Germany and to West Berlin's integrity, it also hoped to stabilize Europe and thus wanted to explore the possibility of a Berlin settlement with the Soviets.[23] But moves in that direction—as well as moves toward a general détente with Moscow—were viewed with suspicion in Bonn. When the United States and the Soviet Union came to terms on the Nuclear Test Ban Treaty in 1963, Adenauer exhibited "vast discontent" and "complained bitterly."[24]

The chancellor and the rest of Europe also had concerns about the Kennedy administration's plans to alter the American nuclear strategy. The Eisenhower administration had declared a policy of massive retaliation. Since the West could not match the conventional military forces of the Soviet bloc, the United States would rely on its superiority in nuclear forces.[25] Kennedy, in contrast, adopted a policy known as flexible response. Responding to Soviet provocations with one of two alternatives—either launching a nuclear attack or backing down—was unappealing to him. Thus, he sought to build up America's conventional forces and have its allies do the same, providing the United States with more options. This new approach was not controversial within the administration, as both the State and Defense Departments were in agreement. In Europe, however, "American motives were suspect." Allies saw the United States trying to back out of its security commitments, weakening deterrence against the Soviets.[26]

When Kennedy and Adenauer first met in April 1961, the psychological and emotional elements were clear. Although the German chancellor publicly expressed his eagerness to meet with the president and championed unity, reports from Bonn cautioned that Adenauer "had a grandfatherly mistrust of the new young man in the White House." Compared with Eisenhower's, Kennedy's guarantees were viewed as "pallid" and "half-hearted."[27] Part of Adenauer's concern sprang from statements the president had made while still a senator. Kennedy was not focused on the reunification of Berlin and believed that fixating on the issue hindered attempts to build better relations with the Soviets. Such views were what Adenauer "feared most." And JFK did not endear himself to the chancellor when he declared in *Foreign Affairs* that "the age of Adenauer is over." No wonder there were reports that West Germany had hoped Richard Nixon would defeat Kennedy.[28]

From the start, Kennedy would be hard-pressed to reassure Adenauer. From the US perspective, the Germans were suffering from severe psychological trauma. Henry Kissinger, then a part-time White House adviser, argued that a nation that had endured an economic catastrophe, fought and lost two wars, and experienced the horrors of the Nazi years was "bound to suffer from deep psychological scars." He told Kennedy that West Germany was "a candidate for a nervous breakdown. The fear of being alone or sold out is, in some sense, a quest for emotional security."[29] Thus, when dealing with Germany, the psychological was as important as the political. Adenauer had "an almost pathological fear" that the United States would sell out Germany to the Soviets. This was "not the kind of fear which can be exorcised by rational argument. It is always at the back of the Chancellor's mind." A short visit would not solve the problem, but the administration believed that talks at the highest levels would "have a psychologically reassuring effect."[30]

On the eve of their talks, Kennedy sent Dean Acheson, former secretary of state and a longtime acquaintance of the chancellor's, to the Federal Republic. According to Acheson, Adenauer "wanted to see me very badly."[31] During the visit, he sought to convince the chancellor that Kennedy was steadfast and would not betray West Germany. The mission was successful, and Adenauer declared that Acheson had "lifted a stone from my heart."[32]

Days later, the president and the chancellor met. By most accounts, the encounter went well. When they talked privately, Kennedy spoke of the "great respect" he and all Americans had for Adenauer and West Germany and reassured him that the United States "was prepared and determined to stand by its commitments."[33] The chancellor took away a positive impression of the young president and said he was "deeply moved" when Kennedy praised him as a historic figure.[34]

Kennedy's job as counselor, however, was never-ending. The Bay of Pigs fiasco happened less than a week after the meeting with Adenauer, and the president's handling of it did not inspire confidence in Europe.[35] Even without the botched mission, Kennedy would have spent his time in office continually seeking to bolster Adenauer, but crises made the need more acute. For example, after the Berlin Wall went up in August 1961, Kennedy wrote to the chancellor and told him that the United States was "prepared to do whatever is necessary to meet this challenge, rather than capitulate, or make damaging concessions."[36]

When the two leaders met for the second time in November 1961, it was again Kennedy's job to reassure Adenauer "that the U.S. Government has a clear sense of national purpose, firm leadership and a capacity not to be deflected from basic goals by particular crises."[37] A successful visit also depended on the president's ability to make the chancellor feel politically relevant. Adenauer arrived fresh off an electoral victory for his party, but forming a new government had proved difficult and hurt the chancellor's domestic standing. He had "lost both in prestige and power," Rusk noted, "and he will undoubtedly regard his early visit here as an important factor in recouping his position." This was nothing new for Adenauer, who had used past White House visits to boost his political standing and "self-confidence." After the challenges of forming a new cabinet, Rusk warned, the chancellor would be "particularly sensitive" to any signs that Kennedy had lost respect for him.[38]

Kennedy took the advice to heart, and at the end of Adenauer's visit, both sides hailed it a success. On the second day, the two leaders met for an hour and forty-five minutes with just their interpreters. Throughout their discussions, Kennedy reassured Adenauer that there would be no recognition of East Germany, that Western forces would remain in Germany, and that ties between West Berlin and West Germany would be strengthened. He conveyed unity of purpose and the sense that the fate of their two nations was intertwined. The chancellor emerged pleased and declared publicly that their talks had been "excellent."[39] Privately, he told the president in a letter, "When I took my leave of you I said that I have seldom gone away from the White House with such a feeling of satisfaction and assurance as this time. . . . I should like to say again how much support and reassurance I have derived from my talks with you . . . the earnestness of your determination, Mr. President, have made a deep impression on me."[40] Weeks later, still buoyed by his visit, the chancellor told Kennedy that their talks "convinced [him] . . . the West will survive the trials that lie ahead."[41]

The two men's third meeting came in November 1962, only weeks after the Cuban missile crisis, which many feared was the prelude to a Soviet attack on Berlin. Adenauer initially offered strong support of Kennedy, but that quickly turned to doubt. As he prepared to leave for the United States, he said the Kennedy administration had achieved only a "qualified success" during the crisis, while the Soviets had done "quite well." From the chancellor's perspective, the confrontation had not cowed Khrushchev, and there was no guarantee the Soviets would remove all their missiles from Cuba.[42] It was clear the president needed to reaffirm American support, strength, and commitment.

Kennedy also needed to make Adenauer feel special, as the chancellor again found himself in a politically weakened position. He faced an intensifying political scandal that involved his defense minister and the newspaper *Der Spiegel.* In addition, at age eighty-six, Adenauer was facing pressure to step aside in the coming year.[43] Weeks earlier, the chancellor's political rival Willy Brandt had made a successful visit to Washington, and Adenauer hoped his upcoming trip would counteract it. The administration was willing to help. Well aware of his "susceptibilities to pomp, circumstance and flattery," it believed that giving Adenauer the "red-carpet treatment . . . would probably pay dividends" and help him overcome "his reported sensitivity" over Brandt's visit.[44]

Kennedy welcomed Adenauer with a colorful ceremony on the South Lawn of the White House that included a nineteen-gun salute and an honor guard. Later that day, the president praised the chancellor as "an old, valued and courageous friend."[45] In private, the two discussed Adenauer's concerns about the removal of missiles from Cuba. The president admitted that it was impossible to know with absolute certainty that all the missiles were gone, but he was confident the threat was over. Both agreed that the Cuban issue needed to be fully resolved before any new initiatives on Berlin, although Kennedy seemed more optimistic about the possibility of an agreement. They released a joint statement that emphasized cooperation and their determination to defend Berlin "in all circumstances and with all means."[46] But as one journalist mused, the visit, overall, was "a polite fiasco." After successfully dealing with the Cuban missile crisis, Kennedy probably had little desire to take advice from someone old enough to be his grandfather.[47] Importantly, however, the president still tried to allay the chancellor's concerns.

In June 1963 Kennedy and Adenauer met for the final time when the president visited West Germany and West Berlin. More than on any of Kennedy's other trips abroad, psychological and emotional elements took center stage. It was the first time an American president had visited Berlin since 1945, when Harry Truman attended the Potsdam Conference. Kennedy was also the first leader of a NATO country to visit the city. The administration believed the president's visit demonstrated "in impressive and personalized form" America's closeness to the city and would "give Berliners themselves [a] helpful . . . psychological lift."[48] The trip was overwhelmingly about public displays. Kennedy's presence and public remarks were intended to remind the people of West Germany and Berlin—as well as the rest of Europe—of America's commitment to defend the Continent.[49]

Kennedy's trip was part of a larger ten-day journey that took him to Ireland, the United Kingdom, and Italy. But the German portion of the trip took center stage. On Kennedy's first day in West Germany, an estimated one million came out to greet him, and about twenty million watched him on television.[50] Adenauer welcomed Kennedy warmly, thanking him for coming and declaring that the president "could not have done anything more effective to strengthen the cohesion within the Alliance." In response, JFK reaffirmed America's commitment: "So long as our presence is desired and required, our forces and commitments will remain. For your safety is our safety, your liberty is our liberty, and any attack on your soil is an attack upon our own."[51]

On June 26, 1963, Kennedy arrived in Berlin, the "emotional climax" of the trip, where he received a rousing welcome.[52] Riding in an open car with Adenauer and Brandt, the president traveled all over the city, stopping at iconic locations such as the Brandenburg Gate and Checkpoint Charlie as cameras captured his every move. Millions came out to see him, and when he delivered a speech in front of city hall (one of three he gave that day), an estimated 300,000 showed up. It was there that Kennedy delivered his most famous line ("*Ich bin ein Berliner*"), declaring his solidarity with the city's residents.[53]

In the afterglow, Kennedy told close adviser Theodore Sorensen, "We'll never have another day like this one as long as we live."[54] Indeed, as the *Los Angeles Times* reported, Kennedy "came, he saw and—judging by the response to his presence and his words—he conquered."[55] The excitement was palpable. The press reaction was glowing, and West Germans and Berliners were just as enthusiastic. According to a public opinion poll conducted for Brandt's office, 58 percent of West Berliners had come out to see the president. When asked to rate Kennedy's "effort" and "reliability," 63 percent gave him an A, and 29 percent a B. According to one pollster, this was a significant feat because "as school-masters Berliners tend to be slow with praise. . . . No foreign or West German leader has ever done this well in West Berlin." The pollster added that Kennedy's visit "convinced and reassured people who formerly were skeptical."[56] An added bonus was that Kennedy's visit forced Khrushchev to make an impromptu trip to East Berlin less than two days later to bolster morale for his side. His reception, however, failed to match Kennedy's, as only about 10,000 showed up and offered "feeble" praise.[57]

Adenauer "needed constant reassurance; he saw a lot of shadows," Rusk remembered.[58] But providing support was not always easy. "Jack really got irritated with the Germans," Jackie Kennedy recalled. No matter what he did to lift Adenauer's spirits, it never seemed to be enough. "What do you have to do to show the Germans that you care?" he lamented. Despite his frustration, Kennedy continued to try to soothe the West German leader—and not because he was particularly fond of the chancellor. JFK referred to Adenauer as a "bitter old man" and admitted that "he got awfully fed up with" him. But as president, Kennedy's job was to handle not only West Germany's military needs but also its psychological ones. It was thankless work, but he deemed it necessary to promote US national security.[59]

KENNEDY AND THE SHAH

Just as Kennedy continually comforted his European partners and reassured them of American steadfastness, he did the same for non-Western allies, who were often more desperate for economic and military aid and had a tenuous hold on power. The shah of Iran was a prime example. From the administration's perspective, the shah was even more emotional and insecure than Adenauer. His fears were not entirely unfounded. Iran's northern neighbor was the Soviet Union, and during World War II it had occupied part of Iran.

After the war the Soviet Union refused to withdraw from Iranian territory and supported separatist elements in the country. Although the Soviets eventually yielded and Iran regained all its territory, the crisis lasted more than a year and was one of the first Cold War conflicts outside of Europe. It brought the United States and Iran closer together and was a reminder of Iran's perilous geopolitical position.

Like the Kennedy-Adenauer relationship, the Kennedy-shah connection was not warm. Indeed, the two men shared a mutual contempt. During the 1960 election, the shah had hoped for a Nixon victory, as he feared (correctly) that a Democratic administration would push him on domestic reforms and, in his mind, downplay the communist threat.[60] Importantly, however, regardless of their animosity, the two men could not avoid each other. To get the economic and military aid he wanted, the shah needed Kennedy. And despite all the shah's flaws, Kennedy believed he was the best hope for stability in a strategic nation bordering the Soviet Union.

When Kennedy took office, the shah's military and political concerns appeared to be worsening, so in early 1962 the administration began discussing a state visit. It was known that the shah wanted an invitation, and the State Department believed it would enhance the Iranian leader's mental health: "An invitation is essential to bolster the Shah's morale and confidence in Western support against Soviet threats and subversive pressures."[61] The visit was originally planned for late September, but because of the shah's "depressed mood," it was moved up to April.[62] The press was not privy to the administration's view of the shah's psychological state, but it was common knowledge that the Iranian leader felt underappreciated and frustrated with US support.[63]

The State Department and the White House were not avid supporters of the shah, but they saw no alternative. "The internal stability of Iran, as well as its foreign policy," the State Department advised, "is for the present and the near future almost entirely dependent upon the resolution, courage, and common sense of the Shah."[64] From the US perspective, they needed to bolster the shah's spirits to counteract other internal and external forces that wanted the Iranian leader to change his pro-Western positions.

It all came down to the president. Other American officials could offer words of encouragement, but as one National Security Council (NSC) staffer asserted, "only JFK himself will be able both to reassure him [the shah] as to our continued backing and tell him gently a few home truths."[65] Thus, in February 1962 Kennedy wrote to the shah and invited him to the United States.

Advised that "the Shah's capacity for absorbing flattery is as unlimited as is his need for reassurance," the president took the opportunity to praise him.[66] "I have long observed," Kennedy wrote, "the role you have played in leading the Iranian people through the years toward material progress, national unity, and the preservation of the independence and integrity of your nation. Your personal observations on world conditions and on matters of cooperation between our two nations would be of great value to me in these difficult times."[67] The shah's thoughts might have been genuinely interesting to Kennedy, but the primary goal was to make the Iranian leader feel important because, according to the administration, he was "vastly impressed by being made privy to top-level thinking on vital world problems, particularly when it appears that his advice is being sought."[68]

As the shah's visit approached, the administration emphasized the president's role as counselor, noting that the Iranian's "current despondency and talk of abdication . . . arise out of what he regards as insufficient United States support of Iran and him personally. . . . He badly needs United States reassurance." This was complicated, because the shah had a lot on his mind. He was "moody and insecure, preoccupied with military affairs, fearing for his country and his throne, and jealous of possible competitors for power."[69] The shah's focus on military security particularly irritated the administration. He had an "almost psychotic obsession" with it, and even though Iran was in a geographically hazardous neighborhood, the shah constantly overestimated the Soviet threat.[70] The United States wanted Iran to downsize its military, believing that a smaller, modern force would be more beneficial. Using his "personal warmth," Kennedy needed to "calm" the Iranian leader and convince him that the odds of a Soviet assault were slim. The shah could "rest assured" that Iran was under US protection and that, if attacked, the United States would assist it.[71]

Given such a "particularly delicate exercise in reassurance," Kennedy's NSC staff thought the president should have multiple strategy sessions before the visit. The aim was to determine how to approach the Iranian leader and what kind of aid JFK should offer. The administration also considered the need for positive press coverage, which it deemed essential for a successful visit. The shah obsessed over "every word . . . written about him" and had the "unshakable conviction" that negative stories had the US government's consent. He believed if the administration wanted to end the bad press, it could.[72] Writing to White House press secretary Pierre Salinger, NSC staffer Robert

Komer inquired whether there was anything the administration could do to "give the Shah a good press." Admittedly, the Iranian leader was not a sympathetic figure, but since "the visit is largely an exercise in psychotherapy," the administration needed to "build him up, not tear him down."[73]

The US ambassador to Iran, Julius Holmes, believed that the more flattering the American press's portrayal of the shah, the bigger the impact in Iran, thus increasing the shah's prestige and quelling domestic dissent. To that end, he advised the administration to emphasize that the shah was a "reformist monarch" trying to build a modern state and better his people's lives.[74] The shah himself could help, the State Department believed, by not wearing a military uniform, except on certain occasions; not buying expensive items such as jewelry and cars; and not giving extravagant gifts.[75]

Another issue that arose during planning was whether the shah should speak before a joint session of Congress. Initially, he was scheduled to do so, but about two weeks before the visit, some members of Congress raised concerns. As Senator Stuart Symington told the State Department, a speech might backfire. He noted that the shah had spoken to Congress before and was not a polished orator. Symington predicated that if a speech by the Iranian leader were scheduled, very few members of Congress would attend, which would be "humiliating" for the shah.[76]

Ambassador Holmes had a different take. He believed that telling the shah he could not give a speech would cast a pall over the entire visit, negating any benefits the administration hoped to achieve. According to Holmes, the shah knew exactly which other leaders had given speeches before Congress, and the fact that the president of Brazil would be addressing Congress just a few days before the Iranian leader's arrival made it very difficult to tell him no. Additionally, since the shah had addressed Congress before, he would be expecting to do so again. If the shah's speech was canceled, Holmes warned, it would "at least plunge him again into dark mood depression in which he will be convinced that he ranks below neutrals in [the] esteem of [the] US and is considered a second-class ally." If the choice was between the shah addressing an empty chamber and not speaking at all, the ambassador preferred the former. In the end, the speech took place, and Symington's prediction proved correct. Attendance was poor, with the House chamber being only about half full.[77] But Holmes was also right. The paltry turnout did not seem to sour the trip.

The effort the administration put into planning the shah's visit and considering his mental state was not altruism but self-interest. It believed that improving the Iranian leader's mood would advance US foreign policy objectives. As Holmes argued:

> The Shah should be treated not as an anachronism—which he is—nor as a man who has, perhaps, more responsibilities than he is able to bear well and without flinching—which he is—but as a chief of an allied state whom we respect and will treat as we would, for example, the chief of state of a NATO country. By so treating him we will encourage him as much as by any other means to behave in the manner in which we would like to see him behave. He needs such encouragement. . . . By such a flattering approach we can help encourage the Shah to be the kind of monarch that he says he is, that he wants to be and that we want and need him to be.[78]

Kennedy followed this advice. Throughout the visit, he praised the shah and provided repeated assurances of America's goodwill.

At the arrival ceremony, the president declared the visit "most valuable" and offered gushing praise: "Occupying as you do in Iran a most important strategic area . . . your country has been able to maintain its national independence century after century, until we come to the present date, where under great challenges you, Your Majesty, lead that historic fight."[79] At the state dinner, the president continued this theme, calling the Iranian leader "a friend and a very valiant fighter." "We are quite aware," Kennedy toasted, "that were it not for the leadership that he has given . . . this vital area of the world . . . would long ago have collapsed."[80] The president said the same thing in private. The United States could survive regardless of who was president, he declared, but the same was not true of Iran. The shah was the "keystone" that held Iran and the Middle East together.[81]

The shah appeared to be content when he left, but the visit was not an unqualified triumph. As Komer warned, "With a man like the Shah, it is hard to tell how long this effect will last."[82] Indeed, the shah was not an easy man to reassure. In a speech before the National Press Club, he made some revealing remarks. "This king business," the shah said, "has given me personally nothing but headaches. During the whole of these twenty years of my reign, I have lived under the strain and stress of my duties." He urged Americans to think twice before criticizing him and his country, as defending against such attacks drained him and gave comfort to the enemy.[83] The speech revealed that the shah had never been comfortable in his role as king. He had assumed the throne during World War II, after the Allies forced his father to abdicate; his rule was challenged during the Mossadeq years, and then the CIA sought to make him the unquestioned leader. Even so, the shah never felt secure. This insecurity, combined with serious economic and security concerns, made it clear why the Iranian leader needed constant reassurance.

Less than six months after the shah's visit, the administration sent Vice President Lyndon Johnson to Cyprus, Greece, Italy, Lebanon, Turkey, and Iran. Between August 22 and September 7, he traveled to these countries, acting as a proxy for Kennedy and trying to boost morale. "There is a real need for reassurance as to US support . . . [and] that US interest in them [the countries on LBJ's itinerary] remains high," Komer told Kennedy.[84] The shah welcomed Johnson heartily, and the visit appeared to accomplish its goal of raising his spirits.[85] When LBJ returned, he reported to the president. Because of their location, the nations he visited were vulnerable to communist aggression, he noted, but "their heads are still high." However, he continued, "there are disquieting indications that the governments and peoples of these countries are beginning to feel the strain of their exposed position, and to question what is in our hearts toward them—what our real intentions are." Crises such as those in Berlin and Cuba might take precedence, but the vice president urged the administration not to neglect these other nations. A visit by the vice president might be comforting, but it was a temporary fix. As Johnson warned Kennedy, "it would be unrealistic to assume that this fear [of US neglect and withdrawal] has been erased by a single effort."[86]

And there lies the rub of the president's role as counselor. The job is never complete. As the shah illustrates so well, many leaders need constant reassurance. The Iranian leader had a personal support session with the president in April, but by the end of August, he already needed more encouragement. And as Johnson's warning indicated, he would need even more in the future.

In the second half of the twentieth century, it was not enough for presidents to simply meet or correspond with world leaders. As Kennedy's experience with Adenauer and the shah demonstrate, occupants of the White House had to actively tend to their counterparts' emotional and psychological needs. Kennedy's efforts were not unique; other presidents tried to soothe foreign leaders' anxieties as they pursued policies that were at odds with those of their allies. However, Kennedy's charm certainly assisted his endeavors. As Max

Frankel wrote in the *New York Times,* Kennedy's style and personality were "the supreme political weapon abroad," bolstering the presidency's prestige and allure.[87]

But tending to foreign leaders' mental states became the new job of all modern presidents in the post–World War II era, even those lacking Kennedy's charisma. Whether they were dealing with security, economic, or political concerns, presidents took it upon themselves to ease the minds of their foreign counterparts. This was done not necessarily out of any deep affection, although that might have been a factor in some instances. Instead, playing the role of counselor was a tool that presidents and their advisers used to advance US foreign policy. The success of this strategy varied, and presidents used it on some leaders more than others. World leaders did not necessarily see the president performing this task. Many would have taken umbrage at the idea that they needed psychological support—especially from the American president. But the White House, for better or worse, fulfilled this function.

4. Lyndon Johnson and the Imperatives of the International Arena

The mourning had barely begun for the fallen president. But matters of state stopped for no one. It had been three days since John F. Kennedy's assassination, and as the country struggled to understand the tragedy, many things weighed on the mind of the new president, Lyndon B. Johnson. With the Cold War still raging and scarcely a year removed from the Cuban missile crisis, Johnson knew that other crises would erupt sooner rather than later, and foreign leaders would test him. Many saw Johnson as a philistine who was ignorant of foreign affairs, compared to his urbane and internationally minded predecessor. Would Johnson continue Kennedy's policies? How would he respond to global crises? What kind of leader would he be? Foreign governments, both friend and foe, were eager learn the answers.[1]

Recalling his first days as president, LBJ wrote, "The most important foreign policy problem I faced was that of signaling to the world what kind of man I was and what sort of policies I intended to carry out. It was important that there be no hesitancy on my part—nothing to indicate that the U.S. government had faltered."[2] When numerous world leaders came to the United States for Kennedy's funeral in November 1963, Johnson had an opportunity to reassure them. On the advice of national security adviser McGeorge Bundy, he met privately with select foreign leaders. The purpose of the meetings, Bundy told the president, was to "restate . . . the basic position of the United States and to pick up threads of your own personal acquaintance of these men." The State Department disagreed. It argued that meeting privately with only certain foreign leaders would be inappropriate, as the others might be offended. Bundy was unconvinced: "To have them [foreign leaders] come and go and not to meet with them would be equally foolish." Johnson did not seem to care one way or the other and was willing to do whatever Bundy wanted him to.[3]

The new president met individually with dozens of world leaders who attended Kennedy's funeral. The impact of this early venture in leader-to-leader diplomacy is hard to measure. It is clear, however, that some people in the administration, like Bundy, considered it a valuable exercise necessitated by the nature of international politics. As one reporter put it, LBJ's funeral di-plomacy was a "sharp reminder that, in a world torn by big and little conflict and shrunk by jet travel, practical personal diplomacy is an enormous part of being President; domestic problems may be subject to delay, but world issues are less likely to wait."[4]

Though Johnson took office amid tragedy and uncertainty, the demanding nature of foreign affairs guaranteed that he would soon have to turn his atten-tion to global problems. In this, he was not alone; all postwar presidents felt the burdens of confronting a complex world. But for Johnson, this burden was particularly acute. The ever-worsening situation in Southeast Asia ravaged his presidency and—along with other international crises—diverted his attention from his beloved Great Society.[5]

This chapter examines how the demands and crises of the international arena pushed the presidency toward personal diplomacy. The United States was the dominant power in the postwar era, and as it waged the Cold War, its commitments spanned the globe. When crises occurred and issues of war and peace were at stake, it often fell to the US president to become personally involved and interact with other heads of state and government. Personal di-plomacy did not always diffuse these crises, but presidents and their advisers often believed it would help.

In many ways, Johnson is the exception that proves the rule. Compared with his predecessor and successor, he found his interactions with foreign leaders less enjoyable. Later in his presidency this changed, as he sought to use summitry to bolster his legacy, but early on, his advisers often had to per-suade him to employ personal diplomacy. Thus, even a president like LBJ, who would have preferred to focus on the home front, frequently found him-self engaging with his foreign counterparts, often compelled to do so by in-ternational developments and crises that demanded the president's personal attention.

JOHNSON'S STRUGGLES

"'If it hadn't been for Vietnam'—how many times this phrase has been spoken in conversations assessing Johnson's place in history," historian Doris Kearns Goodwin has written. "For it is impossible to disconnect Johnson from that war."[6] Vietnam influenced nearly all of LBJ's diplomacy, especially after 1965.

It led to disagreements with other world leaders and made his leader-to-leader contacts less effective than they might have been. For example, when British prime minister Harold Wilson came under increasing domestic political pressure over Vietnam, he sought to mediate the conflict. This angered Johnson. He did not know how to stop Wilson's efforts but was adamant that he would never cooperate.[7] With Canadian prime minister Lester Pearson, the disagreement over Vietnam became physical. After Pearson delivered a speech at Temple University in Philadelphia and suggested a bombing pause, Johnson became irate. He immediately requested (demanded) that Pearson have lunch with him at Camp David, where he told the prime minister that his speech was "awful." As the Canadian ambassador recalled, after "expostulating, upbraiding, reasoning, [and] persuading," the president "strode up to him [Pearson] and seized him by the lapel of his coat, at the same time raising his other arm to the heavens." Then Johnson told the prime minister, "You don't come here and piss on my rug."[8]

Vietnam might have adversely affected Johnson's engagement with world leaders, but he frequently used personal diplomacy, even in Vietnam. In early 1967, as the war dragged on and he became increasingly desperate, LBJ tried to communicate directly with North Vietnam's Ho Chi Minh. The idea was not new. In the fall of 1966 the president was planning to meet with a group of Southeast Asian leaders in Manila, and national security adviser Walt Rostow had a "wild idea." He suggested that Johnson send a secret letter to Ho, inviting him to meet while LBJ was in the region. "You win if he refuses or if he accepts," Rostow believed.[9] Nothing came of the idea, but in February 1967 the president "decided that perhaps the only way to find a path to peace was through direct contact." LBJ sent a letter to Ho, stating that for years his administration had tried to convey its desire for peace. That effort had failed, he suggested, because their respective positions had been "distorted or misinterpreted as they passed through various channels." Therefore, it was time for direct communication. The president suggested secret negotiations between their representatives, but Ho was unreceptive, and his reply had an "unyielding tone." The president wrote a second time, but again he was disappointed. The second letter was returned to the US embassy in Moscow, with no response. The letter had been opened, however, and the administration was sure that Hanoi's leadership had read its text.[10]

This failed attempt encapsulates much of Johnson's personal diplomacy. Confronted with a global dilemma, he engaged with foreign leaders but rarely got satisfaction. "Foreign affairs devour his days," Lady Bird Johnson said of her husband in 1965. "True, he takes less joy in them" than domestic issues, but "[international] problems are harder to solve."[11] Despite LBJ's frequent frustration, his personal diplomacy was on a par with that of other modern presidents. He might not have enjoyed it as much as some did, but he engaged in it. And the impetus to do so was often the international challenges and crises confronted by all modern presidents.

THE "JOHNSON TREATMENT" ON THE WORLD STAGE

In the days and weeks following Kennedy's assassination, political pundits speculated about the kind of president LBJ would be. The biggest difference between them, popular thinking went, would be their political style and intellectual temperament. As one reporter disparagingly wrote, in comparison to Kennedy, LBJ was "clearly a man of less intellectual depth and imagination, of less inspiring speaking style, of folksy and almost corny habits of speech and action."[12] In terms of policy, however, most did not expect any significant changes. Domestically, observers believed that Johnson would push to implement Kennedy's unfinished programs, most notably in the areas of civil rights and tax reform. Internationally, with no global crises requiring prompt action, the new president was likely to follow his predecessor's path as well.[13]

Despite the popular view that Johnson lacked the diplomatic sophistication of his predecessor, he was no stranger to statesmanship. As vice president, he had traveled widely, making eleven trips to thirty-three countries. Perceptions at the time were that JFK was simply keeping LBJ busy, and State Department officials and reporters who followed the vice president's journeys were not impressed. Johnson, "constrained and frustrated in the isolation booth of the vice-presidency," let loose on these trips, where his "pent-up energies and excesses of personality burst forth."[14] He frustrated State Department officials by breaking with protocol and acting more like a politician on the campaign trail than a statesman. Regardless of this criticism, LBJ's travels had utility, and Kennedy sent him on too many diplomatic missions for them to be mere attempts to keep him occupied. Despite his eccentricity, Johnson did more good than harm, particularly in the developing world. Because of his experience growing up in rural Texas—where poverty and daily struggle were common—he was better able to connect with the people in those countries than were the Ivy Leaguers in the Kennedy administration.[15]

Though Johnson was no stranger to foreign affairs, he clearly preferred domestic policy. Early in his presidency, when advisers proposed meeting with foreign leaders, they had to give him a good reason for doing so. And during his first year in office, LBJ refused to go abroad. He may have been tempted by the pageantry and glamour of foreign travel, but he rejected the idea of going abroad merely for ceremony, and he thought Eisenhower's and Kennedy's world travel had produced little of benefit.[16] So when he met with leaders at Kennedy's funeral, he told them that only an "exceptional situation, maybe a summit or something, that was really imperative" would cause him to leave the country. Johnson worried that if he visited one country, there would be pressure to visit others. "If I start going to one place," LBJ said, "I'll have to go meet others. I can't have any legitimate excuse for not meeting a bunch of other heads of state that want me to. They'll be glad to meet me somewhere."[17] Johnson also had an ambitious legislative agenda, and with the international scene relatively quiet, he saw no pressing need to leave the country. And because 1964 was an election year, he would be busy on the campaign trail. Adding to his reluctance to travel abroad was that, in the years before the Twenty-Fifth Amendment established how to fill a vacancy in the vice presidency, Johnson had no one to take on presidential duties in his absence.[18]

Johnson's early hesitation, however, did not mean he had no interest in personal diplomacy. Indeed, he became quite "a summitry enthusiast," according to one scholar, and took full advantage of the range of techniques for engaging in leader-to-leader interactions.[19] This was evident early on. Speaking to Secretary of State Dean Rusk less than a month into office, he suggested that since the Canadian prime minister was scheduled to visit the following month, they should invite the Mexican president as well. "I just thought it would be a nice gesture," LBJ told Rusk, "since Canada is coming" and the Mexicans have "an inferiority complex, and they're always being mistreated."[20]

Johnson, more so than his predecessors, made frequent use of the telephone. He "launched the era of telephonic summitry," and foreign leaders took notice.[21] In June 1964 Johnson learned that French president Charles de Gaulle wanted better communication, and the possibility of a telephone call came up. Even though de Gaulle rarely used the device, Bundy told LBJ, "I think that the old boy [de Gaulle] is using the telephone because he thinks *you* want to."[22] Not everyone approved of this move toward "telephone summitry." Johnson's opponent in the 1964 presidential election, Barry Goldwater, charged that the "implications of such a 'person-to-person' approach are, to say the least, frightening." LBJ had taken this approach in the Senate, but foreign matters were more critical than domestic ones and should not be entrusted to the "personal whims" of one man. "Telephone summits," argued Goldwater, are "not the kind of presidential activity that inspires confidence."[23]

Another defining feature of Johnson's personal diplomacy was the use of his Texas ranch.[24] He relished its relaxed, informal atmosphere, and it is where he hosted his first foreign visitor, West German chancellor Ludwig Erhard, in December 1963. The ranch also played a role in image building, which Johnson used strategically. As a historian of LBJ's "Texas White House" writes:

> To Europeans especially, and foreign visitors in general, the ranch served as a symbol of this mythically genuine America, where people were "just plain folk" and a handshake was as good as a written contract. It was as if the world of the Western movie had come to life. The conviviality of the Johnson barbecues and the manufactured ambience of authenticity created a seductive environment that disarmed even the most suspicious of visitors. In this setting, Johnson could work his personal magic and could utilize the charisma that underlay his political career with a style and comfort level that he simply did not possess in the nation's capital. In the setting at the ranch . . . Johnson seemed at home, genuine in a manner foreign to the Washington, D.C., environment. He was a real American in the real America—a seductive concept for Europeans familiar with American mythology as well as for national leaders from elsewhere around the globe.[25]

While the use of the ranch was a calculated ploy, it was also a bit ironic. For a president whose sophistication was often questioned, playing up the Texan image seems like an odd choice. And the ranch's informal atmosphere did not appeal to some foreign leaders. In January 1965 Canadian prime minister Lester Pearson arrived wearing a black suit, while Johnson was dressed as a cowboy. Rather than wide-ranging, free-flowing conversations, the president took Pearson—with the press in tow—on a tour of the ranch. During the visit, "the president dispensed drinks liberally and swore loudly," and dinner was "hurried and informal." The Canadian prime minister was not impressed.[26]

For American pols, Pearson's experience was a familiar one: it was known as the "Johnson treatment." The president would flatter, pressure, and back-slap mercilessly in an attempt to get what he wanted. But many questioned whether world leaders would "really [be] susceptible to the kind of eye-ball-to-eyeball, arm-around-the-shoulder manipulation that works so well with businessmen and senators from the Midwest?"[27] Critics thought that Johnson failed miserably, but Rusk believed that, "in general the President got along very well with foreign leaders."[28]

Johnson demonstrated particular skill with European leaders. His inter-actions with Charles de Gaulle were emblematic of his finesse. During the Kennedy years, relations with France had been delicate, as de Gaulle became increasingly critical of the United States and more determined to act inde-pendently. When he attended JFK's funeral, some interpreted it as a sign that he wanted to repair relations. It was not to be. Although LBJ thought his meet-ing with de Gaulle went well, the Frenchman referred to the president as a "cowboy-radical."[29] Johnson had known de Gaulle for years and "had no illu-sions about his flexibility," and throughout LBJ's presidency, de Gaulle con-tinually criticized US policy. Yet, despite the caricature of LBJ as unhinged and uncouth, he refused to "indulge in petty bickering." He believed that respond-ing to every French attack, especially in a vindictive manner, would only make matters worse and further harm the Western alliance. Instead, he tried to ig-nore de Gaulle. "I am not going to fuss at him or fuss over him," LBJ said.[30]

Despite the personal bitterness, Johnson worked with the French leader whenever he could, as he did with Harold Wilson of Great Britain and Lester Pearson of Canada.[31] This gets to the heart of Johnson's approach. He "would not let us criticize any foreign leader by name," Rusk recalled. He did not want "to inflame difficult relations with personal invective. LBJ wasn't responding to my coaching; he probably learned that in the Senate."[32] Johnson was more concerned with the political than the personal. According to him, if he under-stood one thing, it was power—"where to look for it, and how to use it."[33] He believed "the behavior of world leaders was influenced by the same grammar of power; whatever their countries' sizes or shapes, they shared a common concern with questions of rulership: which groups to rely on, which advisers to rely on, and how to conduct themselves amid the complex intrigues of pol-itics."[34] Thus, he did not need to be friendly with other leaders to understand what motivated them.

MANAGING GLOBAL CRISES

"Cyprus, unhappily, along with Vietnam and Panama, is my husband's diet these days," Lady Bird wrote in her diary in January 1964.[35] After a brief lull since assuming office in November 1963, Johnson faced challenges around the globe. "Suddenly, sooner than he or anyone else expected, the great men of the world and their problems are crowding into Washington again," Max Frankel of the *New York Times* wrote. "Sooner than he wished, Mr. Johnson, has found that he must conduct foreign policy, or at least set the pace, because the world plays on apace."[36]

The first crisis occurred in Panama, where a dispute over displaying the American flag in the Canal Zone led to riots. The Canal Zone police were unable to control the protesters, and Panamanian forces did little to help. It fell to US military troops stationed in the Canal Zone to maintain security, but the rioting turned to shooting, leaving four American soldiers and twenty Panamanians dead. Panama quickly broke diplomatic relations with the United States. "Get me the President of Panama—what's his name—on the phone," Johnson ordered. With diplomatic relations severed, an aide questioned the wisdom of a call. "Why the hell can't I?" LBJ snapped. "Come on, now, get him on the phone."[37] In his conversation with President Robert Chiari, Johnson pushed the Panamanian leader to calm the situation and end the violence. According to LBJ, Chiari resisted and tried to use the violence as leverage to revise the canal treaty. Johnson, however, would not consider any changes until things had calmed down. "I was cold and hard and tough as hell," he told Senator Richard Russell.[38]

The president's tough talk did not solve the problem. "Things are going like hell . . . we're in trouble," Johnson warned ten days after talking to Chiari.[39] Although the violence died down, Panama still demanded a treaty revision. It formally requested that the Organization of American States hear charges of aggression against the United States, and Chiari warned there would be more riots without a new treaty.[40] It was an election year, and Johnson was determined to project strength and not yield to pressure. "We're not giving them a damn thing," he told Russell.[41] Eventually, the situation calmed. Diplomatic relations were restored in April, and negotiations quietly took place for a new Canal Zone agreement.[42] But this was only the first of many global headaches for Johnson.

During the mid-1960s the United States would have preferred to stay away from Cyprus. The American public was uninformed about the situation and was not pushing for action, and no matter what the administration did, it was bound to alienate either Greece or Turkey or possibly both NATO allies, thus harming US interests.[43] "Cyprus was about to demonstrate," foreign affairs correspondent Philip Geyelin wrote, "that what had been for a thousand years only a Mediterranean trouble spot, reserved for Mediterraneans . . . could suddenly erupt into a matter of crucial concern to the United States, requiring urgent U.S. action."[44]

Initially, the administration hoped Britain would take the lead. Cyprus had been a British colony and had been given independence only in 1960. The island's residents were predominantly Greek, but there was a sizable Turkish population. In November 1963 the president of Cyprus, Archbishop Makarios III, proposed altering the constitution. The Greek majority supported this proposal, but the Turkish minority felt threatened. Fighting broke out in late December, and Britain, Turkey, and Greece held a conference in January 1964.

Johnson did not seem particularly interested in the issue at the outset, apart from its public relations aspects.[45] But as efforts to resolve the crisis faltered, Cyprus occupied more of the president's time, especially after Britain announced that it would no longer take the lead in keeping peace on the island. Johnson was not pleased. "Goddamn them," he fumed. "I'm ashamed of them."[46] With Britain unable or unwilling to intercede, the options were either a NATO peacekeeping force or taking the matter to the United Nations. The UN option was unappealing because it would give communist nations a chance to meddle in what the administration considered a NATO issue. Reluctantly, Johnson agreed to a NATO force, but Makarios opposed it, preferring the UN option. A UN force arrived in March 1964, but this was only a temporary solution. As the administration continued to search for a permanent settlement, this led to presidential personal diplomacy.

In February 1964 Johnson called Cyprus "the most dangerous thing" since the Cuban missile crisis.[47] By the following month, however, the situation seemed to have calmed. "Cyprus is still tense but quiet," Rusk reported. "I think it is under reasonable control."[48] But by June, conditions had deteriorated, as Turkish Cypriots considered declaring an independent state with military help from Turkey. The fear of a Turkish invasion prompted the president to send a letter to Turkey's prime minister, Ismet Inönü, which Undersecretary of State George Ball later called "the diplomatic equivalent of an atomic bomb."[49] In blunt language, Johnson laid out the consequences if Turkey invaded Cyprus. He said that military action in Cyprus "gravely concerned" him and would harm Turkey's relations with NATO, the United Nations, and the United States. Given the possibility of "such far-reaching consequences," Johnson asked Inönü to halt any military action until the two of them could have "the fullest and frankest consultation."[50] Johnson's letter had the desired effect—Turkey stood down—but it soured relations. "Your message, both in wording and content," Inönü wrote to Johnson, "has been disappointing."[51] The two men would soon have an opportunity to discuss their disagreements in person when the prime ministers of both Turkey and Greece visited LBJ in the same week.

The diplomatic initiative made Johnson wary. "I think that we got in trouble the other night when we suggested to him [Inönü] . . . I'd be glad to see him," the president told Rusk. "When I got home and thought about it a little bit, I thought, 'Now, what in the hell's Lyndon Johnson doing inviting this big mess right in his lap?' . . . I have no solution. I can't propose anything. He'd come over here looking for heaven, and he'd find hell." Though the outcome was unknown, meeting with these leaders seemed to be the best option to control an explosive situation. "We were absolutely desperate," Johnson acknowledged, so he let the invitation stand.[52]

According to National Security Council (NSC) staffer Robert Komer, the aim of meeting with the Greek and Turkish leaders was "to convince our two reluctant dragons to play." Rusk believed the visits would give Johnson "the opportunity to seize the initiative at the outset to shake both leaders off their fixed positions and move them toward negotiation."[53] The administration was not going to propose any plans. Instead, it wanted to get both sides to agree to secret, direct talks overseen by former secretary of state Dean Acheson.

Inönü visited first. "This will be the easier half of your chore," Komer told the president, in part because, according to Ball, the Turkish leader was "desperate." With the Turkish Cypriot position continuing to crumble, Turkey's "only real card" was military action, something adamantly opposed by both the United States and the United Nations. So LBJ's job was "to convince Inonu that it would be folly to play this card."[54]

Johnson was successful, as the Turkish prime minister agreed to secret talks.[55] But Greek prime minister Georgios Papandreou would be a "far tougher nut to crack." Getting him on board "will be no mean trick," advisers cautioned Johnson.[56] Papandreou felt the Greek position was strong, and as the CIA reported, he "has great faith in the power of words, as well as in his ability to use them." The prime minister was confident he could win Johnson over to his side.[57] It was up to the president, then, to enforce his will with either reasoned argument or scare tactics. "I am convinced that it will be your own personal impact which will be determining here," Komer told the president. "This man thinks he's going to snow you, which makes it all the more important you sell him."[58]

Johnson's salesmanship, however, came up short, as Papandreou resisted the US proposal. Greece's and Turkey's positions were so far apart, he argued, that an exchange of views would "lead to war."[59] Instead, he wanted to continue working through the United Nations. The CIA reported that the prime minister was "disappointed and 'a little angry'" after the talks. The lack of an American proposal that went beyond getting the two sides together to talk bothered him.[60]

Despite Papandreou's lack of enthusiasm for American-led negotiations, Dean Acheson still got involved. Officials in charge of the UN mediation asked for an unofficial American representative to meet with both sides. That person was Acheson, who became the key figure in the talks.[61] In the end, his efforts proved unsuccessful. Turkey was willing to go along with his plan, but Greece and Cyprus were not.

By August, Secretary of Defense Robert McNamara told the president that Cyprus was "blowing up."[62] Johnson saw Greece as the main obstacle. At one point, he lost control and scolded the Greek ambassador: "America is an elephant. Cyprus is a flea. Greece is a flea. If these two fellows [Makarios and Papandreou] continue itching the elephant, they may just get whacked by the elephant's tail, whacked good." Johnson was adamant that the ambassador deliver his message to Papandreou. "Don't forget," he said, "to tell old Papa-what's-his-name what I told you—you hear?"[63] Fortunately for LBJ, the worst-case scenario, a Turkish invasion, never occurred—at least on his watch. Turkey would take military action in Cyprus in 1974, creating a division of the island that continues to this day. Johnson's diplomacy did just enough to prevent greater hostilities but failed to develop a long-term solution.

The administration had a similar experience in Yemen. In 1962 a civil war divided the nation, leading to a proxy battle between Egypt and Saudi Arabia. Kennedy tried personal diplomacy to ameliorate the situation, and Johnson followed suit. Soon after JFK's assassination, Walt Rostow advised LBJ to send messages to President Gamal Abdel Nasser of Egypt and Crown Prince Faisal of Saudi Arabia (the center of power and future king), urging both to show restraint. Rostow proposed sending a letter to the crown prince, which he thought might "be the key . . . [to] forestalling any ugly crisis at the end of the year." He advised sending Nasser a verbal message "designed to remind him . . . that you, like President Kennedy, are personally interested in Yemen." The administration viewed such communications as vital. "This personal Presidential diplomacy has been a crucial element in enabling us to control the Yemen crisis," Rostow declared, and "such evidence of your own determination to continue weighing in will have a major calming effect."[64]

Throughout his term, Johnson continued to engage both Faisal and Nasser, but the dynamics with each man were different. Whereas Faisal headed a country that was a US ally, Nasser did not. Johnson tried to continue JFK's more conciliatory policy toward the Egyptian president, but the administration came to have very little faith in Nasser. Events in Yemen, Egypt's increasing reliance on Soviet arms, the US affinity for Israel, and LBJ's personal dislike of Nasser hindered any improvement in relations.[65]

Though Johnson was on better terms with Faisal, that did not mean the administration's task was easy; it had the burden of trying to prevent a wider conflict while reassuring an ally. The president's early letter to Faisal received a positive response. The crown prince said he hoped the "frank rapport" he had enjoyed with Kennedy would continue, strengthening ties and taking relations to "new heights." Regarding Yemen, Faisal agreed to a two-month extension of a disengagement agreement.[66] Still, LBJ needed to reassure Faisal frequently (a common occurrence in personal diplomacy). "Our oil-rich friend has been very cooperative," Komer told the president, "but gets periodically nervous about whether we're still interested in him and whether Khrushchev and Nasser aren't in cahoots." The US ambassador in Saudi Arabia was "pleading" for the president to calm the Saudi leader. Because the United States did not give much aid to Saudi Arabia, LBJ's "personal relationship" with Faisal "is our best instrument of policy," Komer advised Johnson, who approved the sending of another letter.[67]

Johnson's hopes of a permanent settlement proved illusory. By 1966, the Yemen situation remained unsettled, and hostilities between Saudi Arabia and Egypt endured. In June Faisal traveled to the United States to meet with the president—a delicate task for the administration. "King Faisal's visit will depend—more than usual—as much on the tone you set as on the substance," Rostow told Johnson. The king was worried about "Zionist influence" on US policy and feared communist incursions into the Middle East. American outreach to Nasser also concerned Faisal, who believed the administration wanted to make the Egyptian leader its "chosen instrument" in the region, which only amplified his resentment. The president had to reassure Faisal on all these fronts, in the belief that this would prevent greater turmoil in the Middle East.[68]

Johnson had to perform a delicate balancing act. He needed the king to feel that LBJ was "his friend without thinking he has a blank check to pick a fight with Nasser."[69] In a private eighty-minute meeting with just Faisal and an interpreter, Johnson followed that advice and skillfully showed understanding and sympathy for the king's troubles. When the two men joined their advisers, the president declared that "they had a delightful talk . . . he did not know when he had so enjoyed such a visit and that he and the King had established real rapport."[70] While this was partly LBJ bluster, Faisal appeared to be satisfied with the visit. The US ambassador to Saudi Arabia reported that the king "expressed . . . deep appreciation for the President's warm reception which very much impressed him."[71]

Like in Cyprus, the situation in Yemen was not satisfactorily resolved during Johnson's tenure. Saudi Arabia and Egypt never had a direct confrontation, but that was due to other events as much as to Johnson's diplomacy. In the aftermath of the Six-Day War in 1967, Egypt withdrew its forces, removing a significant source of tension with Saudi Arabia. Fighting continued in Yemen until 1970, when both sides agreed to end hostilities. The role of presidential personal diplomacy in preventing a direct conflict between Egypt and Saudi Arabia is debatable, but Johnson's urgings gave both sides pause. However, the impact of LBJ's diplomacy in Cyprus and Yemen is beside the point. The Johnson administration felt compelled to prevent these two situations from deteriorating, and it believed that the president interacting with his foreign counterparts was the best way to achieve that objective.

SUPERPOWER DIPLOMACY

Within days of taking office, Johnson sent Soviet leader Nikita Khrushchev a letter. As LBJ recalled, he was "extending the hand of peace."[72] In the president's mind, the dangers and pressures of the Cold War made such overtures vital. "I was totally convinced . . . that the more the Soviet leaders and I understood each other's thinking," he wrote in his memoir, "the better it would be for all concerned."[73] Johnson believed personal diplomacy was the best means of avoiding misperception and increased hostility, something he felt had happened to Kennedy, ironically, as a result of JFK's personal diplomacy at Vienna in 1961. When a reporter inquired about a summit in early 1964, Johnson did not foreclose the option. "I am ready and willing to meet with any of the world leaders at any time there is an indication a meeting would be fruitful and productive," he replied.[74]

Johnson never met Khrushchev, although they did conduct a regular correspondence. By the fall of 1964, LBJ felt they had begun to understand each other, but then Khrushchev was forced from power in October. "All the careful work, the exchanges of letters, and the gradual understanding of Khrushchev's thinking and reactions had been undone," Johnson lamented. "I knew I would have to start all over again and get to know the new man, or men, who decided Kremlin policy."[75] So LBJ began a new round of personal diplomacy with Khrushchev's replacement, Alexei Kosygin.

Johnson's messages to the Soviet leadership were frequently informal documents sent outside of regular diplomatic channels. This format allowed a freer exchange of ideas, and the White House did not widely share the content of this "pen pal" correspondence. According to one NSC staffer, the value of these exchanges was "psychological as well as political," and they were especially important "during times of crisis."[76] Others were not as enthusiastic. Llewellyn Thompson, US ambassador to the Soviet Union, had "reservations." He believed that many of the routine issues discussed could be better handled through regular diplomatic channels.[77]

As pen-pal messages went back and forth between the White House and the Kremlin, talk of a summit continued. In his 1965 State of the Union address, Johnson expressed "hope" that the new Soviet leadership could visit the United States and learn about the country "firsthand."[78] A month later, he again expressed a desire for Soviet leaders to visit: "As I have said so often before, the longest journey begins with a single step—and I believe that such visits would reassure an anxious world that our two nations are each striving toward the goal of peace."[79]

Behind the scenes, there were discussions about whether a summit should occur in the United States or the Soviet Union. By February 1965, the Soviets seemed willing to come to the United States, but they wanted a signal that the president would make a return visit. But, as happened so often with Johnson's foreign policy agenda, Vietnam intruded. When LBJ began bombing North

Vietnam, Kosygin was in Hanoi. Chagrined, the Soviets became cool to the idea of a summit.[80]

Johnson would not meet Kosygin until 1967, and even then, the talks were not planned but rather the consequence of a local conflict that turned into a Cold War confrontation. In June 1967 war broke out between Israel and its Arab neighbors, most prominently Egypt. In the month leading up to hostilities, the administration had tried to calm the situation, sending presidential communications to Egyptian president Nasser and Israeli prime minister Levi Eshkol. "I would like to emphasize in the strongest terms the need to avoid any action on your side which would add further violence and tension in your area," Johnson wrote to Eshkol on May 17.[81] However, the situation continued to deteriorate, and when it appeared that Israel was going to take military action against Egypt, Johnson sent another message to the prime minister, urging restraint. As a result of the president's intervention and assurances of support, Eshkol agreed to refrain from taking action—at least temporarily.[82]

To Nasser, Johnson implored, "your task and mine is not to look back, but to rescue the Middle East—and the whole human community—from a war I believe no one wants."[83] The administration believed this type of presidential communication was critical. "Nasser feels cut off from the United States," Rostow said. "He is an informal rather than formal man, and State Department communications are, for him, no substitute for informal, high-level—Presidential letters and emissaries."[84] But the Egyptian president's response to LBJ's message was "quite uncompromising," and the two leaders' views remained far apart, although Nasser remained open to dialogue.[85]

Despite US efforts, war broke out on June 5 when Israel preemptively attacked Egypt. Within six days, the fighting was over and Israel had thoroughly defeated its Arab neighbors, but not before the United States and the Soviet Union got involved in the conflict. Between June 5 and 10, Johnson and Kosygin exchanged twenty messages over the post–Cuban missile crisis hotline—the first time it was used other than for test messages and New Year's greetings.[86] The two men agreed that hostilities should end, but each backed a different client. So when Israel appeared to violate a UN cease-fire, the Soviets threatened unilateral intervention. "A very crucial moment has now arrived," Kosygin told Johnson, "which forces us, if military actions are not stopped in the next few hours, to adopt an independent decision. We are ready to do this." Kosygin knew that Soviet action would result in "a clash, which will lead to a grave catastrophe," but if Israel did not comply, he was prepared to take the "necessary action . . . including military."[87]

The message created a situation of the "utmost gravity," according to Ambassador Thompson. Johnson worded his response carefully and sought to assuage Soviet concerns. Israel's compliance with the UN cease-fire was essential, he declared, and his administration had already expressed this to the Israelis, who promised to abide by the agreement.[88] To the White House's relief, the situation calmed, and the threat of Soviet intervention passed as the fighting stopped.

"The hot line proved a powerful tool," Johnson recalled, "not merely, or even mainly, because communications were so rapid." Its most valuable aspect "was that it engaged immediately the heads of government and their top advisers, forcing prompt attention and decisions," even though the White House "had to weigh carefully every word and phrase."[89] Kosygin also found the hotline to be of great value, proclaiming that they "had accomplished more on that one day [the first day of the Six-Day War] than others could accomplish in three years."[90]

The cease-fire was not the end of Johnson's interaction with Kosygin. About a week later, the Soviet premier came to New York to discuss the recent Middle East conflict at an emergency session of the UN General Assembly. With Kosygin in the United States, the question on everyone's mind was whether he and Johnson would meet. The president's key advisers seemed to be of one mind on the question. Defense Secretary McNamara was in favor, telling the president that, "at a minimum you would take from the meeting an appraisal of Kosygin which should enable you to better predict his behavior and he, in turn, would better understand your character and the resolve which you approach our commitments in Vietnam."[91] McGeorge Bundy, now a special adviser to the president, concurred. A meeting would allow Johnson to get "a measure" of the Soviet leader, but more importantly, "Kosygin will get a measure of you," he told the president. "You really do speak, on topics like Vietnam, wider contact, and the Middle East itself, in tones which are significantly different from those of your Secretary of State."[92]

The administration believed the Soviets had similar motives for holding a summit. "There is surely a great drive to see first-hand what makes Lyndon Baines Johnson tick," the president's senior adviser on Soviet and eastern European affairs noted. The Soviets also coveted the prestige connected to a summit with the American president. They were "still Number 2," which "must have been painfully obvious" after the sound defeat of their Arab clients. A summit would allow the Soviet Union to feel like a superpower and be perceived as the United States' equal.[93]

If there was consensus about Johnson meeting with Kosygin, there was also agreement that nothing substantial would be achieved by such a summit. "Very little of substance can come from the meeting, and it may even lead to a hard-nose standoff," Bundy warned. McNamara believed that the chance of any progress on major issues such as Vietnam and arms control was "less than even."[94] But even if tangible results remained elusive, the consensus was that the meeting had to take place. The American public expected it, and if it did not happen, the president would pay a political price. The defense secretary told the president, "unless the failure to meet is clearly his [Kosygin's], the domestic and international price to you of a failure to meet could be substantial." Looking ahead to Johnson's reelection bid in 1968, Rostow advised him, "at home it will cover your flank to the left and among the columnists. If you don't do it, they will blame every difficulty that follows on the lack of a meeting. The Republicans will run on: I will go to Moscow."[95] Indeed, as Johnson recalled, after Kosygin announced his trip to New York, there was enormous pressure for the two men to meet. For his part, Johnson saw value in a "frank exchange of views [that] might help clear the air . . . and might even pave the way for solution of serious problems."[96]

Once the administration decided to hold a summit, the question became where the two leaders would meet. Johnson made it clear that Kosygin was welcome to come to Washington, but the Soviet premier thought the president should come to New York. Neither man wanted to give the impression of paying homage to the other. After almost a week, they finally settled on somewhere in the middle: Glassboro, New Jersey.[97]

At Glassboro, there was no fixed agenda, but the discussion centered on the Middle East, Vietnam, and arms control, as well as a general discussion of US-Soviet relations. During their tête-à-tête, Kosygin told Johnson that "a great deal of clarification [was] needed in order to understand each other's actions," and he hoped their talks would make American intentions plain. The president agreed.[98] After their meeting, Johnson reported that Kosygin was "friendly, jolly and warm," despite complaining that the US bombing of Hanoi in 1965 coincided with his visit there. The president repeatedly tried to discuss critical issues such as arms control but "got no positive reaction."[99] LBJ attributed this to the Soviet leader's political situation, given that he had no authorization from other Kremlin leaders to engage with the president. The war in Vietnam continued to hinder LBJ. Kosygin noted that he "failed to see true possibilities" for arms-control talks while the war in Southeast Asia raged and the Middle East remained volatile.[100]

In their talks, LBJ also suggested that US-Soviet summits become institutionalized. Perhaps they could "set aside a week every year during which all problems would be discussed." Kosygin did not commit himself, noting that the hotline was available for any necessary discussions. The president agreed but pointed out that yearly meetings would allow for a regular overview of relations, rather than ad hoc contact only during times of crisis.[101]

When Glassboro was over, Johnson had "mixed feelings." No breakthroughs materialized, but the talks were cordial and the atmosphere positive. The president was hopeful that understanding between the adversaries had improved.[102] The summit also boosted Johnson domestically, countering critics who viewed him as an ineffective diplomat. "Glassboro may well make it clear," the *New York Times* wrote, "that Mr. Johnson can handle himself and the nation's affairs in direct confrontation with major foreign leaders." Looking ahead to the 1968 presidential election, Vietnam was still an albatross, but if relations with the Soviets improved because of LBJ's diplomacy, the war might be less of a campaign issue.[103] Indeed, in the wake of Johnson's handling of the Six-Day War and the summit, pollster Louis Harris found that his approval rating had jumped eleven points to 58 percent. Additionally, 67 percent of those surveyed gave LBJ a positive assessment for his role in "working for peace in the world," and he held a 12 percent edge over potential Republican challengers George Romney and Richard Nixon.[104]

The long-term impact of Glassboro was negligible, but it demonstrates a crucial aspect of presidential personal diplomacy. In the post–World War II international system, where crises awaited around every corner, personal engagement with Soviet leaders might have a calming effect. As Johnson said after the summit, "The world is very small and very dangerous." His talks with Kosygin "made it a little smaller still, but also a little less dangerous."[105]

LBJ'S LAST GASP

By March 1968, any post-Glassboro bump in LBJ's popularity was long gone. With the war in Vietnam still raging and his approval rating cratering, Johnson announced that he would not run for reelection. LBJ may have been a lame duck, but his personal diplomacy did not reflect it. He had visions of one last summit with the Soviets, preferably in Moscow, which would be the "grand climax" of his presidency.[106]

Events in Czechoslovakia crushed Johnson's summit dream. In early 1968 a reform-minded government led by Alexander Dubček came to power in Prague, causing alarm in Moscow. As tension between Dubček and the Soviets increased, some administration officials had second thoughts about a summit. "I don't believe I'd go near Kosygin during the time that Czechoslovakia is still hot," Secretary of Defense Clark Clifford advised, fearing that the president would get "caught up" in the brewing crisis.[107]

But even as the situation in Czechoslovakia deteriorated, Johnson continued to push for a summit. On August 20 the administration was on the verge of formally announcing a meeting. Then came the news that the Soviets had invaded Czechoslovakia. For the Soviets, the summit and their military actions were separate issues. For Johnson, they were not. Meeting with Soviet leaders now would be seen as condoning and sanctioning the Kremlin's aggression. A couple of weeks after the invasion, the president confirmed what many already suspected: there would be no summit.[108] Just as world crises can lead to personal diplomacy, they can also prevent it.

Talk of a summit did not die, however. The secretary-general of the United Nations, U Thant, still pushed for one. Rather than seeing the crisis in Czechoslovakia as a reason to shun diplomacy at the highest level, he thought it increased the need for a summit. For its part, the administration sent mixed signals. In early October Rusk said the invasion made a summit unlikely. Simultaneously, the press believed the president was still open to a summit, which would allow his last act to be one of peace, not war.[109] As NBC's John Chancellor put it, LBJ wanted "to hang a diplomatic coonskin on the wall" during his last months in office. Indeed, by December, Rusk's tune had changed, and he stated on CBS's *Face the Nation* that he would not "rule out the possibility of a meeting at the top level."[110]

"Moscow is clearly ready to go—and eager," Rostow told the president in mid-November. Johnson was eager as well.[111] However, Richard Nixon would be sworn in as the nation's thirty-seventh president in just two months, and Johnson tried to obtain his support. The Soviets now appeared to be ready to discuss strategic missiles, LBJ told Nixon, something the United States had been pushing for close to a decade. Now that the Soviets were ready, there should be no delay. The Kremlin was also worried that the recently signed Treaty on the Non-Proliferation of Nuclear Weapons was losing momentum. Coordinated action was needed to get more nations on board.[112] Johnson invited Nixon to attend any potential talks, but the president-elect reportedly called a summit "most unwise" and did not want to be constrained by negotiations of the outgoing president.[113]

Everyone recognized that it would be extraordinary for an outgoing president to conduct major talks with only months left in his term. The *New York Times* declared, "the world can only benefit by having talks begin as soon as possible," but one of its prominent journalists called the idea of a last-minute summit "lunacy."[114] By mid-December, both the Soviets and Johnson were having second thoughts.[115] LBJ realized that his time was quickly coming to an end, and given Nixon's lack of enthusiasm, the Soviets thought it best to wait.

Johnson's failure to hold a lame-duck summit with the Soviets is not surprising. What is amazing is that he even considered it. LBJ's desire for a legacy-defining diplomatic accomplishment partly explains why he pushed so hard.[116] But there was more to it. In the second half of the twentieth century, when the next international crisis was always lurking around the corner and issues of war and peace dominated the public consciousness, there was the feeling that personal diplomacy was necessary—even if it came at the end of a presidency.

As the administration finalized plans for a summit in August 1968, LBJ's approval rating was 35 percent. But even though a majority of Americans disapproved of the president, an October poll showed that 57 percent favored talks with the Soviets. And this was *after* the Soviets invaded Czechoslovakia. What accounts for these seemingly contradictory results? Johnson's approval rating improved in September—rising to 42 percent—but that was hardly overwhelming support.[117] For many Americans, LBJ included, the world was a dangerous place, and the heads of the superpowers needed to engage. Nuclear arms, the Middle East, and Vietnam were just a few of the many issues that could benefit from an exchange of views, the administration believed, and the urgency of these problems explains why Johnson pushed for a summit with so little time left. As Rostow told the president, he might "regret" not meeting the Soviets more than any other decision. Agreements on nuclear issues and missiles did not happen every day, and he feared that the new administration would not prioritize the Non-Proliferation Treaty. "Time will pass. Men and situations will change. And mankind may move down the wrong fork in the road for what will, with hindsight, look like relatively trivial reasons," Rostow worried. After reading the memo, Johnson wrote at the bottom, "I agree," and he drew a line connecting to the word "regret," which he circled.[118]

"His days are so full of trouble," Lady Bird told her diary in May 1965.[119] From the agony of Vietnam to flare-ups in Panama, Cyprus, and the Middle East—not to mention protests and riots at home—Johnson confronted a never-ending series of problems. But this was not unique to LBJ. All modern presidents faced international and domestic crises. Some were luckier than others, but trouble always loomed. And when there was a global emergency, modern presidents frequently resorted to personal diplomacy. During the Cold War, when world crises were a way of life, it fell to the US president—as leader of the world's dominant power—to mediate, lower tensions, and prevent wider conflict. Sometimes he was successful; other times, he was not. Johnson's outreach often fell short. But despite the uneven results, he used personal diplomacy because of the pressures placed on him by international events. Even when the odds of success were slim, personal diplomacy was often seen as the best option to manage an increasingly dangerous and complex world.

5. Richard Nixon and the Domestic Politics of Personal Diplomacy

"An election loss," Richard Nixon told Chinese premier Zhou Enlai, "was really more painful than a physical wound in war. The latter wounds the body—the other wounds the spirit."[1] Having felt the sting of electoral defeat before, Nixon was determined to avoid that fate again in 1972. To achieve victory, he sought to leverage every available resource—whether legal or not. Domestically, this led to abuses such as the Watergate scandal. Internationally, it led to historic acts of personal diplomacy with China and the Soviet Union.

Driven by a realistic outlook—a perspective he shared with his national security adviser Henry Kissinger—Nixon sought to avoid idealistic policy and focus on what he deemed the national interest. Weakened by Vietnam as other nations grew stronger, the United States was no longer the dominant power it had once been. The bipolarity of the global arena that had existed since the end of World War II was breaking down. With the United States' overwhelming dominance diminished, Nixon and Kissinger sought a way to move forward and stabilize the nation's global position. The administration thus pursued a policy of détente with the Soviets and rapprochement with China, and it attempted to end the Vietnam War.

But these moves were not made out of desperation. In absolute terms, American power—economic, military, and technological—was still supreme. To stunt the relative decline of US strength, however, Nixon and Kissinger sought new approaches. They saw their various policies and actions as interconnected. The duo believed success in one area would lead to improvement in another. Rapprochement with China would strengthen America's position against the Soviet Union, and détente with the Soviets would enhance America's posture in relation to China. Improved relations with the two communist powers would help in Vietnam, and ending the conflict in Southeast Asia would further US relations with both nations. Nixon and Kissinger were confident their efforts would enhance America's strategic position and, as a result, the nation would emerge from this tumultuous period stronger, with its dominance intact.[2]

Yet, as Nixon carried out his geopolitical strategy, domestic considerations were never far from his thoughts. When he traveled to Beijing and Moscow in 1972, part of his goal was to establish a productive working relationship with Soviet and Chinese leaders that would advance his foreign policy agenda. At the same time, interacting with his communist counterparts bolstered his reelection bid. Diplomacy is a type of "theater," and personal diplomacy between world leaders is diplomatic drama at the highest level. Nixon's journeys to meet with Mao Zedong, Zhou Enlai, and Leonid Brezhnev created a spectacle that captivated Americans. China and the Soviet Union became a stage, and its leaders were props in a theatrical performance in which the president was the star and the American voting public the audience.[3]

Presidents are hesitant to acknowledge when domestic political considerations creep into their foreign policy, fearing they will be portrayed as selfish or calculating. But all presidents are politicians. "The president's trip [to China] may not have been politically motivated," noted NBC newsman Garrick Utley, "but it is politically convenient."[4] Indeed, Nixon used these high-profile summits—and the spectacles they created—not only to further US foreign policy but also for domestic political gain.

With Nixon's poll numbers sliding in 1971 and his reelection prospects endangered, he used personal diplomacy to change the narrative. He created a media event and cultivated the image of world statesman par excellence. This strategy was not unique to Nixon. As a group, modern presidents have used foreign travel and interactions with world leaders to bolster their domestic positions. Such activities have often garnered significant media coverage, allowing White House occupants to look "presidential." Writing in the 1980s, journalist Hedrick Smith noted:

> [The Reagan administration] created a storybook presidency, using the pageantry of presidential travel to hook the networks and captivate the popular imagination. They projected Reagan as the living symbol of nationhood. And there was a payoff for policy: The more Reagan wrapped himself in the flag, the harder it became for mere mortal politicians to challenge him, the more impossible he was to defeat come reelection, the more worthy he seemed of trust and latitude on policy.[5]

Nixon was the father of this strategy. He was the first "image-is-everything president."[6] Reagan adopted Nixon's techniques, and although Reagan had his own image makers, such as Michal Deaver, his administration was full of former Nixon officials who contributed their expertise in public relations. Nixon lacked Reagan's natural charm and grace, and as a result, his image building seemed forced and sometimes rang hollow. Reagan executed the strategy better than Nixon, but Nixon provided the template. Nixon was Reagan before Reagan, and in 1972 he sought to create his own storybook presidency by crafting a diplomatic drama in which he portrayed the world's leading apostle of peace.[7]

This chapter examines how Nixon used foreign travel and interactions with world leaders to bolster his domestic standing. In 1972 he was quite successful in this endeavor. Personal diplomacy, however, could not save him in the years to come. As the Watergate scandal destroyed his presidency, Nixon once again looked to leader-to-leader diplomacy to help him at home. It failed, but the allure remained. Nixon's successor, Gerald Ford, tried to repeat the success of 1972 with his own flashy acts of personal diplomacy, but to less dramatic effect.

TELEVISION, SPECTACLE, AND IMAGE MAKING

"Jack doesn't stand a ghost of a chance," Vice President Richard Nixon boasted to a cheering crowd of up to 140,000 on the eve of Halloween, a little more than a week before the 1960 presidential election.[8] But when the votes were tallied, he had lost one of the closest elections in US history. Senator John F. Kennedy had defeated him by less than 120,000 votes (49.7 to 49.5 percent). The bitter Nixon blamed his loss not on his policies or ideas but on "showbiz politics."[9] The young, charming senator from Massachusetts had strategically turned himself into a celebrity and deftly used television and the media to sell his personality. Indeed, Kennedy attracted huge crowds on the campaign trail. In the waning days of the presidential contest, an estimated 500,000 came to see him in New York City. The throngs frequently overran police barricades to get closer to JFK. "Kennedy spoke often," the *Chicago Daily Tribune* reported, "but it was the man and not his words the people seemed interested in."[10]

Kennedy's image and mystique left an indelible mark on Nixon. His loss to Kennedy in 1960 and his failed attempt to win the California governorship in 1962 convinced him that what mattered to the American public was not substance or qualifications but the ability to craft an appealing, glamorous image through the mass media, particularly television.[11] Nixon saw television as a tool that could more easily be manipulated than the print media, allowing him to project a favorable image to voters. His chief of staff, H. R. Haldeman, encouraged this. Haldeman had previously worked in advertising; he knew how to sell an image and was a strong advocate of television. During the 1968 campaign he advised his boss on new ways to use the medium, noting that, in "political campaigning—its techniques and strategies," the time had come "to move out of the dark ages and into the brave new world of the omnipresent eye." Once in office, Nixon and Haldeman spent a lot of time crafting a public relations strategy.[12]

In the second half of the twentieth century, the presidency became the center of American government, and the public focused on the individual occupying the White House. "Since the president has become the embodiment of government," presidential scholar Theodore Lowi observed, "it seems perfectly normal for millions upon millions of Americans to concentrate their hopes and fears directly and personally upon him."[13] But even the most competent presidents have found it difficult to meet such high expectations. Regardless of their actions or policies, it is never enough. Thus, according to Bruce Miroff, "presidents turn to gestures of spectacle to satisfy their audience." Spectacles are symbolic events that present "intriguing and often dominating characters not in static poses, but through actions that establish their public identities."[14] These events are concerned primarily with sending signals to the public.

This was Nixon's goal in 1972. His trips to China and the Soviet Union were spectacles on a grand scale that portrayed him as a statesman and a peacemaker, which he believed would improve his image domestically and boost his reelection prospects. Even before 1972, the president's aides were pondering how to leverage image making, spectacle, and foreign affairs for electoral advantage. Early on, the administration was concerned with creating an "aura" and "mystique" around the president, and foreign affairs offered one way to accomplish this.[15] In February 1971 special assistant to the president Dwight Chapin recommended that, over the next twenty months, the administration spend at least a third of its time emphasizing foreign policy and highlighting Nixon's interactions with foreign leaders. The focus should be on the president's role as a world leader, his vast knowledge of global issues, the respect shown to him by foreign counterparts, and his image as a statesman. To further these aims, Chapin suggested the administration strive for greater television coverage of state visits. Chapin saw the media as a tool the administration could exploit "to build [a] Presidential image of capability, strength, leadership, and command," and foreign policy was central to this endeavor.[16]

As Nixon told an aide in the fall of 1971, "International affairs is *our* issue." The following year, the administration planned to build up the president's image as "Mr. Peace" by improving relations with China and the Soviet Union. This provided an opportunity for presidential spectacle—"splashy, headline-grabbing, camera-pleasing event[s] that would drive home his international successes" to American voters.[17]

PERSONAL DIPLOMACY'S POLITICAL BENEFITS

It is ironic that Nixon, an introverted and socially awkward man, would rely so heavily on interactions with world leaders to create presidential spectacle. Nixon's fascination with foreign affairs partially explains this strategy, but he also believed that personal contact with world leaders could advance American interests. "I have learned that there is an intangible factor which does affect the relations between nations," Nixon said. "When there is trust between men who are leaders of nations, there is a better chance to settle differences than when there is no trust."[18] However, he realized there were limits to what leader-to-leader diplomacy could achieve.

When Nixon became president in 1969, he already had a wealth of experience engaging with heads of state and government. As Eisenhower's vice president, he had traveled overseas seven times, visiting fifty-four countries and meeting numerous world leaders. According to the political opposition, these trips were not merely diplomatic missions. Paul Butler, chairman of the Democratic National Committee, claimed that the vice president's travels toward the end of the Eisenhower years were "nothing more than cleverly concealed propaganda campaigns designed to keep him on Page 1 of the newspapers as a preliminary to the 1960 Presidential campaign."[19]

Nixon's most famous journey as vice president came in 1959, when he traveled to the Soviet Union to attend the opening of an American cultural exhibit and hold talks with Soviet leader Nikita Khrushchev. With the upcoming election only a year away, Nixon had a personal stake in the trip's outcome. "Mr. Nixon's trip behind the Iron Curtain has, as everyone knows, been planned and prepared as a triple wager," prominent journalist Walter Lippmann wrote. "It is a flyer in propaganda, a flyer in diplomacy, and a flyer in his own personal presidential politics."[20]

Because Nixon was the highest-ranking American official to visit the Soviet

Union since Franklin Roosevelt attended the Yalta Conference in 1945, interest in the trip was immense. Nixon received mostly positive press coverage, and before his departure, newspapers wrote approvingly of his extensive preparation and his plans to talk "tough" with Khrushchev.[21] Once Nixon came face-to-face with the Soviet leader, he generated even greater headlines. In what became known as the "kitchen debate," the two men engaged in a spirited discussion about the merits of their respective countries' systems of government. The debate was front-page news around the globe.[22] It also became a television event when it was discovered that cameras had recorded sixteen and a half minutes of the clash. The three television networks (ABC, CBS, and NBC) promptly aired the footage. Influential Republicans such as Senate minority leader Everett Dirksen and numerous political commentators praised Nixon's performance and acknowledged the boost to his political fortunes. In the end, though, it was not enough to get him elected president in 1960, demonstrating the limits of personal diplomacy.[23]

Despite losing the election, Nixon recognized the opportunity for image building offered by personal diplomacy. After losing the race for California governor in 1962, he spent the next five years rehabilitating his image, an effort that relied heavily on journeys overseas. During his years in the so-called political wilderness, Nixon was a frequent traveler. In 1967 alone he visited Europe, Asia, Latin America, Africa, and the Middle East, meeting with foreign leaders at each stop. These trips allowed him to portray himself as an experienced statesman with both knowledge and gravitas, which was becoming "increasingly important to voters," according to the *Wall Street Journal*. Elaborating on the political benefits, the paper told readers:

> As part of his effort to develop a less partisan image, Mr. Nixon has minimized his party appearances. Each of his four foreign tours since the first of the year has kept him out of the country two to three weeks. These trips . . . refreshed his acquaintance with crucial foreign policy areas. In the months ahead he will be able to sprinkle his speeches with remarks such as "when I was in Indonesia last April . . . " or "as President de Gaulle told me in June. . . . "[24]

Given that his travels and meetings with foreign leaders did not lead to victory in 1960, it is unclear how much the statesman image helped in Nixon's 1968 presidential victory. But there is no question that once he became president, he sought to make his mark internationally, and as he moved to reorient American foreign policy, personal diplomacy was part of that mission. During his first year in office, Nixon told his staff he wanted to communicate regularly with various foreign leaders. "Sometime ago I suggested that I would like to start a practice of writing a letter from time to time to some of the major leaders we have met on our trips abroad or on their visits here," he told Kissinger. "I still think this would be a very good idea. . . . For example, a letter to the Pope, to [Willy] Brandt, perhaps [Georges] Pompideau [*sic*], etc. on various subjects in which they would be interested and which would serve our purposes might be extremely helpful."[25] To that end, White House staff prepared a list of possible leaders for Nixon to correspond with, which he then edited. He was also eager for face-to-face interactions. A month into office, he went on a tour of Europe, visiting five countries and the Vatican. Five months later he went to Asia, stopping in six nations and holding state visits in five of them.[26]

Nixon's early trip to Europe was the first by a US president in five and a half years. It represented an attempt to reset relations after years of complaints about US neglect and questions about American reliability. With almost two hundred journalists traveling with the president, the trip generated extensive media coverage, most of it positive. Beforehand, the State Department characterized the press's reporting as overwhelmingly favorable, and once the trip began, all three television networks provided "special coverage." NBC's morning show devoted thirty minutes each day to the president's journey, and the station's nightly news show was extended from thirty minutes to an hour.[27]

Although there were no agreements or major announcements, Nixon accomplished his goal of restoring a spirit of cooperation and goodwill. He also demonstrated his skill in cultivating the camera. As one reporter observed, "Nixon proved an adept television performer. He is always aware of cameras and microphones and openly plays to them. His microphone technique is almost flawless." And because of "a kind of circular illogic that a person's merely being on TV makes that person important," the administration was able to use television "to stress to each citizen that Mr. Nixon, elected by a small margin, is now the President of the United States."[28]

Back home, Nixon continued to occupy the media spotlight when he addressed the nation on television. He spoke for five minutes about his European travels before answering reporters' questions for fifty minutes—the longest presidential press conference ever televised up to that point. Nixon's remarks were carried on each of the networks and numerous other independent stations. According to one estimate, as many as 75 million Americans watched the president, and most agreed that they had witnessed an exceptional performance. Speaking without notes, Nixon handled a total of twenty-six questions with ease and aplomb. The *New York Times* wrote that he was "impressive in scope and grasp . . . it was a *tour de force.*" The *Los Angeles Times* echoed those sentiments: "The American public had seldom been so impressed . . . [Nixon] emerged as a vitally healthy world leader in complete command of the situation."[29] All this positive press affected the American people, who overwhelmingly viewed the trip as enhancing relations between the United States and western Europe.[30]

Overall, the trip demonstrated two aspects of Nixon's conduct of foreign policy. First, his administration would rely on television—"electronic statecraft"—to get its message across and project an image of leadership. Second, in carrying out foreign policy and electronic statecraft, interactions with foreign leaders would play an important role. "His visits to the West European capitals," one reporter noted, "offered all the proof that is needed that the American people have a new President who relishes personal diplomacy and feels at home abroad."[31] In 1972 this penchant for foreign travel would reach new heights, as Nixon's trips to China and the Soviet Union became grand productions.

NIXON GOES TO CHINA

During the first two years of Nixon's presidency, his approval rating hovered in the high fifties to low sixties. It is hard to pinpoint the role played by his early forays into personal diplomacy, but polls taken as he departed for Europe and about a week after his return showed an increase in his approval rating from 60 to 66 percent. By June 1971, any boost from the European trip was long gone. Only 48 percent of Americans now approved of Nixon's job performance. Faced with a worsening economic situation as both inflation and unemployment rose, the president was becoming increasingly unpopular. His failure to end the Vietnam War and his escalation of the conflict into Cambodia and Laos generated widespread protests and spelled trouble for his reelection bid.[32]

To combat the growing economic discontent, Nixon reversed some long-held convictions. He instituted price and wage controls, allowed a floating exchange rate, and stopped converting dollars into gold. Nixon had once opposed all these policies, and they upset the global economic order that had been in place since the end of World War II. But the president was more concerned about the domestic impact than the international one. These moves were popular at home, and although economic troubles eventually returned, the economy improved and boosted Nixon's reelection prospects in the short term.[33]

In the realm of foreign policy, he also went against his previous reputation. As a young congressman, Nixon had made his name as the coldest of cold warriors. During campaigns for the House and Senate, he attacked his opponents by implying they secretly held radical views or were closet communists. Once in Congress, Nixon rose to fame as a member of the House Un-American Activities Committee (HUAC). In 1948 he led the HUAC investigation of Alger Hiss, a former State Department employee accused of being a communist spy. Though Hiss never admitted to espionage, uncovered documents suggested that he was a spy or, at the very least, had contact with communists—something he denied. Hiss was convicted of perjury, and the intense media spotlight on these hearings made Nixon a national figure.

By the time he assumed the presidency, he was calmer and more restrained but was still viewed as a staunch anticommunist. However, with the world in flux, the goal of preserving America's global influence required a new approach. Rather than being guided by a reflexive hatred of communism, Nixon and Kissinger took a realistic outlook and focused on issues of power and security instead of ideological compatibility or moral dilemmas. They believed that engagement with communist foes in Beijing and Moscow would better serve American interests than continued hostility.

Nixon previewed his thinking on China in a 1967 article in *Foreign Affairs.* While recognizing the danger China posed, he argued that, in the long term, the United States could not "afford to leave China forever outside the family of nations."[34] Once in office, Nixon moved in that direction. Months after the inauguration, Secretary of State William Rogers proclaimed that the United States was open to improved relations with China and would work to make it a reality. Other moves accompanied that announcement, such as halting aggressive naval actions regularly conducted near the Chinese coast and easing travel restrictions to China. The administration also sought to establish a secret back channel through intermediaries such as Yahya Khan, Pakistan's leader.[35]

By the spring of 1971, the secret Pakistani back channel had yielded enough progress that a high-level meeting between American and Chinese officials was considered desirable. Chinese premier Zhou Enlai suggested that a special envoy, or even Nixon himself, come to Beijing. The president quickly accepted the proposal. However, before he visited, he wanted to lay the groundwork with a preliminary meeting between Kissinger and Chinese officials, which he insisted be kept "*strictly secret.*"[36]

Nixon would eventually push for as much publicity as possible, but at this early stage, such exposure was seen as dangerous. As Kissinger later recalled, if his visit to China had been made public, the administration would have been "caught between those who wanted a catalogue of concessions and others who wanted guarantees of our intransigence."[37] Internationally, nations that opposed improved US-China relations might have attempted to undermine the visit. Perhaps most important, announcing the trip ahead of time would have given domestic opponents time to mobilize. By the early 1970s, the once influential "China lobby" had declined in prominence, but some vocal members could still cause trouble for the president. And while relations with China seemed to be on the upswing, there was no guarantee of success. "It is difficult to recapture now the sense of mutual ignorance of the United States and China in those days," Kissinger remembered. "We had no contact of any sort with the Chinese leadership . . . we had no idea what we would find in Peking [Beijing]."[38] This explains why Nixon's trip to China captivated the American public: the communist nation was a great mystery. But until he was sure that the dramatic diplomatic initiative would pay off, Nixon wanted to keep it a secret. The opening to China would become a spectacle, but it would happen on the president's terms.

In July 1971 Kissinger left for China. Stopping first in Pakistan, he feigned illness while there, and once he was out of the press spotlight, he was secretly shuttled into China. Kissinger met extensively with Zhou, discussing relevant issues and details about the president's trip. When the visit was over, Kissinger was jubilant. Despite the difficulties ahead, he was confident the foundation had been set for Nixon and Chinese leaders "to turn a page in history."[39]

Once Kissinger returned, Nixon informed an unsuspecting world on live television about the clandestine trip and revealed that he would visit China the following year. The statement was brief, but it sent shock waves around the globe. The objective was peace, Nixon said, and he conveyed the implicit message that he was the conduit of that peace: "I will undertake what I deeply hope will become a journey for peace, peace not just for our generation but for future generations on this earth we share together."[40]

Nixon's bombshell was guaranteed to dominate the news cycle, but the administration strove to maximize coverage. In conversations with Zhou, Kissinger had pushed for the announcement of Nixon's trip (which would occur simultaneously in China) to take place on July 15, a Thursday evening. Because this was less than five days after their talks, Zhou thought this might be too soon, not allowing enough time to prepare for the announcement. But Kissinger's mind was on something else. "The weekly news magazines such as *Time* and *Newsweek* are printed on Friday and Saturday," he noted. "Therefore, if the announcement is made on Thursday night, they can do a better job of reporting it than if it were Friday night." Though it was not a sticking point, he told the Chinese premier that a Thursday announcement would mean better coverage in the newsmagazines and the Sunday newspapers, which are "very big" in the United States.[41] To the Americans' delight, Zhou consented.

Within a month of announcing the trip, Nixon's political fortunes quickly improved. Whereas a June Gallup poll had showed him trailing Edmund Muskie (his presumed Democratic opponent in 1972) 41 to 39 percent, an August poll found him on top 42 to 36 percent. China and the theme of peace were proving to be political winners, and lest anyone try to steal his thunder, Nixon made it clear to the Chinese that he expected them to restrict American political visitors until after his trip. He wanted the public to believe that he alone was capable of this dramatic undertaking and that he understood the issue of peace better than anyone.[42]

For Nixon, image was key. Deeds were great, but unless they were promoted and shaped into a triumphant narrative, there was little domestic political benefit. "What the people want is the appearance of action," Nixon told his advisers. As Haldeman recorded in his diary, the president wanted to focus not so much on concrete issues but rather on notions of "leadership: boldness, courage, etcetera," and depictions of "the President as the world leader for peace[,] the biggest leader in the world."[43] Thus, as the Nixon administration turned the China trip into a grand production, presenting the American public with political and diplomatic theater at the highest level, the focus was more on Nixon himself than on US-China relations. "This country is soon to be flooded with more news from China than will be easily digested," CBS newsman Eric Sevareid commented, "but it won't really be the story of China. It'll be the story of President Nixon in China."[44]

In crafting Nixon's story and creating a presidential spectacle, the maximization of media coverage, particularly television exposure, was crucial. "For most Americans at home the dramatic journey will be a TV spectacular which the White House obviously wants. One picture may not be worth ten thousand words," Sevareid mused, "but the White House is betting it's worth ten thousand votes."[45] The administration scheduled events to ensure they could be televised in prime time back in the United States, and the president was especially anxious about his arrival and departure. As Haldeman recorded in his diary, Nixon wanted his arrival to "be handled flawlessly since that will be the key picture of the whole trip." Returning home, "he definitely does not want to arrive in Washington at noon, but rather at 9:00 at night to make prime time television." The advance team worked out every detail, including the optimal spot to land on the runway to ensure the best angle for photos—and there would be plenty of photos. The administration received more than 2,000 applications from the press, and Nixon—who favored television over print—personally chose the journalists who would accompany him.[46]

From his arrival to the lavish opening banquet to his meeting with Chinese leaders and his visit to the Great Wall, Nixon created a spectacle that dominated American media and wreaked havoc on the campaigns of his two primary challengers.[47] In New Hampshire, site of the year's first primary, Nixon dominated print, radio, and especially television. "To his opponents here in New Hampshire it must have seemed as if the president were everywhere," NBC's Doug Kiker reported; he was "the most active candidate in this primary this week even though he was half a world away."[48] Nationally, the story was the same. A Gallup poll taken days after the visit showed that 97 percent of Americans had heard or read about the trip.[49] Whether they regularly paid attention to politics or not, Americans could not escape the president's trip to China.

The State Department compared Nixon's journey to the moon landing—both "venture[s] into the unknown." And "like a moon flight," the department noted, "the voyage to China was a media phenomenon, tightly scripted and edited by time and technology, of a new kind scarcely imaginable before the age of television and communications satellites."[50] The trip's unprecedented nature boosted Nixon's image as the peace candidate, as most Americans believed it would play an important role in improving global harmony.[51] One might have thought that, having already gone to the diplomatic equivalent of the moon, Nixon would have been satisfied. But the peace candidate had another spectacle to perform.

THE MOSCOW SUMMIT

While diplomacy with China was new terrain, dealing with the Soviets was well-trod—if hazardous—ground. The United States had had little to no contact with China for more than two decades, but it communicated frequently with the Soviet Union. For Nixon, it was important that a meeting at the highest level produce tangible results. If he met with Soviet leaders and nothing of substance was accomplished or, even worse, tensions rose, the public would be disillusioned and his political opponents would pounce. "I am greatly concerned," Nixon told his ambassador to the Soviet Union, "about the adverse effects of a meeting that ends in deadlock even if it is surrounded by agreeable social functions. In this respect, top level meetings between US and Soviet leaders are different from other top level meetings."[52] It was fine for the China summit to be mainly symbolic, but a US-Soviet summit had to be substantive. Thus, to lay the groundwork, Nixon directed Kissinger to engage in back-channel discussions with Soviet ambassador Anatoly Dobrynin.[53]

For the administration, lessening tensions with the Soviets was an important step toward ending the Vietnam War. If relations improved, the Soviets would likely aid the United States as it tried to extricate itself from Southeast Asia. There were other issues to discuss, such as arms control, but neither side wanted to appear desperate for a summit. In Nixon's first years in office, the Soviets floated the idea of meeting multiple times, only to have the administration reject it. In the view of Nixon and Kissinger, the Soviets overestimated the president's desire for a summit and tried to extract numerous concessions for merely agreeing to meet.[54] As reelection neared, however, the administration became more eager.

The path to a summit, however, was not smooth. On the critical issue of Vietnam, the Soviets were no help, although the two sides made some progress on arms control. By the spring of 1971, there was a "conceptual breakthrough" in the Strategic Arms Limitation Talks (SALT), as well as negotiations over antiballistic missile (ABM) systems. Yet they still could not agree on a date for a summit. From the administration's perspective, the Kremlin was dithering. But once news broke of Nixon's planned trip to China, the Soviets quickly agreed to a date for their own summit. Dobrynin tried to persuade Kissinger that the president should visit Moscow before going to Beijing, but he rejected that idea. The visits would take place in the order they had been agreed to.[55]

For the Soviets, news of a US-China rapprochement was worrisome. Once allies, the two communist powers had become adversaries by the 1970s. And as their monthlong border skirmish in 1969 made clear, the threat of a Sino-Soviet war was real. Kissinger tried to assure Dobrynin that improved American-Chinese relations were not a threat to the Soviet Union, but in reality, the division between the communist rivals served American purposes: each side worried that the other might develop closer ties to the United States.

Months before the Moscow summit, Nixon told a Soviet official that his talks with Leonid Brezhnev "could be the most important heads-of-government meetings in this century."[56] Though Nixon was guilty of a bit of self-aggrandizement, he and Brezhnev did sign two arms control agreements—an ABM treaty and a SALT accord. They also concluded various other agreements dealing with environmental protection, medical science and public health, and cooperation in space, science, and technology. Perhaps most important was the "Basic Principles" document, which defined relations between the United States and the Soviet Union. For the Soviets, this was particularly significant because they believed it signaled that the Americans now viewed them as equals. Nixon also became the first American president to speak on Soviet television.[57]

Like the trip to China, the president's Moscow visit furthered geopolitical goals and domestic ones as well. Shortly before the trip, pollster Louis Harris found that a large part of the president's improved standing with voters was attributable to his initiatives with America's communist foes. "In a period marked by little confidence in political leadership of nearly any stripe," Harris wrote, "Nixon's announcement of journeys to Moscow and Peking [Beijing] met with remarkably high acceptance from the American public." More than 70 percent of Americans approved of the summits, and almost 60 percent believed Nixon was "working for peace in the world."[58]

Upon returning home, Nixon took a dramatic helicopter flight from Andrews Air Force Base to the Capitol, where he delivered a thirty-five-minute, nationally televised address to Congress. Only about half the members were present, but Nixon's real audience was the American people. Playing up the theme of peace, he stated that for both the United States and the Soviet Union, there was "an overriding desire to achieve a more stable peace in the world," and having embarked on that course, "history now lays upon us a special obligation to see it through."[59] And clearly the statesman best able to guide America down that path was Nixon.

By improving relations with the two major communist powers, both summits furthered the administration's goals of stabilizing the international environment and strengthening America's position in it. At the same time, they were spectacles and personal successes for Nixon, as he became the first president to visit the capitals of America's two major adversaries. Given his reputation as a hard-line anticommunist and an American public that was anxious for peace, these journeys presented the perfect forum for diplomatic stagecraft. Of the two, China provided greater theater—"a technicolor picture story," according to CBS. But the Soviet summit also provided drama. Nixon at the Kremlin was something "few soothsayers would have dared to predict." CBS labeled it a "political soap opera." Global headlines also heralded the president, with one Paris paper calling the Soviet trip "another sensation. . . . Mr. Nixon is in the process of taking his place among the great Presidents of the U.S." In the aftermath of the Moscow summit, the president's popularity rating hit a two-year high, rising from 53 percent two months before the trip to 61 percent, an even greater boost than he saw after his China trip.[60]

Nixon easily won reelection in 1972, beating George McGovern with 60.7 percent of the popular vote and 96.7 percent of electoral votes. Whether Nixon's trips played a decisive role is debatable, but they were prominently highlighted in campaign ads. In one television commercial titled "Passport," the narrator extolled Nixon's personal diplomacy: "President Nixon's travels represent a new foreign policy for the United States, a policy that calls for . . . peaceful negotiations with our enemies, all for a single purpose, world peace. But there are still places to go and friends to be won. That's why we need President Nixon. Now more than ever." Another ad featured a cheery song proclaiming, "Nixon Now." As a woman sang "Reaching out across the sea / making friends where foes used to be / giving hope to humanity," images of Nixon with Mao and Brezhnev flashed across the screen.[61]

It is impossible to know how the summits influenced voters, as multiple factors are in play when choosing a president.[62] But the media clearly saw the trips as an attempt to influence public opinion. "The China visit, part diplomacy, part contrived public relations circus, drove up his [Nixon's] popularity several points in the opinion polls," Sevareid noted.[63] Others were convinced the trips were crucial to the president's electoral triumph. Nixon adviser Chuck Colson believed the president's "election is in the hands of Peking [Beijing]." And while the Soviet press criticized the China trip as "little more than a publicity stunt on the part of Mr. Nixon designed to get him reelected," that attitude changed when he went to Moscow. As Brezhnev told deputy national security adviser Alexander Haig, the Soviets "were doing everything to help the President get re-elected." Regardless of what was actually on voters' minds as they cast their ballots, the visits to Beijing and Moscow began the process of changing the public's perception of Nixon and led to some very visible successes.[64]

WATERGATE AND THE LIMITS OF IMAGE MAKING

Nixon and Brezhnev met again in 1973, this time in the United States. After the drama and achievements in Moscow, the Soviet leader's visit was lackluster by comparison and less politically beneficial to the president. "In 1972, your trip to Moscow took place on the crest of your successful China visit and firm stance in Vietnam," the State Department told Nixon. "This year, our allies and the American public will be more prone to subject the results of your meetings with Brezhnev to skeptical examination, searching for signs of weakness on our part."[65] By this time, SALT was under attack from conservatives and hard-liners such as Washington senator Henry Jackson. The fact that SALT allowed the Soviets to have more land-based and submarine-launched missiles was anathema to Cold War hawks. In late 1972 Jackson secured passage of a resolution that required parity in any future arms control agreements. He also hindered détente by holding up a trade agreement with the Soviets unless they allowed unlimited Jewish emigration. Nixon's attempts to negotiate another SALT agreement became increasingly challenging.

Even without dedicated opponents of détente, Nixon was in trouble, as Watergate threatened to destroy his presidency. In mid-1973, with his domestic position crumbling and the congressional investigation of the scandal intensifying, Senator Jackson publicly stated that the upcoming summit with Brezhnev should be postponed. But as Kissinger recalled, that was not an option: "We had no choice except to pretend that our authority was unimpaired . . . we needed to project self-confidence no matter what we felt." Thus, the summit went ahead as planned. According to Kissinger, the president also had a more "personal motive" for not wanting to postpone: "For him to concede that his ability to govern had been impaired would accelerate the assault on his Presidency. He could not bring himself to admit the growing disintegration of what he had striven all his life to achieve."[66]

The summit, however, did nothing to bolster Nixon's approval ratings, and some feared the desperate president would "be under terrible pressure to report new and favorable turns in US-Soviet relations if only to counteract the running horror of the Watergate headlines." At the same time, according to one survey, 78 percent of Americans approved of the summit, and most believed it furthered the cause of world peace. At the very least, the meeting gave Nixon some respite from Watergate. Congressional hearings were postponed for the week, allowing him to play the role of statesman once again.[67]

As historian David Greenberg has written, Nixon's peacemaker image "constituted a key plank in his Watergate defense."[68] As the scandal reached its peak in 1974, the embattled president embarked on a heavy schedule of foreign travel, visiting Europe, the Middle East, and the Soviet Union again. These trips provided a brief reprieve and gave the beleaguered administration a "noticeable morale boost," reported ABC newsman Tom Jarriel. Nixon was feted in Egypt, where an official told an NBC reporter that his government wanted to give Nixon "the biggest reception any American president ever had, anywhere."[69]

During these sojourns, both Nixon and his staff played up his relationships with world leaders and stressed how vital those connections were to world peace. While in the Soviet Union, the president proclaimed in a toast that the lessening of tensions was the result of "a personal relationship that was established between" Brezhnev and himself, and "because of our personal relationship, there is no question about our will to keep these agreements and to make more."[70] For those listening back home, the not so subtle message was that if Nixon were no longer in power, the country would lose the advantages of his close bond with Brezhnev, leading to increased hostilities with the Soviet Union.

If Nixon thought such statements would influence the public, he was mistaken. The summit "turned into a pale imitation of the first two," Kissinger recalled. Some believed the whole trip had been designed to distract Americans from Watergate. Critics worried that a weakened president eager for success would make harmful concessions. The trip produced some minor agreements, and in retrospect, Kissinger believed it was beneficial. But given Nixon's previously orchestrated diplomatic spectacles, anything less would likely fail to gain the public and media traction he needed to improve his image.[71]

Brezhnev would be the last foreign leader Nixon met with. A little over a month later, he resigned. In the span of two years, he went from the height of popularity to leaving the presidency in disgrace. Diplomatic spectacle—foreign travel and interactions with world leaders—had helped Nixon reach the pin-nacle of success. But ultimately, the role of statesman and peacemaker could not save him. Presidential spectacles can help domestically, but they cannot work miracles. Just as a president can use personal diplomacy for domestic political gain, domestic troubles can hinder diplomatic effectiveness. "The strategy of the Nixon Administration presupposed a decisive President willing to stake American power to resist Soviet expansionism and ready to negoti-ate seriously if the Soviets would accept coexistence on this basis," Kissinger recalled. But Nixon's ability to perform the role of bold statesman was "de-stroyed by our domestic passion play."[72] Though his administration worked hard to produce diplomatic theater at the highest level and create grand spec-tacles of summitry, there were limits to what it could achieve domestically, especially when faced with a scandal as toxic as Watergate.

FORD'S NIXON IMITATION

When Gerald Ford assumed the presidency, the shadiness of the Nixon era came to an end. But the new president continued to pursue his predecessor's international agenda, particularly détente.[73] Détente was not the only strategy Ford borrowed from Nixon. Like his predecessor, he sought to leverage per-sonal diplomacy for domestic political gain. And Ford needed the help. When he took office in August 1974, his approval rating was 71 percent; by mid-December 1975, it had sunk to 39 percent.[74] This was unwelcome news mere weeks before the start of a presidential election year.

A constellation of forces conspired to make Ford unpopular. Shortly after taking office, he offended a vast swath of Americans when he pardoned Nixon. His inability to deal with the nation's economic malaise, increasing attacks from the right and left for following the policy of détente, and a resurgent and combative Congress all made his political life difficult. Ford's political advisers also worried that Kissinger's continuing prominence (by this time, he was both national security adviser and secretary of state) raised questions about Ford's foreign policy leadership. Kissinger's outsized role led to attacks by presidential hopefuls Ronald Reagan and Jimmy Carter, who claimed that Kissinger, not Ford, was the driving figure in the White House. Personal di-plomacy offered a way to bolster Ford's image.[75] Three months after taking office, he traveled to Japan, South Korea, and Vladivostok, where he met with

Brezhnev to discuss a SALT II agreement. Like Nixon's trips, Ford's was about more than domestic politics. A second strategic arms agreement was a long-held US foreign policy objective, and the trip gave the new president a chance to assert himself.

At home, however, some questioned whether Ford should be going on the trip at all. With the vice presidency vacant and the economy in dire straits, some members of Congress thought the president should stay home. Others criticized Ford's move for being too much like Nixon's. The president "was mindlessly following the scenario of the Nixon presidency's most success-ful policy, inappropriate though it might be today," one Republican senator grumbled.[76] Other critics saw no need for the trip. There was nothing specific to discuss in Japan, and there was concern that leftist protesters would mar the visit. South Korea was an authoritarian regime, so why reward it with a presi-dential visit? And a meeting in Vladivostok, near the disputed Soviet-Chinese border, might harm US-China relations. In contrast, the White House be-lieved that if the president did not make the trip, it would signal to the rest of the world "domestic instability" and a weakened presidency.[77] Presenting such an image was anathema to the administration. "We must make strong deci-sions," Ford said weeks before his trip, "whether they're supported by Con-gress or not." Kissinger concurred. If Ford could offer strong leadership and "defend the national interest," he could "win in '76."[78]

Despite all the misgivings, Ford's trip went well. The Japanese emperor welcomed him, and Ford became the first US president to visit Tokyo. Protests occurred and there was a heavy police presence, but talks with Prime Minister Kakuei Tanaka were friendly, and they released a joint communiqué pledging cooperation. However, they concluded no major agreements, and Kissinger oversold the visit's importance when he declared that it had "achieved per-haps the optimum of what one had hoped for."[79] In South Korea, hundreds of thousands came out to welcome the president, and he reaffirmed the US commitment to the nation's defense.[80]

But Ford's meeting with the Soviet leader was most important. According to Kissinger, Ford's style was "a new experience for the Soviets." Whereas Nixon dealt in generalities and let others (like Kissinger) handle the specifics, Ford "came straight to the point and conducted much of the technical discussion himself."[81] Brezhnev and Ford developed a rapport and agreed to new arms limits, furthering progress on SALT II. According to Thomas A. Schwartz, the talks "proved the highpoint of détente during the Ford Administration."[82]

Although the summit produced tangible results, the White House exaggerated its accomplishments. The agreement reached "was something that Nixon couldn't do in three years, but Ford did it in three months," press secretary Ron Nessen boasted. The president would return home "in triumph" he predicted. But what Ford accomplished at Vladivostok was "essentially an agreement to seek an agreement."[83]

After Ford met with Brezhnev, Kissinger headed to Beijing, where the Chinese extended an invitation for the president to visit the following year. A trip to China and an arms control agreement with the Soviets were "an attempt to steal from Nixon's playbook and repeat the same foreign policy maneuvers for the election in 1976," according to Schwartz. And like Nixon, Ford wanted drama and spectacle.[84] Kissinger initially recommended that Ford visit the ancient Chinese capital of Xi'an, but he ultimately decided that Ford's trip to China should be vastly different from his predecessor's. "Don't stay long, don't go to another city," he told the president. "Any other city visit, even if it's different from where Nixon went, will look like a repeat to the American people." Kissinger also thought Ford should visit some other countries while in Asia. If Beijing was his only stop, the Chinese "will have you by the balls," he warned, because the journey would be judged solely by what happened in China.[85]

As Ford tried to differentiate himself from Nixon, there was one clear contrast: Chinese feelings toward the United States had soured since 1972. Beijing perceived a weakened United States, and it was increasingly suspicious of the US-Soviet détente. So Ford got his wish, and his summit was different from his predecessor's. Whereas Nixon's journey to Beijing was "the week that changed the world," Ford's was "slightly starchy hospitality plus a dash of tedium," according to one newspaper reporter.[86]

Even though the trip failed to match the glamour of Nixon's, there was still a heavy media presence. Whether that would benefit Ford domestically was questionable, however. Ford's political advisers cautioned that an image as a world leader was "no asset for the 1976 campaign."[87] And a month before the trip, the president's political standing suffered a self-inflicted wound. In what came to be known as the "Halloween massacre," Ford fired Secretary of Defense James Schlesinger and CIA Director James Colby, forced Vice President Nelson Rockefeller to declare that he would not be Ford's running mate in 1976, and removed Kissinger from his role as national security adviser. Ford thought these actions would show his command. Instead, the White House appeared to be in turmoil.[88]

So a politically weakened Ford left for a trip that was, in his words, of "great significance." Although the Soviets were happy with the president's decision to remove Schlesinger, who opposed détente, the Chinese were unhappy because it eased the way for closer US-Soviet cooperation. Nevertheless, the objective of the trip remained the same: normalization of relations.[89] Once in China, most of Ford's discussions were with Vice Premier Deng Xiaoping, as Zhou Enlai was ill and Mao Zedong was now an octogenarian. He did, however, meet with Mao for an hour and fifty minutes. Ford was keen to stress to Chinese leaders that the United States had the determination and strength to confront the Soviets. The Chinese called the talks "earnest and significant."[90] Publicly, US officials agreed. Privately, they were less sanguine. The Chinese wanted to improve relations, but Ford's talks with Chinese leaders "blazed no new ground." Relations were "waning," according to Kissinger.[91] But that did not stop Ford from proclaiming the trip a success, both in public and in private. "I am damned pleased," he told Kissinger.[92]

From China, Ford went to Indonesia and the Philippines. He was greeted warmly at both stops, and as NBC's Tom Brokaw said of his visit to Indonesia, "it's good domestic politics for the president to be seen with a strong anti-communist like Suharto after a week with China's revolutionary heroes."[93] The domestic benefit of the entire trip, if any, was unclear. Less than a week before leaving the country, Ford's approval rating was 41 percent. Days after he left China, it was up to 46 percent. However, Ford returned home to polls that showed a drop in support among Republican voters: 40 percent now wanted Ronald Reagan to be their nominee, as opposed to 32 percent who supported Ford.[94]

Ford's trips to China and the Soviet Union may have emulated Nixon, but his use of an economic summit for domestic political gain was a new strategy. With the global economy spiraling downward and established institutions and methods unable to stop the hemorrhaging, French president Valery Giscard d'Estaing and German chancellor Helmut Schmidt proposed that the leaders of the industrialized democracies meet informally to discuss their major economic problems. At the end of 1974, Giscard and Schmidt approached the Ford administration with the idea and received a positive response. A little less than a year later, the first meeting was held in Rambouillet, France.[95]

The Group of Seven (G-7) summit was not intended to be a formal annual event, but members of the Ford administration saw its value, and within five months of the first meeting, they began to discuss a second. "In both the monetary and trade areas there are major storm warnings on the horizon," said one National Security Council staffer.[96] But there were other motivations as well. Ford hoped to use a second summit for political purposes—at least that was what many in the press corps suspected.[97] The G-7 summit transitioned from an intimate get-together among leaders to a "great show," according to NBC's Marvin Kalb in 1983. The host nation "play[ed] impresario, generally against a backdrop of pageantry and history, attracting at first hundreds and now thousands of reporters and cameras."[98] In 1976 these changes had not yet taken hold, but they explain why the G-7 was seen as a useful forum for presidential image making.

The 1976 economic summit took place between the end of the Republican primary season and the Republican National Convention. At the time, Reagan was challenging Ford for the Republican nomination, and an economic summit was something the former California governor "could not duplicate."[99] The administration pushed back against the insinuation that the meeting in Puerto Rico was political. Press secretary Nessen declared that election-year politics played no role in Ford's call for a summit. It was Alan Greenspan, chairman of the President's Council of Economic Advisers, who had first suggested it. Kissinger agreed: "It can't be a political ploy because they're [industrial nations] not involved in our politics."[100]

While denying the summit's political aspects, some of those involved in the planning wondered whether an economic summit could be held in the United States during such a politically charged time.[101] The press wondered this too. To deflect criticism, the administration referred to the talks as Rambouillet II, an effort to portray the gathering as merely a follow-up to the first economic summit. But to critics, "the only purpose of the new summit is political, an effort to sharpen the image of Mr. Ford as economic manager and world leader during the election campaign."[102]

Still, it was doubtful how much political mileage Ford could get out of the summit. Hundreds of reporters would be covering the talks, but the seven leaders had "no surprises to announce," according to NBC's John Cochran.[103] They released an upbeat joint communiqué stating that "economic recovery is well under way" and touting the "substantial progress" some nations had made toward lowering inflation and unemployment.[104] Ford also achieved his top priority: a pledge from the other leaders to fight inflation. But in the end, the G-7 gathering did not help the president politically. While in Puerto Rico, Ford's delegate lead over Reagan was reduced to only 25, with 182 uncommitted delegates up for grabs at the upcoming convention.[105] Days after the summit, the appraisal by the *New York Times* was harsh: the talks "may well have produced a sharp deflation in the value of summitry as a political device," resulting in increased "disillusionment, mixed with cynicism."[106]

A month and a half after returning from the G-7 summit, Ford narrowly won the Republican nomination, but he went on to lose a close general election to Jimmy Carter. The headwinds of a dismal economy and his connection to the Nixon administration were too much to overcome. And Ford did himself no favors in the final presidential debate when he declared that the Soviets were not dominating eastern Europe.[107] Like Nixon, no amount of summitry could save Ford.

Geopolitical objectives drove Nixon to open to China and pursue détente with the Soviet Union. He believed that doing so put the United States in a better strategic position, preserving and furthering America's dominant place in the world order.[108] Diplomacy at the highest level advanced these moves but also presented domestic political opportunities. Nixon's prepresidential career provided him with numerous examples of how television and personal diplomacy could enhance a politician's image. Thus, in 1972 he was well aware of how visits to Beijing and Moscow—and the accompanying newspaper and television coverage—could influence the voting public. Perhaps CBS's Eric Sevareid best captured Nixon's need for popular approval, as well as his attempts to use the international sphere to strengthen his domestic position: "This president has never had the solid, unquestioning majority support that . . . Eisenhower enjoyed. Mr. Nixon is a stronger president, but with a weaker mandate, and he requires periodic drama. World affairs provide a much handier stage for it than domestic affairs."[109]

The drama of the international stage led to images of the president as a bold statesman and peacemaker. It shifted perceptions and improved Nixon's electoral prospects. Nixon is an extreme example of a president manipulating personal diplomacy for domestic political gain, but he is not alone in doing so. Other modern presidents, including Ford, sought to bolster their images as statesmen through personal diplomacy.[110]

Political scientists have shown that foreign travel and high-level diplomacy with world leaders generally enhance a president's approval rating. The sizable bounce in popularity that Nixon received after his election-year summits is rare, however. More common is a small increase that quickly diminishes.[111] But as presidential scholar George Edwards argues, the "greatest source of influence for the president is public approval." And Bruce Miroff notes that the public and the media expect spectacle, and they use such performances to judge a president's leadership.[112] Given the enormous expectations of those who sit in the Oval Office, presidents take whatever help they can get to raise their approval ratings, strengthen their political power, boost their reelection prospects, and secure a place in history. Thus, even if the spectacle of foreign travel and personal diplomacy failed to pay substantial domestic dividends, postwar presidents leveraged them for personal political gain.

6. Jimmy Carter and the Demand for Presidential Time

A little less than a year before resigning from office, Richard Nixon hosted Romanian president Nicolae Ceauşescu at the White House. The visit illustrated Romania's relative independence from Moscow and provided Ceauşescu the opportunity to enhance his image as a statesman and promote his country. He had hoped the Nixon administration would offer "visual evidence of a highly-special" US-Romanian relationship, but it could not deliver. To compensate, advisers told Nixon that Ceauşescu would "attach particular importance to the quality of the personal relationship he will have established with you."[1] At this point, the two men had met multiple times. In 1969 Nixon traveled to Romania, becoming the first American president to visit a communist state since 1945. A year later Ceauşescu came to the United States, hoping to deepen his connection with the president.[2]

For Ceauşescu, intimate and frequent contact with Nixon was a boon for himself personally and for his country. By the time Jimmy Carter came to office in 1977, the Romanian leader was accustomed to close contact with the American president. A month after Carter's inauguration, Ceauşescu sent a personal emissary to Washington to make it clear that Romania desired to continue its close relationship with the United States. As Deputy Secretary of State Warren Christopher told the president, part of the mission was "to convey President Ceausescu's desire to establish with you the kind of personal relationship he had with Presidents Nixon and Ford." Christopher believed the Romanian emissary might "be fishing for an invitation" for Ceauşescu to visit. No invitation was forthcoming in 1977, but a year later the Romanian president was in Washington for a state visit.[3]

Ceauşescu was not alone. Political and economic benefits, as well as enhanced prestige, made interaction with the American president worth pursuing. For example, Indonesian president Suharto had enjoyed a personal connection with Nixon and Ford and sought to form close ties with Carter.[4] When Suharto's outreach was unsuccessful, it negatively affected US-Indonesia relations. By Carter's last year in office, the State Department warned, "Suharto . . . [has] an impression that the U.S. is neglectful of Indonesia, possibly ill-willed toward Suharto's continuance in power, and ungrateful for Indonesian support and cooperation on a range of issues important to us." The number-one reason for the current state of relations was "insufficient personal contacts" and the failure to invite Suharto for a state visit. Suharto believed "he had a personal relationship with previous U.S. presidents, and his resentment over this perceived slight (plainly visible to his political constituency) has reinforced his reaction to other U.S. actions."[5]

This illustrates the potential consequences when American presidents do not reciprocate foreign leaders' interest in personal contact. Presidents have a finite amount of time and an infinite number of demands, and they cannot satisfy every leader. But in the postwar period, as the US presidency became the key institution in the international arena, foreign leaders became increasingly interested in meeting with the holder of that office. Most heads of state and government believed that no other person could deliver the same economic, military, or political benefits. This forced presidents to interact with foreign leaders more than they might have wished, and sometimes they became overwhelmed. As a memo from the vice president's office cautioned Carter, the list of potential visitors for the upcoming year had "too many proposed visits, including visits by leaders from nations whose relations with us are of such modest proportions that I question their being given priority over the domestic demands on your 1978 schedule."[6]

Though this was sage advice, during the Cold War, US relations with very few parts of the world could be deemed of "modest proportions." No longer were relationships confined to a limited number of traditional partners. The United States had interests in every corner of the globe, and foreign heads of state and government knew it. Some world leaders wanted to meet with the president because of legitimate security concerns or economic needs made acute by the Cold War. Others were more opportunistic, seeking to profit from America's decades-long struggle against communism. Either way, presidents felt compelled to interact personally through invitations to visit the United States, trips abroad, correspondence, and telephone calls. This did not mean that presidents had no choice in the matter, but when approached by foreign leaders, presidents often erred on the side of more personal diplomacy rather than less. A president could refuse, but he did so at his own peril. As the case of Suharto illustrates, the Carter administration's lack of personal attention created friction in US-Indonesia relations. In other contexts during the Cold War, a presidential rebuff of overtures by a neutral or nominally

Western aligned leader could lead to flirtations with the Soviets. Refusing to engage with an ally could publicly strain relations, and this was anathema to Cold War leaders focused on solidarity, or at least the perception of it.

Using the Carter administration's relationship with Japan and Egypt, this chapter explores how foreign leaders pushed presidents toward personal diplomacy in the second half of the twentieth century. Whether they were simply maneuvering for an invitation to visit or pursuing a dramatic reorientation of bilateral relations, foreign leaders sought out the occupant of the White House. Sometimes these overtures were welcomed; sometimes they were not. And when the president was eager to forge a personal relationship, the depth and scope of that connection and the demands it entailed could be greater than anticipated.

CARTER IN CHARGE

Jimmy Carter's presidency started propitiously, but in less than a year, his fortunes began to decline. At or above 60 percent for most of his first year, Carter's approval rating was in the 30s by 1980.[7] Like many of Carter's domestic policies, his conduct of foreign affairs came under frequent attack. In the fall of 1977 national security adviser Zbigniew Brzezinski warned him of "a growing domestic problem." While Brzezinski personally believed that Carter's foreign policy was correct, the public did not. "To put it simply and quite bluntly, it is seen as 'soft,'" he told the president.[8] Carter never overcame this perception. Though accomplishments such as the Camp David Accords would boost his popularity, he could never shake the negative images formed during his first year.

When Carter left office, his approval rating was only 34 percent, and 46 percent of Americans believed posterity would view him as a "below average" or "poor" president. Indeed, historians have been critical.[9] However, like any presidency, Carter's had both failures and successes. He faltered plenty, but he also was unlucky, and many of the challenges he confronted were not of his own making.[10]

One challenge Carter shared with other modern presidents (and one overlooked by scholars) was foreign leaders' demands on his time, which required increasing levels of presidential personal diplomacy. As an adviser told President-elect Carter a little more than a month before his inauguration, he would "inevitably have *direct* dealings with heads of foreign governments. They will not be satisfied dealing through your Secretary of State and will want a *personal* relationship."[11] The administration believed such leader-to-leader interactions would play a crucial role in its ambitious agenda, which included negotiating a new SALT agreement with the Soviet Union, transferring control of the Panama Canal to the Panamanians, normalizing relations with China, negotiating a long-term peace agreement in the Middle East, and dealing with apartheid in South Africa and majority rule in Rhodesia.[12]

Once Carter took office, the value of personal diplomacy was reemphasized. Before the United Nations General Assembly met in 1977, the State Department urged Carter to do more than simply deliver a speech; though past presidents had rarely done so, it encouraged him to consider holding bilateral meetings at the UN. As diplomatic progress was made in the Middle East and Rhodesia, the State Department argued that the "exercise of Presidential leadership through personal diplomacy could have a major impact on the thinking of world leaders" at the UN.[13] Two years later, the administration continued to strategize how to leverage the practice. "As I consider ways to increase the effectiveness of our diplomacy in [the] coming months," Secretary of State Cyrus Vance told Carter, "I am struck with the fact that there is often no more persuasive means at our disposal . . . than even brief visits with you. The extremely positive results coming out of your personal contacts with foreign leaders confirm the great utility of these meetings . . . [and] personal diplomacy by you could make a significant difference" in many parts of the world. Vance proposed that the administration arrange up to two foreign visitors per month, and Brzezinski concurred. Vance acknowledged this would be an added burden on Carter, but he believed it "would be time well spent in furthering our foreign policy objectives."[14]

Thus, from the beginning of his presidency, Carter spent much of his time interacting with heads of state and government. His first year in office he met with fifty leaders in the United States; that included hosting a state visit for the president of Mexico less than a month after inauguration. Less than four months into his presidency, Carter traveled to the United Kingdom and Switzerland, where he met with fifteen heads of state and government and showed "his skill at personal diplomacy with some proud and touchy European leaders," according to one newspaper reporter.[15] At the end of his first year he embarked on another foreign trip, visiting Poland, Iran, India, Saudi Arabia, Egypt, France, and Belgium.[16]

By the end of his presidency, Carter had completed the most extraordinary display of personal diplomacy ever. Although other presidents engaged in dramatic personal diplomacy in the second half of the twentieth century—such as Richard Nixon with Mao Zedong and Ronald Reagan with Mikhail Gorbachev—juxtaposed with Carter's efforts at the center of negotiations between two leaders who did not like each other and whose countries were longtime foes, these other presidential endeavors fail to compare.[17] Though ultimately successful, the talks at Camp David were a huge gamble and occupied a significant amount of time, allowing critics to claim that Carter was neglecting other aspects of his job. But as noted earlier, the administration generally saw personal diplomacy as a good use of the president's time.

In a meeting with the South Korean foreign minister, Brzezinski boasted, "In the first 14 months of his [Carter's] Presidency he met with 67 foreign leaders as opposed to 8 by President Truman and 22 by President Kennedy during a similar period." Yet in that same conversation, the pitfalls of too much leader-to-leader engagement were evident. Explaining why a meeting between Carter and the South Korean president would not be possible, Brzezinski noted that Carter had "already followed a very heavy foreign travel schedule which has compressed the time that he has devoted to Congressional legislation and given rise to criticism that he is neglecting domestic policy. . . . The days at Camp David devoted solely to the Middle East have further exacerbated the situation."[18]

As it did for other presidents, personal diplomacy held both promise and peril for Carter, and the fact that foreign leaders actively sought him out intensified the administration's favorable view of the practice. But wanting to interact with the president did not necessarily mean that foreign leaders liked him or that they got along. For example, Carter's relationship with West German chancellor Helmut Schmidt was awful. Publicly, they were all smiles, and when they met early in 1977, Carter wrote in his diary he "liked" Schmidt. Less than a year later, he was venting about the chancellor's criticism and volatility. Likewise, Schmidt's memoir paints an extremely unflattering portrait of Carter, calling him "fickle" and "bereft" of experience and knowledge in foreign affairs.[19] They differed on numerous issues, ranging from economics to arms control, but they could not ignore each other. In November 1977 Schmidt proposed a four-power gathering of West Germany, the United States, France, and Britain to discuss arms control. The following year, with détente weakening and progress on arms control stalled, Schmidt again suggested an informal meeting, raising the issue with Brzezinski and then with Carter himself.[20] Even though the chancellor did not like the president, he needed him.

A foreign leader did not have to be the president's friend to want to engage with him, and whether friend or not, Carter might or might not welcome the outreach. Even when the president was receptive, these interactions could be more intense than he ever imagined. These dynamics are clear in Carter's diplomacy with the leaders of Japan and Egypt.

CARTER, FUKUDA, AND ŌHIRA

After World War II the relationship between the United States and Japan changed dramatically. Defeated and broken after the war, Japan was, by the start of Carter's presidency, the third-largest economy in the world and America's key Asian ally. The US-Japan relationship, however, was not without tensions. Immediately after the war the United States occupied Japan and sought to restructure its government and society.[21] A new constitution and land reform were part of these changes, but Japan's role in the emerging postwar order was not immediately apparent. Rising conflict between the Americans and the Soviets clarified this role, and the outbreak of the Korean War in 1950 cemented it: Japan would be a strategic Cold War military asset. In 1951 Japan and the United States signed a security treaty. One of its key features was US rights to the Ryukyu Islands, an archipelago south of mainland Japan that included key military bases at Okinawa. Though technically Japanese territory, the archipelago would be under US control.[22]

Problems arose soon after the security agreement went into effect. In 1953 there were significant disturbances on the northernmost island of the Ryukyus, and in 1955 a controversy arose over the possibility of nuclear-armed missiles on American bases. In 1958 the United States and Japan entered negotiations to revise the security treaty. After two years of difficult talks they came to a new agreement that was more to Japan's liking, including a provision requiring "prior consultation" before nuclear weapons could be based on Japanese territory. Not everyone in Japan supported the treaty, and the high-handed tactics used by the prime minister to assure its passage provoked protests. The turmoil became so severe that President Eisenhower's planned visit to Tokyo in 1960 was canceled out of fear for his safety.

This inauspicious start to the 1960s foreshadowed greater tensions that arose later in the decade and continued into the early 1970s. Two decades after the end of World War II, the United States still had political control over Japanese territory, a potentially debilitating situation for US-Japan relations, according to US ambassador Edwin Reischauer. Throughout the 1960s the Kennedy and Johnson administrations explored the reversion of Okinawa to Japanese control. The Nixon administration continued this effort but was also responsible for numerous shocks to American-Japanese relations. The declaration of the Nixon Doctrine in 1969 was an early indication that the administration wanted its allies, including Japan, to take a greater role in their own defense. Nixon's announcement in 1971 that he was going to China stunned the Japanese. It was not the burgeoning reconciliation between Cold War foes that shocked the Japanese as much as the fact that they had not been consulted or informed in advance. Nixon also devalued the dollar and instituted a surcharge on imports, moves that adversely affected the Japanese economy. These developments, combined with the American withdrawal from Vietnam, put US reliability into question.[23]

Skeptical of American security commitments, Japan also began to fear economic reprisals by the 1970s. During the previous decade, Japan's economy had exploded: it witnessed 10 percent annual growth and a doubling of income.[24] This robustness coincided with the economic decline of an overburdened America. By the late 1970s, high unemployment and rising inflation gripped the United States, along with increasing energy costs and an ever-expanding trade deficit. During the Carter years, the US economy was feeble. The United States ran trade deficits with many nations, but as the nation's largest trading partner, Japan was often singled out. American officials regularly sought to even the trade balance, while Japan sought to prevent any new trade restrictions or barriers. Japanese officials frequently tried to appease the United States by pledging to voluntarily restrict exports of one product or another, but the imbalance was never satisfactorily resolved.

Despite these issues, the two nations were close allies and dependent on each other in the realms of economics and security. Because of this interdependence, it was vital not to allow any irritants to become acute. When Carter took office in 1977, it was unclear in which direction he would take US-Japan relations, and the Japanese were eager to feel him out. In his approach toward Japan, as in other aspects of his foreign policy, Carter tried to move beyond the Cold War. Rather than focus on the island nation as a military installation projecting American power, he wanted to concentrate on energy, human rights, economics, and what a post–Vietnam War Asia would look like. But economic relations were always problematic, and by the end of his term, confrontation with the Soviets again took center stage.[25] However, at the outset, Carter had grand aspirations, and even though he did not achieve them all, he elevated the importance of US-Japan relations more than any previous president had.

Months before Carter took office, Jack Watson, director of the president-elect's transition team, told him, "The importance of Japan . . . our most important Asian ally . . . cannot be overemphasized." There were tensions in relations, Watson said, but the issues were "in some ways more matters of style than of content and *it is the style of the relationship which requires early attention by a new President,* in order to set the proper tone or mood."[26] The best way to do this was for Carter to visit Japan, which experts believed would be a highly visible way to demonstrate its importance as an ally. If that was not possible, Carter should have the Japanese prime minister visit the United States, Watson advised.

There was no early presidential trip, but the administration worked quickly to create a favorable impression and show that it valued Japan. Between his election and inauguration, Carter made a well-received phone call to Japanese prime minister Takeo Fukuda and invited him to visit soon after the inauguration.[27] Three days after taking office, Carter sent Vice President Walter Mondale to consult with Japanese leaders and other allies. Because the new president was an unknown quantity, allied leaders welcomed the visit as a chance to learn more about the administration's thinking. As Mondale recognized, his trip could set the right tone in relations.[28] While in Japan, the vice president pushed the country to increase imports and reduce its trade surplus with the United States. He also gave assurances regarding troop withdrawals from South Korea. More important, he clearly communicated the administration's appreciation of Japan. There was "no nation with whom we share a broader range of interests," Mondale said. Japan was "one of the cornerstones" of American foreign policy and "indispensable" to the solution of global problems.[29]

Carter's next step was to meet with the Japanese leader himself. Fukuda clearly wanted to visit the United States, and because of his country's importance, he got an early appointment. The prime minister also felt he deserved an early meeting because he was staunchly pro-American and had steered Japanese policy closer to US preferences on multiple issues.[30] So when Fukuda came to the White House in March 1977, the administration believed his main goal was to enhance his image as a statesman who could manage Japan's most important bilateral relationship. Vance reiterated the point that "style" was key, noting that the visit would build on the positive feelings generated by Carter's preinauguration phone call.[31] The president welcomed Fukuda warmly, and the two men were all smiles when they met. During their talks, Carter reaffirmed US security commitments to Japan, calling them "permanent and unshakeable."[32]

A single meeting, however, was insufficient, and Fukuda pushed for more time with the president.[33] Shortly after their initial talks, they both attended the G-7 summit in London, where Fukuda hoped to have some alone time with Carter. He requested a thirty-minute meeting to discuss proliferation issues before the summit convened in the plenary. After London, Fukuda's advisers tried to set up a private channel between the prime minister and Brzezinski. If Fukuda could not talk directly with the president, his national security adviser was the next best option.[34] "There is so much we can do together," Fukuda wrote to Carter after the economic summit, "and I hope we can keep in close touch [with] each other."[35] Carter reciprocated, telling him a few months later, "If you have any thoughts you wish to convey to me . . . I hope you will feel free to utilize the telephone or the Cabinet line which provides a direct communication link between us."[36]

Sometimes, however, correspondence and phone calls are not enough. These are useful means of keeping in touch, but nothing is more valuable than a face-to-face meeting. As Carter began his second year in office, Fukuda requested another White House visit. The two countries continued to tussle over trade issues, and although Fukuda had made some concessions, they did not go far enough for the United States. Faced with domestic opposition to more concessions, Fukuda wanted to present his case directly to the president, in the hope of preventing any retaliatory measures. A high-profile US visit might also help his sagging poll numbers back home.[37]

Though the Japanese privately requested a visit, they also made their desire known publicly about a week later, putting pressure on the Carter administration to extend an invitation—which it did. According to ABC's Tom Jarriel, the visit was "designed to improve the image of Japan in the eyes of Americans," and the prime minister hoped he could ease bilateral tensions.[38] According to Carter, his meetings with Fukuda "went well," but reporters noted that neither side was "completely satisfied with the outcome."[39] Though Fukuda agreed to implement new measures to adjust the trade imbalance, he was short on specifics. And while the United States agreed to a new monetary accord, it did not intervene to prop up the dollar and prevent a further decline, a major desire of Japan. Fukuda would also be disappointed domestically. If the visit gave him any political boost, it was short-lived. By the end of the year, he was voted out of office.

During his second visit to the White House, Fukuda, pushed Carter to visit Japan. Such a trip would be "appreciated," Fukuda said; he issued a standing invitation for the president to visit and pressed for a firm date. Carter demurred. He wanted to go, he said, but was not sure when he could. Fukuda tried to pin him down, suggesting this year or the next. "Please do not make me promise," Carter responded, before moving on to a different topic.[40]

Fukuda never got the president to commit to a visit, but the administration did see its value, and Carter eventually went to Japan for a state visit in June 1979. In the months following Fukuda's 1978 visit, Mike Mansfield, US ambassador to Japan, noted that despite some economic problems, relations between the two nations were solid, and he stressed the importance of Carter going to the island nation. Mansfield told the president that it would be "a major event in US-Japan relations." It would be only the second presidential visit, and as such, "it will have a significant impact on Japanese—and Asian—perceptions concerning the United States' role in this region," as well as being "a rather dramatic reaffirmation" of the US-Japan alliance. The United States asked a lot of Japan, and more often than not, it "leaned over backwards" to help. We "could not necessarily talk the same way to some of our European allies and get away with it," Mansfield observed.[41] The Japanese knew this too, which only added to their resentment of being treated like a second-class ally. The administration needed to demonstrate that the United States valued and respected Japan and recognize that tone and style were central to bilateral ties. At the very least, high-level meetings with the president helped give the impression of equality with the Europeans.

The Carter administration did itself no favors in this area. In January 1979 the president met with the leaders of Britain, France, and West Germany on the French island of Guadeloupe. Japan's exclusion was no doubt a blow to its pride and increased its sensitivity to differential treatment. Soon after Guadeloupe, the Japanese made it known that the new prime minister, Masayoshi Ōhira, wanted to visit the United States; it was the "one thing which clearly is very much on his mind," Mansfield reported. This was not imperative from the American perspective, but for Ōhira, who was under attack at home for not promoting the US-Japan relationship more vigorously, a presidential meeting was critical.[42] Once again, the Japanese communicated their desire for a visit both privately and publicly, forcing the administration's hand. "Now that Ohira has asked, the trip becomes necessary," one National Security Council (NSC) staffer wrote. "The Japanese are still raw over Guadeloupe. To turn the Prime Minister down would rub salt in that wound, ruin his political standing, and add an irritant to our relationship that we cannot afford. What's worse, the world knows that Ohira has asked to come."[43]

Mansfield supported the visit. He believed it would allow the United States to influence Japan in certain areas and strengthen relations "in a broader political and psychological sense" after recent rumblings about how the two nations were moving apart. Carter, however, was not pleased. "This kind of thing should be worked out privately," Carter complained to Vance, "instead of following the Japanese policy of inviting themselves with a public announcement of unscheduled visits. I resent their taking advantage of us like this."[44] He agreed to see the prime minister, but only after the administration let the president's "displeasure sink in."[45]

Japan got what it wanted, yet it still pushed the Carter administration for more. In early April, as planning for the following month's meeting got under way, Mansfield reported that Japanese officials were arguing that Ōhira needed two meetings with Carter, separate from their scheduled dinner.[46] Almost three weeks later, Vance informed Carter that the Japanese foreign minister was making "a strong plea for two meetings." The Japanese were concerned about having time for both pleasantries and policy discussions, he wrote, "but the principal issue is one of face, that is, whether the holding of only a single meeting will be interpreted by the public as an indication of problems in the relationship or, since you had two meetings with Fukuda, a downgrading of Ohira. This is a peculiar—but—real problem for the Japanese."[47] The National Security Council disagreed: having two meetings "purely for the sake of form is unacceptable trifling with the President's time."[48]

In the end, Carter held two meetings with Ōhira, and despite the public pressure used by the prime minister to secure the invitation, the talks were positive. "I had what all of us agreed was one of the most productive diplomatic sessions of our administration," Carter wrote in his diary. He said the same thing publicly. Ōhira was an adept manager of relations with the United States, and during their meeting, he encouraged Carter to continue his work with "courage and self-confidence." Carter was impressed with Ōhira's sincerity and determination to solve the trade imbalance, and the two leaders agreed on a new method to track progress toward this goal. Additionally, they planned to create a group of "wise men" from both countries to make policy recommendations and address irritants in the relationship.[49]

When Ōhira made another visit to the White House in the spring of 1980, the Japanese again managed to raise American ire. Stopping for a day while journeying to Mexico, the prime minister was scheduled to meet with Carter for about two hours, but the Japanese requested additional time, including a lunch for Ōhira. "We all knew this request for a lunch would come," one chagrined NSC staffer said, "even though the Japanese this time promised that a 2–3 hour meeting would be enough."[50] The State Department supported the idea, believing it would increase the visit's importance and symbolize the closeness of the US-Japan relationship.[51] But Carter objected: "Tell State— There will be no extension of [the] 2 hour time!" he wrote, underlining "no" three times.[52]

These frequent Japanese requests for more time made the White House leery, so when they suggested changes to the agenda to make the meeting run more efficiently, Carter hesitated. Initially, there was supposed to be simultaneous translation during the meeting, but the State Department, the commercial interpreting firm used by the department, and the Japanese all preferred consecutive translation. This might have made the meeting longer, which Carter adamantly opposed. Eventually, the president relented. "At first I thought this effort to return to consecutive interpretation was a ploy designed to lengthen the meeting," Brzezinski explained, but "I no longer believe this is the case." He became convinced that there was real concern about translating between two languages as different as English and Japanese. He urged Carter to allow consecutive translations but assured the president that this change, "per your clear instructions . . . will not be used to extend the meeting."[53]

In addition to this behind-the-scenes wrangling, clouding the meeting was the failed US military operation to free the American hostages in Iran, which had taken place a little over a week before Ōhira's visit. The Japanese prime minister was caught off guard and disappointed there had been no consultation, particularly as he had asked Carter not to use force. "What can the United States be thinking of?" he moaned when news of the botched rescue mission broke.[54] Nevertheless, the meeting went well. The two men signed a five-year deal on scientific cooperation, and Carter promised to help Japan meet its oil needs after it agreed to boycott Iranian oil in response to Iran's seizure of the US embassy in Tehran. The president also pushed Ōhira to approve a military buildup designed by his defense agency and urged him to deal proactively with the growing criticism over Japanese auto imports. Most important, Carter and Ōhira met for only two hours, but they did so during a "working luncheon," giving the Japanese the symbolic meal they wanted.[55]

Despite a variety of irritants, by the end of Carter's time in office, ties with Japan were one of the few bright spots in his foreign policy. Unlike the relationship with European allies, the US-Japan connection "became closer than ever," despite economic tensions, Brzezinski recalled.[56] On a personal level, Carter and Ōhira grew close. "Along with President Anwar Sadat of Egypt, Ohira was a special friend of mine among the foreign leaders I knew," Carter recalled.[57] Regardless of their closeness, the president was not always favorably disposed to grant the prime minister more time. Yet the two men's intimate ties probably emboldened Ōhira to take advantage of their relationship to ask for and receive more time with the president.

As the leaders of a vital American ally, there was no doubt that Fukuda and Ōhira would meet with Carter. But the prime ministers often set the timing and extent of those interactions. Carter could have refused, but an outright rejection would have harmed relations, either in practice or in the public's perception, an outcome that neither Carter nor other presidents could easily ignore.

In the spring of 1979, soon after Ōhira publicly invited himself to the United States, Japan had to deal with its own uninvited visitor. According to a Japanese official, Egyptian president Anwar Sadat had "been making embarrassing public statements about visiting Japan (without checking with the Japanese)." Sadat also talked about the generous amount of aid Egypt would be receiving from Japan. The Japanese government decided to push the visit back to August or September and remained silent on the issue of aid, but officials were "rankled by Sadat's insensitivity." Americans could not help but experience a bit of schadenfreude. As one NSC staffer remarked, "The shoe is on the other foot and it pinches."[58] Though Sadat may have irritated the Japanese, the United States welcomed his outreach. Little did Carter know that interacting with the Egyptian president would result in such intense personal diplomacy. For Sadat, however, that was part of his plan all along.

CARTER AND SADAT

Since the 1950s, US-Egypt relations had been rife with tension. During the Eisenhower years, America's Cold War leaders loathed Egyptian leader Gamal Abdel Nasser's revolutionary nationalism and burgeoning ties with the Soviet Union. Relations improved slightly during the Kennedy years but then deteriorated again under Johnson. When Anwar Sadat became president in 1970, no diplomatic relations existed, and Egypt was considered securely in the Soviet orbit.

Domestically, Sadat faced significant challenges. "The legacy Nasser left me was in a pitiable condition," he recalled.[59] Confronted with a moribund economy, bureaucratic corruption, and food shortages, Sadat tried to initiate a new economic policy in an attempt to attract foreign investment. But growth remained weak, and the need to improve Egypt's economy would motivate much of his foreign policy.[60]

Sadat spent his first year in power combating opponents and Nasser loyalists. After a failed coup attempt in May 1971, he was firmly in power and moved forward with his chief foreign policy objective: a peace settlement with Israel. Since 1948, the year the Jewish state was founded, Egypt and Israel had engaged in four military conflicts. But Sadat now realized that Egypt had more to gain from peace than war. Egypt could regain the Sinai peninsula, which it had lost to Israel during the Six-Day War in 1967, and it could reduce military spending and focus on other sectors of the economy.

Thus, in February 1971 Sadat proposed that if Israel withdrew from the Sinai, he would sign a peace treaty with Israel and reestablish diplomatic relations with the United States. Israel and the United States were cool to the proposal and did not take Sadat seriously. The United States was also distracted in the early 1970s. Secretary of State Henry Kissinger "was not ready to switch his attention from other international problems [e.g., Vietnam] to the Middle East situation, which he believed would be dormant for a long time to come," according to Sadat's foreign minister, Ismail Fahmy. Sadat was "deeply hurt and angered" by America's lack of interest in his initiatives.[61]

US ambivalence was problematic for Sadat. For Egypt and Israel to make peace, he believed, America had to play a central role. But Egypt's relationship with the Soviet Union only pushed the United States closer to Israel. Thus, Sadat began reorienting Egypt's foreign policy. His first major move was to expel Soviet military personnel from his country in July 1972. Sadat's purpose was "not just to get them out but to get the Americans in," said Israeli foreign minister Moshe Dayan.[62] Yet, to Sadat's disappointment, the United States kept its distance. Something more was needed to shatter the status quo.

To get the superpower's attention, Sadat believed that Israel's military complacency had to be broken, which would lead to action on a peace agreement. So in October 1973 Egypt went to war with Israel. Although it was technically a military defeat for Egypt, Sadat changed the dynamics in the Middle East. As the Egyptian foreign minister recalled, "The American position had undergone major changes. . . . The war had created a new military and psychological situation. . . . Washington had no option but to move quickly to defuse the crisis."[63]

In the war's aftermath, Kissinger embarked on his famed shuttle diplomacy, facilitating two disengagement agreements between Israel and Egypt in 1974 and 1975. Kissinger used a step-by-step approach to these negotiations, focusing on specific, limited, attainable objectives. He believed this was the only viable path. The time was not yet right for a comprehensive settlement dealing with all outstanding issues.[64] Thus, by the mid-1970s, Sadat was much closer to his goal. The United States had taken the lead in the quest for peace in the Middle East, furthering Egypt's agenda. Sadat believed that America had "all the cards in its hands," and Israel had to "heed" it.[65]

In 1974 the United States and Egypt reestablished diplomatic ties, but Sadat wanted more. He wanted to broaden and deepen relations beyond military matters, extending into economic, scientific, and cultural areas.[66] As Carter came to office, relations "remained rather delicate," recalled Fahmy. There was a "new friendship" between the two nations, but Egypt believed the United States "was still much more committed to Israel," Fahmy lamented.[67] Sadat had also grown tired of the step-by-step approach. The two agreements Kissinger had helped broker were not peace treaties, so technically, Israel and Egypt were still at war. Looking to 1977, the Egyptian president wanted a comprehensive settlement. "There is no need for any more 'step by step,'" he declared weeks after Carter's election.[68]

According to Carter, the Middle East occupied more of his time than any other region of the world.[69] Fortunately for Sadat, he and the new American president had similar approaches. Carter also favored a far-reaching settlement that addressed all the issues, including the most divisive ones. But there was no guarantee that Sadat would get what he wanted just because the two presidents agreed on the process. Thus, he embarked on a mission to move closer to Carter and deepen US-Egyptian ties.

During the transition, advisers told Carter that Sadat might press for a new US peace initiative. But the options they presented to the president-elect would not have pleased the Egyptian president. One option called for a comprehensive settlement, but others included doing nothing, pushing interim agreements, or working with the Soviet Union.[70] Though committed to an overarching agreement, the United States initially decided to work with the Soviets and convene a peace conference in Geneva. This was not Sadat's first choice, but he went along with it. To maneuver himself closer to Carter, he needed to be seen as cooperative.

Shortly after Carter's inauguration, Egypt's foreign minister began to inquire about a possible Sadat visit. Two months later, in April 1977, he was at the White House.[71] In the buildup to the meeting, the Egyptian leader laid the groundwork for close ties by praising Carter in his public remarks. The two presidents would get along, Sadat proclaimed, because both were "men of faith, deep moral beliefs, and operate from principle."[72] The Egyptian president's feelings may have been genuine, but he was also ingratiating himself to the American president, the person whose goodwill he most needed to achieve his objectives.

The administration was well aware of Sadat's strategy. "Sadat's personal relationship with you," Vance informed Carter, "will be his main preoccupation on this visit. He will want your confidence and your understanding for his aims."[73] Once at the White House, the Egyptian leader made it clear that the American president was key to progress in the Middle East. "You are the man to help end the conflict," Sadat told Carter. At multiple points in their conversation, he emphasized the importance of American involvement. He dismissed Soviet abilities and motivations for peace, arguing that only the United States could "balance everything. . . . Peace in the Middle East should be American."[74] If Sadat hoped to make an impression on the American president, he succeeded. As Carter told his diary, Sadat "was a charming and frank and also very strong and courageous leader" who could become an important ally. Sadat, too, believed he could rely on the American president to help advance his agenda.[75]

But by the fall of 1977, the peace process appeared to be stuck. Sadat reignited negotiations with a historic trip to Jerusalem in November 1977, where he gave a speech before the Knesset. Former Israeli prime minister Golda Meir recalled that it was "as if the Messiah had almost arrived." A captivated Vice President Mondale echoed the sentiment, telling Sadat, "More people watched your speech than almost anything in American history. In 48 hours, in the minds of Americans you became one of the world's leading apostles of peace and statesmen."[76]

After this spark, however, the peace process quickly became moribund. But as movement toward an agreement with Israel stalled, Sadat made progress toward his goal of moving Egypt closer to the United States. The trip to Israel had been intended to advance negotiations, but it was also a way to get into Carter's good graces. The bold gesture was guaranteed to make a favorable impression, especially since Sadat credited the American president with the idea. In an October 21, 1977, letter to the Egyptian president, Carter wrote that it was a "crucial moment" and he needed Sadat's "help. . . . The time has now come to move forward." It was this letter, Sadat declared, that inspired his journey to Jerusalem.[77]

Soon after the historic events in Israel, Carter and Sadat met. In early January 1978, as part of a broader foreign trip, the American president stopped in Egypt to "reestablish and enhance" his bond with Sadat, "something that can only be done in a face-to-face meeting," adviser Hamilton Jordan believed. Visiting Egypt was important because Sadat had made himself the "engine and motivation" of the Middle East peace process. In the past month, Carter had met with four key leaders in the region, but not with Sadat—a glaring omission, considering he was "the man who is personally responsible for opening things up."[78] After the visit, Carter wrote in his diary: it "was perhaps the most exciting" part of his trip "because of my strong friendship toward Sadat and worldwide interest in our resolving the Mideast disputes," and there were "no differences" between the them.[79] The Egyptian president was well on his way to winning Carter over.

Though the two men made progress on the personal front, advancement toward an Israeli-Egyptian agreement remained stalled. Weeks after meeting with the American president, and discouraged by what he believed to be Israeli intransigence, Sadat decided to suspend political talks with Israel. "I am very disappointed with the Israeli attitude," he told Carter in a telephone conversation. "They didn't get the conception of my initiative. They prefer land to peace. . . . They think I want peace at any price."[80] Some saw the decision to discontinue talks as a desperate act by a "glum and secluded" leader. Others saw it as a more calculated maneuver.[81] The sudden nature of the Egyptian president's announcement produced a swift reaction from Carter, who got on the telephone and, in a ten-minute conversation, persuaded Sadat to at least continue military talks, which were occurring alongside the political ones.

Some diplomats saw this prompt action by the American president as the purpose (partially, if not wholly) of Sadat's abrupt cancellation of political talks.[82] Sadat believed that Carter was reluctant to become deeply enmeshed in Middle East peace talks in part because of domestic political concerns that made him unwillingly to challenge Israeli prime minister Menachem Begin.[83] According to news reports, Sadat hoped his announcement would pressure Carter to be bolder. He wanted a trilateral summit with American, Israeli, and Egyptian leaders, where Sadat reportedly believed he could generate enough public pressure to force Carter to take a firmer line with Begin. Carter told the press he disagreed with this analysis, but it seems clear that Sadat, with his flair for the dramatic, was angling for something.[84] Though Sadat was impatient and impulsive, it is not hard to see that his outburst was more than pure frustration. Such a histrionic and sudden action held the promise of not only sparking negotiations but also directing them toward his preferred positions.

Carter was not yet ready for a trilateral summit. But in February 1978, a few weeks after Sadat's suspension of political talks with Israel, he invited the Egyptian president to Camp David, the first time Carter had hosted a foreign leader there. Sadat used the visit to illustrate the growing closeness between the United States and Egypt. In his talks with Carter, he expressed frustration over Begin's intransigence and said he was considering withdrawing from the peace talks entirely. Carter convinced him not to do that, but it was clear that a peace agreement was still a long way from becoming a reality. If Sadat had hoped the visit would result in a dramatic gesture by the United States, he was disappointed. He was successful, however, in charming Carter and other American officials. By the end of the visit, it was apparent that the Egyptian leader had garnered new favor and sympathy from the administration.[85]

Throughout the peace process, Sadat's message to Carter was clear: US leadership was vital. As he stated in June 1978, without the United States "as a witness" and "near or present," direct negotiations between Israel and Egypt would fail.[86] As the months passed and the peace process again seemed to be on the verge of collapse, Sadat finally got his wish. Carter decided to take a significant risk, and he invited both Sadat and Begin to Camp David in September 1978. This was an unprecedented foray into personal diplomacy. Rather than having leaders come together to finalize an agreement or settle a few outstanding issues, Carter planned to have Begin and Sadat engage in negotiations, with no guarantee of success.

It took almost two years of maneuvering by Sadat, but Carter was now deeply involved. From the beginning, Sadat had acted strategically. He had as-pired to be an actor in his youth, and that flair for the dramatic never left him. His theater background, combined with his penchant for personalizing his international relationships, was a key feature of his diplomacy.[87] The admin-istration knew this, but it could not resist being drawn in. "Sensing in Carter a personal friend, Sadat saw in the peace process an opportunity to fashion a new American-Egyptian relationship," Brzezinski recalled, "one in which Egypt might even displace Israel as America's closest ally in the region." If this failed, Sadat had a backup plan. Based on his words, actions, and relationship with Carter, the Egyptian president would "at the very least . . . be well on his way to becoming America's favorite statesman in the region."[88] For the most part, this is what happened. Sadat was the West's darling, and the American public had a very high opinion of him, an extraordinary achievement for an Arab leader in the late 1970s. More important, Sadat got Carter on his side, which gave him confidence. In the weeks leading up to the summit, he contin-ued to move closer to the American president, talking about their "common strategy" and how they could "come out 'victorious'" no matter what hap-pened at Camp David. Sadat's plan worked. At Camp David, Carter told him that even if Israel did not accept an agreement, Egypt and the United States could come to their own understanding.[89]

The relationship between Sadat and Carter not only played a role in bring-ing the American president to Camp David but also forced him to engage in a more intense personal diplomacy than he ever imagined. Initially, Carter thought his role would be simple: he would bring Begin and Sadat together, and once both men saw that the other was sincere in his desire for a fair and just peace, they would work their problems out rationally.[90] Carter was wrong. There was too much history between their nations, and the issues were too emotional, for the men to work together. Thus, it fell to the American presi-dent to save the summit. He was at the center of negotiations, and as the key figure, both Sadat and Begin sought to have Carter on their side.[91]

As the fulcrum on which the negotiations hinged, Carter had to not only work out complicated compromises on previously intractable issues but also convince Sadat and Begin just to stay at Camp David. For example, on the eleventh day of the summit, Sadat planned to leave. To keep any hope of suc-cess alive, Carter got very personal and told Sadat that, if he left, it would dam-age not only US-Egyptian relations but, more importantly, "one of my most precious possessions—his friendship and our mutual trust."[92]

When Carter spoke of friendship, it was not hyperbole.[93] But the relationship did not develop overnight; it was something both men cultivated, especially Sadat. He needed Carter to push Israel to make concessions, and the closer he got to the American president, the more he benefited. At Camp David, Sadat used the trust he and Carter had developed to Egypt's advantage, going so far as letting the American president negotiate for him. "Sadat essentially gave Carter a blank check. He told Carter to do the best he could; he would trust the American President not [to] give away Egypt's interests. That was a technique that Sadat repeatedly used with Carter and used very successfully," recalled US ambassador to Israel Samuel Lewis.[94] While Carter enjoyed having Sadat's trust, he was also somewhat wary of being given such a free hand.[95] But that was the position he found himself in, and by September 1978, Carter had little choice. Because of his intimate involvement in the peace process and with Sadat personally, Carter had put the prestige of his office and his country at stake, and he had to take the plunge into intensive personal diplomacy.

After much cajoling and threatening, a deal was struck at Camp David; it created a framework for the normalization of relations, Israel's withdrawal from the Sinai, and self-government for the Palestinians. But that was just the beginning: a formal treaty was needed. Within two months of Camp David, however, treaty talks between Israel and Egypt were unraveling. According to Brzezinski, the main reason for the breakdown was that Carter was no longer at the center of negotiations.[96] As prospects for a final treaty appeared to be slipping away, Sadat again appealed to the American president, telling Carter in an eight-page handwritten letter that they needed to "devise a joint course of action which could serve our purpose."[97] The administration had hoped its work was done, but it was clear that a final treaty would require another extraordinary effort by the American president. Already heavily invested, Carter went for broke and traveled to the Middle East to finalize an agreement. Most of his advisers opposed the trip, fearing it would look like he was "traipsing around the Middle East, hat in hand."[98] It was a huge risk that put not only Carter's personal prestige on the line but also that of the United States. At this point, however, he was already so deeply involved, in large part because of Sadat, that he had to see it through.[99]

In March 1979 Carter flew to the Middle East. He received an enthusiastic welcome in Cairo but a cooler greeting in Jerusalem. Despite the apparent failure of the talks, he was able to finalize a treaty at the last minute.[100] Although the gamble paid off, implementing the agreement's terms proved no less challenging than negotiating them. The main problem revolved around autonomy for the Palestinians. When attempts to resolve the issue faltered, Carter brought Sadat and Begin to the White House for separate meetings in April 1980. Thus, as the Egyptian leader moved closer to Carter and brought him deeper into the peace process, Sadat also pushed him into increased contact with Begin, amplifying the amount of personal diplomacy required of the American president.

"Carter's relations with Begin were correct," Israeli foreign minister Moshe Dayan recalled, but "with Sadat they were much warmer."[101] Indeed, Carter and Begin were not close and often clashed on policy. But the Israeli prime minister respected and valued the office of the presidency and recognized what it could do for him and his country.[102] And like Sadat, he "had a strong conviction that face-to-face meetings between world leaders can bring about changes in their approaches," according to Ambassador Lewis.[103] But Begin knew that in the tug-of-war for Carter's favor, he fell short.

Even though Sadat played a better personal game than Begin and coaxed Carter into certain actions, the Egyptian leader was also used to a certain degree. Because of their relationship, Carter counted on Sadat to be more flexible and make more concessions. In the end, Sadat got what he wanted: the return of the Sinai. But he was attacked throughout the Middle East, and the Arab League expelled Egypt.[104] As a result, Sadat became even more dependent on the United States. He had "placed all his eggs in the American basket," the State Department noted, and "devoted much energy and personal prestige to attaining peace."[105] The Carter administration tried to bolster Sadat, but ultimately, it could not save him. Islamic extremists assassinated him in 1981.

Carter's fate was not nearly as dire. Despite engineering the historic agreement, by 1980, his diplomatic efforts were forgotten and he lost reelection. In the immediate aftermath of his efforts, Carter's public standing rose, but he never achieved the domestic windfall he had hoped for, as many Americans were distracted by inflation and high gas prices.[106] As Jody Powell, Carter's press secretary, remembered somewhat bitterly, the president got no credit "in the minds of the public . . . for one of the most dramatic and important diplomatic triumphs in recent American history."[107]

Just as American presidents have sought out personal interactions with foreign leaders, foreign leaders, attracted by US power and prestige, have sought out relationships with American presidents. They may have seen interactions with the president as the best way to achieve various aims, including military and economic aid, political support, and enhancement of their own prestige.

Narratives similar to those of Fukuda and Ōhira have played out numerous times with the leaders of various countries in the postwar era. Not all of them received satisfaction, but US presidents often engage with their foreign counterparts due to the latter's initiative. Although the Carter administration occasionally expressed irritation over Japan's frequent requests for presidential time, that is not always the case. Presidents often welcome close contact with other world leaders, especially ones they consider friends. Sadat's example also shows how a foreign leader can involve a president in personal diplomacy to an unprecedented degree. The Egyptian president's words and actions made it difficult for Carter to avoid becoming deeply involved in the Middle East. Carter wanted peace, but his diplomacy's scope and depth were largely due to Sadat, whose persistence also forced the American president to deal with Begin and sometimes put him in an impossible position. "You [Sadat] overestimate our influence with Israel & they overestimate my influence with you," Carter noted after a phone call with the Egyptian president.[108] The Camp David summit is the ultimate example of the unintended demands placed on presidents by personal diplomacy. The summit was scheduled to last for only a few days but went on for thirteen, proving that, as much as presidents try to control and protect their time, foreign leaders often have plans of their own.

7. Ronald Reagan and the Desire for Control

Ronald Reagan came to the White House with little foreign policy experience. During the 1980 presidential campaign, he advocated for a muscular approach. He wanted to increase defense spending and adopted aggressive rhetoric, but other than taking a hard line against the Soviet Union, it was unclear where the president stood on many international issues. "I like President Reagan as a person," German chancellor Helmut Schmidt said six months into Reagan's presidency, "but I can't say that about his foreign policy because I don't know what it is." The administration disputed this notion. Yet halfway through Reagan's first year, he had not yet delivered a major foreign policy address.[1]

"I know I'm being criticized for not having made a great speech outlining what would be the Reagan foreign policy. I have a foreign policy; I'm working on it," a frustrated Reagan wrote in a letter. "I just don't happen to think that it's wise to always stand up and put in quotation marks in front of the world what your foreign policy is. I'm a believer in quiet diplomacy and so far we've had several quite triumphant experiences by using that method. The problem is, you can't talk about it afterward or then you can't do it again."[2]

Reagan's contemporaries considered him an aloof chief executive not overly interested in policy details. He was a figurehead who reigned more than ruled. Months before the 1984 election, *NBC Evening News* ran a special series titled "The Reagan Record," part of which examined the president's leadership style. Reporter Chris Wallace stated, "For all his leadership qualities, there are continuing doubts about Mr. Reagan that boil down to whether he really runs the government. There are charges he relies too much on his staff. That he is too passive." Up to that point in his presidency, Reagan had spent one out of every six days in office on vacation, and top administration officials called Reagan "disengaged," Wallace reported. He spent only one-third of his time on policy and two-thirds on ceremonial activities.[3]

The same caricature has dominated scholarly works, summed up by the critique of historian Gary Wills, who referred to Reagan as "Mr. Magoo."[4] Even close associates who admired Reagan noted his "lack of curiosity" and passivity.[5] Such critiques have merit and aptly describe the president's attitude in many instances. But the portrayal is too simplistic. It overlooks the times when Reagan was deeply involved, knowledgeable, and the driving force behind his administration's policy.[6]

Despite perceptions of an ill-defined foreign policy, Reagan, like his predecessors, frequently engaged in personal diplomacy. By the end of his first year in office, he had met with foreign leaders twenty-nine times in the United States, traveled to Canada for a state visit and the G-7 summit, and attended the International Meeting on Cooperation and Development in Mexico with almost twenty other world leaders. Reagan's early contacts with foreign leaders made it clear that the administration saw value in presidential personal diplomacy. For example, at the economic summit in Mexico, the president's bilateral meetings were considered crucial. Those one-on-one meetings provided an opportunity for Reagan to explain his views to other leaders, advance US objectives, and lay the groundwork for future cooperation.[7] And symbolically, the bilateral meetings suggested an active and engaged president. When the summit was over, Secretary of State Alexander Haig boasted that, as a result of Reagan's efforts, the administration had achieved "in two days what might take literally months of diplomacy."[8]

At the start of Reagan's presidency, some argued against the use of presidential personal diplomacy—a common assertion at the beginning of many postwar presidencies. One former US ambassador urged Reagan to reject his predecessors' "infatuation" with the practice and return to the "normal if underused channels of international intercourse."[9] But like all presidents since Franklin Roosevelt, Reagan saw the usefulness of engaging his foreign counterparts; among other things, it was a means to gain greater control over foreign policy. Reagan was often disinterested in policy matters and delegated responsibility. But when he was motivated, he could be hands-on and dominant. On matters of great significance, Reagan, like other modern presidents, sought as much control as possible. Direct contact with world leaders helped achieve this goal.

Ultimately, the buck stops at the Oval Office. As a member of the Obama administration's National Security Council (NSC) observed, "given that the president would be the one held accountable by the public, press, and Congress" for every action of his administration, "the incentives usually were for the White House to take more control, not less."[10] In the minds of many presidents and their advisers, foreign affairs bureaucracies—though ostensibly existing to facilitate presidential objectives—are obstacles. For routine diplomacy, the bureaucracy works well. But new, bold initiatives usually require direct, sustained presidential involvement, which often means personal diplomacy. This can eliminate bureaucratic lag, avoid distortion of the president's message, and signal to other nations the importance of a particular initiative.

Confidence and hubris, common to all modern presidents, may encourage them to believe that they can shape their foreign counterparts' thinking and actions. Whether relying on their charisma or on the political, military, and economic might of the nation, presidents frequently believe that if they personally control diplomacy, the nation's foreign policy will be better served. Presidents also use the practice to control and advance their political position, as well as their legacy and place in history. Diplomatic breakthroughs are difficult, and if diplomacy were left to the State Department, the status quo would likely remain unchanged. Personal diplomacy can spur a bold diplomatic initiative and give it force. If successful, the result can be legacy-defining images of a beaming president shaking hands with another world leader.

Personal diplomacy also gives presidents more control by allowing a greater understanding of intentions. Through face-to-face meetings, presidents can better assess the seriousness of their counterparts. A secondhand report about another leader, though valuable, is quite different from sitting across the table from that individual and making a personal assessment. And although misperception is possible, studies have found that face-to-face diplomacy is an effective means of evaluating sincerity and generating empathy.[11]

Using Reagan's engagement with the Soviet Union, this chapter shows how presidents use personal diplomacy to exercise more control over their foreign policy. Reagan's journey from cold warrior to peacemaker was not smooth. His policy was ambiguous. Privately, he tried to engage the Soviet Union, while publicly, he challenged it with bellicose language and a military buildup. The administration, taking its cue from the president, was riddled with divisions between moderates and hard-liners. Though Reagan's personal diplomacy developed in fits and starts, he used it to exert control over his Soviet outreach, avoid bureaucratic infighting and stagnation, overcome hard-liners, and secure his place in history.

THE DESIRE FOR CONTROL

According to James Wilson, Ronald Reagan "was fundamentally of two minds about whether to undermine the Soviet Union or to engage with its leaders."[12] He despised communism and dreamed of its demise, but he also recognized the horrors of nuclear war and wanted to reduce the threat. These two objectives required different approaches: unremitting hostility versus engagement. In the end, the fierce cold warrior chose the latter and sought compromise with his Soviet counterparts.

Though his public rhetoric remained hostile, Reagan tried his hand at personal diplomacy with a succession of Soviet leaders behind the scenes. Engagement, however, did not come easy. The Soviets were leery of the new tough-talking president and unwilling to modify their positions. Just as important were challenges within the Reagan administration, including a cautious, slow-moving bureaucracy and a faction of hawks. If it had been up to these groups, Reagan's initiative might never have advanced. Thus, he had to forcefully insert himself into the diplomatic process.

Fractures within the administration were a central problem. There was discord between the State Department and the NSC, as well as between the State and Defense Departments. Memoirs from the Reagan years are full of bitterness over the disputes between the competing agencies, which resulted in a confused policy-making process and individual enmity.[13] "Morale had been damaged" at the State Department, Haig wrote, as "the making of foreign policy had been preempted by the White House. . . . State had increasingly become a housekeeping agency charged with the errands of foreign policy."[14] Haig's successor at State, George Shultz, had similar concerns. Shultz's memoir is replete with references to his issues with the NSC, at one point calling it a "wildcat operation."[15] A member of the NSC staff, Richard Pipes, recalled that the first eighteen months of Reagan's presidency "passed in an atmosphere of unremitting tension" between the bureaucracies. He branded the State Department the "enemy."[16] The result was a foreign policy team that was, according to chief of staff James Baker, "often a witches' brew of intrigue, elbows, egos, and separate agendas."[17]

Causing further tension was Reagan's heavy reliance on his "troika" of personal advisers—James Baker, Michael Deaver, and Edwin Meese—who dominated policy emanating from the White House during Reagan's first term. The president set the broad agenda, but he allowed his staff a considerable amount of power and autonomy. Decisions were frequently made during discussions between the president and his troika. In Haig's view, these three men "perceived their rank in the Administration as being superior to that of any member of the Cabinet" and "regard[ed] themselves as managers of the Presidency."[18] In many respects, they were. They had full access to the president and his complete trust. "The power dynamic is natural enough," journalist Hedrick Smith explained. "Presidents see their staffs, domestic or foreign policy, as extensions of themselves, whereas they look at cabinet secretaries and departments as sometimes difficult allies or even liabilities and nuisances."[19]

In international affairs, White House aides often exploit a president's desire for control and seize the opportunity to centralize policy making and execution. The result is a diminution of the State Department's influence—and foreign governments know this. In this environment, national security advisers become more influential as "they pull the most urgent business into the White House."[20] For world leaders, then, the most powerful and authoritative messages come from the White House, not from the sprawling US foreign policy bureaucracy.

In addition to infighting, Reagan had to confront hard-liners—many whom he had appointed—who resisted any accommodation with the Soviet Union. As he wrote in his diary, "I think I'm hard-line & will never appease but I do want to try," but "some of the N.S.C. staff are too hard line & don't think any approach should be made to the Soviets."[21] Secretary of Defense Caspar Weinberger was one such hard-liner; he never fully embraced the president's agenda and even went so far as to try to undermine him on the eve of a summit with Soviet leader Mikhail Gorbachev. But, at the urging of Secretary of State Shultz, Reagan would engage his Soviet counterparts to a greater degree than many at the time realized.

REAGAN AND THE SOVIET GERONTOCRACY

In his first press conference as president, Reagan said, "So far détente's been a one-way street that the Soviet Union has used to pursue its own aims . . . the only morality they recognize is what will further their cause, meaning they reserve unto themselves the right to commit any crime, to lie, to cheat." The following year Reagan said the Soviet Union would end up on the "ash-heap of history," and in 1983 he labeled it an "evil empire."[22] That same year he proposed the Strategic Defense Initiative (SDI), a space-based missile defense system, and the "zero option" for intermediate nuclear forces (INF) in Europe, whereby the United States would cancel its deployment of Pershing and

Tomahawk missiles if the Soviet Union dismantled its intermediate-range ballistic missiles. But that proposal was "loaded to Western advantage and Soviet disadvantage," according to arms control expert Raymond Garthoff.[23] Western Europe's missiles were exempt, as were sea- and air-based missiles, in which the United States had an advantage. Many regarded it as a disingenuous offer.

Despite this unyielding public posture, Reagan was more flexible behind the scenes and took the lead in reaching out to the Soviets. "For all his distaste for the Soviet system," recalled Jack Matlock, an NSC Soviet specialist and later ambassador to the Soviet Union, Reagan "nevertheless believed that it could change if subjected to sufficient pressure and his personal negotiating skill."[24] Thus, in April 1981, about a month after John Hinckley Jr.'s attempt on his life, Reagan sent two letters to Soviet leader Leonid Brezhnev. The State Department drafted the first, which was official and formal in tone and was sent through normal diplomatic channels. Reagan personally penned the other letter a week after leaving the hospital. As Michael Deaver, deputy chief of staff, noted, the second letter contained "no proposals, just a direct and personal and thoughtful message to try to nudge the process along."[25] Initially, Reagan was not sure whether he would send the letter, but, as he told his diary, he "enjoyed putting some thoughts down on paper."[26] When he informed his advisers about the letter, they were hesitant. Haig "was reluctant to have *me* actually draft it," the president recalled. "If I was going to send a letter, he said the State Department should compose it."[27] Reagan consented to revisions, but when he received the amended letter a few days later, he did not like the results. It was "a somewhat shorter redraft of his letter, something the State Department might have written twenty years ago. Typical bureaucratese," Deaver remembered.[28] The president agreed. The overall effect, he believed, was a "diluting [of] some of my personal thoughts with stiff diplomatic language that made it more impersonal than I'd wanted."[29] Reagan decided to send his original letter, largely unchanged, as well as a formal State Department message.

The letter to Brezhnev was conciliatory and heartfelt. Recalling their first meeting in the early 1970s, Reagan wrote, "You took my hand in both of yours and assured me . . . that you were dedicated with all your heart and mind to fulfilling those hopes and dreams" of people all over the world who yearned for peace. "It is in this spirit" that Reagan was lifting the US grain embargo on the Soviet Union. He hoped this action would lead to a "meaningful and constructive dialogue which will assist us in fulfilling our joint obligation to find lasting peace."[30]

Brezhnev replied with an "icy" letter, Reagan recalled. "So much for my first attempt at personal diplomacy."[31] The Soviet premier's response, however, was not nearly as cold as the president thought. Soviet specialists at the NSC had a more positive assessment at the time, noting that although the reply was "unbending in substance," it was "conciliatory in tone." He "tries to match the constructive tone of your letter," Reagan's national security adviser told him.[32] Indeed, the main thrust of Brezhnev's message was that his nation did "not seek confrontation." He wrote, "We will never set up the fire of war. You know very well, as we do, what such a fire would lead to."[33]

Despite the conciliatory language, little progress was made on arms reduction. In September Haig suggested sending a message to Brezhnev to regain the "political offensive" and demonstrate to the world that while the United States was interested in peace, the Soviet Union was hindering progress toward that goal. Reagan approved. "Although we would not release the text of the letter," Haig said, "we envisage briefing the press on its main themes in order to create the maximum possible impact on Western opinion."[34] In preparing background for the press, national security adviser Richard Allen's staff advised him to emphasize that world tension was the Soviets' fault. Disagreements between the two nations were not the result of misunderstanding: "There is dialogue . . . the Soviets simply do not like what they are hearing." Through the first five months of 1981, the administration noted, there had been fifty-two exchanges between the two nations. Of these, the United States had initiated thirty-six.[35]

As INF talks went nowhere, progress on strategic arms also faltered. In May 1982 Reagan delivered a commencement address at Eureka College in which he put forth his vision for strategic arms reduction talks (START).[36] Like the zero option, Reagan's START proposals were imbalanced: the Soviets would be required to destroy more of their strategic arsenal than the United States, and the technologies that benefited America would be left untouched. Brezhnev was not impressed. He labeled the proposals "one-sided" and unrealistic. They would endanger "the very stability which the U.S. side is allegedly so anxious to ensure," he told the president. The divide between the two men was clear. "He has to be kidding," an incredulous Reagan wrote in the margin of the letter. "He's a barrel of laughs."[37]

Brezhnev's days of frustrating the president were short-lived. In November 1982 he died. Reagan sent Vice President George H. W. Bush to attend the funeral in Moscow, and the president made the "unusual gesture" of going to the Soviet embassy in Washington to sign the condolence book. "It was a signal," Matlock said, "that he was ready to improve communication with the new Soviet leader."[38]

But the new man at the helm of the Kremlin showed no interest in improving communications. The administration had hoped Brezhnev's passing would lead to changes in Soviet policies, but Yuri Andropov seemed determined to follow in his predecessor's footsteps. "It is becoming increasingly clear that the Andropov approach is not marked by significant experimentation or initiative," the US ambassador in Moscow reported.[39] Reagan, however, still sought to engage him. "I decided to experiment with some personal diplomacy using back channels to the Kremlin," he recalled, "outside the spotlight of publicity" so that both men "could speak frankly without the posturing" that had become so typical in relations between the two nations.[40] Reagan was confident in his abilities. "I felt that if I could ever get in a room alone with one of the top Soviet leaders," he wrote, "there was a chance the two of us could make some progress in easing tensions between our two countries."[41] Reagan would have to wait three more years for his chance.

In February 1983, at the urging of Secretary of State Shultz and over the NSC's protests, Reagan finally met with a Soviet official. He spent two hours with Soviet ambassador Anatoly Dobrynin and made it clear that he wanted to communicate directly with Dobrynin's boss. "I told him I wanted George [Shultz] to be a channel for direct contact with Andropov—no bureaucracy involved," Reagan wrote in his diary.[42] To indicate his seriousness about arms reduction and lessening tensions, he considered appointing a "close personal associate" as ambassador to the Soviet Union. This did not happen, but Matlock believed it showed Reagan's desire to improve relations.[43]

More significantly, Reagan began to seriously consider a summit, something he had rejected at the start of his presidency when Brezhnev broached the issue in an address to the Twenty-Sixth Communist Party Congress in February 1981.[44] Brezhnev's proposal was not a serious one; it was a public relations move. In contrast to Reagan's bellicose rhetoric, Brezhnev sought to portray his nation as moderate and eager to reduce tensions. However, the proposal sent the administration "into a scramble," according to NBC's Marvin Kalb. Reagan had to convey that although he was interested in a "dialogue" through normal diplomatic channels, he was not open to a summit, something he took pains to express in an interview with CBS's Walter Cronkite.[45]

Even if Reagan had agreed to an early meeting in 1981, the Soviet Union mostly likely would have stalled, as Brezhnev's health and mental faculties were not up to the task.[46] By 1983, Reagan wanted to explore the possibility of a summit, and he had Matlock draft a memo laying out the pros and cons of meeting Andropov face-to-face. The main downside was that it would raise public expectations to unrealistic levels. However, Matlock argued that if Reagan made it clear that no agreements would come from a summit—that the meeting would merely spur negotiations that might lead to an accord—the public would understand. The key benefit of a summit "lay in the opportunity for direct communication with the Soviet leader and the push such meetings give bureaucracies to work out as many problems as possible in advance." Reagan read the memo with "care" and made notes in the margins. At least to Matlock, it was clear that the president was searching for a way to meet the Soviet leader.[47] Indeed, in January 1983, as the NSC discussed arms control negotiations, Reagan told his diary, "I was wishing I could do the negotiating with the Soviets."[48]

In July the president sent a handwritten letter to Andropov. With all the world's troubles, they needed "a more active level of exchange than we have heretofore been able to establish," Reagan wrote. He suggested that "private and candid" communication between the two of them would be most effective, and if Andropov "wish[ed] to engage in such communication you will find me ready."[49] Though Reagan wanted a more informal and forthright exchange, he never got it. Andropov's "letters were stiff and cold as a Siberian winter, confined to platitudes," according to the president.[50] Matters were made worse by a series of events that raised tensions and risked direct confrontation, including the Soviet downing of a civilian airliner and the North Atlantic Treaty Organization's (NATO's) Able Archer exercise, which frightened the Soviets and convinced them that a nuclear attack was imminent. Reagan did not have to deal with Andropov's perceived intransigence for long, as the Soviet leader died in February 1984. The administration debated whether the president should attend the funeral but in the end decided against it. "I don't want to honor that prick," Reagan said.[51]

Andropov's successor, Konstantin Chernenko, was a hard-line septuagenarian in ill health. Even so, the president was determined to move forward with a summit. "I have a gut feeling I'd like to talk to him about our problems man to man," Reagan told his diary, "and see if I could convince him" of the benefits of changing Soviet behavior. He directed his advisers to pursue a meeting.[52] Reagan might have had a "gut feeling" that it was time to sit down and talk, but his reelection bid in 1984 gave him further incentive. The aggressive rhetoric and military buildup of his first term, combined with his failure to meet with any Soviet leader, gave Democratic challenger Walter Mondale a line of attack. He portrayed Reagan as a loose cannon edging the nation closer to war. "It's been four years, and President Reagan still hasn't met even once with the leaders of the Soviet Union," a Mondale television ad reminded voters. "The tough talk, the political rhetoric—that's one thing. But no talk—that's dangerous. No conference, no meeting, and the nuclear arms race goes on and on. More nuclear warheads, more threats, but no meeting." Mondale built on this message on the campaign trail, promising that, if elected, he would work to implement annual summits with the Soviets, an idea the Reagan administration rejected.[53]

But these attacks failed to gain much traction. Reagan moderated his tone and modified his stance on a summit. He was now "willing to meet and talk any time," and he met with Soviet foreign minister Andrei Gromyko before the election. The president had vowed not to "play political games with this summit," but to most observers, it seemed that this change in tone was very much about politics. This new stance, combined with an improved economy, reassured the president of a landslide reelection.[54]

Throughout 1984 Reagan and Chernenko corresponded privately. In March the president received a lengthy letter. "First of all," Chernenko wrote, "I would like to emphasize that, like yourself, I value the importance of our correspondence which makes possible a direct exchange of views on the cardinal problems of relations between our countries and the international situation." The Soviet leader described his perception of US-Soviet relations and surveyed the state of world affairs. Reagan was impressed. "I think this calls for a very well thought out reply," he wrote on the message, "not just a routine acknowledgment that leaves the status quo as is."[55]

Reagan's early experience with his letter to Brezhnev and the pushback he received from some of his advisers made him acutely aware that elements within his administration could prevent the type of progress he desired. Reagan lamented that every time he wanted to send a letter to a foreign leader, "copies of my message were usually first circulated to a half-dozen or more agencies at the State Department, the Pentagon, the Commerce Department, and elsewhere for comment and suggestions." Though well meaning, these "bureaucrats down the line . . . would try to add or change something—whether it was needed or not. The result: often a blurring of my original intentions."[56] Starting with his reply to Chernenko's March letter, Reagan decided to sidestep the bureaucracy. Instead, he would draft letters with input from a small group of close advisers. He wanted "a more hands-on approach—without help from the bureaucrats." Shultz agreed, noting that going through the bureaucracy took too long. Matlock thought letters drafted through the bureaucratic process were "devoid of personality," which was especially harmful to Reagan, "whose personality and charm were his greatest assets."[57] For the president, a direct exchange outside official diplomatic channels gave him more control and ensured that his messages would be taken seriously. "It is important to recognize that the purpose of establishing a White House–Kremlin channel was to get results," national security adviser Robert McFarlane noted, because "the Soviets had not taken traffic in normal diplomatic channels as authoritative." They considered messages sent through regular channels as "simply grandstanding for domestic consumption."[58]

In April 1984 Reagan sent Chernenko a letter stating that the United States was "ready for a turning point," but it needed to be met halfway. In a handwritten postscript, Reagan reassured the Soviet leader that he was committed to working for peace and acknowledged the psychological trauma of Soviet history: "I have reflected at some length on the tragedy and scale of Soviet losses in warfare through the ages. Surely those losses, which are beyond description, must affect your thinking today. I want you to know that neither I nor the American people hold any offensive intentions toward you or the Soviet people."[59] Chernenko's response was "correct and non-polemical," but it did not move relations or arms negotiations forward. His letter "made clear," Matlock recalled, "that a summit meeting was out of the question."[60]

Reagan was undeterred. "His reply to my letter is in hand & it lends support to my idea that while we go on believing & with some good reason, that the Soviets are plotting against us & mean us harm, maybe they are scared of us & think we are a threat," he wrote in his diary. "I'd like to go face to face & explore this with them."[61] Reagan never got the chance. For the third time in less than three years, the head of the Soviet Union died. The question once again arose: should the president attend the funeral? He wanted to meet the new Soviet leader Mikhail Gorbachev, but if he went to the funeral, his meeting with Gorbachev would be brief, and he would be competing for time with other foreign visitors. Reagan decided to wait.[62]

REAGAN AND GORBACHEV

Vice President Bush again went to Moscow to represent the United States at Chernenko's funeral, and he carried a letter from Reagan inviting Gorbachev to visit. "You can be assured of my personal commitment to work with you . . . in serious negotiations," the president told the new Soviet leader. "I want you to know that I look forward to a meeting that could yield results of benefit to both our countries and to the international community as a whole."[63] Gorbachev responded in a "non-polemical tone," according to Shultz, and was favorably disposed to a summit.[64] Improved relations were "not only extremely necessary, but possible, too," Gorbachev said, and he expressed a "positive attitude" about meeting face-to-face. They would not have to sign a major agreement, he noted; rather, "the main thing is that it should be a meeting to search for mutual understanding."[65]

Both sides professed a desire to meet, but location and timing became an issue. Reagan invited Gorbachev to Washington, but his delay in accepting led some in the administration to propose holding the summit somewhere else. Hard-liners—who wanted no summit at all—took issue. "Uncomfortable with the president's desire to have a face-to-face meeting with the Soviet leader," Matlock recalled, hard-liners "kept insisting that the summit be held in Washington if it was to take place at all." These antisummit forces cited protocol. They argued that because the last two summits had been held in neutral nations and the two before that had been in the Soviet Union, it was the Soviet leader's turn to come to the United States. According to Matlock, "their real reason was to create an image of a Soviet leader begging for concessions."[66] As a meeting in Washington seemed less and less likely, Reagan seriously considered going to Moscow. When the Soviets proposed a neutral site, Shultz, fearing that prospects for a summit were dimming, urged Reagan to accept. The president, "eager, above all, to go head-to-head with the Soviet leader," approved.[67]

Geneva, Switzerland, was the site chosen for the first meeting between a US president and a Soviet general secretary since 1979. But before the November talks, Reagan had to prepare. McFarlane worried about the president's grasp of details, so he had Matlock design "Soviet Union 101," consisting of twenty-one papers, eight to ten pages each, covering Soviet history and psychology.[68] Never one for extensive preparation, Reagan took an uncharacteristic interest in readying himself for his encounter with Gorbachev. He "became a near-Russophile over the course of the next six months, studying each paper throughout and waiting eagerly for the next," McFarlane recalled. "President Reagan was clearly determined to be thoroughly prepared. . . . He worked hard, and by the time he reached Geneva, was thoroughly in command of his brief."[69] The president even did a bit of role-playing, having Matlock take the part of Gorbachev and even having him speak in Russian, giving the president a feel for what a face-to-face meeting with the Soviet leader would be like. By the time he was done, Reagan knew exactly "what he wanted to say and how he would say it."[70]

The administration at large also prepared. It outlined the themes and perceptions it wanted to highlight publicly and compiled a schedule of speeches, events, and meetings with foreign leaders in the lead-up to the summit.[71] Public relations were just as important as policy. As Dan Rather mused, the meeting might be "as much a summit of images as issues." Thus, the administration spent a lot of time on its public message.[72] Reagan even sat down with Soviet journalists for an interview that appeared in the newspaper *Izvestia*, marking the first time members of the Soviet media had questioned an American president since Kennedy. CBS's Mark Phillips called it "remarkable" that the American president's views would be conveyed to the Soviet public in this way.[73]

Privately, Shultz warned the president that the talks "will not be an easy task." He questioned to what extent Gorbachev and his associates were willing to soften their positions. But if Reagan could "develop a personal relationship with Gorbachev" and engage in frank discussions about US-Soviet tensions and how to deal with them, Shultz believed they could "take a substantial step forward."[74] McFarlane sent the president a memo prepared by Matlock along similar lines. The summit would give Reagan a chance to "get a feel for Gorbachev's intentions," and it would allow the Soviet leader to do the same. Though he would probably fiercely criticize US policy, Gorbachev wanted a "successful summit" to bolster his image and political position back home. He wanted to show that he could "deal as an equal" with the American president. Overall, the meeting provided "the occasion to initiate a process of dialogue which can be used, over time, to manage the relationship in a more stable and predictable manner than has been the case in the past."[75]

Another issue that surfaced on the road to Geneva was how to record the summit. The State Department prepared in advance a joint statement that could be issued after the talks. Reagan rejected this. He did not want a "'pre-cooked' summit. . . . He wanted the meeting in Geneva to be *his* meeting," according to Matlock. Reagan wanted any postsummit statement to reflect what actually took place. This worried the bureaucracies of both nations. "The very idea! Reagan was insisting that they do what he and Gorbachev decided!" Matlock sarcastically recalled. "In the mind of bureaucrats in both countries, neither [man] had the knowledge and experience to be trusted with decisions. But the fact was that our respective bureaucracies had spun their wheels for years without tangible result. It was time for the president and general secretary to take charge."[76]

Given Reagan's reputation, taking charge was out of character. But in his engagement with Soviet leaders, that is exactly what he did. Reagan could sometimes be extremely detached, but on major issues that captivated him, he could "be more actively engaged and more involved in minute details than even such notorious micromanagers as Richard Nixon and Jimmy Carter," according to former journalist and foreign correspondent James Mann.[77] In the weeks leading up to Geneva, the president was determined to make the summit his own. This was not an easy task, as he had to battle hard-liners both inside and outside his administration who viewed negotiations with the Soviets as foolish.

When Reagan first proposed a summit in March, reports of rumblings within the administration quickly became public. "There is no laughter here about what officials are calling the outbreak of summit fever," NBC's Chris Wallace reported. There was a "split" in the White House between pro- and antisummit forces. On the eve of the summit, that "split" became "open and bloody warfare." Even though Defense Department officials were banned from giving television interviews, Secretary Weinberger delivered harsh speeches about the Soviet Union and took a hawkish position on arms control.[78] On November 15 he publicly released a letter he had sent to Reagan urging him to take a tough stance with the Soviets. He advised the president to resist pressure to continue adhering to SALT II, as well as any attempts to impose restrictions on SDI. Weinberger was also very concerned about the Soviets' failure to live up to past arms control agreements, and he urged the president to end this practice.[79] Press secretary Larry Speakes branded the letter "almost treasonous, since it was designed to ruin the summit."[80] Reagan was "furious," and he had a right to be. As Matlock recalled, "the letter was a public display of Weinberger's lack of confidence in the president's judgment."[81]

Despite his lack of experience in diplomacy, Reagan was confident in his abilities, and the American public trusted him.[82] As images of past presidential summits with Soviet leaders flashed across the television screen, ABC's Sander Vanocur reported that Reagan was in a "stronger political position than any American president of the past thirty-five years has been on the eve of a summit" with the Soviets. According to an ABC/*Washington Post* poll, his overall approval rating was at 63 percent, and his foreign affairs approval rating was 62 percent, a seven-point increase since September and the highest it had been in four years. Vanocur speculated that if Reagan got lucky in Geneva, he might return to the United States as "the most powerful American president since Franklin D. Roosevelt."[83]

Reagan and Gorbachev spent about eight hours together over two days; for half that time, they met one-on-one with only their interpreters present. In their first private meeting, the president told the Soviet leader they "could really talk now." Rather than discussing arms control specifically, which they would do in plenary sessions, Reagan said their private talks should focus on "eliminat[ing] the suspicions which each side had of the other. The resolution of other questions would follow naturally after this."[84] The two men jostled over various issues, such as human rights and their respective nation's global activities, but the main area of contention was SDI. Neither side would budge, and substantial progress on arms reduction remained elusive.[85]

The main story line coming out of Geneva was the intense personal diplomacy that took place and the president's authority and control, with minimal assistance from advisers. "What was most striking about this summit," NBC's John Chancellor proclaimed, "was Mr. Reagan's dominance of it. He set the themes, and in his remarkable series of personal meetings with Gorbachev he set the style."[86] Indeed, Reagan "glowed with pride and a sense of accomplishment," according to chief of staff Donald Regan.[87]

Reagan and Gorbachev's first private meeting went well beyond the scheduled fifteen minutes. It "excited the h—l out of the Press," the president told his diary.[88] The fact that the two men spent more time in private, informal talks than in sessions with aides was "perhaps the most intriguing development," according to one journalist.[89] This occurred thanks to Reagan's "initiative," resulting in "the most extensive personal diplomacy between an American president and Kremlin leaders since World War II."[90] Officials in Geneva went one step further, claiming that the two leaders' personal diplomacy "had no equals in the annals of previous summit meetings."[91]

Publicly, Gorbachev said he was "optimistic" that the "world has become a safer place." Privately, he was less sanguine. Reagan "does not seem to hear what I am trying to say," he lamented.[92] Upon returning home he said, "Reagan is maneuvering . . . the essence of his policy—the policy of the military-industrial complex—has not changed, there was no increased love toward us." At the same time, however, he thought the president "was a man you could do business with."[93]

Reagan felt similarly, although, on a personal level, he felt more of a connection than the general secretary did. He respected Gorbachev; "in fact, he liked the man," according to Matlock.[94] But Reagan had no illusions. Writing to a friend soon after the summit, he noted that the talks were "worthwhile, but it would be foolish to believe the leopard will change his spots. [Gorbachev] is a firm believer in their system . . . and he believes the propaganda they peddle about us." But Reagan also recognized that the general secretary was "practical" and could be convinced to make a deal.[95]

THE HIGHS AND LOWS OF SUMMITRY

After Geneva, Reagan wanted to quickly follow up with the Soviet leader, and he instructed Matlock to draft a letter. "Eager to avoid the delays of interagency consideration and bickering between Shultz and Weinberger," Matlock recalled, "Reagan intended to copy my draft in his own handwriting," which he did. The president believed that a letter in his own hand would encounter less resistance from the bureaucracies. So, just a week after Geneva, a presidential letter was on its way to Gorbachev. If routine procedures had been followed, with the usual back and forth between the various agencies, it might have taken weeks or even months for a letter to be sent to the Kremlin.[96]

Reagan's message noted that a formal letter through official channels would be forthcoming, but he "wanted to waste no time in giving you some of my initial thoughts on our meetings . . . [because] there are some things I would like to convey very personally & privately." The letter highlighted the value of Geneva, which had allowed them to reach a better understanding of each other. "Both of us have advisers & assistants," Reagan wrote, "but, you know, in the final analysis, the responsibility to preserve peace & increase cooperation is ours." Reagan's letter also tried to assuage Soviet fears over SDI.[97] For domestic reasons, Gorbachev did not want to appear too eager. He took almost a month to reply, and it was not encouraging. From the administration's view, Gorbachev's answer was combative and only rehashed old Soviet arguments.[98]

Despite the disappointing response, Reagan still looked forward to meeting again with Gorbachev and was eager to negotiate an arms reduction agreement.[99] At Geneva, the two had decided that Gorbachev would come to the United States, but the timing of that visit was anyone's guess. Arms control negotiations at lower levels were stalled, and the Soviet leader had difficulties at home, including a nuclear accident at Chernobyl and trouble implementing perestroika. Then, the arrest of a Soviet spy in the United States caused the Soviets to retaliate by arresting an American journalist for espionage. Prospects for a summit seemed dim.[100]

But both men still hoped to make progress. In September 1986 Gorbachev wrote to Reagan and acknowledged that negotiations "will lead nowhere unless you and I intervene personally." He proposed "a quick one-on-one meeting . . . to engage in a strictly confidential, private, and frank discussion."[101] A month later, the two men were face-to-face at a neutral site: Reykjavik, Iceland. Before the meeting, Gorbachev made a litany of concessions, moving significantly toward the American position on an INF agreement.[102] But neither side had much time to prepare, leading to doubts about what could be accomplished. Matlock did not share this concern. He assured the president that his one-on-one talks with Gorbachev, not bureaucratic preparation, were most important because in "Soviet eyes a real leader does not need to be propped up by a lot of 'advisers.'"[103]

Indeed, at Reykjavik, Reagan would make more progress than any of his advisers imagined. Gorbachev proposed to cut strategic arms by 50 percent and eliminate both nations' intermediate-range nuclear forces in Europe. SDI, however, continued to be a problem. Gorbachev wanted to consign it to the laboratory, but this was a nonstarter for the president. As Shultz noted, SDI was "personal" for Reagan. He saw SDI as defensive and could not understand the Soviets' concerns. In a July 1986 letter to Gorbachev, Reagan wanted to include a section about sharing the technology, but the bureaucracy was opposed. "Damn it," Reagan said, "it is my letter, that's what I am going to do."[104] Despite Reagan's assurances about sharing, the Soviets had little faith, and such promises were not enough to overcome their concerns at Reykjavik.

On the second day, the discussions became increasingly heated. Gorbachev felt that Reagan was not making any concessions, and Reagan could not understand Soviet concerns about SDI. After the third session—which was scheduled to be the last—it was announced that the two men would meet for a fourth time. This news shocked some in the American delegation. As one US arms control expert recalled, when Reagan and Gorbachev announced another meeting, "I knew Reykjavik had changed. No longer were the President of the United States and General Secretary of the Soviet Union reading staff papers to one another. No longer were they blessing what their arms control teams had worked out. They would move from headquarters in base camp to the front lines. They would become negotiators-in-chief."[105]

This unscheduled fourth meeting became "the highest stakes poker game ever played," according to Shultz.[106] As the two men went back and forth, they proposed something radical. "It would be fine . . . if we eliminated all nuclear weapons," Reagan proclaimed. "We can do that," Gorbachev replied. "We can eliminate them." But once again, SDI divided the two men, and they could not bridge the gap. Reagan implored Gorbachev to do him a "favor" and accept his view on SDI, but the Soviet leader refused.[107] "I don't know when we'll ever have another chance like this and whether we will meet soon," the president lamented as they parted. "I don't either," Gorbachev glumly responded.[108]

The dominant image from Reykjavik was the somber-faced leaders going their separate ways. "Something had gone wrong," Nancy Reagan recalled thinking after seeing her husband on television. "He looked angry, very angry. His face was pale and his teeth were clenched."[109] This was not the image the administration wanted to present to the world. As press secretary Larry Speakes recalled, the administration went on an "unprecedented news blitz" to avoid the perception of failure. Although US public opinion was with Reagan, western European leaders bristled at the president's proposal to eliminate all nuclear weapons without consulting them first.[110]

But the situation was not as dire as the two leaders' body language suggested. Speaking to reporters after Reagan's departure, Gorbachev said, "It's not a failure; it's a breakthrough." On the plane ride back to the Soviet Union, he expounded on this, saying that both sides now had a better understanding of the other's position, and it was clear that an agreement could be reached. "We need not fall into despair," Gorbachev said. "I am even more of an optimist after Reykjavik."[111] Initially, Reagan and Shultz were extremely disappointed, but Matlock and other assistants assured them that Reykjavik was far from a failure. The Soviets were closer to the US position on arms control than ever before. They appeared ready to make a deal.[112]

Upon returning home, the Reagan administration became ensnared in the Iran-Contra scandal, and arms control talks were put on the back burner for the rest of the year. In February 1987, however, Gorbachev restarted the arms control process. He signaled his willingness to negotiate along American lines, separating an INF treaty from START and SDI, and he invited Shultz to Moscow for talks.

From the beginning, Reagan's commitment to SDI concerned the Soviet leadership. For the Soviet Union, the prospect of an SDI arms race was untenable; it could not keep up with the current arms race, much less a new one. Gorbachev wanted to shelve SDI, but in the end, his retreat on SDI was dependent on a mix of assurances from Soviet scientists, who said SDI was unrealistic, and his understanding that Reagan was deeply committed to the program, and nothing would change that.[113]

An INF agreement took shape over the ensuing months, and Gorbachev came to Washington in December 1987 to sign it.[114] The Soviet leader's visit was the culmination of a long process for Reagan, who had long desired a US summit. In fact, the president had talked so much about a Gorbachev visit that he even irritated Shultz, who was a summit supporter. Upon learning of the president's idea to invite Gorbachev to his California ranch for Thanksgiving, Shultz recalled saying, "Oh, stop. . . . Let the summit idea alone; quit pressing."[115]

Gorbachev's visit came at a propitious moment for Reagan, providing some positive headlines after months of domination by the Iran-Contra affair. But Reagan still found himself parrying attacks from conservatives. For example, the head of the Conservative Caucus called Reagan a "useful idiot for Soviet propaganda."[116] In the days leading up to the summit, the president took a hard line in public, hoping to assuage his critics. While asserting that Gorbachev was "different than past Soviet leaders," he also said he would walk away from a "bad deal." White House press secretary Marlin Fitzwater said the summit should be seen not as "a session to be taken lightly between old friends" but rather as "a summit between old enemies."[117]

More than in their past two meetings, public relations overshadowed their private talks, and the two leaders spent more time doing public events than meeting one-on-one.[118] This was probably for the best, as their private talks did not go particularly well. Reagan reverted to his usual anti-Soviet jokes and stories, which greatly irritated Gorbachev, who felt the president did not appreciate the significant changes he was implementing in the Soviet Union. Reagan's advisers were alarmed by his performance, and the president himself recognized his error. In his next private meeting with Gorbachev, he behaved better.[119]

Reagan's showing behind closed doors did not go well, but publicly he excelled. "The Washington summit was a milestone for its ceremony, symbolism, and public impact," according to James Mann. "The event dramatized to the American public, in a way that no other event had, that the Cold War was subsiding . . . [and] in all of this Reagan led the way. When it came to shaping the public mood, particularly about the Cold War, he was the driving force for his own administration."[120] The focus on public diplomacy paid off. Despite pockets of conservative dismay, the majority of the American public was enamored with the summit in general and with Gorbachev in particular. "Gorby fever" gripped the capital. Newspapers reported that there was an "air of excitement and drama," and the capital was "charged with electricity." Estimates predicated that 6,000 journalists would descend on Washington to cover the event.[121] Vice President Bush, who would be mounting his own bid for president the following year, tried to tap into this public excitement. He made sure to be seen with the Soviet leader as much as possible and met with him three times.[122]

Five months later, Reagan was in Moscow. Yet, as he left for the first presidential visit to the Soviet Union in more than ten years, the Senate still had not approved the INF treaty. A failure to ratify would have been a severe rebuke of Reagan's personal diplomacy. In the end, it passed 93 to 5, but not before conservative elements tried to attach crippling amendments.[123] No substantive agreements were reached during the Moscow talks, as both sides rehashed their standard arguments. But they did so "without heat," and their meetings were "pale and largely ceremonial."[124] Like at the Washington summit, the public aspects of the Moscow summit were paramount—particularly for Gorbachev, who was still in the midst of a colossal struggle to reform the Soviet Union. A successful summit, the thinking went, would strengthen his domestic position and prove that his policies had resulted in peace and enhanced Soviet prestige, thus silencing challenges to his leadership.[125]

Gorbachev wanted help from Reagan and hoped the president would tone down his rhetoric. But Reagan had his own domestic audience to play to and kept up the attacks on the Soviet Union. The general secretary was not pleased, but once in Moscow, Reagan struck a different tone. He said that Gorbachev was a different type of leader, and although disagreements between the two nations remained, they were waning. When asked who should receive credit for the improvement in relations, Reagan replied that most of it should go to Gorbachev.[126]

The iconic moment from the Moscow summit was the two leaders' stroll through Red Square. When a reporter asked the president whether he still considered the Soviet Union an "evil empire," Reagan replied, "No, I was talking about another time and another era."[127] Indeed, in less than three years, the president and the Soviet leader had met four times. "Summitry no longer requires some wrenching act of will. To meet with the Soviet leader will now be the expected thing for American presidents, rather than the exceptional," a former State Department official noted after Moscow. Reagan had given meetings with the head of the Kremlin a "routine quality."[128]

No one would accuse Reagan of being a workaholic or a micromanager. In the lead-up to the 1980 election, he once complained about having to get up early to campaign, to which one of his advisers said, "You better get used to it. . . . When you're president, that fellow from the National Security Council will be there to brief you at seven thirty every morning." Reagan replied, "He's going to have a helluva long wait."[129] But on issues of importance that were close to his heart, he could exhibit considerable interest and a desire to manage and control. Despite having contradictory impulses, improving relations with the Soviets to reduce nuclear stockpiles was one such issue. To make progress, Reagan felt he had to engage with his Soviet counterparts. And although he did not obtain everything he desired—a strategic arms agreement remained elusive—the INF treaty was more than many thought possible at the start of his presidency.

None of this would have happened without Gorbachev, who was the key player in many ways. By the 1980s, the Soviet system was in trouble. Its oppressive government continued to weigh on its people. Its economy was moribund; its bureaucracy sclerotic; its military-industrial complex bloated. The war in Afghanistan was a continuous drain of blood and treasure. But the Soviet Union could have limped along for years, perhaps even into the twenty-first century.[130] Most Soviet officials were against large-scale reform, so although his nation's challenges incentivized his outreach, Gorbachev was the driving force in improved US-Soviet relations.

But Reagan's willingness to engage through personal diplomacy was equally crucial.[131] From the start, Reagan recalled:

> I'd dreamed of personally going one-on-one with a Soviet leader because I thought we might be able to accomplish things our countries' diplomats couldn't

do because they didn't have the authority. . . . I felt that if you got the top people negotiating and talking at a summit and then the two of you came out arm in arm saying, "We've agreed to this," the bureaucrats wouldn't be able to louse up the agreement.[132]

This is an idealized vision of personal diplomacy, but Reagan is describing the rationale of many presidents. Leader-to-leader engagement is an attractive option because it is often seen as the best way to advance both US foreign policy aims and more personal objectives.

Despite the advantages, there are risks. Many observers, particularly professional diplomats, have bemoaned the practice of personal diplomacy by political leaders as ineffective and dangerous. Leaders often do not fully understand the issues at stake and do not know how to negotiate. And what happens if a president makes a mistake? What happens if a president makes a bad deal? Dean Acheson said it best: "When a chief of state or head of government makes a fumble, the goal line is open behind him."[133]

"Although much has been accomplished by the President's leadership . . . to meet the challenge of this crossroad in mankind's destiny, the President must take personal command of the foreign policy agenda for the 1980s."[134] This was the analysis of NSC staffers in 1984. Though self-congratulatory, it encapsulates a vision of the presidency that many have: a leader boldly charting a foreign policy course and actively pursuing it. Yet all postwar presidents have met resistance, whether it has taken the form of international developments beyond the control of the White House, hostile elements within the United States, or bureaucratic stagnation.

With all that could stymie a president, a more hands-on approach became desirable. Controlling both the strategy and the tactics of foreign policy became a trend, and one of its central elements was direct engagement with foreign leaders. Personal diplomacy allowed presidents to give impetus to their agendas, circumvent unresponsive bureaucracies, and send stronger, clearer messages that were taken more seriously than statements at lower diplomatic levels. It was also a way for presidents to take control of building their own legacies. In the end, regardless of who is involved in the creation and execution of foreign policy, the president is ultimately held responsible. That is a strong incentive for presidents to take a hands-on approach. Though not always effective, personal diplomacy is a tool that can help them better manage their foreign policy.

8. George H. W. Bush and Personal Diplomacy at the End of the Cold War

In a little over a month, George H. W. Bush would be president, and personal diplomacy would be the hallmark of his foreign policy. But in December 1988 he was not ready to meet with Mikhail Gorbachev, who was in New York to deliver a major speech at the United Nations pledging huge reductions in the Soviet military presence in eastern Europe.

Months before the US presidential election, Anatoly Dobrynin, former Soviet ambassador to the United States, had recommended that Gorbachev arrange a meeting with the next American president. It is "extremely important to seek mutual understanding with the new President early," Dobrynin advised, and he urged Gorbachev to take "an extraordinary step" and meet with the president-elect before the inauguration. Gorbachev should also meet with Ronald Reagan one last time, Dobrynin suggested, as the outgoing president was popular and could still influence American public opinion.[1]

Bush, however, was worried about committing himself to anything specific before he had the opportunity to thoroughly review US-Soviet relations. Outgoing national security adviser Colin Powell reassured the president-elect that the US side had made it clear that the meeting with Gorbachev was not a summit; there would be no negotiations. Gorbachev would simply bid Reagan farewell and greet the incoming president. As Powell recalled, Bush agreed, "But he was very uneasy about it."[2]

Powell thought the meeting went well, but the conversation between Bush and Gorbachev was not particularly warm. During a private session (which included Reagan) and a luncheon (which included other US and Soviet officials), Gorbachev tried to engage Bush and expressed his desire for "continuity" in US-Soviet relations. Gorbachev was a man in a hurry; with mounting domestic problems, he needed Bush in his corner.[3] Bush indicated that he wanted to build on the progress of the last eight years, but the president-elect informed the Soviet leader that he needed time to review the issues.

Gorbachev left New York disappointed. He made his dramatic announcement about troop reductions and was welcomed to the city by cheering crowds, but Bush's response to his outreach was less than encouraging.[4] As he told the Politburo weeks later, although the new administration would make no moves to increase tensions, it would take no bold action to move relations forward, either.[5]

It would be a year before Bush and Gorbachev met again, but not because of any aversion to leader-to-leader diplomacy on Bush's part. In fact, he embraced the practice more than any other postwar president, and scholars recognize that personal diplomacy was central to Bush's foreign policy.[6] He had a natural affinity for the practice and had honed his skills as UN ambassador, envoy to China, and vice president. Less recognized is that he was drawn to the practice for the same reasons as his predecessors. Throughout his time in office, he engaged heads of state and government to deal with global crises, to exercise more control over his foreign policy, because other leaders sought him out, and for domestic political gain. Additionally, he played the role of counselor, attempting to ease the concerns of both allies and adversaries.

This chapter explores how Bush used personal diplomacy as the Cold War ended and a new global era began. It provides snapshots of Bush's leader-to-leader engagement by examining US relations with communist nations, German unification, the Persian Gulf crisis, and the changing nature of foreign policy in the early 1990s. These cases illustrate that the same forces driving presidential personal diplomacy during the Cold War were still operating as it ended, and they continued to play a role in the post–Cold War era.

BUSH'S APPROACH

From the early days of the Bush presidency, it was clear that personal diplomacy would be central. During his first weeks in office, Bush kept busy and called his foreign counterparts often, at both scheduled and unscheduled times. Three weeks after taking office, he went on his first trip abroad, visiting Canada and meeting with Prime Minister Brian Mulroney, who would become a close friend and ally. Less than two weeks later, the new president embarked on a whirlwind journey to Japan, China, and South Korea. During the transition, Bush had contemplated an early trip to China, but there had been no reasonable justification for one. Then the Japanese emperor died, giving Bush an opportunity to attend the funeral and tack on a trip to China, becoming the first president to travel to Asia before visiting Europe.[7] The trip to

Japan was symbolically important, as the president's attendance at the funeral demonstrated America's commitment to its most important Asian ally. But, as ABC's Peter Jennings reported, "the chance to do business is irresistible." Within hours of landing after a fifteen-hour flight, Bush had planned eight back-to-back meetings. In total, he met with nineteen world leaders.[8]

After the whirlwind diplomacy in Japan, China welcomed Bush as a *lao pengyou*, or "old friend," from his days as US envoy to China in the 1970s. Bush seemed to enjoy being back in the country, and although he was "pursuing serious big power diplomacy," he was also "genuinely enjoying a visit to an old home city," CBS's Dan Rather reported.[9] Secretary of State James Baker reminded Bush that in his talks with Chinese leaders, the "key purpose is to consolidate your personal ties," which would strengthen US-China relations.[10] The president felt "optimistic" about his talks and thought the two sides were developing a level of trust that would allow them to discuss their problems and differences frankly. As Deng Xiaoping told Bush, he hoped for a "new pattern" in relations, one marked by "mutual trust, mutual support, and minimizing as much as possible the problems" between their nations. Bush heartily agreed.[11]

This early trip set the tone for a presidency defined by personal diplomacy. "I think in all of the events of the Bush administration from the end of the Cold War, the collapse of the Soviet Union, liberation of Eastern Europe, reunification of Germany to the Gulf War, that Bush's personal diplomacy played a huge role in all of them in many ways," recalled Bush's CIA director Robert Gates.[12] Others came to similar conclusions. It was clear to journalists that Bush, as well as Secretary Baker, "like[d] to bypass ambassadors, experts and bureaucrats, and deal directly with their counterparts around the globe."[13] Indeed, Bush's memoir is full of episodes involving his interactions with heads of state and government. For him, cultivating relationships was not merely about being amicable; it also advanced the nation's interests. "If a foreign leader knows the character and the heartbeat of the president (and vice versa), there is apt to be far less miscalculation on either side," Bush explained. "Personal relationships may not overcome tough issues dividing two sides, but they can provide enough goodwill to avoid some misunderstandings. . . . It can make the difference between suspicion and giving each other the benefit of the doubt—and room to maneuver on a difficult political issue."[14]

Although Bush frequently met face-to-face with his foreign counterparts, the telephone became central to his personal diplomacy, and he often took the lead in initiating calls.[15] According to national security adviser Brent

Scowcroft, telephone calls augmented regular diplomatic channels, but they also made some diplomats nervous.[16] Leader-to-leader interaction "makes it harder to keep the U.S. government's vast foreign policy apparatus in tune with what's going on at the top," complained one former ambassador during Bush's first year. And when a president speaks on the telephone with another leader, it can be dangerous because he "is performing without a safety net."[17] However, many (but not all) of Bush's counterparts welcomed his approach and appreciated his frequent calls. For others, Bush's surprise calls made them uncomfortable, and they lamented the president's "telephonitis." "Why does he keeping doing this?" complained one foreign official.[18]

Bush's penchant for telephone diplomacy sometimes led to embarrassment. In March 1990 the president was fooled into taking a telephone call from someone claiming to be Ali Akbar Hashemi Rafsanjani, the president of Iran. The Rafsanjani impersonator said he wanted to discuss freeing the American hostages in Lebanon. According to the White House press secretary, the president took the call, even though he thought it was "suspicious in origin." At a press conference, Bush explained why: If there was any possibility the call was legitimate and might help the hostages, he "would be remiss" if he did not take it. "I owe it to the families," he said. But good intentions do not protect a president from being mocked. The real Rafsanjani used the incident to needle Bush. "Iran's stature in the world is so high," the Iranian leader boasted, "that the strongest power in the world and the greatest power on Earth is striving to find an opening with your executive leader even through telephone wires." The president was unfazed. Would he do it again if the situation presented itself? "Yes," he said, "I probably would."[19]

For Bush, the benefits of the telephone outweighed any potential discomfort or embarrassment because it permitted him to be hands-on. He could engage in a frank discussion of issues while gleaning information from his counterparts that the bureaucracy could not provide. It allowed him to be "an activist," he told one cabinet secretary. His domestic accomplishments were limited by a Democratic Congress, but he could call world leaders and "get things done."[20]

CHINA AND THE SOVIET UNION

If Bush's early trip to China left him buoyed, his optimism about US-China relations quickly waned, and questions about the efficacy of personal diplomacy emerged. In June 1989 the Chinese leadership initiated a violent crackdown against protesters in Tiananmen Square. Global condemnation was swift. Bush denounced the violence and announced the suspension of military sales and meetings between US and Chinese military officials, but many thought the president's response was too muted.[21]

The president was trying to walk a tightrope: he abhorred the violence, but he wanted to keep a line of communication open with Beijing. So Bush called Deng Xiaoping, but the Chinese leader refused to take his call. Bush was "a little pissed off" by this, as he told his diary.[22] The president's inability to get in touch with Deng led some in the White House to think he was ill or possibly dead. As Baker noted, "When the President of the United States calls . . . you usually take his call."[23] The simple truth was that Deng did not want to talk. This hurt Bush because he considered the Chinese leader a friend.

With his attempts to get through by telephone stymied, Bush sent Deng a personal message. "I write this letter with a heavy heart," the president began. "I wish there were some way to discuss this matter in person." Bush assured Deng that he was writing "in the spirit of genuine friendship," but he was under pressure to take more punitive actions. He needed the Chinese leadership to work with him, and to that end, he proposed sending an emissary to discuss matters. Bush hoped for a personal reply from Deng because, as he noted, "this matter is too important to be left to our bureaucracies." Indeed, on the US side, only Bush, Baker, Scowcroft, and chief of staff John Sununu knew about the letter, which Scowcroft hand-delivered to the Chinese ambassador.[24]

According to historian Jeffrey Engel, it was a "remarkable letter, interweaving affairs of state with personal remembrances." It was also risky. Deng could have publicized the letter and embarrassed Bush, but to the Americans' surprise, he responded less than twenty-four hours later. He liked the idea of an emissary, so Bush sent Scowcroft to China.[25] There were no breakthroughs, but the fact that the two sides met in the midst of such a crisis was what mattered. For the remainder of Bush's presidency, however, US-China relations "treaded water," according to Baker.[26]

Critics charged that Bush let his personal relationship with Deng prevent him from imposing more severe measures, and he would later admit that his personal ties "colored his every move during the crisis."[27] However, his relatively light-handed approach, in Bush's words, "kept the door open" for dialogue, which paid dividends the following year when Bush was assembling a coalition against Saddam Hussein.[28] But as journalist James Mann noted, "At the time when it mattered, Bush's friendship with Deng Xiaoping didn't count for much."[29]

If Bush's personal diplomacy fell short with one communist power, it helped with another. As noted earlier, President Bush delayed his first official meeting with Mikhail Gorbachev. Scowcroft recalled, "There were definitely advantages to an early summit. It could capture the popular imagination and get us off to a flashy start." But the administration wanted more than publicity; it wanted tangible results. And Scowcroft believed that "poorly prepared or cosmetic summits were dangerous" because they benefited only the Soviets, not the United States.[30]

However, when Gorbachev came to the United States to meet President Reagan and sign the Intermediate-Range Nuclear Forces Treaty in December 1987, Vice President Bush was very interested in the optics. He was assigned to escort the Soviet leader from the Soviet embassy to the White House, but Gorbachev kept him waiting for almost two hours. Bush was irate, but he stayed for a simple reason: being seen with Gorbachev was good politics. When the two men finally made their way to the White House, the streets were lined with cheering crowds. To everyone's surprise, the Soviet leader ordered the limousine to stop, and he darted outside to mingle with the masses. Bush quickly followed Gorbachev's lead, "lest he fail to appear in photos sure to run in the next day's newspapers."[31] Indeed, NBC's Lisa Myers showed the television audience an image of the two men outside the limo smiling and waving, calling it "a political image maker's dream."[32]

Yet, as a presidential candidate, Bush portrayed the Soviet leader in dark terms on the campaign trail. His advisers believed that if Americans had doubts about Gorbachev, it would benefit Bush's campaign. So in January 1988, just weeks after Bush's appearance with Gorbachev, he attacked the Soviet leader as a "committed Marxist" and not a "friend of democracy."[33] In September his campaign ran a television ad featuring Bush and Gorbachev shaking hands as a narrator intoned: the next president "is going to have to find out if Gorbachev is for real. Somebody is going to have to deal with him, and look him in the eye, and not blink. This is no time for uncertainty. No time to train somebody in how to meet with the Russians."[34] The message was clear: the Soviets were still a threat, and an experienced hand was needed in the White House.

Despite the campaign rhetoric and the lack of enthusiasm for an early meeting, the new president wanted to engage Gorbachev. Days before Bush took office, Henry Kissinger was in the Soviet Union, and the president-elect had the former secretary of state deliver a personal note to Gorbachev. In their conversations, Kissinger communicated that Bush was "very interested" in a back channel that would allow them to have confidential exchanges, something Gorbachev had mentioned at their December meeting. Bush saw back channels as a valuable tool, despite their potential to "leave critical people in the dark."[35] However, the proposed back channel to the Soviet leader never materialized; the person Gorbachev designated as his representative became ill and was unable to perform the task.[36]

As the Bush administration undertook a major review of US foreign policy, it lacked an informal channel to the Kremlin. For Gorbachev, the new administration's policy review, known as "the pause," showed "indecisiveness," but he also knew that Bush was "a very cautious politician." The Soviet leader was not deterred and continued to pursue a "dynamic" policy. As he told the Politburo weeks before Bush's inauguration, "We cannot allow the future administration to take a protracted time out and slow down the tempo of our political offensive."[37]

Gorbachev needed Bush for multiple reasons. As his domestic situation deteriorated, the Soviet leader sought external support, both political and economic, for perestroika. As the CIA reported in November 1989, Gorbachev had a "pressing need for a stable international atmosphere" so he could focus on domestic reforms and reduce military spending to meet consumer needs.[38] For the Soviet leader, a personal relationship with Bush could keep tensions low and perhaps make it easier to obtain the president's backing. And as one State Department official noted, engaging Bush allowed the Soviet leader "to polish his international image," thus boosting his political standing back home and making it harder for rivals to challenge him.[39]

But Gorbachev would have to wait nearly a year for a face-to-face meeting. In July 1989, after months of putting it off, Bush decided that with so many "remarkable" changes happening in the world, it was time to sit down with his Soviet counterpart.[40] Upon returning home from a trip to Poland, Hungary, and the G-7 summit in France, the president penned a personal letter to Gorbachev. "I would like very much to sit down soon and talk to you," Bush wrote. "I want to do it without thousands of assistants hovering over our shoulders, without the ever-present briefing papers."[41] Only close aides knew about the letter, and rather than sending it through normal bureaucratic channels, Bush gave it directly to Gorbachev's military adviser, Sergei

Akhromeyev, during a White House visit. The president wanted to keep the proposal a secret and was worried about leaks. And, as he said months later, there was no need to involve the bureaucracy "because I knew exactly what I wanted to do, and I knew how I wanted to go about doing it." Gorbachev was more than willing to meet, but it took months to decide on a location for the talks. Eventually, the two sides agreed to convene aboard ships off the coast of Malta in December 1989.[42]

There were no major breakthroughs on issues such as arms control, human rights, or German unification. Bush did, however, put forth numerous proposals designed to improve US-Soviet relations. Gorbachev welcomed the suggestions, seeing them as proof of the White House's "political will" and serious desire for better ties.[43] They did not agree on all issues, but after two days of talks, both men emerged pleased with the outcome and walked away believing they could trust each other.[44] "I think there was something concrete established here," newsman Dan Rather told TV viewers. "They didn't just talk, it isn't trying to just accentuate the positive, they did establish a real personal rapport here."[45] During the talks, Bush and Gorbachev were not glued to their talking points and conversed without excessively consulting their advisers. Bush saw that Gorbachev was committed to reform, while Gorbachev felt confident that Bush would not exploit developments in eastern Europe or domestic troubles in the Soviet Union. He believed the American president wanted him to succeed. "With Malta," Baker recalled, "the relationship became human and personal," and this was crucial to future international issues such as German unification.[46]

The two leaders met five more times over the next two years. Those meetings deepened the trust established at Malta, facilitated the peaceful unification of Germany within the North Atlantic Treaty Organization (NATO), and witnessed the signing of major accords that reduced conventional forces in Europe and limited strategic weapons. The frequency of their meetings also made US-Soviet summits a routine affair. But as the relationship between the American and Soviet leaders reached an apex, the Soviet Union was collapsing. When the two men met in Washington in the spring of 1990, Jack Matlock, the US ambassador in Moscow, reported that Gorbachev stood "at the center of a crumbling political order" and was "less a man in control and more an embattled leader."[47] It was no surprise that, in the summit's aftermath, Gorbachev stressed to Soviet officials that he had "strong support" in Washington. Publicly, Soviet television's coverage of the meeting was like a

"Gorbachev political campaign" designed "to gain support at home," according to Matlock. But for average Soviets, the summit mattered little. They were more worried about what they were going to eat than high-level summitry.[48]

With the Soviet economy in shambles, its empire in eastern Europe gone, and the country itself disintegrated, Gorbachev resigned as head of the Soviet Union on December 25, 1991. On that momentous day, he called Bush to notify him of his resignation and assure him that control over the Soviet nuclear stockpile would transfer to the new Russian Federation leadership in an orderly manner. "I want you to know at this historic time," he added, "that I value greatly our cooperation together, our partnership and friendship." Bush responded warmly. He thanked Gorbachev for the call and said he hoped to see the Soviet leader soon. "Our friendship," the president said, "is as strong as ever and will continue to be as events unfold. There is no question about that."[49]

From the beginning of Bush's presidency, there had been questions about Gorbachev's longevity, and some criticized the president for his close ties with the Soviet leader.[50] "There was a general feeling that Gorbachev's time was limited," recalled Bush's second ambassador to the Soviet Union, Robert Strauss. "There was criticism in this country that Bush was staying with Gorbachev too long, too close to him and trying to conduct personal diplomacy instead of nation diplomacy."[51] And Gorbachev's handling of various issues did not inspire confidence. For instance, his approach to Baltic independence involved sending Soviet forces into Latvia and Lithuania, injuring hundreds and killing almost two dozen.[52]

It was clear that Gorbachev's days were numbered, but from the administration's standpoint, there was no better alternative. Supporting Soviet hardliners was not an option. The only serious alternative was to back Gorbachev's rival, Russian president Boris Yeltsin. Yeltsin demonstrated a reformist spirit, but many in the administration had misgivings about him. Scowcroft called him "devious," Baker said he was a "flake," and Bush described him as a "real pain." "Everybody deals with him because he's there," said one American official, "but would you deal with him if he weren't in power? No."[53]

In short, when the administration looked at the Soviet political landscape, the alternatives to Gorbachev were unattractive, and the administration challenged the idea that Bush's relationship with Gorbachev unduly influenced his foreign policy. "I can't change my position because Gorbachev might like me," Bush said, "and he damn sure isn't going to change his because I like him."[54]

When he sought to bolster Gorbachev, Bush saw it as advancing American interests, not an act of kindness for a friend.

GERMAN UNIFICATION

Forty-four years after the end of World War II, many European leaders still feared a united Germany. "It is a fact of life that Europeans will always be suspicious of Germany," French president François Mitterrand told Bush.[55] The American president, however, had no such fear. "He just flat believed that the Germans had changed," recalled CIA director Gates.[56] So when the Berlin Wall came down in November 1989, followed weeks later by West German chancellor Helmut Kohl's Ten Point program for German unification, European leaders were leery of how quickly German unity might occur. Yet a year later, West and East Germany were one. Bush was central to the process. He was an early supporter of Kohl's efforts and used personal diplomacy to get other leaders on board.

"Germany's fate was larger than a matter of self-determination," Bush wrote in his memoir. He was acutely aware that European leaders worried that a united Germany "might cause more trouble and tragedy."[57] He worked to convince them otherwise, while being sensitive to their reservations. This was no easy task. Even before the wall fell, British prime minister Margaret Thatcher told Gorbachev that she was "very concerned" about developments in East Germany. Claiming to speak for western Europe, she declared, "We do not want the unification of Germany."[58] Mitterrand admitted he was "divided" on the issue. While proclaiming to understand the "real feelings" of the German people, he opposed "hasty actions which could destabilize" the Continent.[59] Gorbachev felt similarly. "Kohl is in too much of a hurry," he told Bush.[60] The American president faced the challenge of acknowledging these concerns while not becoming hostage to them.

Bush stayed in close contact with Thatcher throughout the winter of 1989–1990. As he told her, it was crucial that they "stay on the same wavelength."[61] The president was particularly sensitive to her anxieties. When Kohl complained to Bush that he could not understand Thatcher, the president responded that although the United States did not "fear the ghosts of the past," it was important to realize that the British did. We must "bend over backwards to consult," Bush said, adding that he had talked to Thatcher for an hour by telephone, "just to listen to her." And he had promised her that if Germany ever posed a threat, the United States would be there.[62] Mitterrand was more accepting of German unity, but he still had concerns. What would a united Germany's role be in NATO? Would it accept the Oder-Neisse line as the border between Germany and Poland, or would it demand changes? Bush made it clear that he took Mitterrand's concerns seriously. When the French president was adamant that Germany could not be a neutral power, Bush offered to send two of his top advisers to discuss the issue with Mitterrand. "Any questions that you have, you could let me know," Bush told him. "I need your advice and counsel."[63]

Bush had to deal not only with personalities but also with process. While West Germany favored an approach to unification dominated by Germans, other nations wanted a say in the matter. The Bush administration came up with "Two-plus-Four": the two Germanys would handle the internal aspects of reunification, while the four powers from World War II (United States, France, United Kingdom, and Soviet Union) would control external matters. This compromise allowed all the nations with the greatest stakes in German unification to have a voice.[64]

Bush also engaged Kohl to make sure the chancellor's plans aligned with American objectives. The day after the opening of the Berlin Wall, the two men talked. The president offered his support and praised the chancellor's handling of fast-moving events. Bush wanted to remain in close consultation to receive "the full benefit" of Kohl's views, especially as Bush was scheduled to meet with Gorbachev in a few weeks.[65] In a telephone call a week later, the president reiterated his "determination to get advice and suggestions . . . personally" from Kohl. Bush made it clear he did not want to exacerbate instability in Europe or have a rush to unification. Kohl agreed, telling the president he would "do nothing that will destabilize the situation."[66] Shortly after making this pledge, however, Kohl announced his Ten Point program for unification without consulting Bush or the other allies. The next day, Secretary of State Baker defined the terms under which the United States could support unification. Overall, the State Department supported Kohl's agenda, but with stipulations. Publicly, the White House was silent, concerned about Gorbachev's reaction. Privately, Bush was supportive, though he continued to underscore that "stability is the key word."[67]

Throughout the unification process, Bush sought to bolster Kohl amid the massive political pressures he faced. In February 1990, as the chancellor prepared to meet Gorbachev, Scowcroft recommended that Bush send Kohl a letter "giving him all the personal support" possible. But the letter was also meant to clarify American "preferences concerning the future of a united Germany."[68] Bush followed Scowcroft's advice. He offered strong backing for the chancellor and his country and urged Kohl to tell Gorbachev that a united Germany would remain in NATO—this was not up for discussion.[69] The president's message appeared to have the desired effect, and Kohl told Bush his letter "will one day be considered one of the greatest documents in German-American history. Your support is invaluable."[70]

During the talks between Kohl and Gorbachev, the Soviet leader acknowledged that the German people would decide on unification, although he continued to oppose a united Germany in NATO. The NATO issue remained central when Bush and Kohl met at Camp David a little more than a week later—the first time a German chancellor had been invited to stay at the mountain retreat. They discussed the unification process, and despite Bush's support for Kohl's agenda, he wanted the chancellor to commit to NATO and accept the German-Polish border.[71] Kohl recognized the "psychological strain" the border issue placed on Poland, but he did not want it to be part of the official negotiations over German unification. He suggested that the United States mediate the boundary issue instead. On NATO, Kohl "floated a disturbing idea," according to Bush.[72] The chancellor said he was committed to the alliance, but he suggested that a united Germany might be like France: a NATO member but not part of its military structure. This was a nonstarter for the president. "I hate to think of another France in NATO," he said. Germany needed to be a full participant in the alliance.[73]

During their talks, Kohl agreed that US troops and nuclear weapons would remain in Germany after unification, and he publicly stated that a united Germany would be a full member of NATO. The Camp David meeting was important for other reasons as well. Scowcroft characterized it as "a great success . . . because it truly solidified the relationship" of the two leaders. Though not every aspect of unification was settled, the talks played a central role in coordinating the administration's approach to the Two-plus-Four negotiations, and the "closeness" and "camaraderie" between Bush and Kohl were great assets in the months ahead as they confronted the challenges of unification.[74]

If Bush was confident that he and Kohl were in accord and that Thatcher and Mitterrand would ultimately accept German unification, the big question was whether Gorbachev would. "The road to unification still led through

Moscow," one administration official declared.[75] It was a bumpy road. In the immediate aftermath of the Berlin Wall's opening, the Soviet leader dashed off a cable expressing his concern over the "chaotic situation" that might lead to "unforeseen consequences." As Bush recalled, Gorbachev's reaction "was one of outright alarm."[76]

Bush planned to deal with Gorbachev's concerns when the two leaders met off the coast of Malta, just days after Kohl had unveiled his plan for unification and asked for US support. As Baker told Bush, the Soviet leader was coming to the summit "seek[ing] reassurances about [US] intentions" and planned to raise objections to events in Germany.[77] Gorbachev questioned the wisdom of rushing toward unification and argued that domestic political calculations were driving Kohl's approach. It was not a well-thought-out strategy and "could damage things," Gorbachev told Bush. The president admitted that politics were a factor, as was emotion. But he argued that Kohl understood the anxieties of other nations, and he promised the United States would do "nothing to recklessly try to speed up reunification." Gorbachev was still wary of German unity and wanted Bush to slow the process, but he signaled grudging acceptance at Malta.[78]

Over the next ten months, Bush continued to reassure Gorbachev. In a February 1990 telephone call, for example, the president told him that Kohl was committed to working with allies, including the Soviet Union, to "promote peace and stability." Bush understood that many in western Europe shared Gorbachev's concerns. However, despite its own violent past with Germany, the United States did not believe it was destined to threaten the Continent again.[79] Similarly, when Gorbachev visited the United States in May 1990, Scowcroft told the president, "It will be important to show that you understand the sensitivity of the German problem for the Soviet Union."[80] But Gorbachev had other concerns too. The Soviet economy was in dire straits, the Baltic states were agitating to regain their independence from the Soviet Union, and Gorbachev's political standing back home was on the decline.[81] This domestic turmoil made it more difficult for the Soviet leader to agree to concessions on the German question. Thus, Bush believed it was important to provide Gorbachev "with face, with standing." This would be "key," Bush told Kohl, in allowing Gorbachev to take bold steps.[82] To that end, Bush welcomed the Soviet leader with a "spectacular" ceremony on the White House lawn. In the words of NBC's John Cochran, he gave Gorbachev the "full treatment," including a military band, a twenty-one-gun salute, an inspection of troops, and a performance by a fife and drum corps dressed in Revolutionary-era uniforms.[83]

At first, the president thought Gorbachev seemed "confident" but also "a bit tense."[84] In private, however, he quickly relaxed. The two men discussed various issues, including a US-Soviet trade agreement, as well as the crucial question of Germany's future. On the German issue, Bush laid out a nine-point plan to address Soviet concerns. The president also repeated his belief that a united Germany in NATO would be a stabilizing force. Gorbachev countered, saying that a united Germany could be a member of both NATO and the Warsaw Pact, or it could be a member of neither. As the conversation continued, Bush asked Gorbachev whether he accepted the principle, enshrined in the Helsinki Final Act, that nations have the right to choose their alliances. The Soviet leader said that he did, which stunned the president's advisers and distressed Gorbachev's. The Soviet leader had just accepted the US position. Recognizing this, a member of the National Security Council (NSC) staff passed a note to Bush, advising him to get Gorbachev to repeat what he had just said, which the Soviet leader did. This marked a significant shift in Soviet policy, but Bush, ever sensitive to other leaders' anxieties and political needs, refused to revel in this victory.[85]

In July 1990, after meeting Kohl, Gorbachev officially accepted full sovereignty for a unified Germany and its membership in NATO. West Germany agreed to provide much-needed financial assistance to the Soviet Union. How much this influenced the Soviet leader's thinking is unclear, but the fact that economic aid and acceptance of German unification occurred at the same summit is telling. Whereas the United States set the security parameters, Kohl's checkbook diplomacy sealed Gorbachev's acquiescence.[86] And throughout the process of German unification, diplomacy at the highest level was employed "to allay fears, persuade the doubting, and build bonds," in the words of Roman Popadiuk, Bush's ambassador to Ukraine.[87] Indeed, Bush's personal contact with his counterparts led to a frank discussion of issues, allowing him to listen to other leaders' concerns and ideas. Even when he did not follow their wishes, they at least felt they had been consulted. As Engel observes, Bush's personal diplomacy was "part symbolic gesture and part substantive plea," where "listening came first, laced with empathy and respect."[88] Bush's efforts during German unification illustrate the president's role as counselor at the end of the Cold War and the beginning of a new era.

THE PERSIAN GULF CRISIS

On August 1, 1990, President Bush was planning to speak by telephone with Iraqi leader Saddam Hussein. For months, tension between Iraq and neighboring Kuwait had been escalating due to Kuwait's refusal to forgive Iraqi debt (accumulated during its war with Iran) and a border dispute over oil. The goal of Bush's call was to lessen the rising hostilities, but it never took place. In the early-morning hours of August 2, while it was still evening in Washington, Iraq invaded Kuwait.[89]

This canceled call was not the end of Bush's personal diplomacy. The invasion of Kuwait kicked off a flurry of leader-to-leader interactions, mainly by telephone. Bush called "everybody," according to chief of staff Sununu. "When he left office his index finger was an inch shorter" from the amount of dialing he had done.[90] During the Gulf crisis, Bush continually consulted his counterparts. On the day of the invasion, for example, he called regional leaders such as King Fahd of Saudi Arabia, King Hussein of Jordan, and Egyptian president Hosni Mubarak. In each call he expressed America's strong opposition to Iraq's aggression and solicited his counterparts' views of the situation.[91] In the weeks and months to come, Bush's personal diplomacy helped assemble a global coalition to push Iraq out of Kuwait with force, if necessary. This was not always an easy sell. Some leaders supported the use of force, but others needed to be persuaded.

On August 13 Jordan's King Hussein called Bush and asked to visit. Days later, the two men were at the president's home in Kennebunkport, Maine. The king was wary of a military option and wanted to find a diplomatic solution. Bush found their talks disappointing.[92] Throughout the Gulf crisis, the president remained frustrated by Hussein's reluctance to break from Saddam and support the coalition. "He's isolated himself with other Arabs. He's apologized for this guy Saddam. He's cooked his goose with America," Bush vented. Adding to the frustration was the fact that the president considered the king a friend. "I've known this guy forever," Bush lamented, but that relationship did not help during the Gulf crisis.[93]

Nearly two months after the invasion, Bush engaged in a particularly frenzied period of personal diplomacy. On September 28 he welcomed the embattled Kuwaiti leader, who was living in exile in Saudi Arabia, to the United States. "The White House did everything it could today to treat the Emir of Kuwait as the reigning leader of an independent country," ABC's Brit Hume told viewers. But what emerged from the meeting, according to Hume, was "deepening doubts about how much is left of the emir's country and an apparently increased willingness to consider force."[94] The next day Bush was in New York at the United Nations, where he met with twenty world leaders over three days. The purpose of this flurry of meetings, according to a White House official, was "to express gratitude for the efforts of countries that have helped us with the Persian Gulf and to send a signal to Saddam Hussein that all the world is united and talking from the same script on the issue of Iraqi aggression."[95]

Bush also went abroad during the crisis. In November, after attending the Conference on Security and Cooperation in Europe, he made stops in Saudi Arabia and Egypt. In addition, he traveled to Geneva, where he met with Syrian leader Hafez al-Assad. However, the president's most noteworthy trip during the Gulf crisis occurred a little more than a month after the invasion, when Bush attended a "hastily arranged" meeting with Gorbachev in Helsinki, Finland. Soviet support was crucial, according to Baker, but it was not always easy to obtain.[96] Even so, within a day of the Iraqi invasion, the United States and the Soviet Union, after back-and-forth negotiations, had issued an "unusual" joint statement condemning the aggression and calling on Iraq to withdraw.[97]

As Bush prepared for his encounter with Gorbachev, he was "taking no chances," according to NBC's Jim Miklaszewski. Bush knew that getting Saddam out of Kuwait would not be easy and might require military force, something the Soviets adamantly opposed. There was no guarantee the Gorbachev would back the US approach or even grudgingly acquiesce. Therefore, on the Sunday before the summit, the president consulted not only his advisers but also a higher power, as he attended two church services and met with the Reverend Billy Graham.[98]

In Helsinki, as in other meetings with the Soviet leader, Bush knew that Gorbachev was facing severe problems at home: economic troubles, social unrest, and political challenges. These domestic dilemmas, Scowcroft told the president, made Gorbachev "likely to seek accommodation" on issues such as the Gulf crisis.[99] From the start of the summit, Bush made it clear that continued US-Soviet cooperation against Saddam was his top priority. As he told a joint session of Congress days later, collaboration was the building block of a new world order of peace and security.[100] Although the Soviet leader agreed on the importance of cooperation and close ties, his approach to Iraq differed. The main area of disagreement was on the use of force, which the American president believed must be an option. The two also sparred over Gorbachev's desire to offer Saddam a concession, such as convening a regional conference to deal with the Arab-Israeli conflict. Bush adamantly opposed this proposal, claiming that "aggression cannot be rewarded in any way."[101] After the meeting, Scowcroft recalled being "filled with foreboding" because Gorbachev's positions seemed to come straight from the pro-Iraqi Soviet bureaucracy.[102] But the Soviet leader did agree to a joint statement reaffirming that Iraq's occupation of Kuwait "must not be tolerated." Additionally, the statement warned that although both leaders desired a peaceful end to the crisis, additional measures would be forthcoming if Saddam did not withdraw his forces.[103]

Overall, Bush and Gorbachev "largely agreed to disagree" at Helsinki. In the months to come, those disagreements caused friction, but the two leaders continued to engage. From Bush's perspective, merely meeting in Helsinki illustrated that the United States and the Soviet Union were working together.[104] The talks "sent a powerful signal," Bush told French president Mitterrand. Saddam "knows he cannot playoff the U.S. against the Soviet Union."[105] But this did not mean that Bush and Gorbachev were necessarily on the same page. Days before the beginning of the air campaign against Iraq, the two men spoke on the telephone. Gorbachev pushed the idea of sending a personal envoy to Saddam, believing the Iraqi leader was "ready to listen to Moscow." Bush was unconvinced.[106] Three days after the commencement of air strikes, the two leaders spoke again for more than an hour. Bush recalled that Gorbachev's tone was "somber."[107] The Soviet leader blamed Saddam for making the use of force necessary and reaffirmed his desire to work closely with the United States. "We will be with you to the very end," he told Bush. However, Gorbachev also wanted to end the air campaign. From his perspective, the bombing had already dealt Saddam a major political and military defeat, so there was no need to continue. The president disagreed: Saddam had not been defeated, and ending the military campaign so soon would be seen as a victory for the Iraqi leader. Once again, the two leaders differed, but as Bush told Gorbachev, "The phone lines are open. Call day or night. It doesn't matter what time of day it is."[108]

The Gulf crisis tested the relationship between the United States and the Soviet Union. Adding to the challenge was that the air campaign's commencement coincided with Gorbachev's decision to intervene in Lithuania. While condemning that incursion, Bush had to balance criticism with the need to maintain Gorbachev's support in Iraq. To critics, the president's muted response indicated that he was too supportive of the man in the Kremlin.[109]

Similarly, Gorbachev's cooperation with the United States made him vulnerable to detractors among hard-liners and the military, who were critical of attacks on a longtime client state. One conservative Soviet paper went further, proclaiming that joining the United States' opposition to Iraq had "ended the U.S.S.R.'s existence as a superpower."[110] Gorbachev never seemed entirely comfortable in the anti-Iraq coalition, and days after the ground war began, he noted in a speech that US-Soviet relations were "very fragile" and warned of increased tensions. But the two leaders' relationship survived, and they continued to emphasize their commitment to cooperation. "You are my friend," Bush told Gorbachev months after the Gulf War ended, "and I want to prove that and work with you."[111]

Other than Gorbachev, the most important leader Bush engaged during the Gulf crisis was King Fahd. After the invasion of Kuwait, there was concern that Saddam would make a move on neighboring Saudi Arabia. The king was angry about Iraq's actions, but when he and Bush spoke on the day of the invasion, the president was afraid Fahd might cut a deal with Saddam. Indeed, US intelligence reported that the Saudis were considering paying off Saddam. This "rang alarm bells" for Bush.[112] In a telephone conversation two days later, Bush pushed Fahd to accept US troops on Saudi soil. The president worried that without a strong military presence to deter him, the Iraqi leader might be tempted to move south and seize Saudi oil fields. The king evaded Bush's request, but the president stressed that Saudi Arabia's security was vital to the United States.

Fahd, along with other leaders in the region, questioned America's commitment. According to one senior State Department official, they wondered whether the United States would "stay the course."[113] Fahd also worried about the optics of having US forces on Saudi territory and the possibility of an American occupation. Bush's personal diplomacy helped overcome these doubts. Speaking in intimate terms, he gave Fahd his "solemn word" that US forces "will stay until we are asked to leave."[114] Fahd easily could have dismissed this pledge, but Bush had spent years building relationships with world leaders, including the king, and the trust developed through numerous face-to-face meetings, telephone calls, and letters made it easier to believe the president.[115] When Secretary of Defense Dick Cheney went to Saudi Arabia soon after the Iraqi invasion, Fahd agreed to accept American forces. As Cheney recalled, the Saudi leader stated, "Okay, we'll do it. We'll do it because I trust George Bush and because I know when it's over with, you'll leave."[116]

The Gulf crisis was the "first test of the post–Cold War era," NSC adviser Richard Haass stated.[117] But Bush handled it similarly to his Cold War predecessors. Though the scale of his personal diplomacy was different, the impetus to personally engage foreign leaders in times of crisis was the same. Bush proved that leader-to-leader diplomacy would remain a tool in a president's post–Cold War arsenal.

TOO MUCH PERSONAL DIPLOMACY

In the heady days of the Gulf War, Bush's approval rating soared to 89 percent in February 1991, the highest ever recorded by a Gallup poll up to that time (George W. Bush's approval rating reached 90 percent after the 9/11 terrorist attacks).[118] But by the start of 1992, an election year, the president's approval rating was only 46 percent. This was largely because of the faltering economy and the perception that Bush had neglected his duties at home. An ABC News/*Washington Post* poll from October 1991 showed that 70 percent of respondents thought Bush spent "too much time on foreign problems." This "spooked" Bush, according to an administration official. Thus, toward the end of 1991 he attempted to recalibrate and focus less publicly on international issues, although the administration denied that this was the case.[119] But if Bush was not avoiding foreign policy, he was certainly trying to highlight its domestic aspects.

This effort began following the off-year elections in November 1991. Republicans picked up the governor's seat in Mississippi, but Bush's handpicked candidate lost a special election to fill a Senate seat in Pennsylvania. Many saw this as a "harbinger of trouble," as administration official Chase Untermeyer told his diary on Election Day.[120] The White House appeared to think so as well. Bush postponed a long-planned trip to Australia and Asia just weeks before his scheduled departure. When a reporter described the White House as being in a "panic" and claimed the trip had been postponed because the administration was "afraid" voters were angry about the president's focus on foreign affairs and neglect of the economy, Bush brushed it off. "That's crazy," he said. The change in plans, he explained, was because he wanted to stay in the country while Congress was still in session.[121]

In any case, the perception that the president was more interested in foreign than domestic affairs was a cudgel the Democrats used to attack him. For example, as Bush prepared to head to Rome for a NATO summit the day after the 1991 elections, the Democratic National Committee started to sell T-shirts that read, "George Bush went to Rome—and all I got was this lousy recession." Representative Vic Fazio of California held up a shirt on the floor of the House and asked, "How can the president see the pain in the face of a father who can't find work when he finds so much time required to be overseas?" The congressman declared, "The president should be in Rome, Miss., where the unemployment rate stands at over 11 percent."[122]

Bush had a problem. The Cold War was over, and the public's interest in foreign affairs ended with it. At the same time, Americans saw a new threat coming from abroad. Instead of a nuclear challenge, it was an economic one from countries like Japan. As Senator Paul Tsongas famously said, "The cold war is over; Japan won."[123] Bush could not avoid foreign policy, but he had to change his approach. Too much public focus on international affairs, including high-profile trips that dealt with traditional issues of politics and security, hurt him. Thus, Bush decided to connect his personal diplomacy to domestic concerns. Instead of using foreign travel and interactions with world leaders to enhance his own gravitas, he would use them to help the US economy.

When the November trip to Australia and Asia was rescheduled for the start of the new year, Bush proclaimed that the journey was all about "jobs, jobs, jobs" and said he planned to pressure allies to lower trade barriers. It was a "bold but risky bid to use diplomacy to bolster the economy," according to the *Los Angeles Times*. Indeed, no president had gone abroad with the specific goal of reviving the nation's economic fortunes, and Bush risked overselling what he could accomplish by "trying to sound more salesman than statesman."[124]

Bush's agenda also caused concern among the allies he was set to visit, particularly Japan. Japanese leaders worried that they would "be receiving a harried President reacting to bad economic news at home in the style of any desperate candidate—grandstanding for a US audience by putting the screws to the most obvious scapegoat." Prime Minister Kiichi Miyazawa was "scrambling furiously" to prevent failure, but expectations for the trip were low. There was also a sense of anger in Japan. "Stooping to this kind of salesmanship is beneath the dignity of an American President," one Foreign Ministry official noted. "It's not what we expect from the leader of the world's predominant power." The Japanese press voiced similar sentiments, with one paper proclaiming that the visit had the tone of "gunboat diplomacy in economic areas."[125]

At home, the trip was seen through a domestic lens. "This is the strangest foreign trip President Bush has taken," declared NBC's John Cochran. "Although he has talked some about foreign policy, his overriding concern in this election year is how the trip is playing, not only in Peoria, but in Peterborough and other towns in New Hampshire, the first primary state."[126] Initially, the visit was meant to show that Asia still mattered to the United States, after European and Middle Eastern issues had dominated the administration's agenda for three years. It was also meant to reaffirm the US-Japan alliance. However, US domestic politics turned the trip into "a blunt sales pitch for American exports and jobs." The administration claimed the trip would be beneficial both politically and diplomatically, but as one official admitted, it "looks more politically expedient than I wanted."[127]

Accompanying Bush were twenty-one corporate executives. This made sense, as the president had characterized the trip as a means to boost American exports. However, this caused consternation in Japan, as well as "complaints from voters who see the highly paid, all-male and nearly all-white group as unrepresentative of American concerns," one journalist wrote.[128] So even as Bush tried to use the trip to show that he cared about average Americans' concerns, his choice of traveling companions muddled the message.

Shortly before the trip, Bush and Miyazawa spoke by telephone. "I want to talk politician to politician," Bush said. "You know there's a bad economic mood here," which made it hard to fight protectionist measures.[129] Days later, Bush told the nation he was going to Asia "to fight for open markets and more opportunities for American workers because exports abroad mean more jobs right here at home. Let there be no mistake, my number one priority is jobs and economic growth. And I'm confident that we will succeed."[130] Despite the public display of optimism, Bush embarked on his twelve-day tour, in the words of one newspaper, "with his backside exposed to Democratic sniping and his feet stuck in an economic quagmire."[131]

At each stop, the president reinforced the message that American jobs were central. In a speech in Seoul before the Korean National Assembly, he proclaimed, "Let me repeat here what I've said in Australia and in Singapore: At home in the United States, especially during tough economic times, my highest priority must be jobs and economic growth."[132] But in the end, the trip did little to produce American jobs or boost the economy. The agreements between Bush and Miyazawa were modest, such as the Japanese promise to buy more American cars.

"The image the White House political advisers wanted to emerge from President Bush's visit to Japan . . . was that of a strong president using his foreign policy skills to wrest trade concessions from the Japanese," one journalist wrote. It was not to be. Instead, the defining image of the trip was Bush falling ill, vomiting, and passing out on the lap of the Japanese prime minister, an "embarrassment" that produced "awful pictures," NBC reported.[133] Although Americans had sympathy for their leader, that episode symbolized the trip's shortcomings. The *Washington Post* called the whole effort "awkward" and a "flop." NBC ran a story with a banner across the television screen proclaiming, "Not Enough." The Japanese press was even harsher. It called Bush rude for coming to their country and demanding concessions, and it mocked him as a salesman.[134] Multiple polls showed that around 60 percent of Americans considered the trip a failure, and one poll found that 53 percent believed it had been "mainly for show" and not about increasing jobs. Adding to Bush's troubles, the unemployment rate hit a six-year high as he returned home.[135]

"The themes just didn't sell," according to a Republican congressional strategist. The trip's agenda "was for political reasons, and it was transparent, and it didn't work."[136] During the Cold War, presidents used personal diplomacy to appear statesmanlike. With the collapse of the Soviet Union and their longtime nemesis gone, Americans shifted their focus to domestic matters. Thus, Bush tried to use personal diplomacy at the highest level to enhance his popularity and bolster his reelection prospects not by strengthening his image as a statesman but by boosting the US economy. This was a herculean task. Bush had lots of foreign "friends," but "the problem is all politics is local," NBC's John Cochran told viewers. Bush wanted Miyazawa "to do something politically unpopular in Japan," and he "refused to do it."[137]

"Do not forget," Kohl told Gorbachev in June 1989, Bush "inherited a difficult domestic political situation, first of all in terms of the economy." The economic challenge would not get any easier for the new president, as the United States would face increasing competition from Europe and Japan in the years to come. "Bush has an overwhelming load of things to do in the social sphere, which could become his Achilles' heel," Kohl noted presciently.[138]

In 1992 domestic issues were the deciding factor in the first presidential election of the post–Cold War era. But foreign policy was Bush's strength, even if voters thought he spent too much time on it. In a survey taken days before the election, the majority of respondents approved of how Bush was "handling foreign policy." Another poll showed that 58 percent believed Bush would do the "best job" in the global arena, compared with only 20 percent who favored his opponent, Bill Clinton. However, only 8 percent of voters told pollsters that foreign policy was the most important factor in determining their vote. On the economy, one poll showed that 75 percent disapproved of Bush's economic stewardship. Americans approved of Bush's handling of foreign policy, but overall, they disapproved of his job performance as president. His approval rating was a mere 29 percent midway through 1992.[139]

Bush lost his reelection bid, but based on his four years in office, it is safe to assume that personal diplomacy would have continued to be a prominent feature of his foreign policy in a second term. He had a natural predilection for the practice, and like his predecessors, he used it for a variety of reasons, whether to deal with an international crisis, assert more control, soothe his foreign counterparts' worries, or give himself a domestic boost. His presidency illustrates how leader-to-leader diplomacy operated at the end of the Cold War and at the beginning of a new era. The nature of American foreign policy changed with the demise of the Soviet Union, but personal diplomacy remained an essential aspect of the president's role as diplomat in chief.

9. The Impact of Presidential Personal Diplomacy

As the preceding chapters have shown, in the second half of the twentieth century, American presidents frequently used personal diplomacy for various reasons. In the process, the practice became institutionalized. Institutionalization occurs when "value and stability" are attained, and as Samuel Huntington describes, the level of institutionalization can be measured by four factors: adaptability, complexity, autonomy, and coherence.[1] Each is evident in presidential personal diplomacy in the post–World War II era.

Adaptability refers to the ability to respond to the external environment and make changes in order to endure.[2] Throughout the second half of the twentieth century, personal diplomacy adapted to fit both the international environment and each president's personal needs. Presidents engaged world leaders when they thought it was necessary to do so, and they used various means. Even as the Cold War faded, they continued to use the practice to handle numerous international challenges, allowing personal diplomacy to endure into the twenty-first century.

Complexity denotes how an organization is structured. The more subunits an institution has and the more functions it performs, the more complex and stable it is.[3] In personal diplomacy, we see complexity in the multiple bureaucracies involved. From producing briefing materials to generating talking points to drafting correspondence, agencies such as the National Security Council and Department of State are critical. Similarly, a travel establishment exists that allows presidents to trek around the globe.[4] Complexity is also evident in how personal diplomacy operates on multiple levels. As shown in this book, there is both a private and a public side to personal diplomacy, and sometimes it can even operate in a liminal space. When Richard Nixon went to China in 1972, the state banquet was televised. It was an obvious public spectacle that allowed viewers worldwide to witness former foes breaking bread. But under the glare of the camera, Nixon and Zhou Enlai also held private conversations. These were not necessarily policy talks, but the socializing and relationship building that occurred while doing something as ordinary as eating dinner were both private and public events. Additionally, presidents can use personal diplomacy for many reasons, ranging from crisis management to ceremonial celebrations, illustrating the practice's multifaceted nature.

Autonomy is the ability to act independently of others. In terms of presidential diplomacy, there is minimal if any reliance on other political actors to make decisions and take action.[5] From the beginning, when members of Congress failed to halt Woodrow Wilson's trip to Europe, other political actors have had little ability to stop a president from engaging with other chief executives. This does not mean that political and public pressure cannot influence a president's personal diplomacy. But the formal mechanisms that exist to challenge the practice are limited.

Coherence is how an organization manages its workload—the more standardized the operating procedures, the more coherence there is.[6] As a practice, personal diplomacy developed a great deal of consistency. All modern presidents use similar methods to engage foreign leaders, and the resources available to each occupant of the White House are constant. All have wide-ranging bureaucratic support that makes interacting with heads of state and government possible. Furthermore, there are patterns to presidential personal diplomacy. Presidents tend to go abroad during particular times, travel to the same places, and invite the same nations' leaders to the United States.[7]

RISKS AND BENEFITS

If personal diplomacy became institutionalized in the second half of the twentieth century, how beneficial was it? Debates over the risks and advantages have existed from the beginning. Since Woodrow Wilson announced he would attend the Paris peace conference in 1919, critics of the practice have questioned its wisdom and utility. Throughout this book, the double-edged nature of leader-to-leader interactions has been evident.[8] Supporters frequently champion the notion that direct interactions allow leaders to become personally acquainted, that knowledge of the other's thinking, concerns, and political constraints can produce greater understanding. A level of trust might be established, making it easier to tackle thorny issues. Warm personal relations between leaders can also result in good relations between states.

Because diplomacy at the highest levels involves the ultimate political decision makers in each country, issues can be settled rapidly, and stalemated problems at lower diplomatic levels can be resolved quickly. This was something that even nineteenth-century statesmen realized: "In one hour," Napoleon told Tsar Alexander I, "we shall achieve more than our spokesmen in several days."[9] Leader-to-leader engagement also has the power to focus domestic and international attention on an issue, and it can signal policy both at home and abroad. The resulting publicity can enhance the images of the leaders involved, potentially providing a political boost back home.

These advantages make the practice attractive, but there are dangers as well. Most world leaders are not trained diplomats. They may be unaware of protocol, unskilled in negotiations, and uninformed on policy. This lack of knowledge might produce shoddy agreements reached in haste, and there is no higher authority to veto a bad agreement. "When a chief of state or head of government makes a fumble," Truman's secretary of state Dean Acheson warned, "the goal line is open behind him."[10]

An overreliance on personal diplomacy can also harm normal diplomatic channels, rendering them obsolete and damaging professional diplomats' morale and the foreign policy bureaucracy. And just because leaders interact personally, there is no guarantee that they are going to get along. As fifteenth-century French diplomat Philippe de Commynes advised, "two great princes who wish to establish good personal relations should never meet each other face to face, but ought to communicate through good and wise emissaries."[11]

The public aspects of personal diplomacy also present risks. Acting is an important aspect of leadership.[12] Leaders who are poor performers may be less effective; they may send the wrong signals to the public and raise doubts about their leadership abilities. Disillusionment is also a risk. Public expectations rise when a leader-to-leader encounter becomes a spectacle; if those expectations are not met, it can lead to public disappointment. To avoid this, a leader might agree to disadvantageous terms simply to show the public that something was achieved. The pomp and ceremony of public spectacles can create other problems. As British diplomat Harold Nicolson warned, such displays can "tire his [the leader's] physique, excite his vanity, or bewilder his judgement."[13] Overall, when personal diplomacy is used too much, its public impact lessens. As the practice became increasingly commonplace in the second half of the twentieth century, it garnered less attention and was less valuable as a means of influencing public opinion.

Despite these hazards, American presidents have generally found the potential benefits of personal diplomacy worth the risks, and many have considered it the best tool at their disposal to advance the nation's foreign agenda. Confident in their abilities, they believed they could minimize the dangers and achieve their objectives. Many international relations scholars would disagree with the notion that personal diplomacy is valuable, arguing that it is nothing but "cheap talk."[14] The challenge of determining its value is that the purpose of leader-to-leader diplomacy is rarely a major treaty or significant agreement. Instead, the aims tend to be intangible, such as understanding and trust, and thus hard to measure. However, some have tried, such as one study that created a model to measure whether state-to-state relations improve when the US president meets with other leaders. It found that they do.[15] But such quantification is unlikely to be a deciding factor for modern presidents, who have made it clear in their public statements and memoirs that they do not need a bunch of number-crunchers to convince them that they should interact with their foreign counterparts.

LESSONS OF PERSONAL DIPLOMACY

The focus here has been on the factors that pushed modern presidents toward personal diplomacy, regardless of their individual characteristics. But when examining diplomacy at the highest level, questions about the practice's impact, both in general and in terms of individual presidential performance, inevitably arise. How can we measure personal diplomacy's importance? What does success look like? How much difference does an individual president make? How do we know when the president's personal involvement is consequential?

As noted, one of the perceived advantages of personal diplomacy is that leaders get to know each other. So, on the surface, one might say that when leaders "get along with" or "like" each other, personal diplomacy is a success. Sometimes heads of state and government go further and call each other "friend." But what does that mean? Aristotle wrote that friendships are based on different principles: utility, pleasure, and virtue. But only those based on virtue lead to real, lasting bonds. In friendships of utility and pleasure, the parties are interested only because "some good accrues" to them or they derive amusement from the relationship. They do not truly appreciate the other's qualities. Only friendships of virtue are selfless. In these relationships, the parties wish "good things" for the other for the "other's sake," not out of any self-interest.[16]

But friendships of virtue are extremely rare, according to Aristotle.[17] If they are uncommon in everyday life, it seems likely that they are even rarer in international politics. World leaders interact to advance and secure their nations' interests. Thus, relationships at the highest level are based mainly if not solely on utility, at least initially. But leaders are people with emotions and unique personalities, and their relationships can evolve into something more.[18] Utility may be the basis for their interactions, but there are examples of leaders who have transcended political friendships and formed bonds closer to friendships of virtue, such as Jimmy Carter and Egyptian president Anwar Sadat. In his private papers, Sadat wrote, "Jimmy Carter is my very best friend on earth," and even after Carter left the White House, Sadat visited him in Georgia.[19] After the Egyptian president's assassination in 1981, a heavy-hearted Carter said, "I have never had a better and closer personal friend than Anwar Sadat." He added, "His family is close to mine. We have visited back and forth. We have shared great events and achievements and we've shared tragedies as well."[20] But as this book demonstrates, even a close relationship like Carter and Sadat's was always tinged with politics.

So, the question remains, how does diplomacy at the highest level affect policy? Foreign policy and diplomacy are intimately connected yet distinct endeavors. Foreign policy constitutes the objectives and goals of a state. Diplomacy is a central means of implementing foreign policy.[21] But when leaders interact, the line between foreign policy and diplomacy blurs. The leader who sets foreign policy also becomes the one to carry it out. Thus, when presidents engage in personal diplomacy, the possibility arises that they are simultaneously crafting foreign policy and executing it.

Throughout this book, there have been numerous examples of presidents formulating policy while interacting with other chief executives. For example, when Carter negotiated the Camp David Accords, he was not only conducting diplomacy to advance the long-held US aim of Middle East peace but also setting foreign policy. The agreement Carter negotiated with Sadat and Israeli prime minister Menachem Begin created new commitments for the United States. The American president pledged billions of dollars in military aid to Israel and Egypt and guaranteed Israel's oil supplies.[22] Carter made it US policy for the nation to be the guarantor of Egyptian-Israeli peace.

When Ronald Reagan met with Soviet leader Mikhail Gorbachev at Reykjavik, he also went beyond diplomacy. The summit's initial aim was to make progress on arms control, an American goal and policy objective of many previous presidents. But when Reagan agreed to eliminate the nation's stockpile of nuclear weapons, he made a foreign policy decision. Without consulting advisers or allies, he agreed to a major shift in US foreign policy from arms control to abolition.

Presidents are within their rights to conduct diplomacy and craft policy during their interactions with foreign leaders. But this is another risk of the practice. In theory, foreign policy should be well thought out, relying on the input of numerous advisers and experts and considering the consequences of pursuing a particular agenda. Every administration has a different policy-making and decision-making process, but when foreign policy is decided during high-level diplomacy, important considerations might be ignored. For example, how would Reagan's willingness to eliminate nuclear weapons affect America's defensive posture? How would allies that depended on America's nuclear umbrella react? How would Congress respond to the president's failure to consult or notify it in advance of a major shift in US policy? What would the American public think? The answers to these questions would determine the success of a policy that abolished nuclear weapons, but Reagan had not thought them through.

Even when a president sticks strictly to diplomacy, interactions with heads of state and government can inform policy. Personal diplomacy offers the president an opportunity to get a better sense of foreign leaders' personalities, which can help a president understand their priorities and red lines and gauge how they might react to US actions. Presidents can use this information as they go forward to create new policies or reconsider old ones. In this way, personal diplomacy provides a type of feedback loop. As presidents seek to implement their foreign policy through engagement with foreign counterparts, they obtain new information and ideas that can influence future policy. For example, Dwight Eisenhower used his interactions with other world leaders to reevaluate global issues.[23] Carter's numerous meetings with Begin and Sadat provided him with information about what would and would not work in a peace agreement. Likewise, George H. W. Bush's frequent telephone calls with foreign leaders increased his understanding of how they might respond to various US policies. Bush put what he learned to good use when he strove to accomplish German reunification without provoking Gorbachev.

The preceding chapters also offer a guide to how personal diplomacy can potentially be made more effective. Franklin Roosevelt's efforts during World War II, Carter's work at Camp David, and Reagan's actions at the end of the

Cold War are frequently touted as examples of successful personal diplomacy. The common factor in all three cases is a president involved in a sustained process. Their success came through repeated engagement face-to-face, through correspondence, and on the telephone. Personal diplomacy is an iterative process; the interactions build on one another. A single meeting or telephone call generally does not produce immediate results, but in the aggregate, these individual interactions can be quite valuable. For example, many considered the Reagan-Gorbachev summit at Reykjavik a failure. But in the aftermath, both men realized it was an important meeting that provided momentum for a future arms control agreement. Likewise, Bush's relationships with other leaders proved invaluable during the Gulf War. Bush's efforts also demonstrate the benefit of establishing ties before a crisis occurs. As a transition adviser told Carter weeks after his election, "*It is important to establish personal contacts and channels with other world leaders before there are major crises or problems. This will not only help you deal with the problems but, equally important, relationships initiated by crises are always colored by the events that drive them— and often adversely.*"[24]

A well-established relationship might bolster a president's foreign policy, but having a long-standing connection does not always lead to success. Bush's ties with King Fahd of Saudi Arabia and Gorbachev came in handy during the Gulf War. However, his longtime acquaintance with King Hussein of Jordan failed to get the monarch to break with Saddam Hussein. Perhaps most painfully, his "old friend" Deng Xiaoping refused to take his call after Tiananmen Square.

Preparation is also key. If a president hopes to use his contacts with foreign leaders to advance American interests, he must have a clear idea what those interests are. A president who enters a meeting or makes a phone call without knowing what he hopes to achieve from the interaction is unlikely to move his foreign policy agenda forward. It will be a wasted opportunity. A meeting's goal does not have to be as lofty as negotiating an arms control agreement or a peace treaty; it can be as simple as making a connection or sizing up a counterpart. But there needs to be some objective. In addition to knowing what he wants to achieve, a president should have a modicum of knowledge about the issues under discussion. A president does not need to be an expert in every international issue; he has a bureaucracy full of experts at his disposal. But a president should at least be able to speak confidently about the basics. How can a president pursue and advance American interests without an understanding of the issues involved? Some presidents (e.g., Eisenhower, Nixon, Bush) come to the White House with an in-depth knowledge of foreign affairs and need little preparation. Others (e.g., Reagan) need to put in more time. Luckily for them, they have plenty of advisers and briefing books to prepare them. Carter, for example, spent much time preparing for Camp David. His success cannot be attributed to extensive study alone, but it is difficult to imagine that the outcome would have been as good had he not thoroughly understood the issues and personalities involved. Reagan was usually not one for extensive preparation, which was sometimes obvious. For example, at the 1983 G-7 summit, British prime minister Margaret Thatcher thought him "poorly prepared."[25] But when Reagan put his mind to it and studied, as he did for his encounters with Gorbachev, the likelihood of success rose.

Related to preparation is choosing one's words wisely, especially in times of crisis. A president's words carry weight, and an offhand remark or careless phrase can have negative consequences. Lyndon Johnson was cognizant of this during the Six-Day War. As he and Soviet leader Alexei Kosygin exchanged messages over the hotline, Johnson had to consider his words carefully, knowing that if anything he said was misconstrued in Moscow, tensions between nuclear-armed superpowers could increase. Similarly, when presidents play the role of counselor, their words should be uplifting. Thus, when John F. Kennedy engaged German chancellor Konrad Adenauer and the shah of Iran, he used language intended to bolster their trust and faith in the United States and in his personal leadership.

Of all the factors that contribute to effective personal diplomacy, perhaps the most important is beyond presidential control. No matter how skillful, knowledgeable, and charming a president may be, and no matter how diligent the effort to engage, it will not amount to much without a committed partner. The other leader needs to be willing to engage productively. Johnson wanted to go in-depth with Kosygin at Glassboro, but the Soviet leader refrained, thus lessening the meeting's potential impact. Rapprochement with China would not have occurred without Mao Zedong's and Zhou Enlai's willingness to engage with Nixon. Carter could not have helped broker the Egyptian-Israeli peace treaty without a willing Sadat. Reagan did not produce an arms control agreement until Gorbachev changed Soviet policy.

Furthermore, interests need to align. No amount of presidential personal diplomacy will convince other leaders to do something antithetical to their nations' interests. That is why Greek prime minister Georgios Papandreou resisted US proposals during the crisis over Cyprus, Begin frequently frustrated Carter, and Deng Xiaoping refused to take Bush's call. Likewise, no amount of enthusiastic engagement, even if it occurs over a long period, will help if the policy the president is trying to promote is misguided, hostile, or embarrassing to a foreign leader. This explains Khrushchev's refusal to hold a Big Four conference in Paris after the U2 incident.

INDIVIDUAL PRESIDENTIAL PERSONALITIES

A final aspect to consider is a president's personality and style. "If individuals vary in personality but perform identically when exposed to common stimuli," Fred Greenstein writes, "we clearly can dispense with the study of their personality differences: a variable cannot explain a uniformity."[26] Thus, when analyzing why modern presidents used personal diplomacy, the need to explore each leader's individual characteristics fades. However, a president's personal qualities do matter when considering outcomes. In everyday life, the more compelling an individual is, the more enjoyable and persuasive he or she is as a companion. The same is true at the highest level of politics. A president's charm, sense of humor, and general demeanor can be an asset. For example, Roosevelt and Kennedy often drew leaders in with their charisma, and Reagan's geniality and warmth helped disarm foreign critics. These qualities can also help with the public aspects of leader-to-leader diplomacy. A self-assured and magnetic president can captivate a crowd and enhance the symbolism of personal diplomacy, such as when Kennedy traveled to Berlin. Merely possessing a winning personality is not going to make a president's personal diplomacy successful, but it cannot hurt.

The opposite is also true. A president's temperament and disposition can rub another leader the wrong way. Carter and German chancellor Helmut Schmidt did not get along. The tension was partly because of policy differences, but Carter was stubborn and could come off as aloof and arrogant. However, Carter had warm relationships with other leaders, such as Sadat and Japanese prime minister Masayoshi Ōhira. Thus, the impact of presidential personality is a wild card and is usually dependent on the other foreign leader's character and temperament as well.

Under what circumstances might a president's personal qualities make a difference? Greenstein provides a useful framework for thinking about the impact of the individual in politics.[27] He distinguishes between action dispensability and actor dispensability. Action dispensability is concerned with cases in which an individual's actions impact outcomes. Would a particular outcome have occurred without an individual's particular actions? Actor dispensability refers to cases in which an individual's personal characteristics influence outcomes. Can an action best be understood as the result of an individual's personal characteristics?

The chance of an individual's actions shaping outcomes depends on how amenable the environment is to restructuring, how strategically placed in that environment the individual is, and the individual's level of skill.[28] Presidents are at the center of the American political universe and occupy an office with the power, resources, and prestige to make them dominant global players. Thus, occupants of the White House are well positioned to make an international impact. To evaluate the opportunity for presidents' actions to shape outcomes, we can look at variables in the international arena. The relative strength of adversaries, relationships with allies, and the state of the global economy, as well as domestic factors such as a president's popularity, the nation's economic strength, and pushback from Congress, are factors that can either help or hurt presidential personal diplomacy. Thus, the concept of action dispensability provides a way to analyze the potential for personal diplomacy to make a difference, regardless of who the president is.

But to determine the circumstances under which an individual president's personal characteristics are most likely to play a significant role in diplomacy, the concept of actor dispensability is valuable.[29] According to Greenstein, "The opportunities for personal variation are increased to the degree that political actors lack socially standardized mental sets which might lead them to structure their perceptions and resolve ambiguities."[30] First, we can think of the knowledge presidents possess when they interact with their counterparts. How much they know about any particular international issue varies, as does how well they prepare for their encounters. Because presidents lack a standardized set of knowledge, there is variation in how they perform when interacting with other leaders, which influences outcomes.

Second, according to Greenstein, an individual's "intense need to take . . . cues from others will tend to reduce the effects of variation."[31] Presidents often meet with other chief executives in large groups, including advisers and numerous officials from both countries. In addition, they usually have private tête-à-têtes with just a few close advisers or only their interpreters. In larger group settings, they may feel more constrained in what they say and how they act. A standard script may be followed. When alone, presidents are more likely to diverge from the standard approach, which means that personal characteristics play a larger role.

Third, "the more demanding the political act—the more it is one that calls for an active investment of effort—the greater the likelihood that it will be influenced by personal characteristics of the actor."[32] Presidents use personal diplomacy for both routine and extraordinary purposes. In the case of everyday interactions, presidents can be expected to act more or less the same. Sending congratulatory messages or best wishes on a special occasion to another leader and performing symbolic functions during a state visit are examples of standard acts of personal diplomacy. However, during a crisis, when decisions must be made quickly and often with incomplete information, the president's individual characteristics move to the fore. Similarly, if a president has grand ambitions and undertakes a major initiative to reshape the international environment, personality will play a greater role.

Last, "even when there is little room for personal variability in the instrumental aspects of actions, there is likely to be variability in their expressive aspects."[33] This is where a president's style comes into play. For example, during a state visit, every president stages a welcoming ceremony full of pomp and delivers kind remarks about the guest of honor. But not every president exudes the same level of energy and evinces the same level of enjoyment in carrying out such duties. Similarly, behind closed doors, presidents might have the same talking points but deliver them differently, affecting how the other leader responds.

As this book has shown, personal diplomacy has its champions and its critics. This is partly because the potential risks are equal to the potential benefits, and judging the practice's impact is not always easy. This chapter has evaluated personal diplomacy's importance by using examples from earlier chapters to illustrate what has worked and what has not worked for presidents. Additionally, it has provided a set of criteria to help assess personal diplomacy's importance and whether the direct interaction between US presidents and foreign leaders can make a difference and result in outcomes that would not have occurred otherwise.

The aim is not to provide timeless lessons. Like the practice of personal diplomacy, the past is complex. Despite commonalities, every presidential interaction with a foreign leader is unique, limiting what the past can teach us. Still, presidents can learn from the experiences of their predecessors.[34] Statecraft is a perilous endeavor, and those in power should use every available resource as they craft and execute an agenda. Thus, studying the record of diplomacy at the highest level—why presidents used it, how they did so, and the outcomes—provides insight that might not guarantee sound and successful policy but can help at the margins. Given the challenges faced by presidents both at home and abroad and the consequences of failure, every bit of assistance is valuable.

Conclusion: Presidential Personal Diplomacy—Past, Present, Future

When Donald Trump spoke with Ukrainian president Volodymyr Zelensky on July 25, 2019, neither man knew he was taking part in what would become the most famous presidential phone call in American history. Trump began by congratulating Zelensky on his party's recent electoral victory. The conversation, however, quickly moved on to other matters. After Zelensky thanked the president for his support against Russian aggression and expressed his desire to buy more Javelin antitank missiles from the United States, Trump responded, "I would like you to do us a favor though." The favor involved opening investigations into a conspiracy theory related to the 2016 election and into the son of a Democratic presidential candidate. Afterward, Trump vigorously asserted that this phone call was "perfect." Others saw it as an abuse of power. The call's revelation set off an investigation in the House of Representatives, where government officials testified that they believed Trump was withholding military aid and a White House meeting until Zelensky announced that the investigations Trump desired were under way. On December 18, 2019, Donald Trump became the third American president to be impeached.[1]

Trump warned that if his call with Zelensky was inappropriate, then no president was safe: "No future President can EVER again speak to another foreign leader!"[2] But no one questioned the president's right to speak with other leaders or that the president should do so on occasion. Instead, critics questioned Trump's s personal diplomacy, which involved numerous awkward moments and diplomatic faux pas. More seriously, he made statements contradicting long-standing US policy and made inappropriate promises. According to one White House official, many of Trump's telephone calls with other heads of state and government "genuinely horrified" senior staff.[3] Similarly, his fawning praise of brutal dictators and his personal insults of allies caused much consternation. But despite the controversy surrounding Trump, personal diplomacy remains central to the presidency.

As this book has demonstrated, since Franklin Roosevelt, American presidents have felt the pull of engagement at the highest level. As a result, the practice of personal diplomacy has become essential to the conduct of US foreign affairs and a key aspect of presidential leadership. This did not come about because of personality or personal preference. Instead, all modern presidents were influenced by the same set of factors: the challenges and crises of the postwar international environment, domestic political incentives, foreign leaders' desire for presidential time, and the never-ending quest for control of foreign policy. Rarely was one of these elements the sole motivating factor; more often, a confluence of factors nudged presidents along. Personal diplomacy thus became part of their job description. This is not to say that the practice's use developed in a straight line. There were plenty of setbacks and pushback from other political actors. But during the second half of the twentieth century, personal diplomacy became an indelible feature of US foreign relations and the presidency and "a way of life" in international politics.[4]

Even with the end of the Cold War, diplomacy at the highest level remained prominent. The Soviet Union's demise ended the bipolarity that had defined international politics for four decades. In the words of Charles Krauthammer, it was America's "unipolar moment." While Krauthammer wanted America to assert its dominance, others advocated retrenchment.[5] Thus, how America should act on the world stage and what should guide US foreign policy in the post–Cold War world were hotly debated. There was "no rulebook after the Cold War," recalled Nancy Soderberg, deputy national security adviser in the 1990s. "The world had fundamentally changed. The way you do business has to change."[6] That was not entirely true. Some things stayed the same, such as the president's use of personal diplomacy.

When Bill Clinton took office, he was inexperienced in foreign policy and focused on the economy. But if Clinton was preoccupied with economic matters early on, "it's a canard that he wasn't interested in foreign affairs," according to Warren Christopher, Clinton's first secretary of state. After a year in office, the president's schedulers tallied up how much time Clinton had spent meeting with foreign leaders and speaking with them on the telephone. Then they compared it with George H. W. Bush's first year in office—and Bush was a president known for his foreign policy focus. "Damned if it wasn't identical," Anthony Lake, Clinton's first national security adviser, recalled.[7] Clinton also seemed to have a natural skill in this area. He "understood [foreign] leaders magnificently, understood them as politicians, as human beings, as world leaders," James Steinberg, deputy national security adviser, remembered. "He understood what made them work and what made them tick and how to get them on his side."[8] This did not mean that Clinton was always successful, as evidenced by his failure to clinch a deal between Israeli and Palestinian leaders at a two-week summit at Camp David, along with the mixed results of his close relationship with Russian president Boris Yeltsin.[9]

George W. Bush followed in his father's footsteps. "I placed a high priority on personal diplomacy," he wrote in his memoir. "Getting to know a fellow world leader's personality, character, and concerns made it easier to find common ground and deal with contentious issues."[10] Bush's belief in the practice manifested itself in his postpresidential passion for painting. He painted more than two dozen portraits of world leaders that were featured at his presidential library in a 2014 exhibition called "The Art of Leadership: A President's Personal Diplomacy."[11]

But where did Bush's belief in personal diplomacy get him? When he first met Russian president Vladimir Putin, he said, "I looked the man in the eye . . . I was able to get a sense of his soul." Based on this, Bush found the Russian leader "trustworthy."[12] By the end of Bush's term, Putin had invaded Georgia, and US-Russia relations were at a nadir. In other areas as well, Bush's personal diplomacy failed him. When seeking support for the invasion of Iraq, he telephoned numerous world leaders but usually came up short.[13] The story was much the same later in his administration as well. "More than many of his predecessors," the *Washington Post* wrote, "President Bush has invested heavily in trying to forge a strong bond with key foreign leaders. But as his term winds down, new crises in Georgia and Pakistan are underscoring the limits of Bush's personal diplomacy."[14]

In many ways, Barack Obama was the anti-Bush (both the elder and the younger). He did not view personal relations with foreign leaders in the same glow. As Jeffery Goldberg wrote in the *Atlantic*, Obama was "famously transactional when it comes to relations with other leaders . . . [he had a] strong belief that countries tend to act in what their leaders perceive to be their core interests, and I've come to see that Obama doesn't place enormous value in the notion that well-developed personal relationships between leaders could ever trump the cold-eyed pursuit of those interests."[15] Obama's view was closer to that of an old associate of George H. W. Bush: Henry Kissinger. The former secretary of state once told Bush, "It doesn't matter whether they [foreign officials] like you or not."[16] More important were shared interests.

But whether presidents were cast in the Bush or the Obama mold, they engaged in personal diplomacy for strategic reasons.[17] As political scientists have shown, there was a clear increase in the number of presidential trips abroad and visits by foreign heads of state and government in the second half of the twentieth century. Harry Truman averaged less than one meeting a month with a foreign leader. By the end of 2007, George W. Bush averaged six and a half. Dwight Eisenhower visited, on average, four countries each year, and he welcomed almost nine visitors a year to the United States. During the presidency of George H. W. Bush, those numbers were fifteen and forty-nine. This growth was not linear, but the trend was one of increasing personal diplomacy.[18]

International travel is an area of particular interest to political scientists, and they have found numerous patterns. Most nations have hosted presidential visits, with the exception of many countries in Africa. A president's first trip is usually to a neighbor. Of the twelve presidents between Eisenhower and Trump, Canada and Mexico were the first international trips for seven of them. During the Cold War, presidents most frequently visited NATO members and countries in Latin America and East Asia, with the top countries being the United Kingdom, Mexico, Canada, France, Italy, and West Germany. Bilateral meetings with foreign leaders were the main reason for travel, representing more than 60 percent of trips abroad. The next most frequent reason to leave the United States was multilateral engagements, such as G-7 summits. A smaller percentage of travel was to attend ceremonial events.[19]

Presidents' first year in office generally sees the least amount of international travel. They often spend the most time out of the country in their second and third years. Presidents also tend to travel abroad more in their second terms. No longer concerned with strategic travel domestically, presidents feel free to go abroad to boost their legacy. Similarly, the domestic political situation can influence when a president leaves the country. Scholars have found that presidential travel abroad increases during times of divided government or when Congress is polarized. If the government is divided, presidents may find their domestic agendas stalled, but they are freer to act in the international arena. When polarization is high, presidents might try to unite the warring factions through foreign policy, believing the old adage: politics stop at the water's edge. Presidents also tend to travel more often when their party's majorities in Congress are large, requiring less involvement from the White House. And although personal diplomacy is a presidential advantage, the legislative branch can factor into a president's calculations. When Congress asserts itself and takes an active interest in foreign affairs, presidents try to avoid provoking the legislature and tend to travel abroad less. Presidents also stay home when the economy is weak, lest they be perceived as more interested in foreign matters than American pocketbooks.[20]

According to Richard Rose, near the end of the Cold War, international travel became even more central to the presidency. During the Cold War, modern presidents were dominant at home and abroad. But by the late 1970s, the world had become increasingly interdependent, and the presidency's dominance was no more. For Rose, this resulted in a postmodern presidency, requiring presidents to "go international" and engage in "bargaining with foreigners on whose co-operation the President depends for success in foreign and economic policy." Failure to do so would be detrimental to American interests.[21]

When Donald Trump, the most unconventional of presidents, took office in 2017, there were questions about how he would change US foreign policy. Indeed, he shifted America's approach on many issues.[22] But as it had for his predecessors, personal diplomacy remained central, and he acknowledged the value of leader-to-leader diplomacy. The *Wall Street Journal* went so far as to declare personal diplomacy the basis for a Trump Doctrine. "It is very important that if you are the president, you should be with the foreign leaders," Trump declared in a video posted on Twitter. "There is nothing to lose and there is a lot to gain."[23] Though he downplayed the potential pitfalls, the underlying sentiment was one other modern presidents would endorse.

Undoubtedly, Trump's interactions with world leaders were unconventional. Still, his use of personal diplomacy was a continuation of past presidential practice. His style and approach broke from tradition, but the basic impetus was the same as it had been for his predecessors.[24] Similar to Lyndon Johnson's attempts to ease crises in Cyprus and Yemen, Trump, when confronted with the humanitarian disaster in Syria, a trade war, or a global pandemic, engaged with his foreign counterparts.[25] Like Richard Nixon's trips to Beijing and Moscow, Trump used international travel to project a statesmanlike image, such as a photo montage of himself at the 2017 G-20 summit that he posted to Twitter, set to a "Make America Great Again" anthem.[26] Despite some misgivings, foreign leaders still saw the advantage of being close to Trump. Even before the inauguration, Japanese prime minister Shinzo Abe came to the United States to meet Trump and continued to cultivate a relationship for four years. Israeli prime minister Benjamin Netanyahu clung to Trump, featuring him in a campaign ad and even naming a settlement after him.[27] Though Abe's and Netanyahu's goals were different, their strategy was the same as Anwar Sadat's when he tried to get close to Jimmy Carter. And like Ronald Reagan, Trump used personal diplomacy to exercise control. His historic meetings with North Korean dictator Kim Jong Un bypassed the US foreign policy establishment, which had long opposed such high-level diplomacy with a brutal regime.[28] But perhaps there is no better example of Trump's desire for control than his telephone call with Zelensky. Regardless of the call's appropriateness, underlying that conversation was the president's use of personal diplomacy to exercise more control and steer American foreign policy in directions that other actors, such as the State and Defense Departments, could not or would not take.

What will personal diplomacy look like after Trump? His style spotlighted the practice and generally cast it in an unfavorable light. To critics, Trump was impulsive and uninformed, and his reliance on his "feel" for other leaders was dangerous.[29] The call with Zelensky demonstrated that Trump saw no difference between foreign policy and domestic politics. Trump was transactional in his dealings with world leaders, yet he personalized everything. His bargaining was often less about advancing America's national interest and more about enhancing his own political fortunes back home.[30] But those dangers have been present throughout the postwar period. By designating the president the nation's diplomat in chief, the Constitution provides few constraints on diplomacy at the highest level. A personality like Trump intensified the concern, but the practice has survived decades of scrutiny and criticism and will continue to do so. It is part of the fabric of international relations and is accepted and expected by the American public, the media, and leaders in foreign capitals.

The backlash to Trump's approach demonstrates personal diplomacy's staying power. Despite the outrage and even his impeachment, Trump's interactions with world leaders continued unabated. The international system that twenty-first-century presidents confront is different from that of their Cold War predecessors. Although the dynamics that motivated presidents from Franklin Roosevelt to George H. W. Bush have changed over the decades, they still motivate presidents today.

Joe Biden enters the White House with a well-defined approach to foreign affairs. "All politics is personal, particularly international relations," he remarked on the campaign trail in 2020. "You've got to know the other man or woman's soul, and who they are, and make sure they know you." But even without such enthusiasm for personal interaction, there would still be reasons for Biden to engage his foreign counterparts. During his nearly fifty years in government, including decades on the Senate Foreign Relations Committee and eight years as vice president, Biden met with, in his words, "every major world leader." But as he made clear, these meetings were not because of any personal qualities he possessed; they occurred "because of the nature of my job."[31] This is even more true now that Biden is president. As this book has shown, interacting with foreign leaders has become an integral part of how the president manages foreign affairs. It is part of the job description. With all its benefits and dangers, personal diplomacy remains central to presidential leadership and American foreign relations and will continue to be so for the foreseeable future.

Notes

WHCF   White House Central File
WP   *Washington Post*
WSJ   *Wall Street Journal*

INTRODUCTION

1. "2,000,000 Cheer Wilson in Paris," *WP*, December 15, 1918; Samuel F. Wells, *The Challenges of Power: American Diplomacy, 1900–1921* (Lanham, MD: University Press of America, 1990), 119; Woodrow Wilson, "Sixth Annual Message," December 2, 1918, APP, https://www.presidency.ucsb.edu/node/207603; Fred J. Essary, "People Acclaim Wilson; Powerful Politicians as Yet Unreconciled," *Baltimore Sun*, December 15, 1918.

2. "President Poincare Coming to America; Kings Will Also Return Wilson's Visit," *WP*, December 15, 1918.

3. On the idea of the "modern presidency," see Fred I. Greenstein, "Change and Continuity in the Modern Presidency," in *The New American Political System*, ed. Anthony King (Washington, DC: American Enterprise Institute, 1978), 45–86. For a critique of the concept, see David K. Nichols, *The Myth of the Modern Presidency* (University Park: Pennsylvania State University, 1994).

4. The relationship between American presidents and British prime ministers has been of particular interest. See, for example, Warren Kimball, *Forged in War: Churchill, Roosevelt, and the Second World War* (New York: William Morrow, 1997); Jon Meacham, *Franklin and Winston: An Intimate Portrait of an Epic Friendship* (New York: Random House, 2004); Anthony Edmonds, *Eisenhower, Macmillan and Allied Unity, 1957–61* (New York: Palgrave Macmillan, 2003); Jonathan Colman, *A "Special Relationship"? Harold Wilson, Lyndon B. Johnson and Anglo-American Relations "at the Summit," 1964–1968* (New York: Manchester University Press, 2004); Richard Aldous, *Reagan and Thatcher: The Difficult Relationship* (New York: W. W. Norton, 2012). On personality and preferences, see Frank Costigliola, *Roosevelt's Lost Alliance: How Personal Politics Helped Start the Cold War* (Princeton, NJ: Princeton University Press, 2012); Philip E. Muehlenbeck, *Betting on Africans: John F. Kennedy's Courting of African Nationalist Leaders* (New York: Oxford University Press, 2012). The literature on particular summits and meetings is vast. Representative works include Lawrence Wright, *Thirteen Days in September: Carter, Begin, and Sadat at Camp David* (New York: Alfred A. Knopf, 2014); Margaret Macmillan, *Nixon and Mao: The Week that Changed the World* (New York: Random House, 2007); Margaret Macmillan, *Paris 1919: Six Months that Changed the World* (New York: Random House, 2003); S. M. Plokhy, *Yalta: The Price of Peace* (New York: Viking, 2010); Michael S. Neiberg, *Potsdam: The End of World War II and the Remaking of Europe* (New York: Basic Books, 2015); Keith Sainsbury, *The Turning Point: Roosevelt, Stalin, Churchill, and Chiang-Kai Shek, 1943; the Moscow, Cairo, and Tehran Conferences* (Oxford: Oxford University Press, 1985); Günter Bischof, Stefan Karner, and Barbara Stelzl-Marx, eds., *The Vienna Summit and Its Importance in International History* (Lanham, MD: Lexington

Books, 2014); Günter Bischof and Saki Dockril, eds., *Cold War Respite: The Geneva Summit of 1955* (Baton Rouge: Louisiana State University Press, 2000).

5. See, for example, David Reynolds, *Summits: Six Meetings that Shaped the Twentieth Century* (New York: Basic Books, 2007); Kristina Spohr and David Reynolds, eds., *Transcending the Cold War: Summits, Statecraft, and the Dissolution of Bipolarity in Europe, 1970–1990* (Oxford: Oxford University Press, 2016); Charles L. Mee Jr., *Playing God: Seven Fateful Moments When Great Men Met to Change the World* (New York: Simon & Schuster, 1993).

6. Most of these works focus on summitry, which is just one aspect of personal diplomacy. See David H. Dunn, ed., *Diplomacy at the Highest Level: The Evolution of International Summitry* (London: Macmillan Press, 1996); Nicholas Bayne, *Hanging in There: The G7 and G8 Summit in Maturity and Renewal* (Aldershot, UK: Ashgate, 2000); Roland Vogt, *Personal Diplomacy in the EU: Political Leadership and Critical Junctures of European Integration* (New York: Routledge, 2017); Kjell Engelbrekt, *High-Table Diplomacy: The Reshaping of International Security Institutions* (Washington, DC: Georgetown University Press, 2016).

7. Elmer Plischke, *Diplomat in Chief: The President at the Summit* (New York: Praeger, 1986).

8. Todd Hall and Keren Yarhi-Milo, "'The Personal Touch': Leaders' Impressions, Costly Signaling, and Assessments of Sincerity in International Affairs," *International Studies Quarterly* 56, 3 (September 2012): 562.

9. Philip Zelikow, interview by the author, October 22, 2019, Washington, DC.

10. Raymond Cohen and Raymond Westbrook, "Introduction: The Amarna System," in *Amarna Diplomacy: The Beginnings of International Relations*, ed. Raymond Cohen and Raymond Westbrook (Baltimore: Johns Hopkins University Press, 2000), 1–2, 6–9; Erik Goldstein, "The Origins of Summit Diplomacy," in Dunn, *Diplomacy at the Highest Level*, 23–37; Reynolds, *Summits*, 11–24.

11. Jefferson quoted in Felix Gilbert, *To the Farewell Address: Ideas of Early American Foreign Policy* (Princeton, NJ: Princeton University Press, 1961), 72.

12. George C. Herring, *From Colony to Superpower: U.S. Foreign Relations since 1776* (New York: Oxford University Press, 2008), 2–3; C. Vann Woodward, "The Age of Reinterpretation," *American Historical Review* 66, 1 (October 1960): 2.

13. Richard Ellis, *Presidential Travel: The Journey from George Washington to George W. Bush* (Lawrence: University Press of Kansas, 2008), 166–198.

14. Grant to James G. Blaine, August 31, 1871, in *The Papers of Ulysses S. Grant*, vol. 22, ed. John Y. Simon (Carbondale: Southern Illinois University Press, 1998), 125; Elmer Plischke, "The President's Right to Go Abroad," *ORBIS* 15 (Fall 1971): 755–783.

15. "President Poincare Coming to America"; "Visits by Foreign Leaders," Office of the Historian, Department of State, https://history.state.gov/departmenthistory/visits.

16. Richard Collin, *Theodore Roosevelt's Caribbean: The Panama Canal, the Monroe Doctrine, and the Latin American Context* (Baton Rouge: Louisiana State University Press, 1990), 123.

17. Raymond A. Esthus, *Theodore Roosevelt and the International Rivalries* (Waltham, MA: Ginn-Blaisdell, 1970).

18. Ellis, *Presidential Travel,* 172.

19. Sasson Sofer, "Old and New Diplomacy: A Debate Revisited," *Review of International Studies* 14, 3 (July 1988): 194–211; Elmer Plischke, "The New Diplomacy: A Changing Process," *Virginia Quarterly Review* 49, 3 (Summer 1973): 321–345.

20. "Mediation for Europe Offer of President," *Christian Science Monitor,* August 5, 1914; "Mr. Wilson's Reply," *Christian Science Monitor,* June 11, 1915.

21. Greg Russell, "Theodore Roosevelt's Diplomacy and the Quest for Great Power Equilibrium in Asia," *Presidential Studies Quarterly* 38, 3 (September 2008): 440; Howard Beale, *Theodore Roosevelt and the Rise of America to World Power* (Baltimore: Johns Hopkins University Press, 1956), 455; Roosevelt to Carnegie, August 6, 1906, in *The Selected Letters of Theodore Roosevelt,* ed. H. W. Brands (New York: Cooper Square Press, 2001), 423.

22. Ellis, *Presidential Travel,* 179–183.

23. Memos by Robert Lansing, "Will the President Go to the Peace Congress," November 12, 1918, and "The President's Going to the Peace Conference," November 18, 1918, Papers of Woodrow Wilson Digital Edition, University of Virginia Press, https://rotunda.upress.virginia.edu/founders/WILS.html.

24. Wilson, "Sixth Annual Message"; Ellis, *Presidential Travel,* 184.

25. Diary of Henry Ashurst, December 3, 1918, Papers of Woodrow Wilson Digital Edition.

26. "Visits by Foreign Leaders"; "Travels Abroad of the President," Office of the Historian, Department of State, https://history.state.gov/departmenthistory/travels/president.

27. Richard Neustadt, *Presidential Power and the Modern Presidents: The Politics of Leadership from Roosevelt to Reagan* (New York: Free Press, 1990). On the challenges presidents face in the American political system, see Charles O. Jones, *The Presidency in a Separated System,* 2nd ed. (Washington, DC: Brookings Institution, 2005).

28. Examples of other works that view the presidency through a personal lens are Erwin C. Hargrove, *Presidential Leadership: Personality and Political Style* (New York: Macmillan, 1966); Fred I. Greenstein, *The Presidential Difference: Leadership Style from FDR to Barack Obama,* 3rd ed. (Princeton, NJ: Princeton University Press, 2009); James David Barber, *The Presidential Character: Predicting Performance in the White House,* 4th ed. (Upper Saddle River, NJ: Prentice-Hall, 1992).

29. Terry Moe, "Presidents, Institutions, and Theory," in *Researching the Presidency: Vital Questions, New Approaches,* ed. George C. Edwards III, John H. Kessel, and Bert A. Rockman (Pittsburgh: University of Pittsburgh Press, 1993), 337.

30. Clinton Rossiter, *The American Presidency* (Baltimore: Johns Hopkins University Press, 1987), 11–12, 14.

31. Aaron Wildavsky, "The Two Presidencies," *Trans-Action* 4, 2 (December 1966): 7–14; Brandice Canes-Wrone, William G. Howell, and David E. Lewis, "Toward a

Broader Understanding of Presidential Power: A Reevaluation of the Two Presidencies Thesis," *Journal of Politics* 70, 1 (January 2008): 4–5.

32. David Lindsey and Williams Hobbs, "Presidential Effort and International Outcomes: Evidence for an Executive Bottleneck," *Journal of Politics* 77, 4 (October 2015): 1090–1091.

33. Terry M. Moe and William G. Howell, "Unilateral Action and Presidential Power: A Theory," *Presidential Studies Quarterly* 29, 4 (December 1999): 850–873.

34. William G. Howell, *Thinking about the Presidency: The Primacy of Power* (Princeton, NJ: Princeton University Press, 2013), 12, 13.

35. Matthew J. Dickinson, *Bitter Harvest: FDR, Presidential Power and the Growth of the Presidential Branch* (New York: Cambridge University Press, 1997), 86–113.

36. Alfred D. Sander, "Truman and the National Security Council: 1945–47," *Journal of American History* 59, 2 (September 1972): 369–388; Mark M. Lowenthal, *The National Security Council: Organizational History* (Washington, DC: Congressional Research Service, 1978), 8.

37. David Rothkopf, *Running the World: The Inside Story of the National Security Council and the Architects of American Power* (New York: Public Affairs, 2004), 29; Bryan Mabee, "Historical Institutionalism and Foreign Policy Analysis: The Origins of the National Security Council Revisited," *Foreign Policy Analysis* 7, 1 (January 2011): 37–41.

38. On the growth of resources for travel, see Michael John Burton, "The 'Flying White House': A Travel Establishment within the Presidential Branch," *Presidential Studies Quarterly* 36, 2 (June 2006): 297–308.

39. Charles A. Stevenson, *America's Foreign Policy Toolkit: Key Institutions and Processes* (Washington, DC: CQ Quarterly Press, 2013), 144–145, 156–159.

40. On institutional development and the layering of the new on top of existing structures, see Jeffrey K. Tulis, *The Rhetorical Presidency* (Princeton, NJ: Princeton University Press, 1987); Eric Schickler, *Disjointed Pluralism: Institutional Innovation and the Development of the U.S. Congress* (Princeton, NJ: Princeton University Press, 2001); Victoria A. Farrar-Myers, *Scripted for Change: The Institutionalization of the American Presidency* (College Station: Texas A&M University Press, 2007).

41. Plischke, *Diplomat in Chief,* 54.

42. "Coolidge Greets Alfonso on Phone," *NYT,* October 14, 1928

43. Coolidge quoted in Nathan Miller, *New World Coming: The 1920s and the Making of Modern America* (New York: Scribner, 2003), 138.

44. Ellis, *Presidential Travel,* 166–167, 200–203, 221–227; Burton, "'Flying White House,'" 300–303.

45. Kenneth N. Watlz, "The Stability of a Bipolar World," *Daedalus* 93, 3 (Summer 1964): 881–909; John Lewis Gaddis, *The Long Peace: Inquiries into the History of the Cold War* (New York: Oxford University Press, 1987).

46. Rothkopf, *Running the World,* 53.

47. David Holloway, "Nuclear Weapons and the Escalation of the Cold War, 1945–1962," in *The Cambridge History of the Cold War,* vol. 1, ed. Melvyn P. Leffler and Odd

Arne Westad (Cambridge: Cambridge University Press), 390–393. For the two men's exchanges, see *FRUS, 1961–1963*, vol. 7 (Washington, DC: GPO, 1996).

48. Canes-Wrone, Howell, and Lewis, "Toward a Broader Understanding of Presidential Power," 5–6.

49. Lake quoted in Aaron David Miller, *The Much Too Promised Land: America's Elusive Search for Arab-Israeli Peace* (New York: Random House, 2008), 77.

50. For historical works on the nexus between foreign policy and domestic politics, see Melvin Small, *Democracy and Diplomacy: The Impact of Domestic Politics on Foreign Policy, 1789–1994* (Baltimore: Johns Hopkins University Press, 1996); Thomas A. Schwartz, "'Henry, . . . Winning an Election Is Terribly Important': Partisan Politics in the History of U.S. Foreign Relations," *Diplomatic History* 33, 2 (April 2009): 173–190; Julian E. Zelizer, *Arsenal of Democracy: The Politics of National Security—From World War II to the War on Terrorism* (New York: Basic Books, 2010); Andrew L. Johns and Mitchell Lerner, eds., *The Cold War at Home and Abroad: Domestic Politics and U.S. Foreign Policy since 1945* (Lexington: University Press of Kentucky, 2018); Campbell Craig and Fredrik Logevall, *America's Cold War: The Politics of Insecurity* (Cambridge, MA: Belknap Press, 2009). Political scientists have also explored the topic. See Peter B. Evans, Harold K. Jacobson, and Robert D. Putnam, eds., *Double-Edged Diplomacy: International Bargaining and Domestic Politics* (Berkeley: University of California Press, 1993); James Lee Ray, *American Foreign Policy and Rational Political Ambition,* 2nd ed. (Thousand Oaks, CA: CQ Press, 2014); Helen V. Milner and Dustin Tingley, *Sailing the Water's Edge: The Domestic Politics of American Foreign Policy* (Princeton, NJ: Princeton University Press, 2015); James M. McCormick, ed., *The Domestic Sources of American Foreign Policy: Insights and Evidence,* 7th ed. (Lanham, MD: Rowman & Littlefield, 2018).

51. Theodore J. Lowi, *The Personal President: Power Invested, Promise Unfulfilled* (Ithaca, NY: Cornell University Press, 1985), 96.

52. Thomas E. Cronin, Michael A. Genovese, and Meena Bose, *Paradoxes of the American Presidency,* 5th ed. (New York: Oxford University Press, 2017).

53. Samuel Kernell, *Going Public: New Strategies in Presidential Leadership,* 4th ed. (Washington, DC: CQ Press, 2007).

54. Bruce Miroff, "The Presidential Spectacle," in *The Presidency and the Political System,* 10th ed., ed. Michael Nelson (Washington, DC: CQ Press, 2014), 231–257.

55. For example, see Elmer Plischke, "The President's Image as Diplomat in Chief," *Review of Politics* 47, 4 (October 1985): 544–565; Robert E. Darcy and Alvin Richman, "Presidential Travel and Public Opinion," *Presidential Studies Quarterly* 18, 1 (Winter 1988): 85–90; Dennis M. Simon and Charles W. Ostrom Jr., "The Impact of Televised Speeches and Foreign Travel on Presidential Approval," *Public Opinion Quarterly* 53, 1 (Spring 1989): 58–82; Agnes Simon, "The Political and Economic Consequences of the Summit Diplomatic Activity of the U.S. President" (Ph.D. diss., University of Missouri, 2012), 39–60. Presidential travel also has the potential to influence the opinions of foreign audiences. See Benjamin E. Goldsmith and Yusaku Horiuchi, "Spinning the Globe? U.S. Public Diplomacy and Foreign Public Opinion," *Journal of Politics* 71, 3 (July 2009): 863–875.

56. Paul C. Light, *The President's Agenda: Domestic Policy Choice from Kennedy to Clinton*, 3rd ed. (Baltimore: Johns Hopkins University Press, 1999); Phillip B. K. Potter, "Lame-Duck Foreign Policy," *Presidential Studies Quarterly* 46, 4 (December 2016): 849–867.

57. Raymond Cohen, *Theatre of Power: The Art of Diplomatic Signalling* (London: Longman, 1987), 44, 46. On presidential symbolism, see Wilfred E. Binkley, "The President as a National Symbol," *Annals of the American Academy of Political and Social Science* 283 (September 1952): 86–93; Barbara Hinckley, *The Symbolic Presidency: How Presidents Portray Themselves* (New York: Routledge, 1990). While personal diplomacy might better communicate policy and enhance the salience of a foreign policy issue, it is unlikely to change policy positions. See Brandice Canes-Wrone, *Who Leads Whom? Presidents, Policy, and the Public* (Chicago: University of Chicago Press, 2006), 19–50, 83–102.

58. Rossiter, *American Presidency*, 25–27.

59. Simon, "Political and Economic Consequences of Summit Diplomatic Activity," 142–165. See also Nitsch Volker, "State Visits and International Trade," *World Economy* 30, 12 (December 2007): 1797–1816.

60. Michael Anderson and Theo Farrell, "Superpower Summitry," in Dunn, *Diplomacy at the Highest Level*, 69–75; Gordon R. Weihmiller and Dusko Doder, *U.S.-Soviet Summits: An Account of East-West Diplomacy at the Top, 1955–1985* (Lanham, MD: University Press of America, 1986), 65.

61. Lewis quoted in Martha Joynt Kumar, "The Office of Communications," in *The White House World: Transitions, Organization, and Office Operations*, ed. Martha Joynt Kumar and Terry Sullivan (College Station: Texas A&M University Press, 2003), 275.

62. Judith G. Kelley and Jon C. Pevehouse, "An Opportunity Cost Theory of US Treaty Behavior," *International Studies Quarterly* 59, 3 (September 2015): 531–543; Lindsey and Hobbs, "Presidential Effort and International Outcomes," 1089–1102.

63. McGeorge Bundy, *The Strength of Government* (Cambridge, MA: Harvard University Press, 1968), 37. On the problem of control, see Terry M. Moe, "An Assessment of the Positive Theory of 'Congressional Dominance,'" *Legislative Studies Quarterly* 12, 4 (November 1987): 480–481.

64. Lord quoted in Rothkopf, *Running the World*, 127.

65. Jimmy Carter, "Being There," *Foreign Affairs* 78, 6 (November–December 1999): 164, 165.

66. David E. Lewis and Terry M. Moe, "The Presidency and the Bureaucracy: The Levers of Presidential Control," in *The Presidency and the Political System*, 11th ed., ed. Michael Nelson (Thousand Oaks, CA: CQ Press, 2018), 378; Terry M. Moe, "The Politics of Bureaucratic Structure," in *Can the Government Govern?* ed. John E. Chubb and Paul E. Peterson (Washington, DC: Brooking Institution, 1989), 279–280.

67. Richard W. Cottam, *Foreign Policy Motivation: A General Theory of a Case Study* (Pittsburgh: University of Pittsburgh Press, 1977), 10. On bureaucratic politics as a determinant of policy, see Graham Allison, *Essence of Decision: Explaining the Cuban Missile Crisis* (Boston: Little, Brown, 1971).

68. Stephen Hess, *Organizing the Presidency* (Washington, DC: Brookings Institution, 1976), 10.

69. Kissinger quoted in Rothkopf, *Running the World,* 118.

70. Clark Clifford, "The Presidency as I Have Seen It," in *The Living Presidency,* ed. Emmet John Hughes (New York: Coward, McCann & Geoghegan, 1973), 315.

71. Ronald L. Jepperson, "Institutions, Institutional Effects, and Institutionalism," in *The New Institutionalism in Organizational Analysis,* ed. Walter W. Powell and Paul J. DiMaggio (Chicago: University of Chicago Press, 1991), 145; Farrar-Myers, *Scripted for Change,* 6, 15; Paul Pierson, *Politics in Time: History, Institutions, and Social Analysis* (Princeton, NJ: Princeton University Press, 2011), 41.

72. Farrar-Myers, *Scripted for Change,* 12.

73. William B. Macomber, *The Angel's Game: A Handbook of Modern Diplomacy* (New York: Stein & Day, 1975), 30–37; Jonathan Mercer, "Emotional Beliefs," *International Organization* 64, 1 (January 2010): 1–31; Barbara Keys, "The Diplomat's Two Minds: Deconstructing a Foreign Policy Myth," *Diplomatic History* 44, 1 (January 2020): 1–21. In the field of US diplomatic history, Frank Costigliola has been at the forefront of examining the role of emotions in foreign relations. See, for example, Frank Costigliola, "'I Had Come as a Friend': Emotion, Culture, and Ambiguity in the Formation of the Cold War, 1943–1945," *Cold War History* 1, 1 (August 2000): 103–128; Costigliola, *Roosevelt's Lost Alliances.*

74. American Psychological Association, "Counseling Psychology," https://www.apa .org/ed/graduate/specialize/counseling.

75. Robert J. McMahon, "Credibility and World Power: Exploring the Psychological Dimension in Postwar American Diplomacy," *Diplomatic History* 15, 4 (October 1991): 455.

76. Barbara Keys and Claire Yorke, "Personal and Political Emotions in the Mind of the Diplomat," *Political Psychology* 40, 6 (December 2019): 1235–1246. On the use of psychology in US foreign relations, see Richard H. Immerman and Lori Helene Gronich, "Psychology," in *Explaining the History of American Foreign Relations,* 3rd ed., ed. Frank Costigliola and Michael J. Hogan (New York: Cambridge University Press, 2016), 334–355. International relations scholarship that acknowledges the value of personal diplomacy includes Marcus Holmes, *Face-to-Face Diplomacy: Social Neuroscience and International Security* (Cambridge: Cambridge University Press, 2018); Seanon Wong, "Emotions and the Communication of Intentions in Face-to-Face Diplomacy," *European Journal of International Relations* 22, 1 (March 2016): 144–167; Keren Yarhi-Milo, *Knowing the Adversary: Leaders, Intelligence, and the Assessment of Intentions in International Relations* (Princeton, NJ: Princeton University Press, 2014); Nicholas J. Wheeler, *Trusting Enemies: Interpersonal Relationships in International Conflict* (Oxford: Oxford University Press, 2018); Hall and Yarhi-Milo, "'Personal Touch.'"

77. Jenny Edkins, *Face Politics* (New York: Taylor & Francis, 2015), 1; Leigh Thompson, *The Mind and Heart of the Negotiator,* 5th ed. (Boston: Prentice Hall, 2009), 320; Christer Jönsson and Martin Hall, *Essence of Diplomacy* (New York: Palgrave Macmillan, 2005), 84; Holmes, *Face-to-Face Diplomacy.*

78. Bush's memoir is littered with examples of his personal diplomacy. See George W. Bush, *Decision Points* (New York: Crown, 2010).

79. Suzanne Goldenberg, "Secret Talks and a Personal Letter: How the US-China Climate Deal Was Done," *Guardian*, November 12, 2014, https://www.theguardian.com /environment/2014/nov/12/how-us-china-climate-deal-was-done-secret-talks-personal -letter; Andrew Restuccia, "Obama Calls Chinese Leader as Climate Talks Blow Past Friday Deadline," *Politico*, December 11, 2015.

80. Donald Trump, Twitter post, August 18, 2018, 3:39 p.m., https://twitter.com/real DonaldTrump/status/1030902046520696832; "Trump Doctrine," *WSJ*, June 30, 2019, https://www.wsj.com/articles/the-trump-doctrine-11561932751.

81. Keven Liptak, "After Nudge from Macron, Trump and Other G7 Leaders Agree on Coronavirus Coordination," CNN, March 15, 2020, https://www.cnn.com /2020/03/16/politics/trump-g7-leaders-cooperation-coronavirus/index.html; Patrick Wintour, "G20 to Hold Emergency Video Summit to Discuss Coronavirus," *Guardian*, March 25, 2020, https://www.theguardian.com/world/2020/mar/26/g20-hold-emergency-video -summit-discuss-coronavirus.

82. Michael Crowley, "'Strategic Empathy': How Biden's Informal Diplomacy Shaped Foreign Relations," *NYT*, July 5, 2020, https://www.nytimes.com/2020/07/05/us/politics /joe-biden-foreign-policy.html.

1. FDR'S WIDE-RANGING PERSONAL DIPLOMACY

1. Valentin Berezhkov, "Stalin and Franklin D. Roosevelt," in *FDR and His Contemporaries: Foreign Perceptions of an American President*, ed. Cornelis A. van Minnen and John F. Sears (New York: St. Martin's Press, 1992), 45–47; Frank Costigliola, *Roosevelt's Lost Alliances: How Personal Politics Helped Start the Cold War* (Princeton, NJ: Princeton University Press, 2012), 199–200; Charles E. Bohlen, *Witness to History, 1929–1969* (New York: W. W. Norton, 1973), 147.

2. Many of FDR's contemporaries held this view. See, for example, William C. Bullitt, "How We Won the War and Lost the Peace," *Life*, August 30, 1948, 83–97, and September 6, 1948, 86–103; Winston S. Churchill, *The Second World War: Triumph and Tragedy* (Boston: Houghton Mifflin, 1953); Robert Sherwood, *Roosevelt and Hopkins: An Intimate History* (New York: Harper & Brothers, 1948).

3. Costigliola, *Roosevelt's Lost Alliances*; George C. Herring, *From Colony to Superpower: U.S. Foreign Relations since 1776* (New York: Oxford University Press, 2008), 545.

4. Scholarship on the wartime conferences and Roosevelt's relations with Churchill and Stalin is voluminous. Representative works include Warren Kimball, *Forged in War: Churchill, Roosevelt, and the Second World War* (New York: William Morrow, 1997); Herbert Feis, *Churchill, Roosevelt, Stalin: The War They Waged and the Peace They Sought* (Princeton, NJ: Princeton University Press, 1957); Joseph P. Lash, *Roosevelt and Churchill, 1939–1941: The Partnership that Saved the West* (New York: W. W. Norton, 1976); Robert Nisbet, *Roosevelt and Stalin: The Failed Courtship* (New York: Regnery Gateway, 1988); Robin Edmonds, *The Big Three: Churchill, Roosevelt & Stalin in Peace and War* (London: Hamish Hamilton, 1991); Keith Sainsbury, *Churchill and Roosevelt at War: The*

War They Fought and the Peace They Hoped to Make (New York: New York University Press, 1994); Keith Eubank, *The Summit at Tehran* (New York: William Morrow, 1985).

5. William Leuchtenburg, *In the Shadow of FDR: From Harry Truman to George W. Bush*, 3rd ed. (Ithaca, NY: Cornell University Press, 2001).

6. "Inaugural Address," March 4, 1933, APP, https://www.presidency.ucsb.edu /node/208712; "Roosevelt Calls for a Real Peace with the League," *NYT*, August 10, 1920; Franklin Roosevelt, "Our Foreign Policy: A Democratic View," *Foreign Affairs* 6, 4 (July 1928): 573–586.

7. James MacGregor Burns, *Roosevelt: The Lion and the Fox* (New York: Harcourt Brace Jovanovich, 1956), 262–263. For FDR's foreign policy outlook and use of public opinion, see Robert Dallek, *Franklin Roosevelt and American Foreign Policy, 1932–1945* (New York: Oxford University Press, 1995); Richard W. Steele, "The Pulse of the People: Franklin D. Roosevelt and the Gauging of American Public Opinion," *Journal of Contemporary History* 9, 4 (October 1974): 195–216.

8. Raymond B. Fosdick, "America Quits Her Shell of Isolation," *NYT*, June 4, 1933; William E. Leuchtenburg, *Franklin D. Roosevelt and the New Deal, 1932–1940* (New York: Harper & Row, 1963), 200–203; David M. Kennedy, *Freedom from Fear: The American People in Depression and War, 1929–1945* (New York: Oxford University Press, 1999), 155–157.

9. Frederick T. Birchall, "America's Influence Wanes in Europe," *NYT*, July 28, 1935.

10. MacDonald to Roosevelt, February 10, 1933, folder: MacDonald, J. Ramsay, 1933–1937, box 38, PSF, DC, FDRL.

11. Donald Watt, "Roosevelt and Neville Chamberlain: Two Appeasers," *International Journal* 28, 2 (Spring 1973): 187; Roosevelt to MacDonald, February (n.d.) 1933, folder: MacDonald, J. Ramsay, 1933–1937, box 38, PSF, DC, FDRL.

12. "Seeks President's Advice and Aid in Attacking World Problems," *WP*, April 6, 1933; Arthur Krock, "M'Donald to Visit Roosevelt Shortly on World Issues," *NYT*, April 6, 1933.

13. "Joint Statement with Prime Minister MacDonald," April 26, 1933, APP, https:// www.presidency.ucsb.edu/node/208094; "Appeal for World Peace by Disarmament and for Relief from Economic Chaos," May 16, 1933, APP, https://www.presidency.ucsb.edu /node/208142; "Answers to the President's Appeal to the Nations," May 17, 1933, APP, https://www.presidency.ucsb.edu/node/208153.

14. Benjamin D. Rhodes, "The British Royal Visit of 1939 and the 'Psychological Approach' to the United States," *Diplomatic History* 2, 2 (1978): 197–211; David Reynolds, "FDR's Foreign Policy and the British Royal Visit to the USA, 1939," *Historian* 45, 4 (1983): 461–472; Peter Bell, "The Foreign Office and the 1939 Royal Visit to America: Courting the USA in an Era of Isolationism," *Journal of Contemporary History* 37, 4 (October 2002): 599–616; Albert E. Kersten, "Wilhelmina and Franklin D. Roosevelt," in van Minnen and Sears, *FDR and His Contemporaries*, 85–96.

15. Watt, "Roosevelt and Chamberlain," 189; Roosevelt to Chamberlain, September 11, 1939, folder: Great Britain, 1937–1938, box 32, PSF, DC, FDRL; Keith Feiling, *The Life of Neville Chamberlain* (London: Macmillan, 1946), 325.

16. Burns, *Roosevelt*, 476.

17. Roosevelt to Mussolini, May 14, 1933, folder: Italy 1933–38, box 41, PSF, DC, FDRL; Mussolini to Roosevelt, November 19, 1936, folder: Italy 1933–38, box 41, PSF, DC, FDRL.

18. Maurizo Vaudagna, "Mussolini and Franklin D. Roosevelt," in van Minnen and Sears, *FDR and His Contemporaries*, 158.

19. Memcon by Welles, March 22, 1939, in *FRUS, 1939*, vol. 2 (Washington, DC: GPO, 1956), 622; telegram from Welles to Roosevelt and Hull, February 27, 1940, folder: Italy, box 3, PSF, Safe File, FDRL.

20. "Message to Czechoslovakia, Germany, Great Britain, and France on the Threat of War," September 26, 1938, APP, https://www.presidency.ucsb.edu/node/209174; "Reply to the President's Message on the Threat of War," September 27, 1938, APP, https://www.presidency.ucsb.edu/node/209182.

21. Telegram from Davies to Roosevelt and Hull, March 21, 1939, folder: Belgium, 1938–41, box 24, PSF, DC, FDRL.

22. David Reynolds, *Summits: Six Meetings that Shaped the Twentieth Century* (New York: Basic Books, 2007), 85–87; telegram from Cordell Hull to Joseph Kennedy, September 28, 1938, in *FRUS, 1938*, vol. 1 (Washington, DC: GPO, 1955), 688.

23. "Message to Adolf Hitler and Benito Mussolini," April 14, 1939, APP, https://www.presidency.ucsb.edu/node/209511.

24. Sigrid Schultz, "Hitler to Scorn Roosevelt," *CDT*, April 16, 1939.

25. Camille M. Cianfarra, "Roosevelt's Plea Resented in Italy," *NYT*, April 16, 1939; David Darrah, "Britons Wonder if U.S. Note Will Prove Appeasing," *CDT*, April 16, 1939; "Roosevelt's Plea Held Bound to Fail," *NYT*, April 17, 1939.

26. Davies to Roosevelt, May 11, 1939, folder: Belgium, 1938–41, box 24, PSF, DC, FDRL; memo from DOS to Roosevelt, "Symposium of Replies Received by 12 Noon April 16, 1939," folder: Italy, Mussolini-Hitler, box 41, PSF, DC, FDRL.

27. "Capitol Hill Comment on Roosevelt Plea for Peace," *WP*, April 16, 1939; Willard Edwards, "Leaders Assail President Peace Plea as Step toward War," *CDT*, April 16, 1939; "Toward War," *CDT*, April 17, 1939.

28. "Appeal to Hitler Backed in Survey," *NYT*, April 23, 1939; Henry Kissinger, *Diplomacy* (New York: Touchstone, 1994), 384.

29. "Message to Adolf Hitler on the Poland Crisis," August 24, 1939, APP, https://www.presidency.ucsb.edu/node/209874; "A Second Letter to Chancellor Hitler," August 25, 1939, APP, https://www.presidency.ucsb.edu/node/209950.

30. Naval message from Commander Squadron to Chief of Naval Operation, March 17, 1940, folder: Germany, Sept. 1939–Mar. 1941, box 2, PSF, Safe File, FDRL.

31. "Hitler's Declaration of War against the United States," in *Historical Dictionary of the 1940s*, ed. James G. Ryan and Leonard Schlup (London: Routledge, 2006), 470.

32. On Roosevelt and de Gaulle's relationship, see Claude Fohlen, "De Gaulle and Franklin D. Roosevelt," in van Minnen and Sears, *FDR and His Contemporaries*, 33–44; Raoul Aglion, *Roosevelt and de Gaulle: Allies in Conflict, a Personal Memoir* (New York: Free Press, 1988).

33. Roosevelt quoted in Dallek, *Roosevelt and American Foreign Policy*, 406.

34. Memo from Elmer Davis to Roosevelt, June 22, 1944, folder: France, de Gaulle, Charles, 1944–45, box 31, PSF, DC, FDRL.

35. Caffery to Roosevelt, February 26, 1945, folder: France, Aug. 1944–45, box 30, PSF, DC, FDRL.

36. King quoted in Marc T. Boucher, "The Politics of Economic Depression: Canadian-American Relations in the Mid-1930s," *International Journal* 41, 1 (Winter 1985–1986): 9, 10.

37. Norman Armour to Cordell Hull, October 25, 1935; memo from Pierre de Lagarde Boal, October 31, 1935, both in *FRUS, 1935*, vol. 2 (Washington, DC: GPO, 1952), 28–30, 31.

38. C. P. Stacey, "The Turning Point: Canadian-American Relations during the Roosevelt-King Era," *Canada* 1 (1972): 1–10.

39. John MacCormac, "America's Eyes upon Canada," *NYT*, July 26, 1936; "Mackenzie King, Roosevelt Talk on Varied Topics," *CDT*, March 6, 1937; "Premier King's Visit," *WP*, March 6, 1937.

40. King to Roosevelt, March 8, 1937, folder: Canada, 1936–37, box 25, PSF, DC, FDRL.

41. King to Roosevelt, March 15, 1945, folder: Canada, 1944–45, box 25, PSF, DC, FDRL.

42. Roosevelt to King, February 18, 1941, folder: Canada, 1941, box 25, PSF, DC, FDRL.

43. Denis Smith, *Diplomacy of Fear: Canada and the Cold War, 1941–1948* (Toronto: University of Toronto Press, 1988), 13.

44. Norman Hillmer, "Defence and Ideology: The Anglo-Canadian Military 'Alliance' in the 1930s," *International Journal* 33, 3 (Summer 1978): 588–612; Warren Kimball, *The Juggler: Franklin Roosevelt as Wartime Statesman* (Princeton, NJ: Princeton University Press, 1991), 111–112; Galen R. Perras, *Franklin Roosevelt & the Origins of the Canadian-American Security Alliance, 1933–1945* (Westport, CT: Praeger, 1988).

45. "Inaugural Address," March 4, 1933.

46. "Mexican President Greets Roosevelt," *NYT*, November 19, 1941. The standard account of the Good Neighbor policy remains Bryce Wood, *The Making of the Good Neighbor Policy* (New York: Columbia University Press, 1961).

47. Instructions to the Delegates to the Seventh International Conference of American States, November 10, 1933, in *FRUS, 1933*, vol. 4 (Washington, DC: GPO, 1950), 44.

48. For FDR's visitors and travels, see Office of the Historian, Department of State, https://history.state.gov/departmenthistory/visits; https://history.state.gov/department history/travels/president. For a fuller discussion of personal diplomacy during the Good Neighbor era, see Tizoc Chavez, "'The One Bright Spot': Presidential Personal Diplomacy and the Good Neighbor Policy," *Presidential Studies Quarterly* (February 4, 2021), https://doi-org.usmalibrary.idm.oclc.org/10.1111/psq.12701.

49. Panamanian Legation to Cordell Hull, September 21, 1933, in *FRUS, 1933*, vol. 5 (Washington, DC: GPO, 1952), 852.

50. "Panaman [*sic*] President off for Washington," *NYT*, October 3, 1933; "People of Panama Pray for Arias's Success Here," *NYT*, October 4, 1933.

51. "Arias, Panama Ruler, Is Guest in White House," *WP*, October 10, 1933 "Joint Statement with President Arias of Panama," October 17, 1933, APP, https://www

.presidency.ucsb.edu/node/207728; Memo of Points Agreed to by Roosevelt and Arias, n.d., in *FRUS, 1933,* 5:866–868; Gerald Martin, "Panama Cheers Aid from U.S., and Then Gasps," *CDT,* October 31, 1933; "Panama Welcomes Arias," *NYT,* October 31, 1933.

52. "Vincent Goes Home after Favorable U.S. Visit," *Chicago Defender,* April 28, 1934; Dallek, *Roosevelt and American Foreign Policy,* 86; "Roosevelt in Haiti Renews His Pledge to Recall Marines," *NYT,* July 6, 1934.

53. Telegram from Norman Armour to Cordell Hull, July 5, 1934, in *FRUS, 1934,* vol. 5 (Washington, DC: GPO, 1952), 298.

54. Vincent to Roosevelt, November 16, 1933, folder: Haiti, 1933–1934, 1944, box 39, PSF, DC, FDRL, http://www.fdrlibrary.marist.edu/_resources/images/psf/psfa0377.pdf.

55. Press conference, June 15, 1934, FDRL, http://www.fdrlibrary.marist.edu/_re sources/images/pc/pc0008.pdf.

56. "Visit Elates Colombia," *NYT,* July 4, 1934.

57. "Cartagena Is Modernized," *NYT,* July 8, 1934.

58. "Remarks in Cartagena," July 10, 1934, APP, https://www.presidency.ucsb.edu/ node/208502.

59. Irwin F. Gellman, *Good Neighbor Diplomacy: United States Policies in Latin America, 1933–1945* (Baltimore: Johns Hopkins University Press, 1979), 38; "President Hailed in Colombia," *NYT,* July 11, 1934.

60. "Remarks in Panama," July 11, 1934, APP, https://www.presidency.ucsb.edu /node/208506.

61. Gellman, *Good Neighbor Diplomacy,* 38; Dallek, *Roosevelt and American Foreign Policy,* 87.

62. John W. Whites, "Argentina Invites Roosevelt to Visit," *NYT,* November 8, 1936; "Address before the Inter-American Conference for the Maintenance of Peace," December 1, 1936, APP, https://www.presidency.ucsb.edu/node/208508.

63. Dallek, *Roosevelt and American Foreign Policy,* 132–133; Walter Trohan, "Rio to Salute Roosevelt as a Hero Today," *CDT,* November 27, 1936.

64. Harold B. Hinton, "Roosevelt Hailed in Uruguay," *NYT,* December 4, 1936.

65. Gellman, *Good Neighbor Diplomacy,* 63, 65; "Roosevelt Departs," *LAT,* December 3, 1936.

66. Robert Kleiman, "Camacho and Almazan Wind up as Mexico Prepares to Choose President," *WP,* June 30, 1940; "Moderate Cabinet Pledged in Mexico," *NYT,* November 28, 1940; Timothy G. Turner, "Mexican Revolt Impulses under Patriotic Restraint," *LAT,* October 20, 1940.

67. John Gunther, "Camacho to Visit U.S., He Announces," *NYT,* October 6, 1940; Arnaldo Cortesi, "Mexico May Offer Bases for U.S. Use," *NYT,* November 14, 1940; "Unity of Americas Is Inaugural Note of Avila Camacho," *NYT,* December 2, 1940.

68. Edwin L. James, "War Move by Mexico Help to United States," *NYT,* May 24, 1942; Roosevelt to Ávila Camacho, May 30, 1942, folder: Mexico, 1941–42, box 44, PSF, DC, FDRL.

69. Daniels to Roosevelt, February 4, 1941, folder: Mexico, 1941–42, box 44, PSF, DC, FDRL.

70. Memo from Messersmith, January 14, 1943, folder: Mexico, 1943, box 44, PSF, DC, FDRL.

71. See multiple letters from Messersmith to Sumner Welles, including March 6, 8, 11, 22, 1943, folder: Mexico, 1943, box 44, PSF, DC, FDRL.

72. Camille M. Cianfarra, "Mexicans See Ties Cemented by Visit," *NYT*, April 22, 1934; Messersmith to Welles, April 30, 1943, folder: Mexico, 1943, box 44, PSF, DC, FDRL.

73. Bertram Hulen, "Mexico Meeting Viewed as Solidarity Gesture," *NYT*, April 24, 1943; Messersmith to Welles, April 30, 1943.

74. "President Pays Mexico Visit," *LAT*, April 20, 1943; "Speeches by Roosevelt and Avila Camacho," *New York Herald Tribune*, April 21, 1943.

75. For example, see Ávila Camacho to Roosevelt, July 9, 1943; Roosevelt to Messersmith, October 25, 1943; Messersmith to Roosevelt, November 30, 1943, all in folder: Mexico, 1943, box 44, PSF, DC, FDRL.

76. Roosevelt to Messersmith, October 25, 1943; Roosevelt to Ávila Camacho, December 29, 1943, folder: Mexico, 1943, box 44, PSF, DC, FDRL; memo from Messersmith, January 7, 1944, folder: Mexico, 1944–45, box 44, PSF, DC, FDRL; "Reveal F.D.R. Planned to Meet Avila Camacho," *CDT*, April 27, 1945.

77. Messersmith to Roosevelt, June 29, 1944, folder: Mexico, 1944–45, box 44, PSF, DC, FDRL.

78. "In Best Clothes, Capital Greets Muscat Sultan," *WP*, March 4, 1938; "Host to a President," *WP*, May 28, 1943.

79. "Barclays' Visit Stirs Washington," *New York Amsterdam News*, May 1, 1943.

80. Kimball, *Juggler*, 127–157; Gerhard L. Weinberg, *Visions of Victory: The Hopes of Eight World War II Leaders* (Cambridge: Cambridge University Press, 2005), 191–193.

81. Roosevelt to Inönü, March 10, 1944, folder: Turkey, box 51, PSF, DC, FDRL.

82. Report from John Magruder to Col. L. Mathewson, "Reports Received in Office of Strategic Services, No. 89," December 21, 1943, folder: OSS Numbered Bulletins, September–December 1943, box 72, Map Room—Military Files, FDRL.

83. Memo from Hull to Roosevelt, December 23, 1943, folder: Iran, box 40, PSF, DC, FDRL.

84. Mohammad Reza Pahlavi to Roosevelt, December 6, 1943, folder: Iran, box 40, PSF, DC, FDRL.

85. Lloyd C. Gardner, *Three Kings: The Rise of an American Empire in the Middle East after World War II* (New York: New Press, 2009), 19–25.

86. For the persistence of "orientalist" stereotypes in US policy toward the Middle East, see Douglas Little, *American Orientalism: The United States and the Middle East since 1945*, 3rd ed. (Chapel Hill: University of North Carolina Press, 2008).

87. "White House Announcement of New Talks," *NYT*, February 21, 1945; "Kings of the Orient," *NYT*, February 22, 1945; "FDR Host to 3 Rulers," *Atlanta Constitution*, February 21, 1945.

88. For the background reports on the three kings, see folder: Naval Aide's Files, Crimean Conference A/16, box 165, Map Room—Military Files, FDRL.

89. Memo from Joseph Grew to Roosevelt, March 10, 1945; Roosevelt to Ibn Saud, April 5, 1945, both in folder: Saudi Arabia, box 50, PSF, DC, FDRL

90. Memo from Harold B. Hoskins to Roosevelt, September 27, 1943, folder: Saudi Arabia, box 50, PSF, DC, FDRL.

91. Memo from Hoskins to Roosevelt, September 27, 1943; Patrick Hurley to Roosevelt, June 9, 1943, folder: Saudi Arabia, box 50, PSF, DC, FDRL.

92. Memcon between Ibn Saud and Roosevelt, February 14, 1945, in *FRUS, 1945*, vol. 8 (Washington, DC: GPO, 1969), 2–3.

93. William Eddy to Cordell Hull, March 3, 1945, in *FRUS, 1945*, 8:7, 8.

94. Ch'i Hsi-sheng, "Chiang Kai-shek and Franklin D. Roosevelt," in van Minnen and Sears, *FDR and His Contemporaries*, 27. An example of their extensive correspondence occurred in the six-month period between January 10 and July 6, 1944, when they exchanged more than twenty messages. See List of Messages, January–July 1944, folder: President-Chiang Kai-shek 1944, box 10, Map Room—Messages, FDRL.

95. John Powell, "China Looks to Chiang to Save It from Chaos," *CDT*, August 10, 1930; Charles Dailey, "'Roosevelt' of China Promises Warlords Doom," *CDT*, November 23, 1926; "Chiang Called Sun's Heir," *NYT*, August 15, 1927.

96. Ch'i, "Chiang Kai-shek and Franklin D. Roosevelt," 127.

97. Chiang to Roosevelt, June 14, 1940, July 20, 1939, folder: China 1939–40, box 27, PSF, DC, FDRL.

98. Telegram from Chiang to Roosevelt, November 6, 1940, folder: China 1939–40, box 27, PSF, DC, FDRL.

99. Currie to Roosevelt, March 15, 1941, in *FRUS, 1941*, vol. 4 (Washington, DC: GPO, 1956), 92.

100. Roosevelt to Chiang, January 23, 1943, folder: President-Chiang Kai-Shek 1943, box 10, Map Room—Messages, FDRL; message from Roosevelt to Chiang, September 16, 1944, folder: President-Chiang Kai-shek 1944, box 10, Map Room—Messages, FDRL.

101. Message from Stilwell to Marshall, April 23, 1943, folder: Naval Aide's File—China, A 16-3, box 165, Map Room—Military Files, FDRL.

102. Memo from Roosevelt to Marshall, March 8, 1943, folder: Naval Aide's File—China, A 16-3, box 165, Map Room—Military Files, FDRL.

103. Elliott Roosevelt, *As He Saw It* (New York: Duell, Sloan & Pearce, 1946), 154.

104. Telegram from Chiang to Roosevelt, April 13, 1942, folder: President-Chiang Kai-shek 1941–42, box 10, Map Room—Messages, FDRL.

105. Message from Chiang to Roosevelt, November 14, 1942, folder: President-Chiang Kai-shek 1941–42, box 10, Map Room—Messages, FDRL.

106. Chiang to T. V. Soong, April 19, 1942, in *FRUS, 1942, China* (Washington, DC: GPO, 1956), 33; Ronald Ian Heiferman, *The Cairo Conference of 1943: Roosevelt, Churchill, Chiang Kai-shek and Madame Chiang* (Jefferson, NC: McFarland, 2011), 40.

107. Intelligence report, "Chinese Official's Opinion on the Advantages of a Chiang-Roosevelt Meeting," May 21, 1943, folder: President-Chiang Kai-shek 1943, box 10, Map Room—Messages, FDRL.

108. Messages from Roosevelt to Chiang, June 30, October 27, November 10, 1943, folder: President-Chiang Kai-shek 1943, box 10, Map Room—Messages, FDRL.

109. Stimson quoted in Heiferman, *Cairo Conference,* 51.

110. "China's Triumph," *NYT,* December 3, 1943; Arthur Krock, "China Gets Her Place in 'Big Four' Councils," *NYT,* December 5, 1943.

111. Madame Chiang to Roosevelt, December 5, 1943, folder: China, 1943, box 27, PSF, DC, FDRL; "China Is Jubilant as Chiang Returns," *NYT,* December 3, 1943.

112. Louis Mountbatten, *Report to the Combined Chief of Staffs by the Allied Supreme Commander Southeast Asia: 1943–1945* (London: His Majesty's Stationery Office, 1951), 29; Heiferman, *Cairo Conference,* 155.

113. Chiang to Roosevelt, December 9, 1943, in *FRUS, 1943, China* (Washington, DC: GPO, 1957), 181.

114. Heiferman, *Cairo Conference,* 158, 166–167.

115. Ch'i, "Chiang Kai-shek and Franklin D. Roosevelt," 138.

116. "The President and U.S. Aid to China," n.d., folder: Naval Aide's File—Chiang, A 16-3, box 165, Map Room—Military Files, FDRL.

117. "Two Presidents," *NYT,* January 31, 1943; Paul Schubert, "Value of Conferences," *WP,* December 6, 1943; Thurston Macauley, "At Last, a Full Year of Military Progress," *WP,* December 26, 1943.

118. "Cut the Comedy," *CDT,* December 3, 1943; "The Grand Tour Ends," *CDT,* December 18, 1943.

2. TRUMAN, EISENHOWER, AND THE RETREAT AND RESURGENCE OF PERSONAL DIPLOMACY

1. Telegram from Roosevelt to Stalin, April 4, 1945, in *FRUS, 1945,* vol. 3 (Washington, DC: GPO 1968), 745, 746; telegram from Roosevelt to Winston Churchill, April 11, 1945, in *FRUS, 1945,* vol. 5 (Washington, DC: GPO, 1967), 210.

2. T. V. Soong to Truman, August 30, 1945, folder: China, 1945, box 151, PSF, Foreign Affairs, HSTL; telegram from Amman to DOS, March 4, 1951, folder: State Department, Correspondence, 1951–52 (2 of 6), box 42, WHCF, Confidential File, HSTL; telegram from Churchill to Truman, June 16, 1945, doc. 72, in *FRUS: The Conference of Berlin 1945,* vol. 1 (Washington, DC: GPO, 1960), 104.

3. Telegram from Truman to Churchill, April 13, 1945, in *FRUS, 1945,* 5:211; Harry Truman, *Off the Record: The Private Papers of Harry S. Truman,* ed. Robert H. Ferrell (New York: Harper & Row, 1980), 16.

4. "Hopkins Visits Truman, Gives Diplomatic Data," *New York Herald Tribune,* May 5, 1945.

5. Telegram from Truman to Churchill, April 13, 1945.

6. Telegram from Churchill to Truman, May 27, 1945, doc. 141, in *FRUS: Conference of Berlin,* 1:156; memo from Charles Bohlen, May 26, 1945, doc. 24, in *FRUS: Conference of Berlin,* 1:28.

7. Harry Truman, *Memoirs*, vol. 1, *Year of Decisions* (Garden City, NY: Doubleday, 1955), 110, 257.

8. Telegram from Hopkins to Truman, May 28, 1945, doc. 36, in *FRUS: Conference of Berlin*, 1:86.

9. Andrew J. Rotter, *Hiroshima: The World's Bomb* (New York: Oxford University Press, 2008), 161–162; Eben A. Ayers, *Truman in the White House: The Diary of Eben A. Ayers*, ed. Robert H. Ferrell (Columbia: University of Missouri Press, 1991), 51.

10. Truman, *Memoirs*, 341–342; Truman, *Off the Record*, 53.

11. Frank Costigliola, *Roosevelt's Lost Alliances: How Personal Politics Helped Start the Cold War* (Princeton, NJ: Princeton University Press, 2012), 362.

12. Michael Neiberg, *Potsdam: The End of World War II and the Remaking of Europe* (New York: Basic Books, 2015), 249–251; Harry S. Truman, *Dear Bess: The Letters from Harry to Bess Truman, 1910–1959*, ed. Robert Ferrell (Columbia: University of Missouri Press, 1998), 521; Truman, *Off the Record*, 53.

13. "Radio Report to the American People on the Potsdam Conference," August 9, 1945, APP, https://www.presidency.ucsb.edu/node/230985.

14. John M. Hightower, "Any More Talks with Attlee and Stalin Vetoed by Truman," *WP*, November 30, 1945.

15. Costigliola, *Roosevelt's Lost Alliances*, 363–365; Truman, *Off the Record*, 54; Arnold A. Offner, *Another Such Victory: President Truman and the Cold War, 1945–1953* (Stanford, CA: Stanford University Press, 2002), 137; "President's News Conference," May 31, 1946, APP, https://www.presidency.ucsb.edu/node/231763; "President's News Conference," November 29, 1945, APP, https://www.presidency.ucsb.edu/node/230174.

16. Clayton Knowles, "Big Parties to Avoid Foreign Policy Fight," *NYT*, August 15, 1948; Thomas Morrow, "Dewey Sketches Policies," *CDT*, June 26, 1948.

17. "Fact Sheet no. 10: The Yalta and Potsdam Conferences with Russia," Democratic National Committee Research Division, August 17, 1948, folder: 1948 Pres. Campaign Foreign Affairs, box 33, Papers of George M. Elsey—Speech File, HSTL. For the politics of Yalta in the first postwar decade, see Athan G. Theoharis, *The Yalta Myths: An Issue in U.S. Politics, 1945–1955* (Columbia: University of Missouri Press, 1970).

18. Roscoe Drummond, "State of the Nation," *Christian Science Monitor*, January 31, 1946.

19. For Churchill's belief in and use of personal diplomacy, see Klaus Larres, *Churchill's Cold War: The Politics of Personal Diplomacy* (New Haven, CT: Yale University Press, 2002).

20. "Personal Diplomacy," *Daily Boston Globe*, November 7, 1951.

21. Dean Acheson, *Present at the Creation: My Years in the State Department* (New York: W. W. Norton, 1987), 480.

22. On Potsdam, see Neiberg, *Potsdam*; Herbert Feis, *Between War and Peace: The Potsdam Conference* (Princeton, NJ: Princeton University Press, 1960).

23. For Truman's foreign travel and visitors, see Office of the Historian, Department of State, https://history.state.gov/departmenthistory/travels/president/truman-harry-s and https://history.state.gov/departmenthistory/visits.

24. Memo from Joseph Satterwaite to Stanley Woodward, "Invitation by the President to the Shah of Iran to Visit the United States," January 13, 1949, folder: Iran, box 158, PSF, Foreign Affairs, HSTL.

25. John C. Wiley to Truman, October 25, 1949, folder: Iran, box 158, PSF, Foreign Affairs, HSTL.

26. Memo from Acheson to Truman, "Proposed Message to Prime Ministers of India and Pakistan Urging Arbitration of a Truce in Kashmir," July 5, 1949, folder: State Department, Correspondence, 1949 (1 of 3), box 40, WHCF, Confidential File, HSTL.

27. Percy Wood, "India, Pakistan Cool to Truman Kashmir Plea," *CDT*, September 5, 1949; "Nehru 'Surprised' at Truman Move," *NYT*, September 5, 1949; memo from James E. Webb to Truman, "Proposed Letter to Prime Minister of Pakistan Commending His Attitude in Kashmir Dispute," October 31, 1949, folder: State Department, Correspondence, 1949 (1 of 3), box 40, WHCF, Confidential File, HSTL.

28. Division of Press Intelligence, Office of Government Reports, "Editorial Reaction to Current Events: President's Trip to Mexico," March 14, 1947, folder: Mexico, March 3–6, 1947 (2 of 2), box 88, PSF, Trip File, HSTL.

29. David McCullough, *Truman* (New York: Simon & Schuster, 1992), 645–646; Dwight Dickinson to George Marshall, "Visit of President Truman to Mexico," March 15, 1947, folder: Mexico, March 3–6, 1947 (1 of 2), box 88, PSF, Trip File, HSTL.

30. Airgram from Ray Atherton to George Marshall, June 13, 1947, folder: Canada, Ottawa, June 9–12, 1947, box 88, PSF, Trip File, HSTL.

31. C. P. Trussell, "1,000,000 Acclaim Truman on Entry in Brazil's Capital," *NYT*, September 2, 1947; "Rolling Down to Rio," *NYT*, August 8, 1947.

32. "Closer Ties for U.S. and Britain Seen," *LAT*, October 27, 1951; telegram from DOS to London, November 21, 1951, folder: Foreign Relations, Churchill-Truman Conference, January 1952, box 59, Papers of George M. Elsey—Subject File, HSTL.

33. "Welcome for Churchill," *WP*, January 5, 1952.

34. "Remarks of Welcome to Prime Minister Churchill at the Washington National Airport," January 5, 1952, APP, https://www.presidency.ucsb.edu/node/231426; "Truman Toasts Churchill as 'Great Man of the Age,'" *NYT*, January 8, 1952; James Reston, "Truman, Churchill Agree on 3 Points as Parley Closes," *NYT*, January 9, 1952. For Truman and Churchill's talks, see *FRUS, 1952–1954*, vol. 6, pt. 1, docs. 337–340, 344 (Washington, DC: GPO, 1986), 763–786, 794–802.

35. "Notes from the Right," *WP*, January 16, 1952.

36. Works highlighting Eisenhower's personal diplomacy include Michael R. Beschloss, *Mayday: Eisenhower, Khrushchev, and the U-2 Affair* (New York: Harper & Row, 1986); E. Bruce Geelhoed and Anthony O. Edmonds, *Eisenhower, Macmillan and Allied Unity, 1957–1961* (New York: Palgrave Macmillan, 2003); E. Bruce Geelhoed, *Diplomacy Shot Down: The U-2 Crisis and Eisenhower's Aborted Mission to Moscow, 1959–1960* (Norman: University of Oklahoma Press, 2020).

37. Dwight D. Eisenhower, "Annual Message to the Congress on the State of the Union," February 2, 1953, APP, https://www.presidency.ucsb.edu/node/231684.

38. "Yalta in Review," *CDT*, February 24, 1953.

39. Eisenhower quoted in Emmet John Hughes, *The Ordeal of Power: A Political Memoir of the Eisenhower Years* (New York: Atheneum, 1963), 151. For Eisenhower's travels, see Office of the Historian, Department of State, https://history.state.gov /departmenthistory/visits.

40. "Big Four to Meet?" *Christian Science Monitor*, January 2, 1953; Drew Pearson, "Ike-Churchill Highlights Disclosed," *WP*, January 16, 1953; "No Promises to Churchill, Senators Told," *WP*, January 3, 1953; Dwight Eisenhower, *The Eisenhower Diaries*, ed. Robert H. Ferrell (New York: W. W. Norton, 1981), 222.

41. Memo, Eisenhower and Churchill meeting, June 26, 1954, doc. 473, in *FRUS, 1952–1954*, 6(1):1098–1099.

42. "The President's News Conference," May 14, 1953, APP, https://www.presidency ucsb.edu/node/231779.

43. Eisenhower to Anthony Eden, May 31, 1955, folder: Eden 4/6/55–12/31/55 (6), box 21, Papers of the President (AWF)–International Series, DDEL.

44. Telegram from Ankara to DOS, January 29, 1958, folder: Dulles, John Foster Jan. '58 (1), box 9, AWF–Dulles-Herter Series, DDEL.

45. Eden to Eisenhower, May 6, 1955, doc. 103, in *FRUS, 1955–1957*, vol. 5 (Washington, DC: GPO, 1988), 164.

46. Dulles to Roger Makins, May 6, 1955, doc. 104, in *FRUS, 1955–1957*, 5:165–167; Dwight D. Eisenhower, *The White House Years: Mandate for Change, 1953–1956* (Garden City, NY: Doubleday, 1963), 506.

47. Telegram from Dulles to DOS, May 8, 1955, doc. 107; telegram from DOS to Dulles, May 15, 1955, doc. 115, both in *FRUS, 1955–1957*, 5:170–171, 179–180.

48. Notes on a Bipartisan Conference, July 12, 1955, doc. 157, in *FRUS, 1955–1957*, 5:306.

49. "Radio and Television Address to the American People Prior to Departure for the Big Four Conference at Geneva," July 15, 1955, APP, https://www.presidency.ucsb .edu/node/233264.

50. Memo from Rockefeller to Eisenhower, "Psychological Strategy at Geneva," July 11, 1955, doc. 154, in *FRUS, 1955–1957*, 5:298.

51. Kenneth Osgood, *Total Cold War: Eisenhower's Secret Propaganda Battle at Home and Abroad* (Lawrence: University Press of Kansas, 2006), 181–213; Günter Bischof and Saki Dockril, eds., *Cold War Respite: The Geneva Summit of 1955* (Baton Rouge: Louisiana State University Press, 2000); "West European Press Hails Arms Proposal," *WP*, July 23, 1955; "Press of Europe Hails Eisenhower," *NYT*, July 23, 1955; James E. Warner, "Eisenhower Plan Hailed in Congress," *NYT*, July 22, 1955; Foreign Affairs Survey, National Opinion Research Center, University of Chicago, August 1955, iPoll.

52. In his memoirs Eisenhower boasted that during his time as president he hosted thirty-seven official visits by world leaders and 210 meetings, both at home and abroad. See Eisenhower, *White House Years: Mandate for Change*, 237.

53. Eisenhower to Dulles, May 31, 1954, folder: Dulles, John Foster, Aug. 1954 (2), box 4, AWF–Dulles-Herter Series, DDEL; memo from Eisenhower to Dulles, "Visit to the United States of President Magloire of Haiti," June 16, 1954, folder: Dulles, John Foster, Aug. 1954 (2), box 4, AWF–Dulles-Herter Series, DDEL.

54. David M. Kennedy, *Freedom from Fear: The American People in Depression and War, 1929–1945* (New York: Oxford University Press, 1999), 687–691; "Memorandum for an Allied Command, for Lord Louis Mountbatten," September 14, 1943, in *The Papers of Dwight David Eisenhower: The War Years*, vol. 3, ed. Alfred D. Chandler, Stephen E. Ambrose, Joseph P. Hobbs, Edwin Alan Thompson, and Elizabeth F. Smith (Baltimore: Johns Hopkins University Press, 1970), 1420; Bernard L. Montgomery, *The Memoirs of Field-Marshal the Viscount Montgomery of Alamein* (Cleveland, OH: World Publishing, 1958), 484.

55. Cabell Phillips, "Talks with Nehru Typify U.S. 'Personal Diplomacy,'" *NYT*, December 23, 1956.

56. James Reston, "The President's Talks," *NYT*, March 28, 1956; William H. Stringer, "President Plays Role," *Christian Science Monitor*, March 30, 1956.

57. Phillips, "Talks with Nehru"; Elmer Plischke, *Diplomat in Chief: The President at the Summit* (New York: Praeger, 1986), 151.

58. Hagerty quoted in Chalmers M. Roberts, "Ruiz Cortines and St. Laurent Fly to Talks at W. Va. Resort," *WP*, March 27, 1956; Eisenhower quoted in W. H. Lawrence, "Eisenhower Elated at 3-Power Talks," *NYT*, March 29, 1956.

59. "Hospitable Diplomacy," *NYT*, March 29, 1956; "The Little Summit," *WP*, March 29, 1956.

60. John C. Baumgartner, *The American Vice Presidency Reconsidered* (Westport, CT: Praeger, 2006), 32, 121.

61. Memo from Dulles to Eisenhower, "Suggested Message to Prime Minister Nehru of India," April 18, 1957, Folder: India, P.M. Nehru 1957–61 (1), box 29, AWF–International Series, DDEL.

62. Telegram from DOS to London, January 6, 1958, folder: Macmillan-President, December 1957–May 30, 1958 (6), box 22, AWF–International Series, DDEL; Elmer Plischke, "Eisenhower's 'Correspondence Diplomacy' with the Kremlin—Case Study in Summit Diplomatics," *Journal of Politics* 30, 1 (February 1968): 139. Eisenhower sent thirty-one messages; the Soviets sent forty-one.

63. Eisenhower to Arturo Frondizi, December 1, 1959, folder: Argentina (3), box 1, AWF–International Series, DDEL.

64. "Radio and Television Remarks on the Good Will Tour Delivered at the Pageant of Peace Ceremonies," December 23, 1959, APP, https://www.presidency.ucsb.edu/node/235188. For Eisenhower's account of his goodwill trips, see Dwight D. Eisenhower, *The White House Years: Waging Peace, 1956–1961* (Garden City, NY: Doubleday, 1965), 485–513.

65. Memo, December 26, 1960, folder: [ACW] Diary, December 1960, box 11, AWF–Ann Whitman Diary, DDEL.

66. Eisenhower, *White House Years: Waging Peace*, 336.

67. Khrushchev quoted in William Taubman, *Khrushchev: The Man and His Era* (New York: W. W. Norton, 2003), 407; Chester J. Pach Jr. and Elmo Richardson, *The Presidency of Dwight D. Eisenhower*, rev. ed. (Lawrence: University Press of Kansas, 1991), 200.

68. Taubman, *Khrushchev*, 403.

69. Taubman, *Khrushchev*, 415; memcon, "Khrushchev's Visit to the United States," September 17, 1959, doc. 12, in *FRUS, 1958–1960*, vol. 9 (Washington, DC: GPO, 1993), 31.

70. Telegram from DOS to Paris, August 1, 1959, folder: DeGaulle, June 1958–October 30, 1959 (1), box 13, AWF–International Series, DDEL; Eisenhower, *White House Years: Waging Peace*, 412.

71. Scope paper, "President's Trip to Europe: August–September 1959, the Khrushchev Visit and the Aftermath of the Geneva Conference," n.d., folder: European Trip–General Aug./Sept. 1959, box 4, AWF–International Meetings Series, DDEL.

72. Eisenhower, *White House Years: Waging Peace*, 413.

73. Telegram from Bonn to DOS, August 10, 1959, doc. 1, in *FRUS, 1958–1960*, 9:2.

74. "President's Trip to Europe, August–September 1959: Talks with Macmillan, Key Questions," n.d., folder: London Visit—Aug. 27 to Sept. 2, 1959 (1), box 4, AWF–International Meetings Series, DDEL.

75. "President's Trip to Europe: Talks with De Gaulle, Key Questions," n.d., folder: Paris Visit—Sept. 24, 1959 (1), box 4, AWF–International Meetings Series, DDEL; Eisenhower, *White House Years: Waging Peace*, 426.

76. Eisenhower, *White House Years: Waging Peace*, 418.

77. Telegram from Paris to DOS, September 15, 1959, folder: Paris Visit—Sept. 24, 1959 (2), box 4, AWF–International Meetings Series, DDEL.

78. Telegram from London to DOS, September 8, 1959, folder: London Visit—Aug. 27 to Sept. 2, 1959 (1), box 4, AWF–International Meetings Series, DDEL.

79. Drew Middleton, "Tour by Eisenhower a Personal Triumph," *NYT*, September 6, 1959; "The President's Achievement," *NYT*, September 6, 1959; Drew Pearson, "Ike Now His Own Secretary of State," *WP*, September 5, 1959.

80. Memcon, "President's Private Conversation with Mr. Khrushchev," September 15, 1959, doc. 111, in *FRUS, 1958–1960*, vol. 10, pt. 1 (Washington, DC: GPO, 1993), 409.

81. Eisenhower, *White House Years: Waging Peace*, 444; memo, "President Eisenhower's Talks with Chairman Khrushchev at Camp David," n.d., folder: Khrushchev Visit Sept. '59 (1), box 52, AWF–International Series, DDEL.

82. Eisenhower, *White House Years: Waging Peace*, 446.

83. Gallup poll, August 20–25, 1959, iPoll.

84. Drew Middleton, "Khrushchev Voices Hopes to British on the Summit," *NYT*, May 10, 1960; Elie Maissi, "Khrushchev Writes West to Save Summit," *WP*, May 10, 1960. On the U-2 incident, see Beschloss, *Mayday*.

85. Memcon, "Pre-Summit Problems among the Four Powers," May 16, 1960, doc. 168, in *FRUS, 1958–1960*, 9:445, 451, 452.

86. Memcon, "Summit Situation," May 16, 1960, doc. 172, in *FRUS, 1958–1960*, 9:456.

87. Thomas P. Ronan, "World Reaction," *NYT*, May 22, 1960. For Eisenhower's recollection of the failed summit, see Eisenhower, *White House Years: Waging Peace*, 543–559.

88. Before Paris, this trip to Asia was supposed to include a visit to the Soviet Union. For his account of the trip, see Eisenhower, *White House Years: Waging Peace*, 560–566.

89. Eisenhower conferred with the leaders of Ghana, Nepal, Lebanon, Yugoslavia,

Togo, India, Egypt, the United Kingdom, Cambodia, and Canada. For his account, see Eisenhower, *White House Years: Waging Peace,* 582–586.

90. "Mr. Eisenhower's Return," *WP,* May 20, 1960; "Summitry," *NYT,* May 22, 1960.

91. Bill Henry, "Japan Approves U.S. Treaty," *LAT,* June 19, 1960; "Ike Arrives in Okinawa," *CDT,* June 19, 1960. On Okinawa's role in US-Japan relations in the second half of the 1950s, see Nicholas Evan Sarantakes, *Keystone: The American Occupation of Okinawa and U.S. Japanese Relations* (College Station: Texas A&M University Press, 2000), 91–111.

92. Russell Baker, "2 Parties' Congress Chiefs Support Eisenhower Trip," *NYT,* December 1, 1959; George Gallup, "Poll Gives President Huge Confidence Vote," *LAT,* January 17, 1960.

93. George Gallup, "Gallup Poll Eyes Far East," *Boston Globe,* July 3, 1960.

94. Robert J. Donovan, "President Flies from Hawaii to Washington," *Boston Globe,* June 26, 1960.

95. Roscoe Drummond, "No More Trips for Eisenhower," *Boston Globe,* June 24, 1960.

96. Memo from Walter J. Stoessel Jr. to A. J. Goodpaster, "Summitry," September 19, 1960, with attachment "The Future of Summitry," folder: Herter, Christian, October 1960 (2), box 13, AWF–Dulles-Herter Series, DDEL.

97. Memo of Conference—October 2, 1960, October 6, 1960, folder: Macmillan, Harold, 8/10/60 to 1/20/61 (5), box 25b, AWF–International Series, DDEL.

98. Eisenhower, *White House Years: Waging Peace,* 586.

99. "Letter in Reply to a Proposal for a Meeting of the President and Chairman Khrushchev," October 2, 1960, APP, https://www.presidency.ucsb.edu/node/235440.

100. Memo from Walter J. Stoessel Jr. to A. J. Goodpaster, "President's Farewell Messages to Heads of State," January 6, 1961; memo from Walter J. Stoessel Jr. through A. J. Goodpaster to John S. D. Eisenhower, "President's Farewell Message to Heads of State," January 12, 1961, folder: Farewells/Replies: DE/Heads of State A–L (1), box 2, AWF–Presidential Transition Series, DDEL. A select group of seventeen leaders received signed originals, including the prime ministers of Canada, Britain, India, and Japan; the presidents of Mexico and France; the German chancellor; and the pope. See memo from John S. D. Eisenhower to Walter J. Stoessel, January 17, 1961, folder: Farewells/Replies, DE/Heads of State A–L (1), box 2, AWF–Presidential Transition Series, DDEL.

101. "Radio and Television Report to the American People on the Trip to the Far East," June 27, 1960, APP, https://www.presidency.ucsb.edu/node/234965. Eisenhower also used his memoirs to defend his personal diplomacy. The two volumes are replete with his interactions with foreign leaders and his views on presidential personal diplomacy. In one particular passage, he forcefully makes the case not only for his own actions but also for future presidents to act similarly. He declared the president's "right" to engage in personal diplomacy, and critics who saw no value in the practice were "either woefully ignorant of facts or attempting to use powers of objective analysis, without noticeable success." See Eisenhower, *White House Years: Mandate for Change,* 504.

102. "A Clear View of Personal Diplomacy," *LAT,* June 30, 1960.

103. "Every Man a Summiteer," *WP,* October 2, 1959.

104. W. H. Lawrence, "Kennedy Prefers Quiet Diplomacy to Summit Talks," *NYT*, January 24, 1961. According to sources in the administration, Rusk's promotion of "quiet diplomacy" mere days after the inauguration was meant to discourage the Soviets from pressing for an early summit and to discourage other world leaders from trying to get invitations to visit Kennedy.

105. "Return to Quiet Diplomacy," *NYT*, January 25, 1961; Walter Lippmann, "Quiet Diplomacy," *WP*, January 10, 1961; Walter Lippmann, "Rusk on Quiet Diplomacy," *WP*, January 26, 1961.

3. JOHN F. KENNEDY AND THE PRESIDENT AS COUNSELOR

1. Scope paper, "President's Trip to Ottawa, May 16–18, 1961," May 2, 1961, folder: President's Trip to Ottawa, 5/61, Briefing Book, Ottawa Trip, 5/16/61–5/18/61, box 233, NSF, Trips and Conferences, JFKL; "Harmony with Canada," *WP*, May 19, 1961. On US-Canada relations, see Asa McKercher, *Camelot and Canada: Canadian-American Relations in the Kennedy Era* (New York: Oxford University Press, 2016).

2. Telegram from Rome to DOS, January 12, 1963, folder: Italy, Subjects, Fanfani Visit, 1/16/63–1/17/63, 1/7/63–1/15/63, box 122, NSF, Countries, JFKL.

3. Memo from Schlesinger to Kennedy, January 12, 1963, folder: Italy, Subjects, Fanfani Visit, 1/16/63–1/17/63, 1/7/63–1/15/63, box 122, NSF, Countries, JFKL.

4. Telegram from Rome to DOS, January 21, 1963, folder: Italy, Subjects, Fanfani Visit, 1/18/63–1/25/63, box 122, NSF, Countries, JFKL.

5. Richard H. Immerman and Lori Helene Gronich, "Psychology," in *Explaining the History of American Foreign Relations*, 3rd ed., ed. Frank Costigliola and Michael J. Hogan (New York: Cambridge University Press, 2016), 344. See also Robert J. McMahon, "Credibility and World Power: Exploring the Psychological Dimension in Postwar American Diplomacy," *Diplomatic History* 15, 4 (October 1991): 455–471; Deborah Welch Larson, *Origins of Containment: A Psychological Explanation* (Princeton, NJ: Princeton University Press, 1984).

6. Andrew Warne, "Psychoanalyzing Iran: Kennedy's Iran Task Force and the Modernization of Orientalism, 1961–3," *International History Review* 35, 2 (April 2013): 413.

7. Kennedy's time in office also coincided with a surge of interest in psychology among both the public and policy makers. See Warne, "Psychoanalyzing Iran," 404–406; James H. Capshew, *Psychologist on the March: Science, Practice, and Professional Identity in America, 1929–1969* (Cambridge: Cambridge University Press, 1999), 241–258.

8. Kathleen Hall Jamieson, *Packaging the Presidency: A History and Criticism of Presidential Campaign Advertising*, 3rd ed. (New York: Oxford University Press, 1996), 141.

9. "Excerpts of Remarks by Senator John F. Kennedy, New York Coliseum," November 5, 1960, APP, https://www.presidency.ucsb.edu/node/274453.

10. George E. Sokolsky, "The Visitations," *WP*, June 1, 1961; Dean Rusk, "The President," *Foreign Affairs* 38, 3 (April 1960): 361.

11. Wallace Carroll, "Kennedy Is Easing His Aversion to Foreign Trips and Summitry," *NYT*, May 14, 1961. Kennedy's change of heart led to numerous articles debating the merits of summits. For example, see Robert T. Hartmann, "Are the Summit Trips Worth the Hike?" *LAT*, May 28, 1961; Sokolsky, "Visitations."

12. On Kennedy and Khrushchev's relationship, see Michael R. Beschloss, *The Crisis Years: Kennedy and Khrushchev, 1960–1963* (New York: HarperCollins, 1991).

13. "The Inflation of Summit Hopes," *LAT*, May 17, 1961.

14. "Where Angels Fear to Tread," *CDT*, June 2, 1961.

15. Don Shannon, "Kennedy Moves to the Big Leagues," *LAT*, May 21, 1961.

16. Kennedy quoted in George C. Herring, *From Colony to Superpower: U.S. Foreign Relations since 1776* (New York: Oxford University Press, 2008), 799.

17. Memo from C. V. Clifton to McGeorge Bundy, March 6, 1962, folder: USSR, Khrushchev Correspondence, Vol. II-C, 3/3/62–3/10/62, box 183, NSF, Countries, JFKL.

18. For JFK's visitors and trips, see Office of the Historian, Department of State, https://history.state.gov/departmenthistory/travels/president; https://history.state.gov/departmenthistory/visits.

19. Marquis Childs, "JFK's 335 Notes in Invisible Ink," *WP*, April 8, 1963. Childs notes that in 1959, at the height of Eisenhower's personal diplomacy, he sent 281 letters to foreign leaders; in 1962 Kennedy sent 335.

20. On US-German relations during the 1950s and the tensions that existed, see Steven J. Brady, *Eisenhower and Adenauer: Alliance Maintenance under Pressure, 1953–1960* (Lanham, MD: Lexington Books, 2010); Jill Davey Colley Kastner, "The Ambivalent Ally: Adeanuer, Eisenhower, and the Dilemmas of the Cold War, 1953–1960" (Ph.D. diss., Harvard University, 1999); James G. Hershberg, "Explosion in the Offing: German Rearmament and American Diplomacy, 1953–1955," *Diplomatic History* 16, 4 (Fall 1992): 511–549.

21. Theodore C. Sorensen Oral History Interview—JFK #3 and #4, April 15, 1964, JFKL, https://www.jfklibrary.org/sites/default/files/archives/JFKOH/Sorensen%2C%20Theodore%20C/JFKOH-TCS-03/JFKOH-TCS-03-TR.pdf.

22. Arthur M. Schlesinger Jr., *A Thousand Days: John F. Kennedy in the White House* (New York: Mariner Books, 2002), 403–404.

23. Lawrence Freedman, *Kennedy's Wars: Berlin, Cuba, Laos, and Vietnam* (New York: Oxford University Press, 2000), 113.

24. Dean Rusk Oral History Interview—JFK #5, March 30, 1970, JFKL, https://www.jfklibrary.org/sites/default/files/archives/JFKOH/Rusk%2C%20David%20Dean/JFKOH-DDR-05/JFKOH-DDR-05-TR.pdf; Schlesinger, *Thousand Days*, 917, 918. For the sometimes testy relationship between Kennedy and Adenauer and their differences in policy, see Frank A. Mayer, *Adenauer and Kennedy: A Study in German-American Relations, 1961–1963* (New York: St. Martin's Press, 1996).

25. Saki Dockrill, *Eisenhower's New-Look National Security Policy, 1953–61* (New York: St. Martin's Press, 1996), 54–55. The credibility of Eisenhower's approach is debatable. See H. W. Brands, "Testing Massive Retaliation: Credibility and Crisis Management in the Taiwan Strait," *International Security* 12, 4 (Spring 1988): 124–151.

26. Freedman, *Kennedy's Wars*, 48–50.

27. Marquis Childs, "The Deep Rifts Are Still There," *WP*, April 11, 1961.

28. Freedman, *Kennedy's Wars*, 61; John F. Kennedy, "A Democrat Looks at Foreign Policy," *Foreign Affairs* 36, 1 (October 1957): 49.

29. Memo from Kissinger to Kennedy, "Visit of Chancellor Adenauer—Some Psychological Factors," April 6, 1961, folder: Germany, Subjects, Adenauer Visit 4/61, 2/1/61–4/6/61, box 79, NSF, Countries, JFKL.

30. Scope paper, "Chancellor Adenauer's Visit—Washington, April 12–13, 1961," n.d., folder: Germany, Subjects, Adenauer, 4/61, Briefing Book, Parts I–III, box 79, NSF, Countries, JFKL.

31. Dean G. Acheson Oral History Interview—JFK #1, April 27, 1964, JFKL, https://www.jfklibrary.org/sites/default/files/archives/JFKOH/Acheson%2C%20Dean%20G/JFKOH-DGA-01/JFKOH-DGA-01-TR.pdf.

32. Acheson quoted in Mayer, *Adenauer and Kennedy*, 22.

33. Memcon, "NATO and East-West Relations," April 12, 1961, doc. 98, in *FRUS, 1961–1963*, vol. 13 (Washington, DC: GPO, 1994), 272, 273.

34. William J. Jorden, "U.S.-Bonn Talks End with Accord on Major Issues," *NYT*, April 14, 1961; James Reston, "Washington: Kennedy Meets the Test of Personal Diplomacy," *NYT*, April 16, 1961.

35. Freedman, *Kennedy's Wars*, 64.

36. Kennedy to Adenauer, September 4, 1961, folder: Germany, Subjects, Adenauer Correspondence, 1961, box 78, NSF, Countries, JFKL; Freedman, *Kennedy's Wars*, 72–78.

37. Memo from Rusk to Kennedy, "Paper on Objectives and Talking Points," November 18, 1961, folder: Germany, Subjects, Adenauer Visit 11/61, 11/6/61–11/29/61, box 79a, NSF, Countries, JFKL.

38. Memo from Rusk to Kennedy, "Your Meeting with Chancellor Adenauer," November 10, 18, 1961, folder: Germany, Subjects, Adenauer Visit 11/61, 11/6/61–11/29/61, box 79a, NSF, Countries, JFKL.

39. Memcon, "Meeting in the Cabinet Room," November 22, 1961, doc. 221, in *FRUS, 1961–1963*, vol. 14 (Washington, DC: GPO, 1993), 632; "Adenauer Hails Results of Talk with Kennedy," *LAT*, November 24, 1961.

40. Adenauer to Kennedy, November 22, 1961, folder: Germany, Subjects, Adenauer Correspondence, 1961, box 78, NSF, Countries, JFKL.

41. Adenauer to Kennedy, December 11, 1961, folder: Germany, Subjects, Adenauer Correspondence, Miscellaneous and Extra Copies, 10/16/61–12/31/61, box 78, NSF, Countries, JFKL.

42. John A. Callcott, "Adenauer Vows German Support," *WP*, October 27, 1962; David Sells, "Doubts All Missiles Out," *Boston Globe*, November 13, 1962.

43. Flora Lewis, "5 in Adenauer Cabinet Threatening to Resign," *WP*, November 3, 1962; "Adenauer Lands in U.S.," *Boston Globe*, November 14, 1962.

44. Scope paper, "Chancellor Adenauer's Visit to Washington—November 7–9, 1962," October 31, 1962, folder: Germany, Subjects, Adenauer Visit 11/62, 10/12/62–2/5/63, box 79a, NSF, Countries, JFKL.

45. Max Frankel, "Adenauer and Kennedy Discuss Cuba and Berlin," *NYT*, November 15, 1962; "Adenauer and Kennedy Hold 2 Long Talks," *CDT*, November 15, 1962.

46. Memcon, "Conversation between President and Chancellor Adenauer," November 14, 1962, doc. 153, in *FRUS, 1961–1963*, vol. 15 (Washington, DC: GPO, 1994), 427–433; "Joint Statement Following Discussions with Chancellor Adenauer," November 15, 1962, APP, https://www.presidency.ucsb.edu/node/236512.

47. Nora Beloff, "Adenauer's U.S. Visit Was a Polite Fiasco," *Jerusalem Post*, November 20, 1962.

48. Telegram from Berlin to DOS, May 1, 1963, folder: President's Trip, Europe, 6/63–7/63, Germany, 1/17/63–6/10/63 (1 of 2), box 241, NSF, Trips and Conferences, JFKL.

49. Scope paper, "President's European Trip, June 1963—Germany," June 14, 1963, folder: President's Trip, Europe, 6/63–7/63, Salinger Briefing Book (1 of 4), box 239, NSF, Trips and Conferences, JFKL.

50. "Rhineland Gives Rousing Welcome," *NYT*, June 24, 1963.

51. "Remarks upon Arrival in Germany," June 23, 1963, APP, https://www.presidency.ucsb.edu/node/236735.

52. "Cheers & Issues," *NYT*, June 30, 1961.

53. Robert G. Waite, "'Ish bin ein Bearleener'—JFK's 26 June 1963 Visit to Berlin: The Views from East Germany," *Journal of Contemporary History* 45, 4 (2010): 845; "Remarks in the Rudolph Wilde Platz, Berlin," June 26, 1963, APP, https://www.presidency.ucsb.edu/node/236863. For the theatrical elements of Kennedy's Berlin trip, see Andreas Daum, *Kennedy in Berlin*, trans. Dona Geyer (Cambridge: Cambridge University Press, 2008).

54. Kennedy quoted in Theodore C. Sorensen, *Kennedy* (New York: Harper & Row, 1965), 601.

55. "The Presidency," *LAT*, June 30, 1963. Kennedy's European tour was so successful that he was planning a similar trip to the Far East to reassure that region's leaders and people. See Memo from Roger Hilsman to Michael V. Forrestal, "Presidential Visit to the Far East," July 8, 1963, folder: President's Proposed Far East Trip, 7/63–11/63, box 242, NSF, Trips and Conferences, JFKL.

56. Harold Hurwitz, "Berlin Briefing," July 6, 1963, folder: President's Trip, Europe, 6/63–7/63, Germany, 6/11/63–7/12/63 (3 of 4), box 241a, NSF, Trips and Conferences, JFKL. Even without the Berlin trip, Kennedy maintained a high approval rating in West Germany—a not insignificant feat, considering the crises of the early 1960s. See Daum, *Kennedy in Berlin*, 68.

57. "Presidency," *LAT*.

58. Rusk Oral History Interview—JFK #5.

59. Jacqueline Kennedy, *Historic Conversations on Life with John F. Kennedy, Interviews with Arthur M. Schlesinger, Jr. 1964* (New York: Hyperion, 2011), 220, 233.

60. James A. Bill, *The Eagle and the Lion: The Tragedy of American-Iranian Relations* (New Haven, CT: Yale University Press, 1988), 137; James Goode, "Reforming Iran during the Kennedy Years," *Diplomatic History* 15, 1 (Winter 1991): 16.

61. Memo from L. D. Battle to McGeorge Bundy, "Iran: Proposed State Visit by the

Shah of Iran," January 30, 1962, folder: Iran, Subjects, Shah Visit, 1/31/62–3/20/62, box 117, NSF, Countries, JFKL. On the Kennedy administration's use of psychology in US-Iran relations, see Warne, "Psychoanalyzing Iran."

62. Telegram from DOS to Tehran, March 16, 1962, folder: Iran, Subjects, Shah Visit, 1/31/62–3/20/62, box 117, NSF, Countries, JFKL.

63. Caroline Kilpatrick, "Kennedys Will Meet Shah of Iran Arriving Today with Wife on Visit," *WP*, April 11, 1962; "Shah Receives Kennedy Praise as State Visit Begins," *NYT*, April 12, 1962.

64. Memo from Battle to Bundy, "Iran: Proposed State Visit." On the policy of re-assuring the shah to get him to follow US preferences, see Ben Offiler, *US Foreign Policy and the Modernization of Iran: Kennedy, Johnson, Nixon, and the Shah* (Basingstoke, UK: Palgrave Macmillan, 2015), 49–68.

65. Memo from Komer to Bundy, January 31, 1962, folder: Iran, Subjects, Shah Visit, 1/31/62–3/20/62, box 117, NSF, Countries, JFKL.

66. "President's Talking Paper," April 3, 1962, folder: Iran, Subjects, Shah Briefing Book, 4/11/62–4/14/62, Index–Tab III, box 117, NSF, Countries, JFKL.

67. Kennedy to the Shah, February 7, 1962, folder: Iran, Subjects, Shah Visit, 1/31/62–3/20/62, box 117, NSF, Countries, JFKL.

68. "President's Talking Paper," April 3, 1962.

69. Scope paper, "Visit of the Shah of Iran—Washington, April 11–14, 1962," March 27, 1962, folder: Iran, Subjects, Shah Briefing Book, 4/11/62–4/14/62, Index–Tab III, box 117, NSF Countries, JFKL; "President's Talking Paper," April 3, 1962.

70. Background paper, "Analysis of Proposed U.S. Assistance to Iran: Report to the National Security Council," April 3, 1962, folder: Iran, Subjects, Shah Briefing Book, 4/11/62–4/14/62, Tab IV–Tab VI (A), box 117, NSF, Countries, JFKL; April R. Summit, "For a White Revolution: John F. Kennedy and the Shah of Iran," *Middle East Journal* 58, 4 (Autumn 2004): 562.

71. "President's Talking Paper," April 3, 1962; Barry Rubin, *Paved with Good Intentions: The American Experience in Iran* (New York: Penguin Books, 1981), 38, 102; scope paper, "Visit of the Shah of Iran—Washington, April 11–14, 1962."

72. Background paper, "Special Problems," April 2, 1962, folder: Iran, Subjects, Shah Briefing Book, 4/11/62–4/14/62, Tab IV–Tab VI (8), box 117, NSF, Countries, JFKL.

73. Memo from Komer to Bundy, March 21, 1962, folder: Iran, Subjects, Shah Visit, 3/21/62–3/24/62, box 117, NSF, Countries, JFKL; background paper, "Special Problems," April 2, 1962; memo from Komer to Pierre Salinger, March 21, 1962, folder: Iran, Subjects, Shah Visit, 3/21/62–3/24/62, box 117, NSF, Countries, JFKL.

74. Telegram from Tehran to DOS, March 20, 1962, folder: Iran, Subjects, Shah Visit, 3/21/62–3/24/62, box 117, NSF, Countries, JFKL.

75. Telegram from DOS to Tehran, March 21, 1962, folder: Iran, Subjects, Shah Visit, 3/21/62–3/24/62, box 117, NSF, Countries, JFKL.

76. Telegram from DOS to Tehran, March 28, 1962, folder: Iran, Subjects, Shah Visit, 3/29/62–4/5/62, box 117, NSF, Countries, JFKL.

77. Telegram from Tehran to DOS, March 30, 1962, folder: Iran, Subjects, Shah Visit,

3/29/62–4/5/62, box 117, NSF, Countries, JFKL; Robert Young, "Shah of Iran Declares: No 'Neutrality,'" *CDT,* April 13, 1962; "Shah Exhorts U.S. to Keep up Its Aid," *NYT,* April 13, 1962.

78. Telegram from Tehran to DOS, March 20, 1962.

79. "Remarks of Welcome to the Shah and the Empress of Iran at the Washington National Airport," April 11, 1962, APP, https://www.presidency.ucsb.edu/node/236370.

80. "Toasts of the President and the Shah of Iran," April 11, 1962, APP, https://www .presidency.ucsb.edu/node/236407.

81. Memcon, Kennedy and the Shah, April 13, 1962, folder: Iran, Subjects, Shah Visit, 4/16/62–5/14/62, box 117, NSF, Countries, JFKL.

82. Memo from Komer to Kennedy, April 18, 1962, folder: Iran, Subjects, Shah Visit, 4/16/62–5/14/62, box 117, NSF, Countries, JFKL.

83. Max Frankel, "'This King Business' a Headache to Shah," *NYT,* April 14, 1962.

84. Memo from Komer to Kennedy, August 20, 1962, folder: V.P. Trip to Middle East, 8/62–9/62, 5/62–8/62, box 243, NSF, Trips and Conferences, JFKL.

85. Telegram from Tehran to DOS, August 22, 1962, folder: V.P. Trip to Middle East, 8/62–9/62, 5/62–8/62, box 243, NSF, Trips and Conferences, JFKL.

86. Memo from Johnson to Kennedy, September 10, 1962, folder: V.P. Trip to Middle East, 8/62–9/62, 9/62, box 243, NSF, Trips and Conferences, JFKL.

87. Max Frankel, "President Seeks to Bolster Leadership of U.S.," *NYT,* June 23, 1963.

4. LYNDON JOHNSON AND THE IMPERATIVES OF THE INTERNATIONAL ARENA

1. The perception that Johnson lacked foreign policy acumen dominated his time in office. See, for example, Rowland Evans and Robert Novak, *Lyndon B. Johnson: The Exercise of Power* (New York: New American Library, 1966); Philip L. Geyelin, *Lyndon B. Johnson and the World* (New York: Praeger, 1966); Eric F. Goldman, *The Tragedy of Lyndon Johnson* (New York: Alfred A. Knopf, 1968). Mostly negative assessments persisted, as evidenced by two edited volumes published in the 1990s in which most of the contributors expressed an unfavorable view of LBJ's handling of foreign affairs. See Diane Kunz, ed., *The Diplomacy of the Crucial Decade: American Foreign Relations during the 1960s* (New York: Columbia University Press, 1994); Warren Cohen and Nancy Bernkopf Tucker, eds., *Lyndon Johnson Confronts the World: American Foreign Policy, 1963–1968* (New York: Cambridge University Press, 1996); Nicholas Evan Sarantakes, "Lyndon B. Johnson and the World," in *A Companion to Lyndon B. Johnson,* ed. Mitchell Lerner (Malden, MA: Wiley-Blackwell, 2012), 487–503. More recently, a growing number of scholars have recognized merit in some of Johnson's foreign policies, and the 2000s have resulted in several works in this vein. See, for example, Thomas A. Schwartz, *Lyndon Johnson and Europe: In the Shadow of Vietnam* (Cambridge, MA: Harvard University Press, 2003); Mitchell Lerner, "Four Years and a World of Difference: The Evolution of Lyndon Johnson and American Foreign Policy," *Southwestern Historical Quarterly* 107, 1

(July 2003): 68–95; Francis J. Gavin, "Blasts from the Past: Proliferation Lessons from the 1960s," *International Security* 29, 3 (Winter 2004–2005): 100–135; Hal Brands, "Progress Unseen: U.S. Arms Control Policy and the Origins of Détente, 1963–1968," *Diplomatic History* 30, 2 (April 2006): 253–285.

2. Lyndon B. Johnson, *The Vantage Point: Perspectives of the Presidency, 1963–1969* (New York: Holt, Rinehart & Winston, 1971), 22.

3. Michael R. Beschloss, ed., *Taking Charge: The Johnson White House Tapes, 1963–1964* (New York: Simon & Schuster, 1997), 26, 28; Evans and Novak, *LBJ: Exercise of Power*, 347; Philip Geyelin, "Johnson's Diplomacy," *WSJ*, November 27, 1963.

4. Geyelin, "Johnson's Diplomacy."

5. Joseph A. Califano Jr., "The Ship Sails On," in *Lyndon Johnson Remembered: An Intimate Portrait of a Presidency*, ed. Thomas W. Cowger and Sherwin Markman (Lanham, MD: Rowman & Littlefield, 2003), 170; Doris Kearns Goodwin, *Lyndon Johnson and the American Dream* (New York: St. Martin's Press, 1991), 251.

6. Goodwin, *Lyndon Johnson and the American Dream*, 251.

7. Michael Beschloss, ed., *Reaching for Glory: Lyndon Johnson's Secret White House Tapes, 1964–1965* (New York: Simon & Schuster, 2001), 214.

8. Johnson quoted in Andrew Cohen, *Lester B. Pearson* (Toronto: Penguin Canada, 2008), 175.

9. Memo from Rostow to Johnson, September 22, 1966, doc. 242, in *FRUS, 1964–1968*, vol. 4 (Washington, DC: GPO, 1998), 653.

10. Johnson, *Vantage Point*, 252, 592, 255–256.

11. Beschloss, *Reaching for Glory*, 327.

12. Alan L. Otten, "President Johnson," *WSJ*, November 25, 1963.

13. Otten, "President Johnson"; Chalmers M. Roberts, "'Can Do' Man Takes Over," *WP*, December 8, 1963.

14. Evans and Novak, *LBJ: Exercise of Power*, 325.

15. Mitchell Lerner, "'A Big Tree of Peace and Justice': The Vice Presidential Travels of Lyndon Johnson," *Diplomatic History* 34, 2 (April 2010): 357–393; Dean Rusk, *As I Saw It* (New York: W. W. Norton, 1990), 331–332. For a summary of LBJ's vice-presidential travels, including their more unconventional aspects and accomplishments, see Robert Dallek, *Flawed Giant: Lyndon Johnson and His Times, 1961–1973* (New York: Oxford University Press, 1998), 12–20.

16. Joseph S. Tulchin, "The Promise of Progress: U.S. Relations with Latin America during the Administration of Lyndon B. Johnson," in Cohen and Tucker, *Lyndon Johnson Confronts the World*, 224; Robert Thompson, "President Determined to Dodge 'Tourist' Tag," *LAT*, December 27, 1964.

17. LBJ conversation with James Reston, January 8, 1964, tape WH6401.09, citation #1273, PRDE, Miller Center, University of Virginia, http://prde.ei.virginia.edu.

18. Johnson, *Vantage Point*, 468.

19. Elmer Plischke, "Lyndon Johnson as Diplomat in Chief," in *Lyndon Baines Johnson and the Uses of Power*, ed. Bernard J. Firestone and Robert C. Vogt (New York: Greenwood Press, 1988), 257–286.

20. LBJ conversation with Dean Rusk, December 6, 1963, tape K6312.04, program number 18, PRDE.

21. Elmer Plischke, *Diplomat in Chief: The President at the Summit* (New York: Praeger, 1986), 53–54.

22. LBJ conversation with McGeorge Bundy, June 2, 1964, tape WH6406.01, citation #3610, PRDE.

23. Barry Goldwater, "Up to the Summit—by Telephone," *Atlanta Constitution*, February 2, 1965. Goldwater was not a fan of summitry in any form. See Barry Goldwater, *Conscience of a Conservative* (Shepherdsville, KY: Victor Publishing, 1960), 100–103; Barry Goldwater, *Why Not Victory? A Fresh Look at American Foreign Policy* (New York: McGraw-Hill, 1962), 65.

24. For other contributions LBJ made to presidential personal diplomacy, see Plischke, "Lyndon Johnson as Diplomat in Chief," 277.

25. Hal K. Rothman, *LBJ's Texas White House: "Our Heart's Home"* (College Station: Texas A&M University Press, 2001), 167.

26. Greg Donaghy, *Tolerant Allies: Canada and the United States, 1963–1968* (Montreal: McGill-Queen's University Press, 2002), 127.

27. Goodwin, *Lyndon Johnson and the American Dream*, 123; Ernest Conine, "Will Johnson Formula Work on World Stage?" *LAT*, January 3, 1965.

28. Evans and Novak, *LBJ: Exercise of Power*, 386, 387; Dean Rusk Oral History Interview I, July 28, 1969, LBJL, http://www.lbjlibrary.net/assets/documents/archives/oral_histories/rusk/rusk01.pdf.

29. Evans and Novak, *LBJ: Exercise of Power*, 386–387; de Gaulle quoted in Schwartz, *Lyndon Johnson and Europe*, 29.

30. Memcon, "De Gaulle and Relations with France," December 28, 1963, doc. 249, in *FRUS, 1961–1963*, vol. 15 (Washington, DC: GPO, 1994), 648; Johnson, *Vantage Point*, 23; memo, "President Johnson's Private Talks with Chancellor Ludwig Erhard, December 28–29, 1963," December 29, 1963, folder: Germany, Erhard Visit, 12/63 (3 of 3), box 190, NSF, CF, LBJL.

31. Sarantakes, "Lyndon B. Johnson and the World," 497; Jonathan Colman, *A "Special Relationship"? Harold Wilson, Lyndon B. Johnson, and Anglo-American Relations "at the Summit," 1964–1968* (New York: Manchester University Press, 2004); Donaghy, *Tolerant Allies*.

32. Rusk, *As I Saw It*, 358.

33. Johnson quoted in Robert A. Caro, *Master of the Senate: The Years of Lyndon Johnson* (New York: Vintage Books, 2003), xx.

34. Goodwin, *Lyndon Johnson and the American Dream*, 195.

35. Beschloss, *Taking Charge*, 191.

36. Max Frankel, "Foreign Policy Again Takes Front Seat," *NYT*, January 19, 1964.

37. Johnson quoted in Jack Bell, *The Johnson Treatment: How Lyndon B. Johnson Took over the Presidency and Made It His Own* (New York: Harper & Row, 1965), 102.

38. Beschloss, *Taking Charge*, 156.

39. Beschloss, *Taking Charge*, 169.

40. Tad Szulc, "Panama Carries Dispute on Canal to O.A.S. Council," *NYT*, January 30, 1964; "Panama Chief Sees New Riots against U.S.," *LAT*, February 24, 1964.

41. Beschloss, *Taking Charge*, 174.

42. For LBJ's account of the situation, see Johnson, *Vantage Point*, 180–184. See also Mark Atwood Lawrence, "Exception to the Rule? The Johnson Administration and the Panama Canal," in *Looking Back at LBJ*, ed. Mitchell Lerner (Lawrence: University Press of Kansas, 2005), 20–52.

43. H. W. Brands, "America Enters the Cyprus Tangle, 1964," *Middle Eastern Studies* 23, 3 (July 1987): 349–351; telegram from DOS to Ankara, August 16, 1964, folder: Turkey—Presidential Correspondence (4 of 4), box 54, NSF, Special Head of State Correspondence, LBJL.

44. Geyelin, *Lyndon B. Johnson and the World*, 72.

45. LBJ conversation with Dean Rusk (joined by Mac Kilduff), December 25, 1963, tape K6312.17, program number 14, PRDE.

46. LBJ conversation with Robert Komer, January 25, 1964, tape WH6401.21, citation #1547, PRDE; LBJ conversation with George Ball, January 25, 1964, tape WH6401.21, citation #1543, PRDE.

47. LBJ conversation with Oren Harris, February 17, 1964, tape WH6402.17, citation #2104, PRDE.

48. LBJ conversation with Dean Rusk, March 21, 1964, tape WH6403.13, citation #2582 and #2583, PRDE.

49. George W. Ball, *The Past Has Another Pattern* (New York: Norton, 1982), 350.

50. Telegram from DOS to Ankara, June 5, 1964, doc. 54, in *FRUS, 1964–1968*, vol. 16 (Washington, DC: GPO, 2000), 107, 110.

51. Telegram from Ankara to DOS, June 13, 1964, folder: Turkey—Presidential Correspondence (4 of 4), box 54, NSF, Special Head of State Correspondence, LBJL. For how the Turks interpreted and responded to LBJ's letter, see Nasuh Uslu, *The Cyprus Question as an Issue of Turkish Foreign Policy and Turkish-American Relations, 1959–2003* (New York: Nova Science, 2003), 45–53.

52. LBJ conversation with Dean Rusk, June 9, 1964, tape WH6406.05, citation #3664 and #3665, PRDE.

53. Komer to McGeorge Bundy, June 18, 1964, folder: Greece, Papandreou Visit, 6/23–24/64 (2 of 2), box 127 (2 of 2), NSF, CF, LBJL; memo from Rusk to Johnson, "Cyprus—Your Discussion with the Prime Ministers of Turkey and Greece," June 22–25, 1964, folder: Greece, Papandreou Visit, 6/23–24/64 (2 of 2), box 127 (2 of 2), NSF, CF, LBJL.

54. Memo from Komer to Johnson, June 20, 1964, folder: Turkey, Inonu Visit, 6/22–23/64 (1 of 3), box 157, NSF, CF, LBJL; memo from Ball to Johnson, "Talking Points for the Inonu and Papandreou Visits," June 19, 1964, folder: Turkey, Inonu Visit, 6/22–23/64 (1 of 3), box 157, NSF, CF, LBJL.

55. Memcon, "Cyprus," June 23, 1964, doc. 73, in *FRUS, 1964–1968*, 16:148–151.

56. Memo from Ball to Johnson, "Talking Points for the Inonu and Papandreou Visits," June 19, 1964; memo from Komer to Johnson, June 23, 1964, folder: Greece, Papandreou Visit, 6/23–24/64 (1 of 2), box 127 (2 of 2), NSF, CF, LBJL.

57. CIA cable, "Papandreou's and Sossidis' Comments on Papandreou's and Inonu's Visits to the United States," June 17, 1964, folder: Greece, Papandreou Visit, 6/23–24/64 (2 of 2), box 127 (2 of 2), NSF, CF, LBJL; memo from Komer to Johnson, June 23, 1964.

58. Memo from Komer to Johnson, June 23, 1964.

59. Memcon, "Cyprus Problem," June 24, 1964, doc. 74, in *FRUS, 1964–1968*, 16:154.

60. CIA cable, "Reactions of Prime Minister Papandreou to His Talks with President Lyndon Johnson," June 27, 1964, folder: Greece, Papandreou Visit, 6/23–24/64 (1 of 2), box 127 (2 of 2), NSF, CF, LBJL.

61. Brands, "America Enters the Cyprus Tangle," 356.

62. LBJ conversation with Robert McNamara, August 9, 1964, conversation WH6408-14-4832, PRDE.

63. Johnson quoted in Lawrence S. Whittner, *American Intervention in Greece, 1943–1949* (New York: Columbia University Press, 1982), 303.

64. Memo from Rostow to Johnson, December 12, 1963, folder: Saudi Arabia, King Faisal Correspondence Vol. 1 (2 of 2), box 48, NSF, Special Head of State Correspondence, LBJL.

65. LBJ conversation with Dean Rusk, April 9, 1964, tape WH6404.05, citation #2941, PRDE; Douglas Little, *American Orientalism: The United States and the Middle East since 1945* (Chapel Hill: University of North Carolina Press, 2002), 31; Johnson, *Vantage Point*, 290–291.

66. Telegram from Jeddah to DOS, January 12, 1964, doc. 221, in *FRUS, 1964–1968*, vol. 21 (Washington, DC: GPO, 2000), 424–426.

67. Memo from Komer to Johnson, June 13, 1964, folder: Saudi Arabia, King Faisal Correspondence Vol. 1 (2 of 2), box 48, NSF, Special Head of State Correspondence, LBJL.

68. Memo from Rostow to Johnson, June 18, 1966, folder: Saudi Arabia, King Faisal Trip to US, 6/21–7/1/66 (1 of 2), box 155, NSF, CF, LBJL.

69. Memo from Rostow to Johnson, June 20, 1966, doc. 273, in *FRUS, 1964–1968*, 21:520.

70. Memcon, "President's Meeting with King Faisal," June 21, 1966, doc. 276, in *FRUS, 1964–1968*, 21:528. For their private talks, see memcon, "President's Meeting with King Faisal," June 21, 1966, doc. 275, in *FRUS, 1964–1968*, 21:523–527.

71. Memo from Rostow to Johnson, "Faisal—Completely Relaxed," June 25, 1966, folder: Saudi Arabia, King Faisal Trip to US, 6/21–7/1/66 (1 of 2), box 155, NSF, CF, LBJL.

72. Johnson, *Vantage Point*, 25.

73. Johnson, *Vantage Point*, 468.

74. "The President's News Conference," December 18, 1963, APP, https://www.presidency.ucsb.edu/node/241826.

75. Johnson, *Vantage Point*, 468, 469.

76. Memo from David Klein to Bundy, "Another Try at Pen Pals," June 21, 1965, folder: Pen Pal Correspondence Kosygin, box 8, NSF, Head of State Correspondence, LBJL.

77. Memo from David Klein to Bundy, "Talk with Ambassador Thompson about Pen

Pals," March 3, 1965, folder: Pen Pal Correspondence Kosygin, box 8, NSF, Head of State Correspondence, LBJL.

78. "Annual Message to the Congress on the State of the Union," January 4, 1965, APP, https://www.presidency.ucsb.edu/node/241819.

79. "Remarks upon Receiving the Anti-Defamation League Award," February 3, 1965, APP, https://www.presidency.ucsb.edu/node/240901.

80. Memo from Bundy to Johnson, "Conversation with Ambassador Dobrynin," January 5, 1965, folder: Pen Pal Correspondence Kosygin, box 8, NSF, Head of State Correspondence, LBJL; memo from Llewellyn Thompson to Bundy, February 1, 1965, folder: Pen Pal Correspondence Kosygin, box 8, NSF, Head of State Correspondence, LBJL; Schwartz, *Lyndon Johnson and Europe*, 48–49.

81. Telegram from DOS to Tel Aviv, May 17, 1967, doc. 8, in *FRUS, 1964–1968*, vol. 19 (Washington, DC: GPO, 2004), 10. For Johnson's recollection of his prewar diplomacy, see Johnson, *Vantage Point*, 289–297.

82. Telegram from DOS to Tel Aviv, May 27, 1967, doc. 86, in *FRUS, 1964–1968*, 19:162–164; diplomatic note from Avraham Harman to Rusk, May 30, 1967, doc. 102, in *FRUS, 1964–1968*, 19:188.

83. Telegram from DOS to Cairo, May 22, 1967, doc. 34, in *FRUS, 1964–1968*, 19:58.

84. Memo from Rostow to Johnson, May 23, 1967, doc. 42, in *FRUS, 1964–1968*, 19:70–71.

85. Telegram from Cairo to DOS, June 2, 1967, doc. 134, in *FRUS, 1964–1968*, 19:254.

86. Johnson, *Vantage Point*, 287; "Washington-Moscow 'Hot-Line' Exchange," folder: USSR Washington-Moscow "Hot-Line" Exchange, June 5–10, 1967, box 8, NSF, Head of State Correspondence File, LBJL. According to Ambassador Thompson, "the Russians made quite a point that the President be physically present at our end of the hot line before they would start the exchange. They asked more than once when he would be there." See memcon, "Hot Line Exchanges," November 4, 1968, doc. 245, in *FRUS, 1964–1968*, 19:411.

87. Message from Kosygin to Johnson, June 10, 1967, doc. 243, in *FRUS, 1964–1968*, 19:409.

88. Memcon, "Hot Line Exchanges," November 4, 1968, doc. 245, in *FRUS, 1964–1968*, 19:414; Johnson, *Vantage Point*, 302; message from Johnson to Kosygin, June 10, 1967, doc. 246, in *FRUS, 1964–1968*, 19:414.

89. Johnson, *Vantage Point*, 303.

90. Memcon, "Middle East, NPT, Cuban Subversion, Viet-Nam," June 25, 1967, doc. 235, in *FRUS, 1964–1968*, vol. 14 (Washington, DC: GPO, 2001), 555.

91. Memo from McNamara to Johnson, June 21, 1967, doc. 221, in *FRUS, 1964–1968*, 14:498.

92. Memo from Bundy to Johnson, June 21, 1967, doc. 222, in *FRUS, 1964–1968*, 14:499.

93. Memo from Nathaniel Davis to Rostow, "Two Summits and Niagara as the President's Guest," June 24, 1967, folder: USSR, HOLLYBRUSH 6/67, President's Mtg w/ Chairman Kosygin II, box 230, NSF, CF, LBJL.

94. Memo from Bundy to Johnson, June 21, 1967, doc. 222; memo from McNamara to Johnson, June 21, 1967, doc. 221, in *FRUS, 1964–1968*, 14:498, 499.

95. Memo from McNamara to Johnson, June 21, 1967, doc. 221; memo from Rostow to Johnson, June 21, 1967, doc. 223, in *FRUS, 1964–1968*, 14:498, 499, 500.

96. Johnson, *Vantage Point*, 481.

97. "The Summit Minuet," *WP*, June 23, 1967.

98. Memcon, June 23, 1967, doc. 229, in *FRUS, 1964–1968*, 14:514.

99. Record of the President's Debriefing, doc. 230, in *FRUS, 1964–1968*, 14:527, 528.

100. Johnson, *Vantage Point*, 484; paper by Benjamin Read, February 21, 1968, doc. 238, in *FRUS, 1964–1968*, 14:566.

101. Memcon, "Middle East, NPT, Cuban Subversion, Viet-Nam," June 25, 1967, doc. 235.

102. Johnson, *Vantage Point*, 485.

103. Tom Wicker, "In the Nation: Glassboro and 1968," *NYT*, June 25, 1967.

104. Louis Harris, "Dramatic Johnson Comeback Traced to His Peace Efforts," *Atlanta Constitution*, July 3, 1967.

105. "The President's Remarks upon Arrival at the White House Following the Glassboro Meeting with Chairman Kosygin," June 25, 1967, APP, https://www.presidency.ucsb.edu/node/238241.

106. "The President's Address to the Nation Announcing Steps to Limit the War in Vietnam and Reporting His Decision Not to Seek Reelection," March 31, 1968, APP, https://www.presidency.ucsb.edu/node/238065; *ABC Evening News*, August 13, 1968, VTNA; memcon, Rusk and Anatoly Dobrynin, July 1, 1968, doc. 278, in *FRUS, 1964–1968*, 14:655.

107. Record of Meeting, July 29, 1968, doc. 282, in *FRUS, 1964–1968*, 14:666.

108. Telegram from Rostow to Johnson, August 19, 1968, doc. 286, in *FRUS, 1964–1968*, 14:681; memo from Rostow to Johnson, August 20, 1968, doc. 288, in *FRUS, 1964–1968*, 14:683–686; telegram from Bromley Smith to Johnson, August 28, 1968, doc. 291, in *FRUS, 1964–1968*, 14:690–691; *ABC Evening News*, September 18, 1968, VTNA; memo from Charles Bohlen to Rusk, October 15, 1968, doc. 311, in *FRUS, 1964–1968*, 14:738–739; Carroll Kilpatrick, "No Summit, President Indicates," *WP*, September 7, 1968.

109. Early W. Foell, "Thant Urges 2-Stage Summit Meeting of Big Four at U.N.," *LAT*, September 27, 1968; Robert H. Estabrook, "Rusk Says Soviets Dim Summit Hope," *WP*, October 7, 1968; Benjamin Welles, "Johnson Still Considering Parley with Top Russians," *NYT*, November 11, 1968.

110. *NBC Evening News*, August 23, 1968, VTNA; Chalmers M. Roberts, "Summit Is Hinted by Rusk," *WP*, December 2, 1968.

111. Memo from Rostow to Johnson," November 14, 1968, doc. 318, in *FRUS, 1964–1968*, 14:754.

112. Memo from Johnson to Nixon, November 25, 1968, doc. 322, in *FRUS, 1964–1968*, 14:761–762.

113. Rowland Evans and Robert Novak, "Johnson's 'Summit Bug' Worries Nixon, Who Has His Own Ideas," *LAT*, December 13, 1968; Chalmers M. Roberts, "Prospects Diminishing for LBJ-Kosygin Talks," *WP*, December 14, 1968.

114. "Opening the Missile Talks," *NYT*, December 9, 1968; C. L. Sulzberger, "Foreign Affairs: Footnotes to Folly," *NYT*, December 27, 1968.

115. Telegram from Moscow to DOS, November 29, 1968, doc. 327, in *FRUS, 1964–1968*, 14:777; memo from Rostow to Johnson, December 11, 1968, doc. 330, in *FRUS, 1964–1968*, 14:780–781.

116. On Johnson's desire for a summit for domestic political reasons, see Jeremi Suri, "Lyndon Johnson and the Global Disruptions of 1968," in Lerner, *Looking Back at LBJ*, 65–69. John Prado takes the opposite view, arguing that Johnson was not driven by concerns about his own popularity. See John Prado, "Prague Spring and SALT," in *The Foreign Policies of Lyndon Johnson*, ed. H. W. Brands (College Station: Texas A&M University Press, 1999), 32.

117. Gallup poll, August 7–12, 1968; Harris survey, October 1968; Gallup poll, September 26–October 1, 1968, iPOLL.

118. Memo from Rostow to Johnson, December 11, 1968, doc. 330, in *FRUS, 1964–1968*, 14:780–781.

119. Beschloss, *Reaching for Glory*, 322.

5. RICHARD NIXON AND THE DOMESTIC POLITICS OF PERSONAL DIPLOMACY

An earlier version of this chapter appeared as "'One Picture May Not Be Worth Ten Thousand Words, but the White House Is Betting It's Worth Ten Thousand Votes': Richard Nixon and Diplomacy as Spectacle," in *The Cold War at Home and Abroad: Domestic Politics and U.S. Foreign Policy since 1945*, ed. Andrew Johns and Mitchell Lerner (Lexington: University Press of Kentucky, 2018), 146–172.

1. Richard Nixon, *RN: The Memoirs of Richard Nixon* (New York: Grosset & Dunlap, 1978), 573.

2. Fredrik Logevall and Andrew Preston, "The Adventurous Journey of Nixon in the World," in *Nixon in the World: American Foreign Relations, 1969–1977*, ed. Fredrik Logevall and Andrew Preston (New York: Oxford University Press, 2008), 4–8.

3. On diplomacy as performance, see Raymond Cohen, *Theatre of Power: The Art of Diplomatic Signalling* (London: Longman, 1987); Andreas W. Daum, *Kennedy in Berlin* (New York: Cambridge University Press, 2008). For Nixon's use of diplomacy for image building and domestic gain, see David Greenberg, "Nixon as Statesman: The Failed Campaign," in Logevall and Preston, *Nixon in the World*, 45–66.

4. *NBC Evening News*, February 25, 1972, VTNA.

5. Hedrick Smith, *The Power Game: How Washington Works* (New York: Ballantine Books, 1988), 414. On the Reagan team's use of foreign travel to improve his public standing, see Sarah Margaret Grace Thomson, "Presidential Travel and the Rose Garden Strategy: A Case Study of Ronald Reagan's 1984 Tour of Europe," *Presidential Studies Quarterly* 50, 4 (December 2020): 864–888.

6. Richard W. Waterman, Robert Wright, and Gilbert St. Clair, *The Image-Is-Everything*

Presidency: Dilemmas in American Leadership (Boulder, CO: Westview Press, 1999), 50, 53.

7. I would like to thank Nicholas Evan Sarantakes for the suggestion to sharpen the point that "Nixon was Reagan before Ronald Reagan."

8. Robert T. Hartmann, "'Jack Hasn't Ghost of Chance,' Nixon Asserts," *LAT*, October 30, 1960.

9. For the development of "showbiz politics," see Kathryn Cramer Brownell, *Showbiz Politics: Hollywood in American Political Life* (Chapel Hill: University of North Carolina Press, 2014). See also Alan Schroeder, *Celebrity-in-Chief: How Show Business Took over the White House* (Boulder, CO: Westview Press, 2004); Kenneth T. Walsh, *Celebrity in Chief: A History of the Presidents and the Culture of Stardom* (New York: Routledge, 2017).

10. Joseph Hearst, "Kennedy Met by Big Crowds in New York," *CDT*, October 28, 1960; Peter Kihss, "City Crowds Hail Kennedy on Tour; He Gibes at Nixon," *NYT*, October 28, 1960.

11. Kathryn Cramer Brownell, "The Making of the Celebrity Presidency," in *Recapturing the Oval Office: New Historical Approaches to the American Presidency*, ed. Brian Balogh and Bruce J. Schulman (Ithaca, NY: Cornell University Press, 2015), 172.

12. Haldeman quoted in Nixon, *RN*, 303; Lawrence R. Jacobs and Melinda S. Jackson, "Presidential Leadership and the Threat to Popular Sovereignty," in *Polls and Politics: The Dilemmas of Democracy*, ed. Michael A. Genovese and Matthew J. Streb (Albany: State University of New York Press, 2004), 29–54. On how the Nixon campaign sought to portray Nixon during the 1968 election and the techniques it used, see Joe McGinnis, *The Selling of the President 1968* (New York: Trident Press, 1969).

13. Theodore J. Lowi, *The Personal President: Power Invested, Promise Unfulfilled* (Ithaca, NY: Cornell University Press, 1985), 96.

14. Bruce Miroff, "The Presidential Spectacle," in *The Presidency and the Political System*, 10th ed., ed. Michael Nelson (Washington, DC: CQ Press, 2014), 232, 234. On spectacle in politics, see also Murray Edelman, *Constructing the Political Spectacle* (Chicago: University of Chicago Press, 1988).

15. Jacobs and Jackson, "Presidential Leadership," 34.

16. Memo from Chapin to Haldeman, "Schedule Planning," February 1, 1971, doc. no. CK2349697245, USDDO.

17. Nixon quoted in Robert Dallek, *Nixon and Kissinger: Partners in Power* (New York: HarperCollins, 2007), 325, 246; David Greenberg, *Nixon's Shadow: The History of an Image* (New York: W. W. Norton, 2003), 277. For more on the administration's attempt to make Nixon the "peace candidate," see Thomas A. Schwartz, "The Peace Candidate: Richard Nixon, Henry Kissinger, and the Election of 1972," in *US Presidential Elections and Foreign Policy: Candidates, Campaigns, and Global Politics from FDR to Bill Clinton*, ed. Andrew Johnstone and Andrew Priest (Lexington: University Press of Kentucky, 2017), 204–227.

18. "The President's News Conference," March 4, 1969, APP, https://www.presidency.ucsb.edu/node/240867.

19. John C. Baumgartner, *The American Vice Presidency Reconsidered* (Westport, CT:

Praeger, 2006), 32, 121; Robert Blanchard, "Butler Sees Nixon's Tours as 'Propaganda,'" *LAT*, May 17, 1958.

20. Walter Lippmann, "Nixon in Russia," *WP*, July 28, 1959.

21. On Nixon's plans to talk tough, see "Reckoning with His Host, Nixon Is Packing Proverbs," *NYT*, July 19, 1959; Robert Hartmann, "Nixon Plans Tough Talk in Visit to Moscow," *LAT*, July 21, 1959; Roscoe Drummond, "Nixon's New Mission . . . He'll Be Ready for K.'s Arguments," *WP*, July 22, 1959

22. For examples of US coverage, see Willard Edwards, "Khrushchev, Nixon Debate," *CDT*, July 25, 1959; Harrison E. Salisbury, "Nixon and Khrushchev Argue in Public as U.S. Exhibit Opens; Accuse Each Other of Threats," *NYT*, July 25, 1959. In Britain and France, the debate was front-page news. While the British press was critical of both Nixon's and Khrushchev's behavior, the French commended the vice president. See "British Press Is Critical," *NYT*, July 26, 1959; "Paris Reaction Is Favorable," *NYT*, July 26, 1959.

23. Richard F. Shepard, "Debate Goes on TV over Soviet Protest," *NYT*, July 26, 1959; Jack Gould, "TV: Debate in Moscow," *NYT*, July 27, 1959. There was no shortage of positive assessments of Nixon's trip. For example, see "Moscow Trip Boosts Nixon, Dirksen Says," *CDT*, July 27, 1959; James Reston, "Nixon Visit Assessed," *NYT*, July 27, 1959; James Reston, "Nixon's Political Coup," *NYT*, July 30, 1959; Alan L. Otten, "Nixon in Russia," *WSJ*, July 27, 1959; George E. Sokolsky, "Nixon's Value," *WP*, July 31, 1959.

24. Alan L. Otten, "Nixon's New Course," *WSJ*, July 24, 1967.

25. Memo from Nixon to Kissinger, November 24, 1969, folder 9, box 759, NSCF, Presidential Correspondence, RNL.

26. Memo from Haldeman to Kissinger, November 7, 1969, with attachment memo from Kissinger to Nixon, October 25, 1969, folder 3, box 767, NSCF, Presidential Correspondence, RNL.

27. Memo from William Rogers to Nixon, "Subject: Your Trip to Europe—Scope Paper," n.d., folder 5, box 443, NSCF, President's Trip Files, RNL; "Trip Tests President's Diplomacy," *WP*, February 23, 1969; Department of State, "Advance Comment on Pres. Nixon's Trip," February 14, 1969, folder 2, box 444, NSCF, President's Trip Files, RNL. NBC had a seventy-six-person crew to cover Nixon's journey, and CBS interrupted its normal programming for a midday special report on the trip. See "TV Highlights: The President in Europe," *WP*, February 24, 1969; "President's Tour to Get TV Coverage," *LAT*, February 17, 1969; "TV Highlights," *WP*, February 27, 1969.

28. Lawrence Laurent, "Two Looks at Nixon's TV Report," *WP*, March 5, 1969.

29. Don Oberdorfer, "Nixon Reviews World Scene with Deft, Direct Remarks," *WP*, March 5, 1969; Laurent, "Two Looks at Nixon's TV Report"; "Mr. Nixon on Foreign Policy . . . ," *NYT*, March 6, 1969; "Nixon's Report," *LAT*, March 9, 1969.

30. Gallup poll, May 1–6, 1969, iPOLL. For Nixon's use and manipulation of polls, see Lawrence R. Jacobs and Robert Y. Shapiro, "The Rise of Presidential Polling: The Nixon White House in Historical Perspective," *Public Opinion Quarterly* 59, 2 (Summer 1995): 163–195; Lawrence R. Jacobs and Robert Y. Shapiro, "Presidential Manipulation of Polls and Public Opinion: The Nixon Administration and the Pollsters," *Political Science Quarterly* 110, 4 (Winter 1995–1996): 519–538.

31. Oberdorfer, "Nixon Reviews World Scene"; Robert J. Donovan, "Nixon's Trip Shows Promise of New Diplomatic Era in West," *LAT*, March 2, 1969.

32. Gallup polls, February 20–25, 1969; March 12–17, 1969; June 25–28, 1971, iPOLL.

33. See Luke A. Nichter, *Richard Nixon and Europe: The Reshaping of the Postwar Atlantic* (New York: Cambridge University Press, 2015), 36–102.

34. Richard Nixon, "Asia after Viet Nam," *Foreign Affairs* 46, 1 (October 1967): 121.

35. Margaret Macmillan, *Nixon and Mao: The Week that Changed the World* (New York: Random House, 2007), 163–165. For a complete account of Nixon's rapprochement with China, see Chris Tudda, *A Cold War Turning Point: Nixon and China, 1969–1972* (Baton Rouge: Louisiana State University Press, 2012). For the Pakistani back channel, see F. S. Aijazuddin, *From a Head, through a Head, to a Head: The Secret Channel between the US and China through Pakistan* (Karachi, Pakistan: Oxford University Press, 2000).

36. Message from Nixon to Zhou via Hilaly, May 10, 1971, doc. 23, NSA Electronic Briefing Book, no. 66, http://nsarchive.gwu.edu/NSAEBB/NSAEBB66/ch-23.pdf (emphasis in original).

37. Henry Kissinger, *White House Years* (Boston: Little Brown, 1979), 725.

38. Kissinger, *White House Years*, 725.

39. Memo from Kissinger to Nixon, "My Talks with Chou En-lai," July 14, 1971, doc. 144, in *FRUS, 1969–1976*, vol. 17 (Washington, DC: GPO, 2006), 454.

40. "Remarks to the Nation Announcing Acceptance of an Invitation to Visit the People's Republic of China," July 15, 1971, APP, https://www.presidency.ucsb.edu/node/240410.

41. Memcon, Kissinger and Zhou, July 11, 1971, doc. 38, NSA Electronic Briefing Book, no. 66, http://nsarchive.gwu.edu/NSAEBB/NSAEBB66/ch-38.pdf.

42. William Bundy, *A Tangled Web: The Making of Foreign Policy in the Nixon Presidency* (New York: Hill & Wang, 1998), 240–241; memo, "Meeting between President, Dr. Kissinger and General Haig," July 1, 1971, doc. 137, in *FRUS, 1969–1976*, 17:356; Nixon conversation with Barend Biesheuvel, Alexander Haig, and J. William Middendorf, January 26, 1972, tape 656-10, RNL, https://www.nixonlibrary.gov/sites/default/files/virtual library/tapeexcerpts/china-656-10b.pdf.

43. H. R. Haldeman diaries, August 16, 1971, RNL, http://www.nixonlibrary.gov/virtuallibrary/documents/haldeman-diaries/37-hrhd-audiotape-ac12b-19710816-pa.pdf.

44. *CBS Evening News*, February 11, 1972, VTNA.

45. *CBS Evening News*, February 11, 1972.

46. H. R. Haldeman, *The Haldeman Diaries: Inside the Nixon White House* (New York: G. P. Putnam's, 1994), 412; Macmillan, *Nixon and Mao*, 51, 152; Haldeman diaries, February 15, 1971, RNL, https://www.nixonlibrary.gov/virtuallibrary/documents/halde man-diaries/37-hrhd-audiocassette-ac19a-19720215-pa.pdf.

47. All three networks carried Nixon's arrival live. ABC's coverage was fifty minutes, CBS's a little over an hour, and NBC's almost an hour and a half. See ABC Special for Sunday, February 20, 1972; CBS Special for Sunday, February 20, 1972; NBC Special for Sunday, February 20, 1972, VTNA.

48. *NBC Evening News*, February 25, 1972, VTNA.

49. Gallup poll, March 3–5, 1972, iPOLL.

50. US Information Agency, "Foreign Media Treatment of President Nixon's Visit to China: Summary as of February 28, 1972," folder 3, box 501, NSCF, President's Trip Files, RNL.

51. Gallup poll, March 3–5, 1972.

52. Memo from Kissinger to Jacob D. Beam, "Instructions for Your Oral Presentation to Kosygin," March 26, 1969, folder 7, box 765, NSCF, Presidential Correspondence, RNL.

53. On the back channel, see Richard Moss, *Nixon's Back Channel to Moscow: Confidential Diplomacy and Détente* (Lexington: University Press of Kentucky, 2017).

54. Gordon R. Weihmiller and Dusko Doder, *U.S.-Soviet Summits: An Account of East-West Diplomacy at the Top, 1955–1985* (Lanham, MD: University Press of America, 1986), 54–57.

55. Kissinger, *White House Years*, 731; Editorial Note, doc. 94, in *FRUS, 1969–1976*, vol. 1 (Washington, DC: GPO, 2003), 327–329.

56. Memo, "President's Meeting with Soviet Minister of Agriculture Vladimir Matskevich," December 9, 1971, doc. 23, in *FRUS, 1969–1976*, vol. 14 (Washington, DC: GPO, 2006), 71.

57. Weihmiller and Doder, *U.S.-Soviet Summits*, 65, 142; Theodore Shabad, "Nixon Talks on TV to Soviet People and Hails Accord," *NYT*, May 29, 1972.

58. Louis Harris, "Summit Vital to Nixon," *Chicago Tribune*, May 18, 1972.

59. Bernard Gwertzman, "Nixon Flies Home and Tells Nation of Summit Gain," *NYT*, June 2, 1972.

60. *CBS Evening News*, May 22, 1972, VTNA; Louise Hutchinson, "Red Carpet for Nixons; U.S. Flag over Kremlin," *Chicago Tribune*, May 23, 1972; memo from Henry Loomis to Alexander Haig, October 13, 1971, folder 1, box 474, NSCF, President's Trip Files, RNL; George Gallup, "Nixon Popularity Hits 2-Year Peak on Soviet Trip," *WP*, June 4, 1972.

61. Committee to Re-elect the President, "Passport" and "Nixon Now," 1972, Museum of the Moving Image, *The Living Room Candidate: Presidential Campaign Commercials 1952–2012*, www.livingroomcandidate.org/commercials/1972/passport; www.livingroomcandidate.org/commercials/1972/nixon-now.

62. James E. Campbell, *The American Campaign: U.S. Presidential Campaigns and the National Vote*, 2nd ed. (College Station: Texas A&M University Press, 2008); Thomas M. Holbrook, *Do Campaigns Matter?* (Thousand Oaks, CA: Sage Publications, 1996).

63. *CBS Evening News*, March 10, 1972, VTNA.

64. Colson quoted in George C. Herring, *From Colony to Superpower: U.S. Foreign Relations since 1776* (New York: Oxford University Press, 2008), 791; *CBS Evening News*, February 29, 1972, VTNA; telcon, Nixon and Haig, April 21, 1972, doc. 137, in *FRUS, 1969–1972*, 14:512.

65. Memo from Kenneth Rush to Nixon, "Brezhnev Visit to the United States," June 12, 1973, folder 5, box 939, NSCF, VIP Visits, RNL.

66. Henry Kissinger, *Years of Upheaval* (Boston: Little Brown, 1982), 289.

67. John Chamberlain, "Nixon's Dilemma in Brezhnev Talks," *Chicago Tribune,* June 16, 1973; Louis Harris, "Majority See Summit as Breakthru," *Chicago Tribune,* June 23, 1973.

68. Greenberg, *Nixon's Shadow,* 280.

69. *ABC Evening News,* June 18, 1974; *NBC Evening News,* June 11, 1974, VTNA.

70. Greenberg, *Nixon's Shadow,* 282; Robert G. Kaiser and Peter Osnos, "Soviets Greet Nixon Warmly," *WP,* June 28, 1974. Interestingly, in the official Russian translation, the word "personal" was dropped, leading some to believe that the Soviets tried to distance themselves from Nixon. See John Herbers, "Tass Deletion of a Word in Nixon Speech Disputed," *NYT,* June 29, 1974.

71. Kissinger, *Years of Upheaval,* 300, 1177; Aldo Beckman, "It's Perils v. Promises in Moscow," *Chicago Tribune,* June 23, 1974.

72. Kissinger, *Years of Upheaval,* 300.

73. John Lewis Gaddis, *Strategies of Containment: A Critical Appraisal of American National Security Policy during the Cold War,* rev. and expanded ed. (New York: Oxford University Press, 2005), 307–341; Thomas A. Schwartz, *Henry Kissinger and American Power* (New York: Hill & Wang, 2020), 269–345.

74. Gallup poll, August 16–19, 1974, December 12–15, 1975, iPOLL.

75. Schwartz, *Henry Kissinger and American Power,* 273, 340–341.

76. Roland Evans and Robert Novak, "President Ford's First 100 Days," *WP,* November 20, 1974.

77. Godfrey Sperling Jr., "Asia Trip," *Christian Science Monitor,* November 18, 1974.

78. Memcon, "Vladivostok Summit with Brezhnev," November 10, 1974, GRFL, https://www.fordlibrarymuseum.gov/library/document/0314/1552844.pdf.

79. Aldo Beckman, "Ford Lands in Tokyo," *Chicago Tribune,* November 8, 1974. For the two leaders' conversations, see memcon, "President Ford–Prime Minister Tanaka— First Meeting," November 19, 1974, doc. 198, and "President Ford–Prime Minister Tanaka—Second Meeting," November 20, 1974, doc. 199, in *FRUS, 1969–1976,* vol. E-12, https://history.state.gov/historicaldocuments/frus1969-76ve12/d198, https://history.state .gov/historicaldocuments/frus1969-76ve12/d199; "Kissinger Says Ford Visit Achieved Optimum Results," *Hartford (CT) Courant,* November 21, 1974.

80. Matthew Storin, "South Koreans Give Ford Massive Welcome," *Boston Globe,* November 22, 1974; Rudy Abramson, "Ford Meets Brezhnev after Pledging Arm Aid to S. Korea," *Boston Globe,* November 23, 1974.

81. Henry Kissinger, *Years of Renewal* (New York: Simon & Schuster, 1999), 292.

82. Rudy Abramson, "Ford and Brezhnev Rapport Credited for Arms Progress," *LAT,* November 26, 1974; Schwartz, *Henry Kissinger and American Power,* 282.

83. Nessen quoted in John Osborne, *White House Watch: The Ford Years* (Washington, DC: New Republic Books, 1977), 31; Schwartz, *Henry Kissinger and American Power,* 284.

84. Schwartz, *Henry Kissinger and American Power,* 284; memcon, "China; Middle East; Sadat Visit," October 17, 1975, doc. 120, in *FRUS, 1969–1976,* vol. 18, https://history .state.gov/historicaldocuments/frus1969-76v18/d120.

85. Memcon, October 25, 1975, doc. 129, in *FRUS, 1969–1976*, vol. 18, https://history.state.gov/historicaldocuments/frus1969-76v18/d129.

86. Memcon, October 25, 1975, doc. 129; Robert Keatley, "Politesse in Peking," *WSJ*, November 28, 1975.

87. "China Trip Coverage," *WP*, November 28, 1975; Jim Squires, "Ford's Trip to Peking," *Chicago Tribune*, November 30, 1975.

88. Rowland Evans and Robert Novak, "And Miscalculating at the White House," *WP*, November 5, 1975.

89. *NBC Evening News*, November 28, 1975, VTNA; "Schlesinger Ouster Draws a Soviet Welcome," *Christian Science Monitor*, November 5, 1975.

90. Memcon, December 2, 1975, doc. 134, in *FRUS, 1969–1976*, vol. 18, https://history.state.gov/historicaldocuments/frus1969-76v18/d134; memcon, "The Soviet Union; Europe; the Middle East; South Asia; Angola," December 3, 1975, doc. 136, in *FRUS, 1969–1976*, vol. 18, https://history.state.gov/historicaldocuments/frus1969-76v18/d136; Lou Cannon, "Ford, Mao Talk Nearly 2 Hours," *WP*, December 3, 1975.

91. Cannon, "Ford, Mao Talk Nearly 2 Hours"; Kissinger, *Years of Renewal*, 894.

92. Memcon, "SALT Negotiation Procedures; Middle East," December 6, 1975, GRFL, https://www.fordlibrarymuseum.gov/library/document/0314/1553316.pdf.

93. *NBC Evening News*, December 5, 1975; *ABC Evening News*, December 8, 1975, VTNA. A day after Ford's visit, Indonesia invaded East Timor. This led to accusations that Ford had given Suharto the green light and serious charges that the United States was complicit in the atrocities carried out by Indonesia. On the Ford administration's support for the invasion, see "East Timor Revisited: Ford, Kissinger and the Indonesian Invasion, 1975–76," NSA Electronic Briefing Book, no. 62, https://nsarchive2.gwu.edu/NSAEBB/NSAEBB62/.

94. Gallup poll, November 21–24, 1975; December 5–8, 1975, iPOLL; *ABC Evening News*, December 11, 1975, VTNA.

95. For more on the origins of the G-7, see Robert D. Putnam and Nicholas Bayne, *Hanging Together: Cooperation and Conflict in the Seven-Power Summits*, rev. ed. (Cambridge, MA: Harvard University Press, 1987), 27–35.

96. Memcon, "Economic Stabilization of Western Europe," March 26, 1976, doc. 133, in *FRUS, 1969–1976*, vol. 31, https://history.state.gov/historicaldocuments/frus1969-76v31/d133; memcon, "European Economic Stabilization: Rambouillet II," April 6, 1976, doc. 135, in *FRUS, 1969–1976*, vol. 31, https://history.state.gov/historicaldocuments/frus1969-76v31/d135; memo from Robert Hormats to Brent Scowcroft, "Economic Storm Warnings," March 17, 1976, doc. 130, in *FRUS, 1969–1976*, vol. 31, https://history.state.gov/historicaldocuments/frus1969-76v31/d130.

97. Putnam and Bayne, *Hanging Together*, 33, 42.

98. *NBC Evening News*, May 30, 1983, VTNA.

99. "Ford Summit Plan Stirs Speculation," *Christian Science Monitor*, June 1, 1976; "Ford to Attend Economic Summit," *Chicago Tribune*, June 1, 1976.

100. "Economic Summit Set," *Atlanta Constitution*, June 2, 1976; "Ford Plans Economic Summit," *LAT*, June 1, 1976.

101. Memcon, "European Economic Stabilization: Rambouillet II," April 7, 1976, doc. 136, in *FRUS, 1969–1976*, vol. 31, https://history.state.gov/historicaldocuments/frus 1969-76v31/d136.

102. Hobart Rowen, "Politics Denied as Motive for Calling Summit," *WP*, June 4, 1976; Leonard Silk, "New Economic Summit Has Political Air," *NYT*, June 16, 1976.

103. "Son of Rambouillet," *WSJ*, June 7, 1976; Ann Crittenden, "Heads of 7 Nations at Parley Isolated in Tropical Splendor," *NYT*, June 29, 1976; *NBC Evening News*, June 28, 1976, VTNA.

104. "Joint Declaration Following the International Summit Conference in Puerto Rico," June 28, 1976, APP, https://www.presidency.ucsb.edu/node/257686.

105. "Reagan Cuts Ford Delegate Lead to 25," *LAT*, June 28, 1976.

106. "Political Summitry," *NYT*, June 30, 1976.

107. Andrew Priest, "Dealing with Defeat: Gerald R. Ford, Foreign Policy, and the 1976 Election," in Johnstone and Priest, *US Presidential Elections and Foreign Policy*, 244.

108. For the impact of these summits on Cold War competition, see Yafeng Xia and Chris Tudda, "Beijing, 1972," and James Cameron, "Moscow 1972," in *Transcending the Cold War: Summits, Statecraft, and the Dissolution of Bipolarity in Europe, 1970–1990*, ed. Kristina Spohr and David Reynolds (New York: Oxford University Press, 2016), 43–66, 67–91.

109. *CBS Evening News*, March 10, 1972, VTNA.

110. Samuel Kernell, *Going Public: New Strategies of Presidential Leadership*, 4th ed. (Washington, DC: CQ Press, 2007), 125–128; Paul Brace and Barbara Hinckley, "Presidential Activities from Truman through Reagan: Timing and Impact," *Journal of Politics* 55, 2 (May 1993): 387.

111. For example, see Elmer Plischke, "The President's Image as Diplomat in Chief," *Review of Politics* 47, 4 (October 1985): 544–565; Robert E. Darcy and Alvin Richman, "Presidential Travel and Public Opinion," *Presidential Studies Quarterly* 18, 1 (Winter 1988): 85–90; Dennis M. Simon and Charles W. Ostrom Jr., "The Impact of Televised Speeches and Foreign Travel on Presidential Approval," *Public Opinion Quarterly* 53, 1 (Spring 1989): 58–82; Agnes Simon, "The Political and Economic Consequences of the Summit Diplomatic Activity of the U.S. President" (Ph.D. diss., University of Missouri, 2012).

112. George C. Edwards III, *The Public Presidency: The Pursuit of Popular Support* (New York: St. Martin's Press, 1983), 1; Miroff, "Presidential Spectacle," 255.

6. JIMMY CARTER AND THE DEMAND FOR PRESIDENTIAL TIME

1. Memo from Kenneth Rush to Nixon, "Ceausescu Visit: Objectives and Perspectives," November 30, 1973, folder 4, box 936, NSCF, VIP Visits, RNL.

2. Memo from Kissinger to Nixon, "Your Meeting with Romania President Ceausescu, October 26," n.d., folder 2, box 936, NSCF, VIP Visits, RNL.

3. Memo from Christopher to Carter, "Visit of Romanian Special Emissary Vasile Pungan," February 21, 1977, NLC-6-66-627-8, CREST, JCL.

4. Memo from Richard Holbrook to Cyrus Vance, "My Trip to East Asia," April 21, 1977, NLC-26-39-5-4-1, CREST, JCL.

5. Memo from Peter Tarnoff to Zbigniew Brzezinski, "Mini-PRC Meeting on Indonesia," August 25, 1980, NLC-132-83-12-8-2, CREST, JCL.

6. Memo from Walter Mondale to Carter, "Foreign Visit Schedule," February 9, 1978, NLC-133-110-1-1-19-0, CREST, JCL.

7. Erwin C. Hargrove, *The Effective Presidency: Lessons on Leadership from John F. Kennedy to George W. Bush* (Boulder, CO: Paradigm Publishers, 2008), 142–143.

8. Memo from Brzezinski to Carter, "NSC Weekly Report #37," November 18, 1977, folder 5, box 41, Donated Historical Material, Zbigniew Brzezinski Collection, JCL.

9. Douglas Brinkley, "The Rising Stock of Jimmy Carter: The 'Hands on' Legacy of Our Thirty-Ninth President," *Diplomatic History* 20, 4 (October 1996): 508. Critical works include Donald Spencer, *The Carter Implosion: Jimmy Carter and the Amateur Style of Diplomacy* (New York: Praeger, 1988); Richard C. Thornton, *The Carter Years: Toward a New Global Order* (New York: Paragon House, 1991); Burton I. Kaufman, *The Presidency of James Earl Carter Jr.* (Lawrence: University Press of Kansas, 1993).

10. For more positive assessments, see Erwin Hargrove, *Jimmy Carter as President: Leadership and the Politics of the Public Good* (Baton Rouge: Louisiana State University, 1988); John Dumbrell, *The Carter Presidency: A Re-evaluation* (New York: St. Martin's Press, 1995); Robert Strong, *Working in the World: Jimmy Carter and the Making of American Foreign Policy* (Baton Rouge: Louisiana State University Press, 2000); Nancy Mitchell, *Jimmy Carter in Africa: Race and the Cold War* (Stanford, CA: Stanford University Press, 2016).

11. Memo from David Aaron to Carter, "The National Security Council System," December 5, 1976, NLC-7-66-8-8-6, CREST, JCL (emphasis in original).

12. For an internal assessment and overview of the Carter administration's foreign policy goals and vision, see memo from Brzezinski to Carter, "Four-Year Goals: Preliminary Statement," April 29, 1977, NLC-12-26-6-2-2, CREST, JCL.

13. Memo from Vance to Carter, "Your Participation in the 32nd United Nations General Assembly," June 17, 1977, NLC-8-22-3-12-3, CREST, JCL; memo from Peter Tarnoff to Brzezinski, "The President's Participation in the 32nd General Assembly," August 4, 1977, NLC-8-21-2-30-5, CREST, JCL.

14. Memo from Vance to Carter, "Foreign Visitors," September 18, 1979, NLC-133-106-2-3-1, CREST, JCL; memo from Brzezinski to Carter, "Foreign Visitors," September 24, 1979, NLC-133-106-2-3-1, CREST, JCL.

15. Hedrick Smith, "Carter Achieved Success in London by Being a Realist," *NYT*, May 11, 1977.

16. For Carter's trips and visitors, see Office of the Historian, Department of State, https://history.state.gov/departmenthistory/travels/president; https://history.state.gov /departmenthistory/visits.

17. Bill Clinton attempted something similar. In 2000 he also spent two weeks at

Camp David trying to negotiate Middle East peace with Israeli prime minister Ehud Barak and Palestinian leader Yasser Arafat, but the effort failed.

18. Memcon, Brzezinski and Park, September 29, 1978, doc. no. K000272, DNSA.

19. Kristina Spohr, *The Global Chancellor: Helmut Schmidt and the Reshaping of the International Order* (Oxford: Oxford University Press, 2016), 32; Jimmy Carter, *White House Diary* (New York: Farrar, Straus & Giroux, 2010), 69, 172; Helmut Schmidt, *Men and Powers: A Political Retrospective*, trans. Ruth Hein (New York: Random House, 1989), 181.

20. Spohr, *Global Chancellor*, 5, 7, 30; memo from Brzezinski to Carter, "NSC Weekly Report #36," November 11, 1977, doc. no. CK2349099284, USDDO; Zbigniew Brzezinski, *Power and Principle: Memoirs of the National Security Advisor, 1977–1981* (New York: Farrar, Straus & Giroux, 1983), 294–295; Kristina Spohr, "Helmut Schmidt and the Shaping of Western Security in the Late 1970s: The Guadeloupe Summit of 1979," *International History Review* 37, 1 (January 2015): 188n10.

21. For the impact of the US occupation on Japanese society, see John W. Dower, *Embracing Defeat: Japan in the Wake of World War II* (New York: W. W. Norton, 1999).

22. The summary of US-Japan postwar relations is drawn from Frederick L. Shiels, *Tokyo and Washington: Dilemmas of a Mature Alliance* (Lexington, MA: Lexington Books, 1980), 65–92; Nicholas Evan Sarantakes, *Keystone: The American Occupation of Okinawa and U.S. Japanese Relations* (College Station: Texas A&M University Press, 2000).

23. Michael Schaller, *Altered States: The United States and Japan since the Occupation* (New York: Oxford University Press, 1997), 210–244.

24. For the influence of US Cold War strategy and America's role in building the Japanese economy, see Aaron Forsberg, *America and the Japanese Miracle: The Cold War Context of Japan's Postwar Economic Revival, 1950–1960* (Chapel Hill: University of North Carolina Press, 2000).

25. Timothy P. Maga, *Hands across the Sea? U.S.-Japan Relations, 1961–1981* (Athens: Ohio University Press, 1997), 141–142. For Carter's failed attempt to reorient American foreign policy, see Jerel A. Rosati, "Jimmy Carter, a Man before His Time? The Emergence and Collapse of the First Post–Cold War Presidency," *Presidential Studies Quarterly* 23, 3 (Summer 1993): 459–476; David Skidmore, *Reversing Course: Carter's Foreign Policy, Domestic Politics and the Failure of Reform* (Nashville, TN: Vanderbilt University Press, 1996).

26. Memo from Jack Watson to Carter, "Options Papers for Foreign & Defense Policy," November 3, 1976, folder: Transition, State and Defense Options Papers (2), 11/76, box 41, Plains File, JCL (emphasis in original).

27. "Carter Invites Fukuda to Talks," *WP*, January 13, 1977.

28. Bernard Weinraub, "Mondale, in Belgium, Affirms U.S. Links to Atlantic Alliance," *NYT*, January 24, 1977; message from Mondale to Carter, "Visit to Europe and Japan," January 18, 1977, doc. 1, in *FRUS, 1977–1980*, vol. 3 (Washington, DC: GPO, 2013), 1–6; memo from Mondale to Carter, "Results of Visit to Europe and Japan," February 4, 1977, doc. 5, in *FRUS, 1977–1980*, 3:15–23.

29. "Mondale, in Tokyo, Affirms U.S. Links with Japan," *NYT*, January 31, 1977.

30. Joseph Kraft, "Japan's Hopes Are America's Interests," *WP*, February 3, 1977.

31. Memo from Vance to Carter, "Official Visit by Japanese Prime Minister Fukuda," n.d., NLC-15-24-1-21-5, CREST, JCL.

32. *NBC Evening News*, March 21, 1977; *ABC Evening News*, March 21, 1977, VTNA.

33. For Fukuda's foreign policy approach, see Bert Edström, *Japan's Evolving Foreign Policy Doctrine: From Yoshida to Miyazawa* (New York: St. Martin's Press, 1999), 90–100.

34. Memo from Henry Owen to Carter, "Prime Minister Fukuda," April 29, 1977, folder: Japan, 1–4/77, box 40, National Security Affairs, Brzezinski Material, CF, JCL; memo from Mike Armacost to Brzezinski, "Direct Channel to Japanese Prime Minister's Office," May 16, 1977, folder: Japan, 5–7/77, box 40, National Security Affairs, Brzezinski Material, CF, JCL.

35. Fukuda to Carter, May 23, 1977, folder: Japan: Prime Minister Takeo Fukuda, 2–12/77, box 11, National Security Affairs, Brzezinski Material, President's Correspondence with Foreign Leaders File, JCL.

36. Carter to Fukuda, July 15, 1977, folder: Japan: Prime Minister Takeo Fukuda, 2–12/77, box 11, National Security Affairs, Brzezinski Material, President's Correspondence with Foreign Leaders File, JCL.

37. "Fukuda Asks for Carter Meeting," *NYT*, January 12, 1978; William Chapman, "Fukuda's Journey to U.S. Linked to Domestic Politics," *WP*, February 23, 1978.

38. "Fukuda Asks for Carter Meeting"; *ABC Evening News*, May 1, 1978, VTNA.

39. Clyde H. Farnsworth, "Carter and Fukuda Agree to Bolster Monetary Process," *NYT*, May 4, 1978.

40. Memcon, "Summary of the President's Meeting with Prime Minister Fukuda (Tete-a-Tete)," May 3, 1978, NLC-26-31-2-4-2, CREST, JCL.

41. Memo from Mansfield to Carter and Mondale, "U.S.-Japan Relations—Update," October 21, 1978, folder: Japan, 6–12/78, box 40, National Security Affairs, Brzezinski Material, CF, JCL.

42. Telegram from Tokyo to DOS, "Prime Minister's Desire to Visit Washington," February 20, 1979; Mansfield to Carter, March 1, 1979, both in folder: Japan, 1–4/79, box 41, National Security Affairs, Brzezinski Material, CF, JCL.

43. Henry Scott-Stokes, "Ohira Defends Japan on Trade Record," *NYT*, February 23, 1979; William Chapman, "Ohira Expects Spring Parley with President," *WP*, February 23, 1979; memo from Nicholas Platt to Brzezinski, "Ohira Visit—Is This Trip Necessary?" February 23, 1979, folder: Japan, 1–4/79, box 41, National Security Affairs, Brzezinski Material, CF, JCL.

44. Mansfield to Carter, March 1, 1979. Carter's message to Vance was handwritten on the letter he received from Mansfield.

45. Note from Karl Inderfurth to David Aaron, March 5, 1979, folder: Japan, 1–3/79, box 24, National Security Affairs, Brzezinski Material, Brzezinski Office File, Country Chronological, JCL.

46. Telegram from Tokyo to DOS, April 3, 1979, folder: Japan, Prime Minister Ohira, 4/30/79–5/6/79, Cables and Memos, box 9, National Security Affairs, Brzezinski Material, VIP Visit File, JCL.

47. Memo from Vance to Carter, "Prime Minister Ohira's Visit," April 23, 1979, folder: Japan, Prime Minister Ohira, 4/30/79–5/6/79, Cables and Memos, box 9, National Security Affairs, Brzezinski Material, VIP Visit File, JCL.

48. Memo from Nick Platt to Brzezinski, "Meetings with Prime Minister Ohira, May 2, 1979," April 5, 1979, doc. no. CK2349514127, USDDO.

49. Carter, White House Diary, 317; Clyde H. Farnsworth, "U.S., Japan Urge Trade Harmony," NYT, May 3, 1979; Seizaburō Satō, Ken'ichi Kōyama, and Shunpei Kumon, Postwar Politician: The Life of Former Prime Minister Masayoshi Ōhira, trans. William R. Carter (New York: Kodansha International, 1990), 200, 467. For Ōhira's foreign policy approach, see Edström, Japan's Evolving Foreign Policy Doctrine, 101–110.

50. Note to David Aaron, n.d., folder: Japan, Prime Minister Ohira, 4/30/80–5/1/80, Briefing Book, box 9, National Security Affairs, Brzezinski Material, VIP Visit File, JCL.

51. Memo from Donald Gregg to Brzezinski, "Planning for the Ohira Visit," March 28, 1980, folder: Japan, Prime Minister Ohira, 4/30/80–5/1/80, Briefing Book, box 9, National Security Affairs, Brzezinski Material, VIP Visit File, JCL.

52. Memo from Frank Press and Brzezinski to Carter, "Signing of US-Japan S&T Agreement," April 17, 1980, folder: Japan, Prime Minister Ohira, 4/30/80–5/1/80, Briefing Book, box 9, National Security Affairs, Brzezinski Material, VIP Visit File, JCL.

53. Memo from Brzezinski to Carter, "Interpreting for the Ohira Meeting," April 22, 1980, folder: Japan: 4–5/80, box 25, National Security Affairs, Brzezinski Material, Brzezinski Office File, Country Chronological, JCL.

54. Bernard Gwertzman, "Ohira Asks Carter to Resolve Hostage Crisis Peacefully," NYT, May 2, 1980; Ōhira quoted in Satō, Kōyama, and Kumon, Postwar Politician, 534.

55. Sam Jameson, "Carter Offers to Help Japanese Meet Oil Needs," LAT, May 2, 1980; Robert Reinhold, "U.S. and Japan Sign Science Agreement," NYT, May 2, 1980.

56. Brzezinski, Power and Principle, 314.

57. Jimmy Carter, Keeping Faith: Memoirs of a President (New York: Bantam Books, 1982), 113.

58. Memo from Gary Sick to Brzezinski, "Japan in the Middle East," April 24, 1979, folder: Japan, 1–4/79, box 41, National Security Affairs, Brzezinski Material, CF, JCL.

59. Anwar Sadat, In Search of Identity: An Autobiography (New York: Harper Colophon Books, 1977), 210.

60. Ralph Israeli, Man of Defiance: A Political Biography of Anwar Sadat (Totowa, NJ: Barnes & Noble Books, 1985), 183; Sadat, In Search of Identity, 213–215; Melvin A. Friedlander, Sadat and Begin: The Domestic Politics of Peacemaking (Boulder, CO: Westview Press, 1983), 2, 4–6; Ali E. Hillal Dessouki, "The Primacy of Economics: The Foreign Policy of Egypt," in The Foreign Policies of Arab States, ed. Bahgat Korany and Ali E. Hillal Dessouki (Boulder, CO: Westview Press, 1984), 124–126.

61. Ismail Fahmy, Negotiating for Peace in the Middle East (Baltimore: Johns Hopkins University Press, 1983), 37; Henry Bellmon to Richard Nixon, November 16, 1971, doc. no. CK2349572991, USDDO.

62. Dayan quoted in Kenneth W. Stein, Heroic Diplomacy: Sadat, Kissinger, Carter, Begin, and the Quest for Arab-Israeli Peace (New York: Routledge, 1999), 65.

63. Fahmy, *Negotiating for Peace*, 66; Felipe Fernandez-Armesto, *Sadat and His Statecraft*, 2nd ed. (London: Kensal Press, 1983), 135–136.

64. Henry Kissinger, *Years of Upheaval* (Boston: Little, Brown, 1982), 615.

65. Memcon, June 1, 1975, doc. no. KT01650, DNSA.

66. Memcon, "Dr. Kissinger's Middle East Briefing," May 31, 1974, GRFL, https://www.fordlibrarymuseum.gov/library/document/0314/1552715.pdf.

67. Fahmy, *Negotiating for Peace*, 152, 155.

68. "Sadat: New Overtures for Peace," *Time*, November 29, 1976.

69. Carter, *Keeping Faith*, 429.

70. Memo from Jack Watson to Carter, "Options Papers for Foreign & Defense Policy," November 3, 1976, folder: Transition, State and Defense Options Papers (2), 11/76, box 41, Plains File, JCL.

71. Telegram from Cairo to DOS, "Possible Sadat Visit to U.S.," February 2, 1977, folder: Egypt, 1–3/77, box 17, National Security Affairs, Brzezinski Material, CF, JCL. Sadat was not the only Middle Eastern leader Carter met with early in his administration. Within four months he had met with Sadat, Israeli prime minister Yitzhak Rabin, King Hussein of Jordan, and Syrian president Hafez Assad. For summaries of Carter's meetings with these leaders, see William B. Quandt, *Camp David: Peacemaking and Politics* (Washington, DC: Brookings Institution, 1986), 44–58.

72. Memo from Jim Fallows to Carter, "Sadat Visit: Welcoming Statement," March 31, 1977, folder: Egypt, 1–3/77, box 17, National Security Affairs, Brzezinski Material, CF, JCL.

73. Memo from Vance to Carter, "Official Working Visit by Egyptian President Anwar Sadat," March 25, 1977, NLC-128-11-19-2-5, CREST, JCL.

74. Memcon, "President's Meeting with President Anwar Sadat of Egypt, Cabinet Room," April 4, 1977, NLC-25-109-8-2-3, CREST, JCL.

75. Carter, *White House Diary*, 38; Anwar Sadat, *Those I Have Known* (New York: Continuum, 1984), 98–99.

76. Meir quoted in Stein, *Heroic Diplomacy*, 227; memcon, "President's Meeting with President Anwar Sadat," February 4, 1978, doc. 211, in *FRUS, 1977–1980*, vol. 8 (Washington, DC: GPO, 2013), 995.

77. Carter to Sadat, October 21, 1977, JCL, https://www.jimmycarterlibrary.gov/assets/documents/campdavid25/cda04.pdf; memcon, "President's Meeting with President Anwar Sadat," February 4, 1978, doc. 211, in *FRUS, 1977–1980*, 8:992; *CBS Evening News*, December 4, 1977, VTNA; Sadat, *In Search of Identity*, 301–302.

78. Jordan to Carter, December 30, 1977, NLC-126-10-15-8-6, CREST, JCL; Stein, *Heroic Diplomacy*,10.

79. Carter, *White House Diary*, 161.

80. Memcon, "Telephone Conversation between President Carter and President Sadat, January 18, 1978, 2:07–2:17 P.M.," NLC-128-11-18-3-5, CREST, JCL.

81. Don A. Schanche, "Sadat Pictured as Dejected Man," *LAT*, January 19, 1978.

82. Murrey Marder, "Sadat's Sudden Drama Seen Calculated," *WP*, January 19, 1978.

83. For the influence of domestic politics on Carter, see memo from Hamilton Jordan

to Carter, "Domestic Political Implications of Foreign Policy," June 1977, folder: Foreign Policy/Domestic Politics Memo, HJ Memo, 6/77, box 34A, Staff Offices, Chief of Staff (Jordan), JCL; Daniel Strieff, *Jimmy Carter and the Middle East: The Politics of Presidential Diplomacy* (New York: Palgrave Macmillan, 2015).

84. Murrey Marder and Edward Walsh, "Carter Calls Mideast Breakdown Temporary, Urges Private Moves," *WP*, January 21, 1978.

85. Memo from Sidney Sober and Harold H. Saunders to Vance, "Analysis of Arab-Israeli Developments, no. 364," February 2, 1978, NLC-25-109-6-9-9, CREST, JCL; Carter, *Keeping Faith*, 307–308; Hedrick Smith, "Sadat Makes an Impression," *NYT*, February 8, 1978.

86. Telegram from Cairo to DOS, "Meeting with Sadat, June 11," June 11, 1978, folder: Israel, 5–6/78, box 35, National Security Affairs, Brzezinski Material, CF, JCL. See also memo from Quandt to Brzezinski, "Sadat's Motivations," July 31, 1978, folder: Middle East–Negotiations (7/29/78–9/6/78), box 13, Donated Historical Material, Zbigniew Brzezinski Collection, Geographic File, JCL.

87. Joseph Finklestone, *Anwar Sadat: Visionary Who Dared* (London: Frank Cass, 1996), 8, 123, 146, 195; Stein, *Heroic Diplomacy*, 4–6.

88. Brzezinski, *Power and Principle*, 236.

89. Mohamed Ibrahim Kamel, *The Camp David Accords: A Testimony of Sadat's Foreign Minister* (London: KPI, 1986), 283; Lawrence Wright, *Thirteen Days in September: Carter, Begin, and Sadat at Camp David* (New York: Alfred A. Knopf, 2014), 52; memcon, "Meeting with President Sadat re Camp David," August 26, 1978, NLC-133-223-5-7-4, CREST, JCL; Wright, *Thirteen Days*, 116.

90. Wright, *Thirteen Days*, 185, 284, 285.

91. Memo from Brzezinski to Carter, "Strategy for Camp David," n.d., folder: Middle East–Negotiations (7/29/78–9/6/78), box 13, Donated Historical Material, Zbigniew Brzezinski Collection, Geographic File, JCL; memo from Vance to Carter, "Camp David Talks," n.d., NLC-133-62-3-11-0, CREST, JCL.

92. Carter, *Keeping Faith*, 392.

93. Douglas Brinkley, *The Unfinished Presidency: Jimmy Carter's Journey to the Nobel Peace Prize* (New York: Penguin Press, 1998), 106; Sadat, *Those I Have Known;* Cyrus Vance, *Hard Choices: Critical Years in America's Foreign Policy* (New York: Simon & Schuster, 1983), 175; Brzezinski, *Power and Principle*, 24; Herman F. Eilts, interview by William Brewer, August 12, 1988, Foreign Affairs Oral History Collection of the Association for Diplomatic Studies and Training, Library of Congress, https://tile.loc.gov /storage-services/service/mss/mfdip/2004/2004eilo1/2004eilo1.pdf.

94. Samuel W. Lewis, interview by Peter Jessup, August 9, 1988, Foreign Affairs Oral History Collection of the Association for Diplomatic Studies and Training, Library of Congress, https://tile.loc.gov/storage-services/service/mss/mfdip/2004/2004lew 03/2004lewo3.pdf.

95. Stein, *Heroic Diplomacy*, 11; Wright, *Thirteen Days*, 53.

96. Memo from Brzezinski to Carter, "Initial Reaction to the Latest Middle East Difficulty," November 30, 1978, folder: Middle East–Negotiations (9/75–12/78), box 14, Donated Historical Material, Zbigniew Brzezinski Collection, Geographic File, JCL.

97. Sadat to Carter, n.d., folder: Egypt, 11/77–11/81, box 1, Plains File, JCL.

98. Lewis interview.

99. For newspaper coverage of the risk Carter was taking, see Hedrick Smith, "Carter's Bold Stroke," *NYT*, March 6, 1979; Edward Walsh and Martin Schram, "Mideast Trip," *WP*, March 6, 1979; Karen Elliott House, "Carter to Put Prestige on the Line in Trip to Mideast Described as Do-or-Die Effort," *WSJ*, March 6, 1979. For why Carter was in too deep to stop, see Hedrick Smith, "This New Gamble for a Treaty Actually Began at Camp David," *NYT*, March 11, 1979.

100. Thomas W. Lippman, "Egyptians Hail Carter on Train Route," *WP*, March 10, 1979; Jonathan Kandell, "Carter Gets a Muted Greeting in Jerusalem," *NYT*, March 11, 1979; Bernard Gwertzman, "For the Peacemakers, a Hopeful Turn on a Twisting Road," *NYT*, March 14, 1979; John Maclean, "Last-Minute Phone Call Turned Tide in Mideast," *Chicago Tribune*, March 15, 1979.

101. Moshe Dayan, *Breakthrough: A Personal Account of the Egypt-Israel Peace Negotiations* (New York: Alfred A. Knopf, 1981), 156.

102. Carter, *White House Diary*, 56; Brzezinski, *Power and Principle*, 255; memo from Robert Lipshutz to Carter, "Israel-Egypt Negotiations," March 1, 1979, folder: Middle East, 12/78–3/79, box 3, Plains File, JCL.

103. Telegram from Tel Aviv to DOS, "Begin's Visit to Washington: Begin the Individual," July 1, 1977, folder: Israel, Prime Minister Begin, 7/19–20/77, Cables and Memos, 6/21/77–7/15/77, box 6, National Security Affairs, Brzezinski Material, VIP Visit File, JCL.

104. Wright, *Thirteen Days*, 276–277.

105. Memo from William G. Bowlder and Harold H. Saunders to Vance, "Analysis of Arab-Israeli Developments," August 14, 1978, NLC-SAFE 17 B-12-66-4-5, CREST, JCL; memo from Saunders and Bowlder to Vance, "Analysis of Arab-Israeli Developments," May 1, 1978, NLC-SAFE 17 A-35-56-1-5, CREST, JCL.

106. A Gallup poll conducted a week before the Camp David summit showed Carter's approval rating at 42 percent. A couple of days into the summit, it stood at 56 percent; by the end of the two-week parley, it was down to 50 percent. When Carter traveled to the Middle East in 1979 to try to finalize a treaty, his approval rating was 39 percent; two weeks later, after he clinched the deal, it shot up to 47 percent. See Gallup polls, September 8–11, 19, 22–29, 1978; March 2–5, 16–19, 1979, iPOLL.

107. Jody Powell, *The Other Side of the Story* (New York: William Morrow, 1984), 102.

108. Telcon, Sadat and Carter, February 27, 1979, NLC-128-11-18-11-6, CREST, JCL. Carter wrote these remarks on the transcript.

7. RONALD REAGAN AND THE DESIRE FOR CONTROL

1. Schmidt quoted in Flora Lewis, "Foreign Affairs: A Voice at the Top," *NYT*, July 10, 1981; Lou Cannon, "White House Lists Much Plus, a Bit Minus," *WP*, July 17, 1981.

2. Reagan to John O. Koehler, in *Reagan: A Life in Letters,* ed. Kiron K. Skinner, Annelise Anderson, and Martin Anderson (New York: Free Press, 2003), 375.

3. *NBC Evening News,* August 13, 1984, VTNA.

4. Gary Wills, "Mr. Magoo Remembers," *New York Review of Books,* December 20, 1990, 29.

5. Peggy Noonan, *What I Saw at the Revolution: A Political Life in the Reagan Era* (New York: Random House, 1990), 151; Martin Anderson, *Revolution: The Reagan Legacy* (Stanford, CA: Hoover Institution Press, 1990), 290; Jack F. Matlock, *Reagan and Gorbachev: How the Cold War Ended* (New York: Random House, 2004), 62.

6. While recognizing Reagan's faults, scholars have recently seen a more active and engaged president with a clear foreign policy vision. For example, see Beth A. Fischer, *The Reagan Reversal: Foreign Policy and the End of the Cold War* (Columbia: University of Missouri Press, 1997); James Graham Wilson, *The Triumph of Improvisation: Gorbachev's Adaptability, Reagan's Engagement, and the End of the Cold War* (Ithaca, NY: Cornell University Press, 2014); Hal Brands, *What Good Is Grand Strategy? Power and Purpose in American Statecraft from Harry S. Truman to George W. Bush* (Ithaca, NY: Cornell University Press, 2014), 102–143; Chester J. Pach Jr., "Sticking to His Guns: Reagan and National Security," in *The Reagan Presidency: Pragmatic Conservatism and Its Legacies,* ed. W. Elliot Brownlee and Hugh David Graham (Lawrence: University Press of Kansas, 2003), 85–112.

7. Memo from Alexander Haig to Reagan, "Your Meetings with Other Heads of State or Government in Cancun, October 21–24," folder: Cancun Economic Summit–Bilateral Mtgs, October 21–23, 1981 (1 of 5) (box 8), box 2 (boxes 8–10), Charles P. Tyson Files, RRL.

8. Haig quoted in Lee Lescaze, "Reagan Uses Hotel Like White House," *WP,* October 25, 1981.

9. Robert J. Schaetzel, "The Dreaded Diplomatic Disease," *LAT,* January 13, 1981.

10. Derek Chollet, "What's Wrong with Obama's National Security Council?" *Defense One,* April 26, 2016, http://www.defenseone.com/ideas/2016/04/whats-wrong-obamas-national-security-council/127802/. For how presidents can better control foreign policy, see Peter W. Rodman, *Presidential Command: Power, Leadership and the Making of Foreign Policy from Richard Nixon to George W. Bush* (New York: Alfred A. Knopf, 2009).

11. See, for example, Marcus Holmes, *Face-to-Face Diplomacy: Social Neuroscience and International Security* (Cambridge: Cambridge University Press, 2018); Todd Hall and Keren Yarhi-Milo, "The Personal Touch: Leaders' Impressions, Costly Signaling, and Assessments of Sincerity in International Affairs, *International Studies Quarterly* 56, 3 (September 2012): 560–573; Seanon S. Wong, "Emotions and the Communication of Intentions in Face-to-Face Diplomacy," *European Journal of International Relations* 22, 1 (March 2016): 144–167.

12. Wilson, *Triumph of Improvisation,* 5.

13. Robert C. McFarlane with Zofia Smardz, *Special Trust* (New York: Cadell & Davies, 1994).

14. Alexander M. Haig, *Caveat: Realism, Reagan, and Foreign Policy* (New York: Macmillan, 1984), 62–63.

15. George P. Shultz, *Turmoil and Triumph: My Years as Secretary of State* (New York: Charles Scribner's Sons, 1993), 822; see also 12, 166–167, 306–318, 902–904.

16. Richard Pipes, *Vixi: Memoirs of a Non-Belonger* (New Haven, CT: Yale University Press, 2003), 153.

17. James A. Baker III, *Politics of Diplomacy: Revolution, War, and Peace, 1989–1992* (New York: G. P. Putnam's Sons, 1995), 26.

18. Haig, *Caveat,* 77, 150.

19. Hedrick Smith, *The Power Game: How Washington Works* (New York: Ballantine Books 1988), 590.

20. Smith, *Power Game,* 562, 592.

21. Ronald Reagan, *The Reagan Diaries,* ed. Douglas Brinkley (New York: Harper-Collins, 2007), 142.

22. "President's Press Conference," January 29, 1981; "Address to Members of the British Parliament," June 8, 1982; "Remarks at the Annual Convention of the National Association of Evangelicals in Orlando, Florida," March 8, 1983, APP, https://www.pres idency.ucsb.edu/node/246569, https://www.presidency.ucsb.edu/node/245236, https://www.presidency.ucsb.edu/node/262885.

23. Raymond L. Garthoff, *Détente and Confrontation: American-Soviet Relations from Nixon to Reagan* (Washington, DC: Brookings, 1985), 1024. For the hard-line positions and intransigence of the Reagan administration's arms control efforts in this period, see Strobe Talbott, *Deadly Gambits: The Reagan Administration and the Stalemate in Nuclear Arms Control* (New York: Alfred A. Knopf, 1984).

24. Matlock quoted in Melvyn P. Leffler, *For the Soul of Mankind: The United States, the Soviet Union, and the Cold War* (New York: Hill & Wang, 2007), 355.

25. Michael Deaver with Mickey Herskowitz, *Behind the Scenes: In Which the Author Talks about Ronald and Nancy Reagan . . . and Himself* (New York: William Morrow, 1987), 262.

26. Reagan, *Reagan Diaries,* 13.

27. Ronald Reagan, *An American Life* (New York: Simon & Schuster, 1990), 270.

28. Deaver, *Behind the Scenes,* 263.

29. Reagan, *American Life,* 271.

30. Reagan, *American Life,* 272, 273.

31. Reagan, *American Life,* 273.

32. Memo from Richard Allen to Reagan, "Leonid Brezhnev's Letter of May 25, 1981," May 28, 1981, folder: USSR, General Secretary Brezhnev, box 38, Executive Secretariat, NSC, Head of State File, RRL.

33. Brezhnev to Reagan, May 25, 1981, folder: USSR, General Secretary Brezhnev, box 38, Executive Secretariat, NSC, Head of State File, RRL.

34. Memo from Haig to Reagan, "Letter to Brezhnev," September 18, 1981, folder: USSR, General Secretary Brezhnev, box 37, Executive Secretariat, NSC, Head of State File, RRL.

35. Memo from Dennis Blair and Richard Pipes to Allen, "Press Backgrounder on President's Letter to Brezhnev, 22 September 1981," September 21, 1981, folder: USSR, General Secretary Brezhnev, box 37, Executive Secretariat, NSC, Head of State File, RRL.

36. "Address at Commencement Exercises at Eureka College," May 9, 1982, APP, https://www.presidency.ucsb.edu/node/245666.

37. Brezhnev to Reagan, May 20, 1982, folder: USSR, General Secretary Brezhnev, box 38, Executive Secretariat, NSC, Head of State File, RRL.

38. Jack F. Matlock Jr., *Reagan and Gorbachev: How the Cold War Ended* (New York: Random House, 2004), 49.

39. US ambassador quoted in Wilson, *Triumph of Improvisation*, 69.

40. Reagan, *American Life*, 567.

41. Reagan, *American Life*, 567.

42. Reagan, *Reagan Diaries*, 131.

43. Matlock, *Reagan and Gorbachev*, 74.

44. W. W. Kulski, "The Twenty-Sixth Congress of the Communist Party of the Soviet Union," *Polish Review* 28, 1 (1983): 48, 49.

45. *NBC Evening News*, February 26, 1981; *CBS Evening News*, March 3, 1981, VTNA.

46. Matlock, *Reagan and Gorbachev*, 30.

47. Matlock, *Reagan and Gorbachev*, 65.

48. Reagan, *Reagan Diaries*, 125.

49. Reagan to Andropov, July 11, 1983, folder: USSR, General Secretary Andropov, box 38, Executive Secretariat, NSC, Head of State Files, RRL.

50. Reagan, *American Life*, 575.

51. Quoted in Matlock, *Reagan and Gorbachev*, 87.

52. Reagan, *Reagan Diaries*, 220, 223.

53. "Table," Mondale/Ferraro Committee Inc., 1984, Museum of the Moving Image, *The Living Room Candidate: Presidential Campaign Commercials 1952–2012*, http://www .livingroomcandidate.org/commercials/1984/table; "White House Rejects Call for Annual Summits," *Boston Globe*, June 13, 1984.

54. Quoted in Hedrick Smith, "Summit Fever," *NYT*, June 17, 1984; James Mann, *The Rebellion of Ronald Reagan: A History of the End of the Cold War* (New York: Viking, 2009), 224.

55. Chernenko to Reagan, March 19, 1984, folder: USSR, General Secretary Chernenko, box 39, Executive Secretariat, NSC, Head of State File, RRL.

56. Reagan, *American Life*, 595.

57. Reagan, *American Life*, 595; memo from Shultz to Reagan, "Response to Chernenko's March 19 Letter," n.d., folder: Head of State Correspondence (US-USSR) March 1984 (2 of 2), box 64, Jack F. Matlock Files, RRL; Matlock, *Reagan and Gorbachev*, 62.

58. McFarlane, *Special Trust*, 298.

59. Reagan to Chernenko, April 16, 1984, folder: USSR: General Secretary Chernenko, box 39, Executive Secretariat, NSC, Head of State File, RRL.

60. Memo from Shultz to Reagan, "Chernenko's June 6 Letter and Dobrynin's Talking Points: Analysis," June 14, 1984, folder: USSR, General Secretary Chernenko, box

39, Executive Secretariat, NSC, Head of State File, RRL; Matlock, *Reagan and Gorbachev,* 89.

61. Reagan, *Reagan Diaries,* 247.

62. Matlock, *Reagan and Gorbachev,* 108.

63. Reagan to Gorbachev, March 11, 1985, folder: USSR, General Secretary Gorbachev, box 39, Executive Secretariat, NSC, Head of State File, RRL.

64. Memo from Shultz to Reagan, March 25, 1985, folder: USSR, General Secretary Gorbachev, box 39, Executive Secretariat, NSC, Head of State File, RRL. See also Shultz, *Turmoil and Triumph,* 534.

65. Gorbachev to Reagan, March 24, 1985, folder: USSR, General Secretary Gorbachev, box 39, Executive Secretariat, NSC, Head of State File, RRL; Reagan, *American Life,* 612–614.

66. Matlock, *Reagan and Gorbachev,* 124.

67. Matlock, *Reagan and Gorbachev,* 127.

68. Wilson, *Triumph of Improvisation,* 96; Matlock, *Reagan and Gorbachev,* 133–135.

69. McFarlane, *Special Trust,* 308.

70. Matlock, *Reagan and Gorbachev,* 134–135.

71. Memo from Donald T. Regan and Robert C. McFarlane to Reagan, "Approaching Geneva: Current Assessment," n.d., folder: FO 006-09 (Begin-326934), box 1, White House Office of Records Management, Subject Files, RRL.

72. *CBS Evening News,* November 14, 1985, VTNA; Matlock, *Reagan and Gorbachev,* 145, 147.

73. *CBS Evening News,* November 4, 1985, VTNA.

74. Memo from Shultz to Reagan, "Your Meetings with Gorbachev in Geneva," n.d., folder: Briefing Book Material [Talking Points] (1 of 3), box 46, Jack F. Matlock Files, RRL.

75. Memo from McFarlane to Reagan, "Your Meeting with Gorbachev in Geneva," n.d., folder: President's Trip to Geneva November 19, 1985 (3 of 4), box 46, Jack F. Matlock Files, RRL.

76. Matlock, *Reagan and Gorbachev,* 143, 144. Shultz makes the same point about Reagan not liking a "fully stage-managed" summit. See Shultz, *Turmoil and Triumph,* 751.

77. Mann, *Rebellion of Ronald Reagan,* 90.

78. *NBC Evening News,* March 14, November 16, November 13, 1985, VTNA.

79. "Weinberger Letter to Reagan on Arms Control," *NYT,* November 16, 1985.

80. Larry Speakes with Robert Pack, *Speaking Out: The Reagan Presidency from Inside the White House* (New York: Charles Scribner's Sons, 1988), 127.

81. *NBC Evening News,* November 16, 1985, VTNA; Matlock, *Reagan and Gorbachev,* 150.

82. Wilson, *Triumph of Improvisation,* 98.

83. *ABC Evening News,* November 7, 1985, VTNA.

84. Matlock, *Reagan and Gorbachev,* 155; memcon, Reagan and Gorbachev, "First Private Meeting," November 19, 1985, folder: Geneva Negotiations–Summary Comments (4 of 5), November 19, 1985 [Geneva memcons], box 54, Jack F. Matlock Files, RRL.

85. William Taubman, *Gorbachev: His Life and Times* (New York: W. W. Norton, 2017), 284–286.

86. *NBC Evening News*, November 21, 1985, VTNA.

87. Donald Regan, *For the Record: From Wall Street to Washington* (New York: Harcourt Brace Jovanovich, 1988), 310–311.

88. Reagan, *Reagan Diaries*, 369.

89. Raymond Coffey, "Hint of Progress at Summit," *Chicago Tribune*, November 21, 1985.

90. Terry Atlas, "The Geneva Summit," *Chicago Tribune*, November 21, 1985.

91. Joseph Lelyveld, "Leaders Are Leaving the Fine-Tuning to Others," *NYT*, November 22, 1985.

92. Gorbachev quoted in Jack Nelson, "'Constructive' Steps toward Peace Taken, President Says," *LAT*, November 22, 1985; Andrei Grachev, *Gorbachev's Gamble: Soviet Foreign Policy and the End of the Cold War* (Cambridge: Polity, 2008), 64.

93. Conference at the Central Committee on the Communist Party of the Soviet Union [CPSU] in Preparation for the 27th Congress of the CPSU, November 28, 1985, doc. 27, NSA Electronic Briefing Book, no. 127, http://nsarchive.gwu.edu/NSAEBB/NSA EBB172/Doc27.pdf; Mikhail Gorbachev, *Memoirs* (New York: Doubleday, 1996), 405.

94. Reagan, *American Life*, 639; Matlock, *Reagan and Gorbachev*, 169.

95. Reagan to George Murphy, December 19, 1985, in Skinner, Anderson, and Anderson, *Reagan: A Life in Letters*, 415–416.

96. Matlock, *Reagan and Gorbachev*, 169, 170.

97. Reagan to Gorbachev, November 28, 1985, folder: USSR, General Secretary Gorbachev, box 40, Executive Secretariat, NSC, Head of State File, RRL.

98. Matlock, *Reagan and Gorbachev*, 172; Taubman, *Gorbachev*, 291.

99. Matlock, *Reagan and Gorbachev*, 175.

100. Leffler, *For the Soul of Mankind*, 389–391.

101. Gorbachev to Reagan, September 15, 1986, folder: USSR, General Secretary Gorbachev, box 40, Executive Secretariat, NSC, Head of State File, RRL.

102. Wilson, *Triumph of Improvisation*, 111; Taubman, *Gorbachev*, 294–295.

103. Matlock quoted in Wilson, *Triumph of Improvisation*, 112.

104. Shultz and Reagan quoted in William C. Wohlforth, ed., *Witnesses to the End of the Cold War* (Baltimore: Johns Hopkins University Press, 1996), 35, 43–44.

105. Kenneth L. Adelman, *The Great Universal Embrace: Arms Summitry—A Skeptic's Account* (New York: Simon & Schuster, 1989), 63. Despite all the one-on-one negotiating, some argue that the failure to reach an agreement at Reykjavik was because Reagan's and Gorbachev's aides prevented the two leaders from making crucial compromises on SDI. See Jay Winik, *On the Brink: The Dramatic, Behind-the-Scenes Saga of the Men and Women Who Won the Cold War* (New York: Simon & Schuster, 1996), 515; Richard Rhodes, *Arsenals of Folly: The Making of the Nuclear Arms Race* (New York: Alfred A. Knopf, 2007), 261–262.

106. Shultz quoted in Frances Fitzgerald, *Way out There in the Blue: Reagan, Star Wars, and the End of the Cold War* (New York: Simon & Schuster, 2000), 351.

107. Memcon, Reagan and Gorbachev, October 12, 1986, doc. 15, NSA Electronic Briefing Book, no. 203, https://nsarchive2.gwu.edu/NSAEBB/NSAEBB203/Document15 .pdf. According to John Lewis Gaddis, Reagan "was the only nuclear abolitionist ever to have been president." See John Lewis Gaddis, *The Cold War: A New History* (New York: Penguin Press, 2005), 226; Beth A. Fischer, "A Question of Morality: Ronald Reagan and Nuclear Weapons," in *Reagan and the World: Leadership and National Security, 1981–1989,* ed. Bradley Lynn Coleman and Kyle Longley (Lexington: University Press of Kentucky, 2017), 31–49.

108. These parting words are in the Soviet transcripts of the talks but not in the US version. See Russian transcript of Reagan-Gorbachev Summit in Reykjavik, October 12, 1986, doc. 16, NSA Electronic Briefing Book, no. 203, https://nsarchive2.gwu.edu/ NSAEBB/NSAEBB203/Document16.pdf.

109. Nancy Reagan, *My Turn: The Memoirs of Nancy Reagan* (New York: Random House, 1989), 345.

110. Speakes, *Speaking Out,* 148; Matlock, *Reagan and Gorbachev,* 239.

111. Gorbachev quoted in Leffler, *For the Soul of Mankind,* 395; "Gorbachev's Reflections on Reykjavik," October 12, 1986, doc. 19, NSA Electronic Briefing Book, no. 203, https://nsarchive2.gwu.edu/NSAEBB/NSAEBB203/Document19.pdf.

112. Wilson, *Triumph of Improvisation,* 114.

113. Gaddis, *Cold War,* 227; Wohlforth, *Witnesses to the End of the Cold War,* 36–37, 39, 47–48; Serhil Plokhy, *The Last Empire: The Final Days of the Soviet Union* (New York: Basic Books, 2014), 13; Holmes, *Face-to-Face Diplomacy,* 104.

114. Taubman, *Gorbachev,* 393–401.

115. Shultz, *Turmoil and Triumph,* 904.

116. Lou Cannon, *President Reagan: Role of a Lifetime* (New York: Simon & Schuster, 1991), 778–781; Conservative Caucus quoted in Mann, *Rebellion of Ronald Reagan,* 276.

117. Reagan quoted in Tom Redburn, "Gorbachev Is 'Different,' Reagan Asserts," *LAT,* December 2, 1987; George de Lama and Terry Atlas, "Reagan: I'll Avoid a 'Bad Deal' on Arms," *Chicago Tribune,* December 1, 1987; Fitzwater quoted in Lou Cannon, "Reagan Toughens Tone on Summit to Reassure Right," *WP,* December 3, 1987.

118. Matlock, *Reagan and Gorbachev,* 273.

119. Cannon, *President Reagan,* 776; Taubman, *Gorbachev,* 401–404.

120. Mann, *Rebellion of Ronald Reagan,* 272.

121. Cannon, *President Reagan,* 774; "Gorbachev Arrives in U.S.; Summit Fever Grips Capital," *LAT,* December 7, 1987; John Mintz and Saundra Saperstein Torry, "Summit Fever Electrifies, Snarls Washington," *WP,* December 8, 1987; Eleanor Randolph, "NBC's Coup on Gorbachev Interview Sends Rival Journalist Scrambling," *WP,* December 1, 1987.

122. Mann, *Rebellion of Ronald Reagan,* 276–277.

123. Mann, *Rebellion of Ronald Reagan,* 290; Matlock, *Reagan and Gorbachev,* 284; Cannon, *President Reagan,* 780–781.

124. Matlock, *Reagan and Gorbachev,* 298; Cannon, *President Reagan,* 787.

125. Matlock, *Reagan and Gorbachev,* 300; Wilson, *Triumph of Improvisation,* 140; Mann, *Rebellion of Ronald Reagan,* 272; Matlock, *Reagan and Gorbachev,* 290.

126. Mann, *Rebellion of Ronald Reagan*, 284–285, 304–305; Matlock, *Reagan and Gorbachev*, 302.

127. Quoted in Mann, *Rebellion of Ronald Reagan*, 304.

128. Hodding Carter, "Reagan's Triumph," *WSJ*, June 2, 1988.

129. Quoted in Cannon, *President Reagan*, 144.

130. Archie Brown, "Gorbachev and the End of the Cold War," in *Ending the Cold War: Interpretations, Causations, and the Study of International Relations*, ed. Richard K. Hermann and Richard Ned Lebow (New York: Palgrave Macmillan, 2004), 48–49; John Prados, *How the Cold War Ended: Debating and Doing History* (Lincoln: University of Nebraska Press, 2011), 105–139.

131. Archie Brown, *The Human Factor: Gorbachev, Reagan, and Thatcher, and the End of the Cold War* (New York: Oxford University Press, 2020).

132. Reagan, *American Life*, 634.

133. Dean Acheson, *Present at the Creation: My Years in the State Department* (New York: W. W. Norton, 1987), 480.

134. Memo from Richard S. Beal, William F. Martin, and Roger W. Robinson to Robert C. McFarlane, "Foreign Policy Background for the President's Trip to Europe," May 18, 1984, folder: Foreign Policy Background for President's Trip to Europe Notebook (1 of 2) (RAC box 8), box 5 (RAC boxes 8, 9), Executive Secretariat, NSC, Trip File, RRL.

8. GEORGE H. W. BUSH AND PERSONAL DIPLOMACY AT THE END OF THE COLD WAR

1. Memo from Dobrynin to Gorbachev, September 18, 1988, doc. 2, NSA Electronic Briefing Book, no. 261, https://nsarchive2.gwu.edu/NSAEBB/NSAEBB261/sov02.pdf.

2. Colin Powell Oral History, Miller Center, University of Virginia, https://miller center.org/the-presidency/presidential-oral-histories/colin-powell-oral-history -chairman-joint-chiefs-staff.

3. Memcon, Bush and Gorbachev, December 7, 1988, doc. 8, NSA Electronic Briefing Book, no. 261, https://nsarchive2.gwu.edu/NSAEBB/NSAEBB261/us08.pdf; memcon, Bush and Gorbachev, doc. 9, update to NSA Electronic Briefing Book no. 261, https:// nsarchive2.gwu.edu//dc.html?doc=5448836-Document-X4-Memorandum-of-Conversation-The; Jeffrey A. Engel, *When the World Seemed New: George H. W. Bush and the End of the Cold War* (Boston: Houghton Mifflin Harcourt, 2017), 49.

4. Engel, *When the World Seemed New*, 64–68.

5. Minutes of the Meeting of the Politburo of the Central Committee of the Communist Party of the Soviet Union, December 27–28, 1988, CWIHP, https://digitalarchive .wilsoncenter.org/document/112478.

6. Two recent examples are Engel, *When the World Seemed New*; Jon Meacham, *Destiny and Power: The American Odyssey of George Herbert Walker Bush* (New York: Random House, 2015).

7. Engel, *When the World Seemed New*, 96; George H. W. Bush and Brent Scowcroft, *A World Transformed* (New York: Alfred A. Knopf, 1998), 62, 91.

8. *ABC Evening News*, February 23, 1989, VTNA; David Hoffman, "President's Fast-paced Asian Tour to Emphasize Personal Diplomacy," *Hartford (CT) Courant*, February 23, 1989. For a list of the leaders Bush met with, see Office of the Historian, Department of State, https://history.state.gov/departmenthistory/travels/president.

9. *CBS Evening News*, February 25, 1989, VTNA.

10. Memo from Baker to Bush, "Your China Visit," February 16, 1989, doc. 4, NSA Electronic Briefing Book, no. 47, https://nsarchive2.gwu.edu/NSAEBB/NSAEBB47/doc4 .pdf.

11. Bush and Scowcroft, *World Transformed*, 97; memcon, Bush and Deng, February 26, 1989, GHWBL, https://bush41library.tamu.edu/files/memcons-telcons/1989-02-26-- Xiaoping.pdf.

12. Robert Gates Oral Interview, Miller Center, University of Virginia, https://miller center.org/the-presidency/presidential-oral-histories/robert-m-gates-deputy-director -central.

13. David Hoffman and Don Oberdorfer, "Bush Makes Personal Contact Hallmark of His Diplomacy," *WP*, April 13, 1990.

14. Bush and Scowcroft, *World Transformed*, 60.

15. Roman Popadiuk, *The Leadership of George Bush: An Insider's View of the Forty-First President* (College Station: Texas A&M Press, 2009), 142–143.

16. Bush and Scowcroft, *World Transformed*, 62.

17. Doyle McManus, "Bush's Personal Diplomacy Faces Tough Test at Summit," *LAT*, December 2, 1989.

18. Foreign official quoted in McManus, "Bush's Personal Diplomacy."

19. Press secretary quoted in David Hoffman, "Fitzwater: Bush Knew Call Was 'Suspicious,'" *WP*, March 10, 1990; "The President's News Conference," March 13, 1990, APP, https://www.presidency.ucsb.edu/node/264692.

20. Bush quoted in Popadiuk, *Leadership of George Bush*, 135, 143.

21. "The President's News Conference," June 5, 1989, APP, https://www.presidency .ucsb.edu/node/262908.

22. Bush quoted in Meacham, *Destiny and Power*, 374.

23. Baker quoted in Jeffrey A. Engel, ed., *The China Diary of George H. W. Bush: The Making of a Global President* (Princeton, NJ: Princeton University Press, 2008).

24. Bush and Scowcroft, *World Transformed*, 100, 102–103.

25. Engel, *When the World Seemed New*, 188, 191; Bush and Scowcroft, *World Transformed*, 103.

26. Engel, *When the World Seemed New*, 196; James A. Baker, *The Politics of Diplomacy: Revolution, War and Peace, 1989–1992* (New York: G. P. Putnam's Son, 1995), 112.

27. Engel, *When the World Seemed New*, 191.

28. George H. W. Bush, *All the Best, George Bush: My Life in Letters* (New York: Scribner, 2013), 431.

29. James Mann, *About Face: A History of America's Curious Relations with China, from Nixon to Clinton* (New York: Vintage, 2000), 191.

30. Bush and Scowcroft, *World Transformed*, 46.

31. Michael R. Beschloss and Strobe Talbott, *At the Highest Levels: The Inside Story of the End of the Cold War* (Boston: Little, Brown, 1993), 8–9; Engel, *When the World Seemed New*, 2–3.

32. *NBC Evening News*, December 12, 1987, VTNA.

33. Bush quoted in Beschloss and Talbott, *At the Highest Levels*, 9.

34. "Gorbachev," Bush-Quayle '88, 1988, Museum of the Moving Image, *The Living Room Candidate: Presidential Campaign Commercials 1952–2012*, http://www.livingroom candidate.org/commercials/1988/gorbachev.

35. Bush and Scowcroft, *World Transformed*, 26; Record of Conversation between Gorbachev and Kissinger, January 17, 1989, CWIHP, https://digitalarchive.wilsoncenter .org/document/134823.

36. Bush and Scowcroft, *World Transformed*, 27.

37. Minutes of the Meeting of the Politburo, December 27–28, 1988.

38. CIA, "The Soviet System in Crisis: Prospects for the Next Two Years," National Intelligence Estimate 11-18-89, November 1989, https://www.cia.gov/readingroom/docs /DOC_0000397625.pdf.

39. Memo from Douglas P. Mulholland to Baker, "Soviet Thinking on the Eve of Malta," November 29, 1989, doc. 5, NSA Electronic Briefing Book, no. 298, https://nsar chive2.gwu.edu/NSAEBB/NSAEBB298/Document%205.pdf.

40. Bush quoted in Beschloss and Talbott, *At the Highest Levels*, 93.

41. Bush to Gorbachev, July 21, 1989, doc. ID 2157793823, DNSA.

42. Beschloss and Talbott, *At the Highest Levels*, 94; Engel, *When the World Seemed New*, 231–233; "The President's News Conference," October 31, 1989, APP, https://www .presidency.ucsb.edu/node/264379.

43. Memcon, Bush and Gorbachev, December 2, 1989, GHWBL, https://bush41li brary.tamu.edu/files/memcons-telcons/1989-12-02--Gorbachev%20Malta%20First%20 Expanded%20Bilateral%20Meeting%20GB%20and%20Gorbachev%20in%20Malta .pdf; Engel, *When the World Seemed New*, 298.

44. Engel, *When the World Seemed New*, 304–305; Beschloss and Talbott, *At the Highest Levels*, 165, 167.

45. *CBS Evening News*, December 3, 1989, VTNA.

46. David Lauter, "Bush and Gorbachev Forge Personal Alliance," *LAT*, December 4, 1989; "Question-and-Answer Session with Reporters in Malta," December 3, 1989, APP, https://www.presidency.ucsb.edu/node/264015; Pavel Palazchenko, *My Years with Gorbachev and Shevardnadze: The Memoir of a Soviet Interpreter* (University Park: Pennsylvania State University Press, 1997), 157; Baker, *Politics of Diplomacy*, 170; Bush and Scowcroft, *World Transformed*, 173.

47. Cable, Moscow to Washington, "Gorbachev Confronts Crisis of Power," May 11, 1990, doc. no. 015714, DNSA.

48. Cable, Moscow to Washington, "Soviet Reactions to the Summit," June 12, 1990, doc. no. 019444, DNSA.

49. Telcon, Bush and Gorbachev, December 25, 1991, GHWBL, https://bush41library .tamu.edu/files/memcons-telcons/1991-12-25--Gorbachev.pdf.

50. "The President's News Conference," October 31, 1989, APP, https://www.presi dency.ucsb.edu/node/264379.

51. Interview with Robert S. Strauss, Association for Diplomatic Studies and Training Foreign Affairs Oral History Project, October 25, 2002, https://cdn.loc.gov/service/mss /mfdip/2007/2007str01/2007str01.pdf.

52. James M. Goldgeier and Michael McFaul, *Power and Purpose: US Policy toward Russia after the Cold War* (Washington, DC: Brookings Institution Press, 2003), 20, 26–29.

53. Scowcroft, Baker, and Bush quoted in Beschloss and Talbott, *At the Highest Levels,* 104, 413; American official quoted in Doyle McManus, "As Yeltsin Steps in, Some Doubt He Can Fill Role," *LAT,* December 23, 1991.

54. "George Bush, Remarks on the London Economic Summit and an Exchange with Foreign Journalists," July 8, 1991, APP, https://www.presidency.ucsb.edu/node/266458.

55. Telcon, Bush and Mitterrand, February 26, 1990, GHWBL, https://bush41library .tamu.edu/files/memcons-telcons/1990-02-26--Mitterrand.pdf.

56. Gates Oral Interview.

57. Bush and Scowcroft, *World Transformed,* 187, 192.

58. Record of Conversation between Gorbachev and Thatcher, September 23, 1989, CWIHP, https://digitalarchive.wilsoncenter.org/document/120816. For Thatcher's opposition to German unity, see Margaret Thatcher, *The Downing Street Years* (London: HarperCollins, 1995), 789–799.

59. Frédéric Bozo, *Mitterrand, the End of the Cold War, and German Unification,* trans. Susan Emanuel (New York: Bergham Books, 2009), 25; Record of Telephone Conversation between Gorbachev and Mitterrand, November 14, 1989, CWIHP, https://dig italarchive.wilsoncenter.org/document/120825.

60. Memcon, Bush and Gorbachev, December 2, 1989, GHWBL, https://bush41li brary.tamu.edu/files/memcons-telcons/1989-12-02--Gorbachev%20Malta%20First%20 Restriced%20Bilateral.pdf.

61. Memcon, Bush and Thatcher, April 13, 1990, GHWBL, https://bush41library .tamu.edu/files/memcons-telcons/1990-04-13--Thatcher.pdf.

62. Memcon, Bush and Kohl, February 24, 1990, GHWBL, https://bush41library .tamu.edu/files/memcons-telcons/1990-02-24--Kohl.pdf; Engel, *When the World Seemed New,* 320.

63. Telcon, Bush and Mitterrand, January 27, 1990, GHWBL, https://bush41library. tamu.edu/files/memcons-telcons/1990-01-27--Mitterrand.pdf.

64. Christopher Maynard, *Out of the Shadow: George H. W. Bush and the End of the Cold War* (College Station: Texas A&M University Press, 2008), 60.

65. Telcon, Bush and Kohl, November 10, 1989, GHWBL, https://bush41library.tamu .edu/files/memcons-telcons/1989-11-10--Kohl.pdf.

66. Telcon, Bush and Kohl, "Telephone Call from Chancellor Helmut Kohl of West Germany," November 17, 1989, GHWBL, https://bush41library.tamu.edu/files/mem cons-telcons/1989-11-17--Kohl.pdf.

67. Maynard, *Out of the Shadow*, 59; Kristina Spohr, "The Caucasus, 1990," in *Transcending the Cold War: Summits, Statecraft, and the Dissolution of Bipolarity in Europe, 1970–1990*, ed. Kristina Spohr and David Reynolds (Oxford: Oxford University Press, 2016), 208; telcon, Bush and Kohl, November 29, 1989, GHWBL, https://bush41library .tamu.edu/files/memcons-telcons/1989-11-29--Kohl.pdf.

68. Bush and Scowcroft, *World Transformed*, 240.

69. Bush and Scowcroft, *World Transformed*, 240–241.

70. Telcon, Bush and Kohl, February 13, 1990, GHWBL, https://bush41library.tamu .edu/files/memcons-telcons/1990-02-13--Kohl%20[2].pdf.

71. Maynard, *Out of the Shadow*, 62–63.

72. Bush and Scowcroft, *World Transformed*, 252.

73. Memcon, Bush and Kohl, February 24, 1990, GHWBL, https://bush41library .tamu.edu/files/memcons-telcons/1990-02-24--Kohl.pdf.

74. Spohr, "Caucasus," 213–214; Maynard, *Out of the Shadow*, 64; Bush and Scowcroft, *World Transformed*, 255.

75. Engel, *When the World Seemed New*, 319–320; official quoted in Philip Zelikow and Condolezza Rice, *Germany Unified and Europe Transformed: A Study in Statecraft* (Cambridge, MA: Harvard University Press, 1997), 196.

76. Gorbachev quoted in Maynard, *Out of the Shadow*, 55; Bush and Scowcroft, *World Transformed*, 150.

77. Memo from Baker to Bush, "Your December Meeting with Gorbachev," November 29, 1989, doc. 6, NSA Electronic Briefing Book, no. 298, https://nsarchive2.gwu.edu /NSAEBB/NSAEBB298/Document%206.pdf.

78. Memcon, Bush and Gorbachev, December 2, 1989, GHWBL, https://bush41li brary.tamu.edu/files/memcons-telcons/1989-12-02--Gorbachev%20Malta%20First%20 Restriced%20Bilateral.pdf; Spohr, "Caucasus," 209.

79. Telcon, Bush and Gorbachev, February 28, 1989, GHWBL, https://bush41library .tamu.edu/files/memcons-telcons/1990-02-28--Gorbachev.pdf.

80. Memo from Scowcroft to Bush, "The Gorbachev Summit May 30–June 3, 1990," n.d., doc. no. 3968, DNSA.

81. Zelikow and Rice, *Germany Unified*, 275.

82. Memcon, Bush and Kohl, February 25, 1990, GHWBL, https://bush41library .tamu.edu/files/memcons-telcons/1990-02-25--Kohl.pdf.

83. Bush and Scowcroft, *World Transformed*, 279; *NBC Evening News*, May 31, 1990; CNN Special, May 31, 1990, VTNA.

84. Bush and Scowcroft, *World Transformed*, 279.

85. Zelikow and Rice, *Germany Unified*, 275–278, 282.

86. On the meeting between Kohl and Gorbachev, see Spohr, "Caucasus." For the role of German economic aid in unification, see Randall E. Newnham, "The Price of

German Unity: The Role of Economic Aid in the German-Soviet Negotiations," *German Studies Review* 22, 3 (October 1999): 421–446.

87. Popadiuk, *Leadership of George Bush*, 142.

88. Engel, *When the World Seemed New*, 347, 353.

89. Engel, *When the World Seemed New*, 383.

90. John Sununu Oral History, Miller Center, University of Virginia, https://miller-center.org/the-presidency/presidential-oral-histories/john-h-sununu-oral-his tory-062000 -white-house-chief.

91. Telcon, Bush and Fahd, August 2, 1990; telcon, Bush and Hussein and Mubarak, August 2, 1990, GHWBL, https://bush41library.tamu.edu/files/memcons-telcons/1990 -08-02--Fahd.pdf, https://bush41library.tamu.edu/files/memcons-telcons/1990-08-02 --Hussein%20I.pdf.

92. Telcon, Bush and Hussein, August 13, 1990, GHWBL, https://bush41library.tamu. edu/files/memcons-telcons/1990-08-13--Hussein%20I%20[1].pdf; Bush and Scowcroft, *World Transformed*, 349.

93. Telcon, Bush and Mulroney, August 4, 1990, GHWBL, https://bush41library .tamu.edu/files/memcons-telcons/1990-08-04--Mulroney.pdf; Chase Untermeyer, *Zenith: In the White House with George H. W. Bush* (College Station: Texas A&M University Press, 2016), 147.

94. *ABC Evening News*, September 28, 1990, VTNA.

95. Maureen Dowd, "Bush Is in New York for the U.N. Conference and a Flurry of Gulf Diplomacy," *NYT*, September 30, 1990.

96. Baker, *Politics of Diplomacy*, 281, 291.

97. Beschloss and Talbott, *At the Highest Levels*, 246–248.

98. *NBC Evening News*, September 2, 1989, VTNA.

99. Memo from Scowcroft to Bush, "Your Meeting with Gorbachev in Helsinki," n.d.; memo, Central Intelligence Agency, "Gorbachev's Position and the Soviet Domestic Scene," September 4, 1990, doc. ID 2157792454, DNSA.

100. "Address before a Joint Session of the Congress," September 11, 1990, APP, https://www.presidency.ucsb.edu/node/264415.

101. Memcon, Bush and Gorbachev, September 9, 1990, doc. ID 2157791884, DNSA.

102. Bush and Scowcroft, *World Transformed*, 366.

103. "Soviet Union–United States Joint Statement on the Persian Gulf Crisis," September 9, 1990, APP, https://www.presidency.ucsb.edu/node/264353.

104. Engel, *When the World Seemed New*, 414; Bush and Scowcroft, *World Transformed*, 361.

105. Telcon, Bush and Mitterrand, September 10, 1990, GHWBL, https://bush41li brary.tamu.edu/files/memcons-telcons/1990-09-10--Mitterrand%20[1].pdf.

106. Telcon, Bush and Gorbachev, January 11, 1991, GHWBL, https://bush41library .tamu.edu/files/memcons-telcons/1991-01-11--Gorbachev.pdf.

107. Bush and Scowcroft, *World Transformed*, 455.

108. Telcon, Bush and Gorbachev, January 18, 1991, GHWBL, https://bush41library.tamu.edu/files/memcons-telcons/1991-01-18--Gorbachev.pdf.

109. Goldgeier and McFaul, *Power and Purpose*, 27–28.

110. Soviet paper quoted in Graham E. Fuller, "Moscow and the Gulf War," *Foreign Affairs* 70, 3 (Summer 1991): 67.

111. Gorbachev quoted in Beschloss and Talbott, *At the Highest Levels*, 341; telcon, Bush and Gorbachev, May 11, 1991, GHWBL, https://bush41library.tamu.edu/files/memcons-telcons/1991-05-11--Gorbachev.pdf.

112. Steve A. Yetiv, *Explaining Foreign Policy: U.S. Decision-Making and the Persian Gulf War* (Baltimore: Johns Hopkins University Press, 2004), 34; Bush and Scowcroft, *World Transformed*, 321.

113. Official quoted in Yetiv, *Explaining Foreign Policy*, 35.

114. Dennis Ross, *Doomed to Succeed: The U.S.-Israel Relationship from Truman to Obama* (New York: Farrar, Straus & Giroux, 2015), 236; Bush and Scowcroft, *World Transformed*, 329; telcon, Bush and Fahd, August 4, 1990, GHWBL, https://bush41library.tamu.edu/files/memcons-telcons/1990-08-04--Fahd.pdf.

115. Engel, *When the World Seemed New*, 407–408.

116. Richard B. Cheney Oral History, Miller Center, University of Virginia, https://millercenter.org/the-presidency/presidential-oral-histories/richard-b-cheney-oral-history.

117. Haass quoted in Beschloss and Talbott, *At the Highest Levels*, 249.

118. RJ Reinhart, "George H. W. Bush Retrospective," December 1, 2018, https://news.gallup.com/opinion/gallup/234971/george-bush-retrospective.aspx.

119. ABC News/*Washington Post* poll, October 16–21, 1991, iPOLL; John E. Yang and Ann Devroy, "Bush Yields Global Stage to Baker," *WP*, December 5, 1991.

120. Untermeyer, *Zenith*, 235.

121. "The President's News Conference," November 6, 1991, APP, https://www.presidency.ucsb.edu/node/266215.

122. James Gerstenzang, "Bush, Criticized on Home Front, Drops Asia Tour," *LAT*, November 6, 1991; Nicholas M. Horrock and Timothy J. McNulty, "Feeling Heat at Home, Bush Delays Asia Trip," *Chicago Tribune*, November 6, 1991.

123. Tsongas quoted in Maureen Dowd, "Voters Want Candidates to Take a Reality Check," *NYT*, February 17, 1992.

124. Michael Wines, "Bush's Asian Trip Recast to Stress Jobs and Exports," *NYT*, December 29, 1991; "A High-Risk Trip—For Very High Stakes," *LAT*, December 23, 1991; John E. Yang, "Economic Results of Bush Trip May Not Match Expectations," *WP*, December 30, 1991.

125. "America's Traveling Salesman," *South China Morning Post*, January 4, 1992.

126. *NBC Evening News*, January 5, 1992, VTNA.

127. Wines, "Bush's Asian Trip."

128. Douglas Jehl, "Bush's Trip Carries Heavy Political Load," *LAT*, January 1, 1992.

129. Telcon, Bush and Miyazawa, December 20, 1991, GHWBL, https://bush41library.tamu.edu/files/memcons-telcons/1991-12-20--Miyazawa.pdf.

130. "Christmas Address to the Nation," December 25, 1991, APP, https://www.pres idency.ucsb.edu/node/266241.

131. "High-Risk Trip."

132. "Remarks to the Korean National Assembly in Seoul," January 6, 1992, APP, https://www.presidency.ucsb.edu/node/266400.

133. *NBC Evening News,* January 8, 1992, VTNA.

134. "The Asia Trip," *WP,* January 10, 1992; *NBC Evening News,* January 9, 1992, VTNA; Alan Murray and Michel McQueen, "Bad Trip," *WSJ,* January 9, 1992.

135. CBS/*New York Times* poll, January 6–8, 1992; *WSJ* poll, January 17–21, 1992; Gallup poll, January 16–19, 1992, iPOLL; Michael Wines, "Bush Returns, Hailing Gains in Japan Agreement," *NYT,* January 11, 1992.

136. Wines, "Bush Returns."

137. *NBC Evening News,* January 13, 1992, VTNA.

138. Record of Conversation between Gorbachev and Kohl, June 12, 1989, CWIHP, https://digitalarchive.wilsoncenter.org/document/120808.

139. CBS News/*New York Times* poll, October 29–November 1, 1992; NBC News/ *Wall Street Journal* poll, October 20–21, 1992, iPOLL; John Dumbrell, "Internationalism Challenged: Foreign Policy Issues in the 1992 Presidential Election," in *US Presidential Elections and Foreign Policy: Candidates, Campaigns, and Global Politics from FDR to Bill Clinton,* ed. Andrew Johnstone and Andrew Priest (Lexington: University Press of Kentucky, 2017), 317; Reinhart, "George H. W. Bush Retrospective."

9. THE IMPACT OF PRESIDENTIAL PERSONAL DIPLOMACY

1. John R. Hibbing, "Legislative Institutionalization with Illustrations from the British House of Commons," *American Journal of Political Science* 32, 3 (August 1988): 682; Samuel P. Huntington, *Political Order in Changing Societies* (New Haven, CT: Yale University Press, 1968), 12.

2. Ted Robert Gurr, "Persistence and Change in Political Systems, 1800–1971," *American Political Science Review* 68, 4 (December 1974): 1484–1485.

3. Lyn Ragsdale and John J. Theis, "The Institutionalization of the American Presidency, 1924–1992," *American Journal of Political Science* 41, 4 (October 1997): 1291.

4. Michael John Burton, "The 'Flying White House': A Travel Establishment within the Presidential Branch," *Presidential Studies Quarterly* 36, 2 (June 2006): 297–308.

5. William Mishler and Anne Hildreth, "Legislatures and Political Stability: An Exploratory Analysis," *Journal of Politics* 46, 1 (February 1984): 30; Robert O. Keohane, "Institutionalization in the United Nations General Assembly," *International Organization* 23, 4 (Autumn 1969): 862.

6. Ragsdale and Theis, "Institutionalization of the American Presidency," 1297–1298; Nelson W. Polsby, "The Institutionalization of the U.S. House of Representatives," *American Political Science Review* 62, 1 (March 1968): 145.

7. James H. Lebovic and Elizabeth N. Saunders, "The Diplomatic Core: The Determinants of High-Level US Diplomatic Visits, 1946–2010," *International Studies Quarterly* 60, 1 (March 2016): 107–123; Amnon Cavari and Micah Ables, "Going Global: Assessing Presidential Foreign Travel," *Congress & the Presidency* 46, 2 (May 2019): 306–329; Ian Ostrander and Toby J. Rider, "Presidents Abroad: The Politics of Personal Diplomacy," *Political Research Quarterly* 72, 4 (December 2019): 835–848.

8. The following paragraphs on the pros and cons of the practice are drawn from the following: D. C. Watt, "Summits and Summitry Reconsidered," *International Relations* 2, 8 (October 1963): 493–504; Keith Eubank, *The Summit Conferences: 1919–1960* (Norman: University of Oklahoma, 1966), 194–209; Elmer Plischke, *Diplomat in Chief: The President at the Summit* (New York: Praeger, 1986), 457–465; Harold Nicolson, *Diplomacy* (London: Oxford University Press, 1960), 76–77; Dean Rusk, "The President," *Foreign Affairs* 38, 3 (April 1960): 353–369; David H. Dunn, ed., *Diplomacy at the Highest Level: The Evolution of International Summitry* (London: Macmillan Press, 1996), 247–268; George Ball, *Diplomacy for a Crowded World: An American Foreign Policy* (Boston: Little, Brown, 1976); Jeffrey G. Giauque, "Bilateral Summit Diplomacy in Western European and Transatlantic Relations, 1956–63," *European History Quarterly* 31, 3 (July 2001): 427–445.

9. Napoleon quoted in David Reynolds, *Summits: Six Meetings that Shaped the Twentieth Century* (New York: Basic Books, 2007), 20.

10. Dean Acheson, *Present at the Creation: My Years in the State Department* (New York: W. W. Norton, 1987), 480.

11. De Commynes quoted in David H. Dunn, "What Is Summitry?" in Dunn, *Diplomacy at the Highest Level*, 4.

12. Thomas E. Cronin, "'All the World's a Stage . . . ': Acting and the Art of Political Leadership," *Leadership Quarterly* 19, 4 (August 2008): 459–468.

13. Nicolson, *Diplomacy*, 100.

14. Todd Hall and Keren Yarhi-Milo, "'The Personal Touch': Leaders' Impressions, Costly Signaling, and Assessments of Sincerity in International Affairs," *International Studies Quarterly* 56, 3 (September 2012): 561; Stephen J. Majeski and Shane Fricks, "Conflict and Cooperation in International Relations," *Journal of Conflict Resolution* 39, 4 (December 1995): 625.

15. Agnes Simon, "The Political and Economic Consequences of the Summit Diplomatic Activity of the U.S. President" (Ph.D. diss., University of Missouri, 2012), 61–103.

16. Aristotle, *Nicomachean Ethics,* trans. Christopher Rowe (Oxford: Oxford University Press, 2002), book 8, 1156a12–13; book 9, 1168b3–4.

17. Aristotle, *Nicomachean Ethics,* book 9, 1171a17–20.

18. Yuri van Hoef, "Interpreting Affect between State Leaders: Assessing the Political Friendship between Winston S. Churchill and Franklin D. Roosevelt," in *Researching Emotions in International Relations,* ed. Maéva Clément and Eric Sangar (Cham, Switzerland: Palgrave Macmillan, 2018), 53.

19. Douglas Brinkley, *The Unfinished Presidency: Jimmy Carter's Journey to the Nobel Peace Prize* (New York: Penguin Press, 1998), 106.

20. Art Harris, "Jimmy Carter: 'I Have Never Had a Better, Closer Personal Friend,'" *WP*, October 7, 1981.

21. On the difference between foreign policy and diplomacy, see Juergen Kleiner, "The Inertia of Diplomacy," *Diplomacy & Statecraft* 19, 2 (2008): 321–349. For multiple definitions of diplomacy, see Elmer Plischke, "Diplomacy—Search for Its Meaning," in *Modern Diplomacy: The Art and the Artisans*, ed. Elmer Plischke (Washington, DC: American Enterprise Institute, 1979), 27–36.

22. William B. Quandt, *Peace Process: American Diplomacy and the Arab-Israeli Conflict since 1967*, 3rd ed. (Washington, DC: Brookings Institution Press, 2005), 235. The guarantee of Israel's oil supply was a reaffirmation and extension of a 1975 US pledge.

23. Cabell Phillips, "Talks with Nehru Typify U.S. 'Personal Diplomacy,'" *NYT*, December 23, 1956.

24. Memo from David Aaron to Carter, "The National Security Council System," December 5, 1976, NLC-7-66-8-8-6, CREST, JCL (emphasis in original).

25. George P. Shultz, *Turmoil and Triumph: My Years as Secretary of State* (New York: Charles Scribner's Sons, 1993), 353.

26. Fred I. Greenstein, *Personality and Politics: Problems of Evidence, Inference, and Conceptualization* (Princeton, NJ: Princeton University Press, 1987), 47.

27. Other scholars have theorized about when a leader's personal characteristics are more likely to influence foreign policy. For example, Margaret Hermann discusses eight situations in which a leader's personality and predispositions are likely to come to the fore, such as when a leader is particularly interested in foreign policy, is charismatic, is facing a crisis, and lacks knowledge of international affairs. See Margaret G. Hermann, "Circumstances under which Leader Personality Will Affect Foreign Policy: Some Propositions," in *In Search of Global Patterns*, ed. James N. Rosenau (New York: Free Press, 1976), 326–333.

28. Greenstein, *Personality and Politics*, 42–46.

29. Greenstein lists eleven circumstances in which an individual's personality is more likely to be central to political outcomes. All could apply to personal diplomacy, but the four discussed here are particularly salient.

30. Greenstein, *Personality and Politics*, 51.

31. Greenstein, *Personality and Politics*, 53.

32. Greenstein, *Personality and Politics*, 54.

33. Greenstein, *Personality and Politics*, 55.

34. On history and statecraft, see Richard E. Neustadt and Ernest R. May, *Thinking in Time: The Uses of History for Decision-Makers* (New York: Free Press, 1986); Ernest May, *"Lessons" of the Past: The Use and Misuse of History in American Foreign Policy* (New York: Oxford University Press, 1973); Hal Brands and William Inboden, "Wisdom without Tears: Statecraft and the Uses of History," *Journal of Strategic Studies* 41, 7 (2018): 916–946; Hal Brands and Jeremi Suri, eds., *The Power of the Past: History and Statecraft* (Washington, DC: Brookings Institution Press, 2016).

CONCLUSION

1. Telcon, Trump and Zelensky, July 25, 2019, https://trumpwhitehouse.archives.gov /wp-content/uploads/2019/09/Unclassified09.2019.pdf; Charlie Savage and Josh Williams, "Read the Text Messages between U.S. and Ukrainian Officials," *NYT*, October 4, 2019, https://www.nytimes.com/interactive/2019/10/04/us/politics/ukraine-text-messages -volker.html; Gordon Sondland, "Opening Statement before the United States House of Representatives Permanent Select Committee on Intelligence," November 20, 2019, https:// intelligence.house.gov/uploadedfiles/sondlandopening.pdf. On Twitter alone, between September 20, 2019, and January 16, 2020, Trump called his phone call "perfect" almost thirty times. See the Trump Twitter archive, http://www.trumptwitterarchive.com/archive.

2. Donald Trump, Twitter post, September 27, 2019, 11:24 a.m., https://twitter.com /realDonaldTrump/status/1177604833538392065.

3. Carol D. Leonning, Shane Harris, and Josh Dawsey, "Trump's Calls with Foreign Leaders Have Long Worried Aides, Leaving Some 'Genuinely Horrified,'" *WP*, October 4, 2019, https://www.washingtonpost.com/politics/trumps-calls-with-foreign-leaders -have-long-worried-aides-leaving-some-genuinely-horrified/2019/10/04/537cc7a8-e602 -11e9-a331-2df12d56a80b_story.html.

4. David Reynolds, *Summits: Six Meetings that Shaped the Twentieth Century* (New York: Basic Books, 2007), 401–435.

5. Charles Krauthammer, "The Unipolar Moment," *Foreign Affairs* 70, 1 (January 1991): 23–33; Hal Brands, *Making the Unipolar Moment: U.S. Foreign Policy and the Rise of the Post–Cold War Order* (Ithaca, NY: Cornell University Press, 2016), 322.

6. Russell L. Riley, *Inside the Clinton White House: An Oral History* (New York: Oxford University Press, 2016), 188.

7. Riley, *Inside the Clinton White House,* 191–192.

8. Riley, *Inside the Clinton White House,* 264.

9. Aaron David Miller, *The Much Too Promised Land: America's Elusive Search for Arab-Israeli Peace* (New York: Bantam, 2008), 278–315; Walter B. Slocombe, "A Crisis of Opportunity: The Clinton Administration and Russia," in *In Uncertain Times: American Foreign Policy after the Berlin Wall and 9/11,* ed. Melvyn P. Leffler and Jeffrey W. Legro (Ithaca, NY: Cornell University Press, 2011), 78–95.

10. George W. Bush, *Decision Points* (New York: Crown Publishers, 2010), 195.

11. "The Art of Leadership," George W. Bush Presidential Center, https://www.bush center.org/exhibits-and-events/exhibits/2014/the-art-of-leadership-a-presidents-per sonal-diplomacy.html.

12. "Press Conference by Bush and Putin," June 16, 2001, http://georgewbush-white house.archives.gov/news/releases/2001/06/20010618.html.

13. Edwin Chen, "Bush Finds His Kind of Diplomacy Goes Only so Far," *LAT*, March 13, 2003.

14. Michael Abramowitz, "Crises Reveal Limits of Bush's Personal Diplomacy on World Stage," *WP*, August 27, 2008.

15. Jeffrey Goldberg, "How Obama Views the Men and Women Who (Also) Rule

the World," *Atlantic*, March 18, 2016, http://www.theatlantic.com/international/archive/2016/03/obama-goldberg-world-leaders/473367/.

16. Kissinger quoted in Jon Meachem, *Destiny and Power: The American Odyssey of George Herbert Walker Bush* (New York: Random House, 2015), 182.

17. James H. Lebovic and Elizabeth N. Saunders, "The Diplomatic Core: The Determinants of High-Level US Diplomatic Visits, 1946–2010," *International Studies Quarterly* 60, 1 (March 2016): 116.

18. Agnes Simon, "The Political and Economic Consequences of the Summit Diplomatic Activity of the U.S. President" (Ph.D. diss., University of Missouri, 2012), 24; Michael J. Smith, "Going International: Presidential Activity in the Post-Modern Presidency," *Journal of American Studies* 31, 2 (August 1997): 226; Brendan J. Doherty, "POTUS on the Road: International and Domestic Presidential Travel, 1977–2005," *Presidential Studies Quarterly* 39, 2 (June 2009): 325–326.

19. Amnon Cavari and Micah Ables, "Going Global: Assessing Presidential Foreign Travel," *Congress & the Presidency* 46, 2 (May 2019): 316; Ian Ostrander and Toby J. Rider, "Presidents Abroad: The Politics of Personal Diplomacy," *Political Research Quarterly* 72, 4 (December 2019): 838, 841; Lebovic and Saunders, "Diplomatic Core," 113; Doherty, "POTUS on the Road," 334–335.

20. Kathryn Dunn Tenpas, Emily Charnock, and James A. McCann, "Second-Term Presidential Travel: The Impermanent Campaign and the Rise of Legacy-Building, 1957–2009" (paper presented at the American Political Science Association annual meeting, 2012), https://papers.ssrn.com/sol3/papers.cfm?abstract_id=2107307; Cavari and Ables, "Going Global," 323, 322; Ostrander and Rider, "Presidents Abroad," 835–848.

21. Richard Rose, *The Postmodern President: The White House Meets the World* (Chatham, NJ: Chatham House, 1988), 8. See also Smith, "Going International."

22. Richard Haass, "Present at the Disruption: How Trump Unmade U.S. Foreign Policy," *Foreign Affairs* 99, 5 (September–October 2020): 24–34. For how Trump departed from presidential norms, see James P. Pfiffner, "Donald Trump and the Norms of the Presidency," *Presidential Studies Quarterly* 51, 1 (March 2021): 96–124.

23. Donald Trump, Twitter post, August 18, 2018, 3:39 p.m., https://twitter.com/realDonaldTrump/status/1030902046520696832; "Trump Doctrine," *WSJ*, June 30, 2019, https://www.wsj.com/articles/the-trump-doctrine-11561932751.

24. Tizoc Chavez, "Personal Diplomacy Has Long Been a Presidential Tactic, but Trump Adds a Twist," *Conversation*, January 23, 2019, https://theconversation.com/personal-diplomacy-has-long-been-a-presidential-tactic-but-trump-adds-a-twist-105031.

25. "Trump Speaks with Erdogan about Crisis in Syria," *Politico*, November 24, 2017, https://www.politico.com/story/2017/11/24/trump-recep-tayyip-edogan-middle-east-259604; Peter Baker and Keith Bradsher, "Trump and Xi Agree to Restart Trade Talks, Avoiding Escalation in Tariff War," *NYT*, June 29, 2019, https://www.nytimes.com/2019/06/29/world/asia/g20-trump-xi-trade-talks.html; Steve Holland, "Trump to Convene G7 Leaders in Video Call to Discuss Pandemic," *Reuters*, April 14, 2020, https://www.reuters.com/article/us-health-coronavirus-trump-g7/trump-to-convene-g7-leaders-in-video-call-to-discuss-pandemic-idUSKCN21W2QI.

26. Donald Trump, Twitter post, July 9, 2017, 8:57 a.m., https://twitter.com/real DonaldTrump/status/884033889613828096.

27. Felicia Schwartz, Farnaz Fassihi, and Mitsuru Obe, "Japan's Shinzo Abe Discusses Security Alliance at Meeting with Donald Trump," *WSJ*, November 18, 2016, https:// www.wsj.com/articles/japans-shinzo-abe-to-address-security-alliance-at-donald-trump-meeting-1479404692; Allison Kaplan Sommer, "Netanyahu Plays Trump Card in Reelection Campaign in Billboards and Video," *Haaretz*, February 3, 2019, https:// www.haaretz.com/israel-news/.premium-netanyahu-plays-trump-card-in-reelection-campaign-using-president-in-billboards-and-1.6899674; Ruth Eglash, "Netanyahu Inaugurates Trump Heights, Israel's Newest Town on the Golan Heights," *WP*, June 16, 2019, https://www.washingtonpost.com/world/netanyahu-inaugurates-trump-heights-israels-newest-town-on-the-golan-heights/2019/06/16/2207cd24-9041-11e9-956a-88c291ab5c38_story.html.

28. Clint Work, "The Biggest Obstacle to a Deal with North Korea Isn't Kim Jong Un," February 25, 2019, *WP*, https://www.washingtonpost.com/outlook/2019/02/25/biggest-obstacle-deal-with-north-korea-isnt-kim-jong-un/.

29. Richard Fontaine, "A Troubling Pattern of Personal Diplomacy," *Atlantic*, December 29, 2018, https://www.theatlantic.com/ideas/archive/2018/12/trumps-pattern-personalized-diplomacy-upended-syria/579145/; Brent D. Griffiths, "Trump: I'll Know 'within the First Minute' if North Korea Is Serious at Summit Meeting," *Politico*, June 9, 2018, https://www.politico.com/story/2018/06/09/trump-north-korea-summit-meeting-one-minute-kim-jong-un-635004.

30. Howard LaFranchi, "Diplomacy Is in Part Transactional. How Is Trump's Different?" *Christian Science Monitor*, October 3, 2019, https://www.csmonitor.com/USA/Foreign-Policy/2019/1003/Diplomacy-is-in-part-transactional-How-is-Trump-s-different.

31. Kevin Liptak, "Glad-handing Biden Begins Foreign Diplomacy with the Telephone," CNN, January 22, 2021, https://www.cnn.com/2021/01/22/politics/joe-biden-foreign-leaders/index.html.

Index